Critical Acclaim for Usability Engineering

Rosson and Carroll's method for scenario-based development offers a promising new approach to usability engineering. Scenarios form a solid basis for design by providing a coherent structure for identifying and assessing the tradeoffs among competing design goals. Rosson and Carroll move beyond the traditional use of scenarios for user task analysis, showing through extensive case studies how the scenario concept can be applied usefully at every level of design. In addition to presenting the scenario approach, the book offers a broad overview of the issues and techniques in human-computer interaction along with a wealth of insights into the design process and the ways that users encounter the software that we build. It will be of great value to students and professionals alike.

—Terry Winograd, Stanford University

Everyone interested in good usability design knows that human-centered, iterative design with field studies, iterative prototypes, and testing is the proper way to proceed. But up to now, learning these skills is not easy, for we have lacked a single, systematic source of information about the methods. This book finally solves the problem. Here, in one comprehensive, easy-to-read text, there is extensive coverage of the multiple stages of a good interface development process. The book is ideally suited for a problem-based curriculum, in which students simultaneously learn good development processes while completing a term project. The book gives excellent guidance, and the case study approach is an excellent organizer and motivator. At last, the proper problem-based textbook.

—Don Norman, Nielsen Norman Group

This is a book that has long needed to be written, and the authors are among the very few who were capable of writing it. It fills a gap in the HCI literature with sufficient depth to serve as a landmark for future efforts. Now, when students ask, "Is there any one book that covers all these issues?", I will point them first to Rosson and Carroll.

—Andrew Dillon, Director of HCI Program, Indiana University

Scenarios have been used by developers of interactive systems for years, but there has been little that explores this technique and places it properly in the perspective of the usability and software engineering lifecycles. *Usability Engineering: Scenario-Based Development of Human-Computer Interaction* by Mary Beth Rosson and John M. Carroll is a textbook that does this. It presents the entire usability engineering life cycle in practical terms, using the example of a virtual science fair to illustrate life cycle and the use of scenarios in development.

Even though scenarios have been in use for some time, many designers and project managers don't recognize their value. They are an important means of communicating product goals in terms of *what the user can do* with a product or system and how they will use it as opposed to the more traditional engineering specifications of *what the product or system will do* and how the product and system does it.

One of the nice things about this book is that it identifies where tradeoffs exist in developing user interfaces. Too many books provide guidelines as if they were absolute—that following the presented guidelines will result in a usable UI. Unfortunately, this is not the case. Tradeoffs must be constantly made, and understanding how one usability objective can impact another is critical to good design.

This textbook provides an additional and important way of approaching and viewing the development of interactive systems.

—John Meads, Usability Architects

USABILITY ENGINEERING

Scenario-Based Development of
Human-Computer Interaction

The Morgan Kaufmann Series in Interactive Technologies

Series Editors:
- Stuart Card, Xerox PARC
- Jonathan Grudin, Microsoft
- Jakob Nielsen, Nielsen Norman Group
- Tim Skelly, Design Happy

Usability Engineering: Scenario-Based Development of Human-Computer Interaction
Mary Beth Rosson and John M. Carroll

Your Wish Is My Command: Programming by Example
Edited by Henry Lieberman

GUI Bloopers: Don'ts and Dos for Software Developers and Web Designers
Jeff Johnson

Information Visualization: Perception for Design
Colin Ware

Robots for Kids: Exploring New Technologies for Learning
Edited by Allison Druin and James Hendler

Information Appliances and Beyond: Interaction Design for Consumer Products
Edited by Eric Bergman

Readings in Information Visualization: Using Vision to Think
Written and Edited by Stuart K. Card, Jock D. Mackinlay,
and Ben Shneiderman

The Design of Children's Technology
Edited by Allison Druin

The Usability Engineering Lifecycle: A Practitioner's Handbook
for User Interface Design
Deborah J. Mayhew

Contextual Design: Defining Customer-Centered Systems
Hugh Beyer and Karen Holtzblatt

Human-Computer Interface Design: Success Stories, Emerging Methods,
and Real World Context
Edited by Marianne Rudisill, Clayton Lewis, Peter P. Polson,
and Timothy D. McKay

USABILITY ENGINEERING

Scenario-Based Development of
Human-Computer Interaction

MARY BETH ROSSON

Virginia Polytechnic Institute and State University

JOHN M. CARROLL

Virginia Polytechnic Institute and State University

MORGAN KAUFMANN PUBLISHERS

AN IMPRINT OF ACADEMIC PRESS
A Division of Harcourt, Inc.

SAN FRANCISCO   SAN DIEGO   NEW YORK   BOSTON
LONDON   SYDNEY   TOKYO

Executive Editor Diane D. Cerra
Publishing Services Manager Scott Norton
Production Editor Howard Severson
Assistant Editor Belinda Breyer
Cover Design Ross Carron Design
Cover Image *Pillar of Education*/© Hans Neleman/Imagebank
Text Design Detta Penna
Illustration Natalie Hill Illustration
Composition TBH Typecast, Inc.
Copyeditor Barbara Kohl
Proofreader Carol Leyba
Indexer Steve Rath
Printer Courier Corporation

Designations used by companies to distinguish their products are often claimed as trademarks or registered trademarks. In all instances in which Morgan Kaufmann Publishers is aware of a claim, the product names appear in initial capital or all capital letters. Readers, however, should contact the appropriate companies for more complete information regarding trademarks and registration.

Morgan Kaufmann Publishers
340 Pine Street, Sixth Floor, San Francisco, CA 94104-3205, USA
http://www.mkp.com

ACADEMIC PRESS
A Division of Harcourt, Inc.
525 B Street, Suite 1900, San Diego, CA 92101-4495, USA
http://www.academicpress.com

Academic Press
Harcourt Place, 32 Jamestown Road, London, NW1 7BY, United Kingdom
http://www.academicpress.com

06 05 04 03 02   5 4 3 2 1

Library of Congress Control Number: 2001090605
ISBN: 1-55860-712-9

This book is printed on acid-free paper.

Foreword

Terry Winograd
Stanford University

Designing good interactive software is neither a science nor an art. It is not yet a matter of routine engineering, yet there is far more involved than native skill and intuition. In years of teaching human-computer interaction design, I have often felt frustrated in trying to capture for students the experience of creating useful, useable, and likeable interactive systems.

Many pitfalls and breakdowns lie on the path to learning good interaction design. First, students need to encompass the breadth of concerns that go into designing any real system. Everything from the social context of the users to detailed keystroke analysis may be of significance, and it might even make the crucial difference between success and failure. A method or approach that focuses on one aspect or discipline may be valuable but is only one piece of the larger picture. Often students end up with a fragmented collage of multiple techniques and concepts with no sense of how to relate them. They are faced with buzzword overload, trying to cope with user-centered design, usability life cycle, heuristic evaluation, participatory design, low-fidelity prototypes, GOMS analysis, systems analysis, object-oriented design, and so on.

This wide breadth of concerns also leads to an endless bog of design choices and details where one is easily lost. Students hope for a guidebook—a list of principles that can be followed to get the "right" design. But guidelines are never sufficient. They are too abstract to offer direct application to any given case. Often two general principles apply, with opposite conclusions arrived at (as in the maxims "Look before you leap" and "He who hesitates is lost"). The easy tendency is to come up with a principle and hold onto it for dear life, in spite of context that makes it inapplicable. General principles cannot give a sense of the need to make tradeoffs, which is at the core of design thinking.

With all of this complexity facing them, students (and many practicing designers) are at a loss as to how to get started. Their tendency is to dive into screen designs and code development. They jump to a likely-sounding solution and start debugging it, without taking the time to understand the alternatives and priorities from the user's point of view. The concreteness of building a prototype provides a clear sense of incremental accomplishment as one piece, then another starts to function. In this software-centric process, it is all too easy to lose sight of the user—of not just what runs but also what matters, what makes sense, and what can be done.

Finally, student designs are often disconnected from previous experience and knowledge, both in the practical world of software and in the research world of relevant explorations. No matter how clever, any design suffers from lack of grounding in the collective knowledge of the discipline.

This is a tough list of problems, and as we like to say in computer science, "There is no silver bullet." Interaction design is inherently the kind of activity that thrives on experience and wisdom, not on having the right answer book. But a book can be of great help, and this one is a fine example. It is built around a few key insights that go a long way.

The first key idea, as the title conveys, is to integrate a design and development process around scenarios. Scenarios have people in them, they are specific, and they are grounded in the real world. By starting with scenario development in all aspects, students (and practitioners as well) can ground their designs in the issues that deserve attention. The scenarios provide concrete starting points and deliverables, and they tie together the different concerns and aspects of design into an understandable sequence.

The second key is the emphasis on understanding tradeoffs. Every decision reflects a set of assumptions, priorities, and alternatives. Rosson and Caroll show how to make this an explicit part of the design process. In addition to the methods in the book, the extensive references to the research literature give a starting point to pursue issues further when greater depth is appropriate.

Third, the extensive use of a coherent worked-out example from actual experience moves the student away from abstraction toward concrete understanding. People learn more readily from example than from generalities, and the science fair example provides the texture and depth to get beyond a vague sense of issues to an experiential sense of what they mean in practice.

And finally, the underlying wisdom of the book is in recognizing that the real benefit of a good methodology does not lie in its ability to give the right answers, but in its ability to provoke the right questions. In the end, interaction design is, as the book's title implies, a kind of engineering. Like all creative engineering, it requires the designer to make discoveries, not just apply formulas. A teacher or book can provide directions and suggest methods, but in the end, success depends on getting each designer to ask the questions that are right for the particular users, for the situation, and for the technologies at hand.

During the time I was reading the manuscript for this book, a student came in for advice on a dissertation project he had begun, focusing on interaction design for a new application in civil engineering. My first reaction was, "You need Rosson and Carroll's book." It was clear to me that its systematic approach to users and usability was sorely missing in his initial software-driven approach. I could think of no better way to get him started down a more productive path than to give him this book. I expect scenes like this to be repeated often in the future, as Rosson and Caroll's work becomes available to a wide audience of both teachers and practitioners.

Contents

Preface

This book grew out of a need for a different kind of textbook. In 1994, Rosson developed an undergraduate course in human-computer interaction at Virginia Tech. The course was intended chiefly for computer science undergraduates, though from the start there was considerable interest from students in many other departments. It was originally created as a technical elective for students with specialized interests. But it has become quite popular; in 2000–2001, about 200 students took the course at Virginia Tech.

The course was designed to be project based. For most students, this course provides their only exposure to HCI. This made it important to integrate concepts and applications in requirements, design, and evaluation of interactive systems. Existing textbooks provide sound coverage of HCI concepts and techniques but offer little guidance for comprehensive semester-long project activities. As we developed and refined the necessary project materials, the specifications became more and more unwieldy and distinct from the text that students were required to read. We needed a single book that integrated key HCI concepts and techniques into an overarching framework for the development of interactive systems.

How This Book is Different

This book differs in several important ways from existing HCI textbooks (such as Shneiderman's *Designing the User Interface* or Preece et al.'s *Human-Computer Interaction*). Our coverage of traditional HCI content is deliberately *minimalist*. We provide a broad view, but we do not attempt to be comprehensive. Instead we present material that we believe is either central to a general appreciation of human needs and preferences, or that provides crucial support for the analysis, design, and evaluation of effective interactive systems. For example, the book contains more content concerning requirements analysis, prototyping, and documentation design than is typical of textbooks in this area. But it also contains fewer pages on human perception and cognition.

The concepts and techniques of HCI are organized and presented through a series of *tradeoffs*. We use this rhetorical device to emphasize that there is never a single answer in the design and development of interactive computer systems. We wish to make it very clear from the start that students must think and reason about user needs. HCI guidelines are useful, but only in the hands of experts who know how to interpret and apply them to many different situations. Introducing HCI material as tradeoffs increases the level of abstraction; students who are hoping for simple answers may find this disconcerting, but it accurately reflects the state of knowledge about humans and their interaction needs.

The HCI content is integrated into a *usability engineering framework* on a chapter-by-chapter basis. We raise HCI issues and concerns as they normally would be encountered during project development. To some extent, this organization is artificial. It implies a waterfall that does not take place in practice (such as requirements to design to evaluation). But we feel that it is important for students in a project-based course to see immediately where and how the HCI issues apply to the analysis and design of interactive systems. The segmentation into chapters is necessary for pedagogical reasons.

The usability engineering framework is founded on the use of *scenarios* as a central representation for the analysis and design of use. A scenario describes an existing or envisioned system from the perspective of one or more users and includes a narration of their goals, plans, and reactions. Other usability engineering frameworks (e.g., Mayhew, 1999) make use of scenarios, but do not use them in the central and systematic way described in this book. The work with scenarios is complemented by many examples of *claims analysis*, a technique we have developed for documenting and reasoning about the pros and cons of design features.

Almost half of the book is devoted to a single, cumulating *design case study*. We use this example (a virtual science fair) to introduce and illustrate the scenario-based methods for requirements analysis, design, and evaluation. We have learned from experience that HCI students learn well from examples. We assume that students' class projects will be cumulative; if so, the case study will be useful as a model. A large set of supporting materials (interview guides, testing materials, etc.) is included, because we have found that students new to HCI need considerable guidance in behavioral methods. This particular design case was selected to be simple and familiar, but also quite open-ended with respect to requirements analysis and the new tasks and interactions it can motivate. It is presented as an example application developed within a larger community network project, the MOOsburg system (*moosburg.cs.vt.edu*). Additional real world case studies will be available through the textbook Web site (*www.mkp.com/ue-sbd*).

Our minimalist presentation of established HCI concepts and techniques is complemented at times with *modules* reporting on both current and classic research studies, design methods, or other topics of interest. These inserts describe HCI activities or concerns that are interesting and relevant, but optional with respect to the main goals of the chapters. We expect to replace or extend these modules in future editions, with the hope of better matching the rapid pace of information technology development.

How To Use This Book

This book was designed for a one-semester course introducing HCI concepts and methods. We are assuming 14 weeks; the book has 10 chapters. This allows one week for most chapters, with more time spent on chapters of most interest to the instructor, and with time left for exams and reviews. The central material is presented in Chapters 1–8, so some instructors may choose to cover only these chapters. In our own course, the material related to design and evaluation is essential, so we devote extra time to this. A suggested 14-week schedule might be:

Week 1   Course overview and SBD introduction (Chapter 1)

Week 2   Requirements analysis (Chapter 2)

Week 3   Activity design (Chapter 3)

Week 4–5   Information design (Chapter 4)

Week 6–7   Interaction design (Chapter 5)

Week 8   Review and discussion, midterm exam

Week 9   Prototyping (Chapter 6)

Week 10–11   Usability evaluation (Chapter 7)

Week 12   Documentation (Chapter 8)

Week 13   Emerging interaction paradigms (Chapter 9)

Week 14   Usability in the real world, review, and discussion (Chapter 10)

The term project should be organized and initiated as soon as possible. We have found that three phases provide a good organization for the project: requirements analysis, design and prototype, and formative evaluation. Students need 3–4 weeks for each of these segments; for example, the first phase might be due during week 5, the second phase during week 9, and the final phase during week 14. The Project Ideas section at the end of each chapter describes portions of an online shopping project that has worked well in our classes; students have enough familiarity with shopping and with Web applications to make progress on this in the short amount of time available. More details regarding project specifications and evaluation criteria are available on the companion Web site. The Web site also contains additional case study materials developed with the support of NSF's program in undergraduate education (NSF DUE-0088396).

Occasional homework or in-class exercises provide a more focused complement to the semester-long projects. The exercises at the end of each chapter are designed to get students thinking about the concepts and methods presented in the chapter. They can be used either for in-class group work and discussion or as homework problems. Sample answers will be made available to instructors via the book Web site.

In addition to a complete list of references, there is a glossary and an appendix that students and instructors may find useful. The glossary defines key HCI concepts. These terms are defined in context as well; each glossary term appears in bold when it is defined in context. There is also an appendix containing a brief introduction to the inferential statistics used in traditional behavioral experiments. These methods are rare in usability engineering practice, so we elected to leave them out of the main textbook content. However, instructors who require their students to carry out formal usability studies should find this material useful.

Acknowledgements

Many people have contributed to the development of this book. We have been much influenced by the other textbooks we have used in our classes, particularly the books by Preece et al. (1994) and by Shneiderman (1998). We have also benefited from our colleague Rex Hartson, who has spent years developing a usability engineering course at the graduate level. His project-based approach to teaching HCI had a formative effect on Rosson's undergraduate course and subsequently this book.

Some of our time developing the book was spent on sabbatical at the Xerox Research Centre in Cambridge, England. We thank our colleagues there for their support, particularly Allan MacLean, who hosted our visit. While there, we had the good fortune to be located near a group of researchers working on mobile and wireless computing, and we thank Mik Lamming, Marge Eldridge, and Mike Flynn, for introducing us to many of the current issues in this area of HCI.

Our development of MOOsburg, the virtual science fair case study, and of scenario-based methods in general has been supported by a number of agencies. We are grateful to NSF (REC-9554206), the Hitachi Foundation, and the Office of

Naval Research (N00014-00-1-0549). Many research associates and students have contributed to these projects over the last few years: Philip Isenhour developed CORK, the software architecture that is used in MOOsburg, as well as many of basic MOOsburg tools; Wendy Schafer developed the map navigation tool; Stuart Laughton, George Chin, Jurgen Koenemann, Dennis Neale, and Dan Dunlap helped us refine our participatory and scenario-based methods; and Christina van Metre and Robert Zinger contributed to some of the early analysis and design work on the virtual science fair. Jennifer Thompson, Wes Lloyd, Vinoth Jagannathan, and Jiunwei Chen worked on the Web-based case study library and browsing tools.

We would also like to thank our many reviewers for their extensive and very constructive comments. We are particularly indebted to John Bennett, Andrew Dillon, Sidney Fels, Doug Gillan, Jeff Johnson, John Meads, Kevin Mullet, and Bonnie Nardi. And of course, we have benefited throughout from the guidance and encouragement of our editors at Morgan Kaufmann: Diane Cerra, Belinda Breyer, and Howard Severson. Lastly we thank our daughter Erin, who has stepped up to many new responsibilities while Mom and Dad were busy working, and our dog Kerby, who in classic yellow lab fashion has happily ignored and energetically diverted much of the stress that comes with a writing project such as this.

1 Scenario-Based Usability Engineering

During the 1990s scenario-based software development techniques became increasingly prominent in software engineering and human-computer interaction. Anecdotal reports suggest that they are pervasive in contemporary software development practice. A study of 15 software companies in northern Europe reported that *all* were using various scenario-based techniques. Most of the projects used scenarios in the iterative development and analysis of prototypes. Scenarios were found to be especially useful in helping development teams reach sufficient agreement to enable work to proceed, and in ensuring consistency with predecessor systems. Two of the projects turned to scenario-based techniques after the standard software development methods they had been employing became too cumbersome! All of the projects surveyed emphasized the need for more comprehensive scenario-based methods (Weidenhaupt, et al. 1998).

───────◦◦◦───────

This introductory chapter discusses the problems in software development that motivate the use of scenario-based development methods. It also provides an overview of the scenario-based framework that forms the basis for the rest of the book and the case study that will be used to illustrate the techniques. We start with a brief example of scenario-based design, then shift to a historical survey of issues in software and usability engineering. We conclude with a discussion of the major phases and methods employed in scenario-based development.

1.1 Design by Scenario: Marissa's Gravity Project

In the mid-1990s, the U.S. government initiated a broad program of research and development in computer networking called the National Information Infrastructure. One target of this program was public education. It was hoped that networking could facilitate collaborative, project-based classroom learning; increase community involvement in public schools; improve access of rural schools to educational opportunities; enhance gender equity in science and mathematics education; and reduce equipment costs and handling.

In response to this national initiative, we created a partnership between Virginia Tech and the local school system to explore the uses of computer networks in science classrooms. Our initial wish list pointed in many directions; we were excited about the potential of computer networks. But many of the people in the new partnership were not software developers. They were not familiar with networking tools and applications. They were teachers, school administrators, parents, and other citizens. We needed to reach a consensus about the problems we would address and the approach we would take. We needed everyone to understand and agree on a plan.

We started by writing a problem scenario. In this context, a **scenario** is simply a story about people carrying out an activity; a problem scenario is a story about the problem domain as it exists prior to technology introduction. The problem scenario for this project (Figure 1.1) describes a hypothetical end-of-class situation in middle school science: Marissa has a question, but her question is not simple and well formed, and in any case time has run out. Will the question be in her mind tomorrow? Will it matter to her a day later? Has an opportunity to make science real for one child just been lost?

Scenarios are good at raising questions. Reading the problem scenario makes you wonder about the other students and what they are thinking. It also makes you think about how science classes work. Why is it important that the class period has ended? Why does this mean Marissa loses access to the teacher? Why can't Marissa work with other students on the problem? It seems a shame to waste Marissa's curiosity and energy.

In parallel, we wrote a design scenario that conveyed a new vision for science learning (Figure 1.2). This scenario describes a different experience for Marissa, where she continues to pursue her questions after school. She uses an online environment to collaborate with two other students, running simulation experiments, making visualizations of results, and writing a report. Of course,

---

- Marissa was not satisfied with her class today on gravitation and planetary motion. She is not certain whether smaller planets always move faster, or how a larger or denser sun would alter the possibilities for solar systems.

- She stays after class to speak with Ms. Gould, but she isn't able to pose these questions clearly, so Ms. Gould suggests that she re-read the text and promises more discussion tomorrow.

Figure 1.1 A problem scenario describing an episode from a science class.

- Marissa, a tenth-grade physics student, is studying gravity and its role in planetary motion. She goes to the virtual science lab and navigates to the gravity room.

- In the gravity room she discovers two other students, Randy and David, already working with the Alternate Reality Kit, which allows students to alter various physical parameters (such as the universal gravitational constant) and then observe effects in a simulated world.

- The three students, each of whom is from a different school in the county, discuss possible experiments by typing messages from their respective personal computers. Together they build and analyze several solar systems, eventually focusing on the question of how comets can disrupt otherwise stable systems.

- They capture data from their experiments and display it with several visualization tools, then write a brief report of their experiments, sending it for comments to Don, another student in Marissa's class, and Ms. Gould, Randy's physics teacher.

Figure 1.2   A design scenario describing our initial vision of a virtual school.

this is just one of many design scenarios that might have been written. We wrote the story to merge the vision of the National Information Infrastructure program with our own starting biases and interests. But any design scenario would have had the same effect—making the new ideas accessible to our partners from the community and the school system.

The full story of this educational technology project is a long one (Chin, Rosson, & Carroll 1997; Carroll et al. 1998; Carroll, Rosson, Neale, et al. 2000; Isenhour, et al. 2000). We worked for six years developing a suite of collaboration tools called the Virtual School (Figure 1.3). The tools allowed students from different classrooms (and occasionally with help from community mentors) to work together on science projects. Sometimes they worked together in real time; at other times they worked on their own at different times.

This system development project led us in many directions. We had to confront problems of running video conferences across school system firewalls, and to create an architecture for collaborative software. We also had to develop and apply participatory design methods that allowed teachers and students to participate in the design of the collaborative software (Carroll, Chin, et al. 2000).

Figure 1.3 A screen shot of some of the tools making up the Virtual School.

The current Virtual School consists of several integrated tools. The main window in Figure 1.3 (upper left) shows which members of a collaborating group are currently logged on, their shared notebooks, and recent project activity. It also is used to initiate text chat, video conferencing, and email. The central window shows a project notebook shared by all group members; the student is working on the Robot Pictures section. The student is placing an annotation in that section, soliciting comments from other group members. One of the student's remote collaborators is working on the Introduction (indicated by the lock on the section tab).

This brief history of the Virtual School project makes a critical point: The system we built is *not* the system envisioned in the design scenario. Of course this is not shocking—the initial design is almost never the one implemented. What is remarkable is that we wasted no resources in this change of direction. We did not have to build and throw away the wrong system, and then start again and build the right one. In fact, we barely noticed that our design changed in fundamental ways. The reason for this is that we used scenarios to raise and evaluate ideas as they came up. Scenarios let everyone contribute to analysis and design, critiquing proposals as they were suggested, comparing them with current classroom practices, mocking them up on paper, and revising them. Scenarios are rich and evocative design representations, but they are also cheap and easy to revise.

1.2   Managing Software Development

Software development is more than writing code. It is the activity of creating software; it is a *process* guided by systematic methods and techniques. The process is challenging because software is very abstract and very flexible; it is difficult to "see," but easy to modify. It is easy to introduce changes that address a specific concern but also undermine the overall design.

In the 1960s, the challenges of software development became enormous. Third-generation computer hardware enabled new applications, leading to software systems of much greater scale and complexity. The resulting failures—cost overruns, late delivery, and ineffective and unreliable systems—were labeled the **software crisis.** This crisis led to the emergence of software engineering as a professional discipline.

The software crisis has not yet been resolved. In the succeeding three decades, hardware costs continued to plummet, even as performance capabilities soared. Software development methods improved and greater attention was paid to software. Nevertheless, software engineering practices still lag behind the increasing scale and complexity of software systems. No single method or technology has yet provided a remedy for the software crisis (see the "No Silver Bullet" sidebar).

1.2.1   Software Engineering

Software engineering is founded on the ideas of structured programming (Mills 1971): Programmers first define the major structures of a software system—the database, the event handler, and the network server, and so on—and then recursively decompose (break down) each structure into substructures. The driving vision is to gain control over design activities by making the software development process explicit and systematic.

An early and influential model for software engineering was the **waterfall:** software development is organized into a series of modular phases, beginning

No Silver Bullet

Fred Brooks (1987) analyzed the perennial yearning for a software technology "silver bullet"—a single innovation that could make software development costs drop in the way hardware costs have. He argued that the essence of software is the abstract construction of data, relationships, and algorithms. Software is complex because these constructions are highly precise, uniquely detailed, and invariant under many representations. This inherent complexity is exacerbated by the fact that software is flexible: It can conform to its context of application, so it typically does, at the expense of undermining its own conceptual integrity; it can be changed and changed again without end, so it changes constantly.

Brooks discussed many breakthroughs in the history of software: high-level languages, time sharing, programming environments, and more recently, object-oriented programming, expert systems, and program verification. But he argued that these breakthroughs have addressed the management of software representations rather than the essence of software con-

struction. High-level languages reduce complexity by allowing programmers to think in terms of problem constructs, instead of being distracted by machine implementations that are not directly relevant to data relations and algorithms. Time sharing addresses complexity by allowing programmers to continuously interact with problems, instead of being interrupted by batch processes. Programming environments make it easier to simultaneously use different programs, including standard tools. None of these technologies offers direct support for the development of better abstractions about data, relationships, or algorithms.

Brooks suggested that one key to the problems of software development is iterative development. He argued that requirements can never be specified completely, precisely, and correctly, and that prototyping is necessary to develop correct conceptual structures. Systems themselves must be grown through incremental development. Finally, the key to successful projects is identifying and supporting great software designers.

with the analysis of functional requirements, and continuing through software design, implementation, testing, and maintenance. Each phase produces one or more documents that are handed off as a specification for the work of the next phase. For example, the software design phase produces a design specification that is used by the implementation phase, which in turn produces the program code used in the integration phase. The waterfall is a wonderful management tool, because projects are organized, tracked, and measured in terms of progress through the phases.

Separating software development into modular phases is a good idea. However, as we will see again and again in this textbook, software development activities are filled with **tradeoffs.** Multiple views of design ideas are common, and progress in part requires understanding and working with competing arguments. In this book we use tradeoffs as a general organizing technique, to identify general issues with competing lines of argument. A major concern for any software development project is the identification, discussion, and resolution of tradeoffs (see the "Tradeoffs in Design" sidebar).

One tradeoff associated with waterfall methods is that many requirements for a system cannot be anticipated and specified in advance (as in the Virtual School example; see Tradeoff 1.1). Unanticipated dependencies or entirely new requirements are often discovered only after clients interact with a running prototype of a system (Brooks 1995). This suggests that requirements analysis must come at both the beginning and the end of the development process; in the extreme this means that you cannot know what to build until you first build the wrong system. At the least, this tradeoff demands some degree of testing and iteration in software development.

Tradeoffs in Design

A truism about design in general is that there is never a single correct answer. Some solutions will be better than others, and some may even seem exactly right at the time, but there are always alternatives. This is what makes design difficult, but also what makes it fun.

One way to acknowledge this is to keep track of all tradeoffs that come up in a design process. For instance, making progress quickly trades off with more thorough analysis and planning. Designing a sophisticated user interface trades off with time to complete the project. Building a system that is incredibly easy to learn will lead to frustration down the line for expert users. And so on. People on a design team are constantly raising alternatives and discussing tradeoffs. Sometimes they even collect precise data to help them choose among alternatives with competing positive and negative arguments.

In this book we emphasize the important role of tradeoffs when thinking about design possibilities. Much of what we know about usability and user interface design can be couched in terms of tradeoffs, and we rely on this format to organize models, theories, and guidelines of human-computer interaction. In the case study materials that accompany each chapter, we show how to analyze and track specific design issues as tradeoffs.

A side effect of writing down and working with tradeoffs in design is the creation of a **design rationale**—documentation showing why specific design ideas are accepted or rejected (Moran & Carroll 1995). Although writing down the design rationale is time consuming (like any documentation effort), it can be very valuable when developing and maintaining complex systems over a long period of time.

TRADEOFF 1.1

 A software development "waterfall" helps to manage complex software development projects, BUT can deprive requirements analysts of critical information that becomes available only later in system development or use.

1.2.2   Prototyping and Iterative Development

The waterfall model offers a framework for addressing the software crisis, but is seen by many as idealized or simplistic. A strict linear flow of design specifications is unlikely to work for systems of nontrivial scale and complexity. Indeed, studies of programming practice have documented that skilled developers deliberately undermine waterfall methods (DeGrace & Stahl 1990).

A complement to structured development is **prototyping**, where designers develop one or more operational models to demonstrate a design idea. A prototype implements ideas that are abstract, making them concrete, viewable, and testable. By turning a proposal into a prototype, designers can test it for usefulness, feasibility, or other project concerns. Prototypes can be built at many phases; they can be used to evaluate requirements, high-level design, detailed software design, and so on (Boehm 1988). The feedback provided by prototyping is used to guide further development, but importantly, it may also be used to transform or reject aspects of the design.

However, prototyping and iteration create their own problems (Tradeoff 1.2). Process management can be difficult if the system evolves too rapidly to document and track the changes. Constant change can also undermine the integrity of a software design. It is difficult to schedule and deploy personnel in this paradigm, because the trajectory of the process unfolds over time, rather than being planned in advance.

TRADEOFF 1.2

 Prototyping encourages iteration in software development, BUT may lead to inefficiency or local optimization of software.

One way to integrate prototyping with structured design is to view prototyping as a requirements analysis method—prototypes are built as trial versions of a system that will be later discarded (Brooks 1995). Another approach is to assume that prototyping will be used to revise design documents. In **iterative development**, design documents are produced as an output of each phase, but they are continually modified through prototyping and testing. The final version of the design specification describes the system that was built (Carroll & Rosson 1985).

1.3 Usability in Software Development

Through the 1970s, it became clear that an important component of software engineering would be the user interface design. As more and more software was developed for interactive use, attention to the needs and preferences of *end users* intensified. In the 1960s, most software users were computing professionals who developed and maintained applications for their organizations. But as computing technology became more powerful, users became more diverse. Application installation and customization were simplified. Office professionals began to assume responsibility for operating their own application software. With personal computers (PCs), it became typical for end users to install and manage their own software. Today, the modal setting for software use is an ordinary person, or group of people, accessing information from the World Wide Web or using a software package installed on their PC.

1.3.1 The Emergence of Usability

As end users became more diverse and less technical, interactive systems came to be compared and evaluated with respect to **usability**—the quality of a system with respect to ease of learning, ease of use, and user satisfaction. The factors that make a system more or less usable are complex and are still the topic of considerable research. However, we can identify three distinct perspectives—human performance, learning and cognition, and collaborative activity—that have contributed to modern views of usability (Figure 1.4). Although these perspectives emerged at different points in time, they are not independent, and their relation is not one of succession. Rather they are complementary, pointing to the increasing richness of the general concept.

Human Performance

Usability entered the software development process at both ends: requirements and system testing. Marketing groups interviewed customers and analyzed competitive products to understand requirements. Quality assurance groups tested whether systems met design specifications regarding human performance with

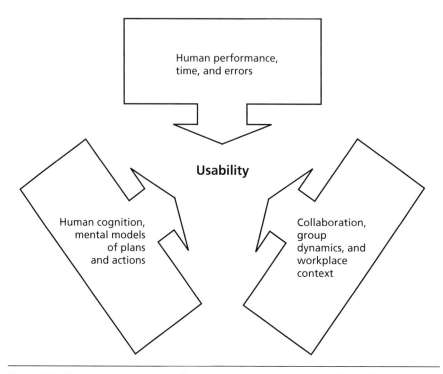

Figure 1.4   Three perspectives contributing to the general concept of usability.

the system; this testing was often summarized as **human factors** evaluation. Unfortunately, the marketing groups rarely talked to people who would actually use the products, instead gathering requirements from management or from similar products. It was also a problem that quality assurance testing occurred at the very end of the development process. The usability evaluators might gather realistic data (performance on a fully functioning system), but the findings were too late to have impact on design.

Solutions to the usability problem were both organizational and technical. Some companies reorganized usability evaluators into testing centers that provided services for both competitive analysis and quality assurance. Even though the quality assurance results still came too late to help redesign the target system, at least both sources of information could be integrated into planning for future systems.

A second piece of the solution was technical. In the 1970s, there was virtually no scientific basis for understanding usability—no general theories, and no standard empirical methods or techniques. But as the diversity of software applications and end-user populations increased, a variety of applied research programs appeared in the social and behavioral sciences and in industrial engineering.

The scientific foundations for studies of human performance are psychology and industrial engineering. The emphasis is on optimal performance—simpler displays and commands, fewer keystrokes, and shorter execution times (Card, Moran, & Newell 1980). Laboratory experiments are the norm, with results organized into guidelines for developers. A limitation of this approach is that the laboratory situations evaluated by researchers must often be simplified. Because users working with interactive systems exhibit great variability, researchers are often able to obtain statistically reliable results only by examining high-level comparisons (e.g., comparing menu versus command-line interaction).

It became clear that optimization of human performance would not be a comprehensive foundation for usability. There were several reasons for this. Although optimal performance is important in some circumstances, it is too narrow an objective. User interfaces that are optimized for keystrokes are not necessarily easier or more satisfying in use. The reliance on formal laboratory experiments was also problematic. Setting up such studies is slow and expensive, and they often produce findings too general to be of practical value.

Nonetheless, the specification and testing of human performance objectives demonstrated that usability could be studied empirically, and that it could play a role in software development. A first generation of experimental methods was developed, and important design variables were identified (e.g., display complexity and length of command strings). The human performance perspective also initiated two enduring themes in usability: (1) the search for broader foundations in science, and (2) the search for more effective roles within the software development process.

Human-Computer Interaction

As the PC era dawned in the early 1980s, new usability challenges emerged. There was far greater variety among users and applications, and in the ways organizations were influenced by usability problems. Rapid learning and self-study became critical, and product development cycles were compressed. This placed a high premium on lightweight methods for improving system usability, including inspection methods based on guidelines or theory. New programming languages and tools were helping to streamline software development. Small and distributed software development organizations became common, and prototyping was used more and more to drive system development.

The increasing prominence of PCs in society made usability more visible. One important new user group consisted of cognitive scientists—psychologists, anthropologists, sociologists, and philosophers interested in how people solve problems and learn new things. In the 1970s, many of these scientists were starting to use computers for their own research activities. Their personal experiences often prompted research programs exploring how people learn to use and solve problems on computers.

Text editing was the first computer-use experience for many of these researchers (e.g., Douglas & Moran 1983). Text editing is a complex task made up of lengthy sequences of planning, building, and modifying text structures. The goals and constraints of text editing change as text is created; text-editing skills develop over weeks and months, not just minutes; and writers possess real job skills, and accomplish real work. Many cognitive scientists felt that the field needed to study complex tasks of this sort. Soon spreadsheets, drawing programs, personal databases, and other applications were also in use. This new area of shared interest between computer science and cognitive science was called **human-computer interaction** (HCI).

A significant early HCI project was GOMS (goals, operators, methods, and selection rules; Card, Moran, & Newell 1983). GOMS is used to analyze the goals, methods, and actions of routine human-computer interaction. This was an advance in human performance testing, because it addressed the mental activities that guide behavior.

Other cognitive scientists studied the learning challenges of interactive systems. Learning requires connecting two sorts of knowledge, the task and the computer. An important issue here is how task needs are mapped to application services. Another issue is the role of the user's prior knowledge—new users try to understand computers by analogy to familiar activities and objects. This observation led to a variety of new user interface ideas, such as the now-pervasive "messy desk" display, and user interactions based on the concept of direct manipulation (Chapters 3 to 5).

A second impact of HCI was on the activity of design itself. Empirical studies of software developers revealed that they are quite opportunistic in their problem solving: Programmers do not just analyze, design, and then implement software. Instead they work on pieces of a solution that seem tractable, and then reconsider their understanding of the entire problem (Guindon 1990). The overall process is piecemeal and locally controlled.

These studies of design problem solving implied that usability input could be useful at any point in system development. As a result, usability evaluators began to use flexible and rich methods that could support a process of continual redesign. Thinking-aloud techniques (users comment aloud as they work through tasks) were shown to be of great use in understanding the mental activities that guide computer use. Such techniques were applied within an iterative development framework that studied end users' reactions early and continually through development (Gould & Lewis 1985).

By the late 1980s, the concept of usability and its role in system development had changed profoundly. Usability was no longer seen as assuring the quality of finished systems, or even as simply making functionality more accessible. It referred to a comprehensive process that included continual prototyping, thinking-aloud evaluation, and regular user involvement in requirements analysis and design. In many development organizations, marketing analysts worked with usability engineers to develop requirements in an iterative fashion. These changes meant that requirements and designs could not be specified in advance. One result was that software development activities became more unstructured and unpredictable.

Collaboration and Group Interaction

In the 1990s, the scope of usability broadened to incorporate social and organizational aspects of system development and use. In part this is due to the success of HCI. As usability specialists were asked to assist and direct a greater range of system development activities, their knowledge and skills expanded. In particular, as they played a larger role in requirements analysis, they began to address the social and organizational context in which people learn and use computers.

The broadening of usability was also caused by the internationalization of computer science in the 1980s. In European traditions, social and organizational aspects of human activity are less separated from cognitive and behavioral aspects than they are in the U.S. (Bjerknes, Ehn, & Kyng 1983). Finally, usability concepts and issues broadened in response to the new technologies for communication and collaboration that swept through the computing industry and society.

Usability came to include more emphasis on understanding the activities of users in the real world (Suchman 1987). This went beyond what is sometimes called task analysis; it involved detailed studies of work practices, roles, and concepts. Field methods were adapted from anthropology and sociology; usability engineers sometimes spent months at a work site collecting the data for requirements analysis. The descriptions such work produces are rich, but not very structured. The scenario-based framework presented in this textbook offers one approach to working with work-oriented methods of this sort.

As a worldwide community of usability engineers emerged, the field's scientific foundations became more diverse. For example, usability engineers became interested in activity theory, which describes how technology is just one part of a complex mix of social factors that influence individuals operating within a community (Nardi 1996; Chapter 2). But while such frameworks lead to a rich understanding of usage situations, the descriptions they produce tend to be ambiguous, because of a strong dependence on language.

Through the 1990s, electronic mail became a pervasive communication tool, and other Internet tools such as newsgroups, multiuser domains, and real-time chat became more accessible. Communication and the coordination of work using networking software had powerful effects on organizations. The portrait of a solitary user finding and creating information on a PC became background to the portrait of groups working together in a variety of times and places.

Computer-supported cooperative work (CSCW) is the current frontier for usability concerns and methods. For example, in the next decade considerable effort will be directed to building rich descriptions of work that can help in writing precise specifications of design solutions. However, usability engineering practice—and correspondingly the view presented in this textbook—continues to incorporate each of the three perspectives discussed here, that is, human performance, human-computer interaction, and computer-supported cooperative work.

1.3.2   Usability Engineering

The term **usability engineering** was coined by usability professionals from Digital Equipment Corporation (Good, et al. 1986). They used the term to refer to concepts and techniques for planning, achieving, and verifying objectives for system usability. The key idea is that measurable usability goals must be defined early in software development, and then assessed repeatedly during development to ensure that they are achieved (Bennett 1984; Gilb 1984).

From the start, usability engineering has relied on user interaction scenarios. For example, early proposals suggested that developers should track changes in performance times, errors, and user attitudes for specific task scenarios (Carroll & Rosson 1985). Such a process would allow developers to measure the impact of particular design changes on usability. Although the focus might be on the general implications of display features or commands, these functions would be considered in a concrete user interaction context.

Initially, usability engineering focused on the design of the user interface—on engineering effective interactive presentations of information and functions. More recently, the management of usability goals has been extended to other software development activities, particularly requirements analysis and system envisionment. This had a notable effect on software development documents: In the early 1980s, increased attention to usability led to the inclusion of user interaction scenarios as appendices in design specifications. By the late 1980s, such scenarios appeared at the front of these documents. Scenarios conveyed design concepts vividly and succinctly, and presented core functions within a meaningful usage context.

In the past 30 years, usability has become a central focus in software development. A 1992 survey of software developers reported that close to 50% of a system's software is devoted to the user interface (Myers & Rosson 1992). But, as we have observed above, the scope of usability is actually far greater than user interface development. Today, usability engineers help to determine what functionality is necessary and appropriate, as well as how it should be presented.

Nevertheless, usability is not everything. Many issues and constraints that bear significantly on the development of usable software fall outside the scope of usability engineering, and are not addressed directly in this book. Examples include team formation, resource assignment, or dependencies on legacy systems. Such concerns may be addressed by the methods of software engineering, or by business activities such as resource planning and scheduling. However, such concerns can have an indirect influence on the final usability of an interactive software system. Table 1.1 lists a number of such concerns; these concerns are often referred to as **nonfunctional requirements**, because like usability, they form external constraints on a project that are not directly related to the functions it will provide (Sommerville 1992). For each concern we briefly indicate how it might influence the goals of usability engineering.

Ultimately, software development is driven by economics. Even in a research setting where systems are designed to demonstrate or explore new concepts, project managers must make wise choices about relative costs and benefits of design features (Bias & Mayhew 1994; Karat 1993). As a simple example, a system that requires communication support can include email with considerably less cost than a collaborative virtual environment. Usability experts may argue persuasively for the latter, but the decision maker must consider usability benefits in light of many other constraints such as those summarized in Table 1.1. While we acknowledge this, the presentation in this book focuses more narrowly on usability issues—the manner in which a system supports users' work activities, the relative ease with which the system is learned and used, and the satisfaction that its users experience.

1.4   Scenario-Based Usability Engineering

Computers do more than just provide information and services for people to use. The design of computing systems is part of an ongoing cycle in which new technologies raise new opportunities for human activity; as people's tasks change in

Table 1.1 Examples of other nonfunctional requirements in a system development project that might interact with usability concerns.

Issue	Potential Impacts on Usability
Team membership	Failure to include usability experts on a team will limit attention to and resolution of usability concerns
Project size	Large complex projects are more difficult to coordinate and may lead to a focus on a few high-level, most critical usability issues; time limits will correspondingly limit the amount of iteration possible
Legacy systems	Prior commitment to existing hardware or software platforms may overconstrain the design space, eliminating some options that would significantly improve usability
Portability	The need to build multiple compatible versions of a system may encourage development of a "lowest common denominator"
Reliability	A need for highly reliable systems may require a distributed or otherwise complex architecture that later is reflected in the user interface
Maintainability	A system intended for a long lifetime may be designed in a modular fashion that separates tasks and activities seen as highly interrelated by users
Software economics	The technology cost of a useful function or user interface technique may be too prohibitive to warrant its inclusion in the design

response to these opportunities, new needs for technology arise (Carroll 2000). The basic argument behind scenario-based methods is that *descriptions of people using technology* are essential in discussing and analyzing how the technology is (or could be) reshaping their activities. A secondary advantage is that scenario descriptions can be created before a system is built and its impacts felt (Rosson, Maass, & Kellogg 1989; Weidenhaupt, et al. 1998).

1.4.1   User Interaction Scenarios

A user interaction scenario is a story about people and their activities (Carroll & Rosson 1990). For example, suppose an accountant wishes to open a folder displayed on his screen in order to open and read a memo. However, the folder is covered by a budget spreadsheet that he also needs to see while reading the memo. The spreadsheet is so large that it nearly fills the display. The accountant pauses for several seconds, then resizes the spreadsheet, moves it partially out of the display, opens the folder, opens the memo, resizes and repositions the memo, and continues working.

This is about as routine a work scenario as one could imagine. Yet even this story conveys important information about window management and application switching: People need to coordinate information sources, to compare, copy, and integrate data from multiple applications; computer displays inevitably get cluttered; and people must find and rearrange windows in these displays. Scenarios highlight goals that are suggested by the appearance and behavior of a system; what people try to do with the system; what procedures are adopted, not adopted, and carried out successfully or unsuccessfully; and what interpretations people make of what happens to them.

Scenarios have characteristic elements (Table 1.2). They include or presuppose a setting or starting state. The accountant scenario describes the starting state for the episode: the relative positions of the folder and spreadsheet and the presence of a single user. Other setting factors are implied by identifying the person as an accountant, and the work objects as budgets and memos.

Scenarios describe the behaviors and experiences of actors: There is just one actor in the example, but many human activities involve several or even many actors. Each actor has task goals. These are changes that the actor wishes to achieve in the circumstances of the setting. Every scenario involves at least one actor and at least one task goal. When multiple actors or goals are involved, some are usually more prominent than others. Often one goal is the highest-level scenario goal; this high-level goal answers the question "why did this story happen?" Similarly, one actor often has a principal role, the answer to the question "who is this story about?"

In the accountant scenario, the high-level goal is to compare the budget and memo information. A lower-level goal (often called a subgoal) is opening the folder that contains the memo; a further subgoal is resizing and moving the spreadsheet to expose the folder. Each goal or subgoal of a scenario is tied to efforts aimed at achieving the goal. Translating a goal into action and making sense of what happens afterward usually take place inside the actor's mind. But sometimes this mental activity is important to a situation, so scenarios usually include information about planning and evaluation. The emphasis on people's changing goals, plans, and understandings is one thing that distinguishes user interaction scenarios from the related software engineering concept of use cases (see "Use Cases" sidebar).

Table 1.2   Characteristic elements of user interaction scenarios.

Scenario Element	Definition	Examples
Setting	Situational details that motivate or explain goals, actions, and reactions of the actor(s)	Office within an accounting organization; state of work area, tools, etc., at start of narrative
Actors	Human(s) interacting with the computer or other setting elements; personal characteristics relevant to scenario	Accountant using a spreadsheet package for the first time
Task goals	Effects on the situation that motivate actions carried out by actors(s)	Need to compare budget data with values questioned in memo
Plans	Mental activity directed at converting a goal into a behavior	Opening the memo document will give access to memo information; resizing one window will make room for another
Evaluation	Mental activity directed at interpreting features of the situation	A window that is too large can be hiding the window underneath; dark borders indicate a window is active
Actions	Observable behavior	Opening memo document; resizing and repositioning windows
Events	External actions or reactions produced by the computer or other features of the setting; some of these may be hidden to the actor(s) but important to scenario.	Window selection feedback; auditory or haptic feedback from keyboard or mouse; updated appearance of windows

Scenarios have a plot; they include sequences of actions and events, things that actors do, things that happen to them, changes in the setting, and so forth. These actions and events may aid, obstruct, or be irrelevant to goal achievement. Resizing and moving the spreadsheet supports the goal of opening the folder. Resizing and moving the memo displays it in a way that enables simultaneous viewing with the spreadsheet. Pausing does not contribute directly to task goals,

Use Cases

At about the same time that usability engineers were developing methods of scenario-based design, software engineers were defining methods for object-oriented development that were based on **use cases**—an enumeration of the complete course of events that can take place given some user input; the case specifies all possible interactions between the user and the system (Jacobson 1990, 1995; Jacobson, et al. 1992). For example, in a telephone-switching system, a use case such as "customer-initiated call" includes events such as "customer picks up handset," "device ID is sent to system," "system sends dial tone," and so on. A fully detailed use case also includes any exception handling that may be required, such as the response sent by the system if an invalid phone number is entered by the customer.

In object-oriented analysis and design, use cases have some of the same features as user interaction scenarios—they decompose a service requested of a system into a series of inputs and system responses. One difference is that a use case is more general, including multiple possible responses to an input (if a user requests a cash withdrawal, the user's balance is first checked

and the response depends on the result of that check). Thus a scenario can be seen as one instance of a use case; it specifies an execution thread for a particular starting state and set of events. Use cases play an important role in identifying software design entities, services, and dependencies. They are also very useful in presenting and negotiating proposed functionality with clients.

Another difference between use cases and user interaction scenarios is the content included in the episode. Use cases are intended to be a complete description of what a system will do. User interaction scenarios specify functionality too, but always *in the context of use*. Scenarios focus less on completeness of coverage, directing attention instead to the design rationale and possible side effects of user–system interactions. Particularly early on in design, scenarios are deliberately underspecified, assuming that the details of a design will be worked out in an iterative process. One way to integrate the two methods is to develop use cases as a functional specification of user–system exchanges, and write scenarios that raise and consider the usability implications of these exchanges.

although it suggests that the accountant's actions were not completely fluent or automatic.

Representing the use of a system or application with a set of user interaction scenarios makes the system's use explicit, and in doing so orients design and analysis toward a broader view of computers. It can help designers and analysts to focus attention on assumptions about people and their tasks. Scenario representations can be elaborated as prototypes, through the use of storyboards, videos, or rapid prototyping tools (Chapter 6).

1.4.2   Why Scenarios?

Design and engineering always involve the management of tradeoffs. For example, the focus in usability engineering is often on "throughput"—optimizing user performance. However, usability engineers typically measure user satisfaction as well, and this does not always improve when performance is made more efficient (e.g., users may be required to learn complex keystroke combinations to speed interaction). Such a disparity between performance and satisfaction is not always problematic. Sometimes efficient performance is the highest-priority goal, and as long as user satisfaction stays within specified limits, the product meets its usability goals. But if a team is trying to optimize both performance and satisfaction, difficult tradeoffs may arise.

Explicit usability objectives—such as a 20% reduction in performance times—are needed to guide the usability engineering process (Bennett 1984; Gilb 1984). They take an abstract usability goal such as "more efficient human performance" and make it concrete and testable. These usability objectives must be clear and specific to be effective. They should be related to what people know and can do and what they wish to accomplish. They should state what will indicate success and what experience a user should have when carrying out a set of task actions and obtaining results.

At the same time, there is no guarantee that the starting goals of an engineering process are appropriate or even attainable. Sometimes good ideas are simply not practical: People may not accept the training needed to fully utilize a system's capabilities. The display hardware may not have the required resolution. Thus, while explicit and measurable goals are necessary, any particular goal may ultimately be discarded.

Scenario descriptions can be very useful in managing the tradeoffs of usability engineering (Figure 1.5). For example, scenarios are both concrete and flexible. A scenario can say what happens in a particular situation without committing to details of precisely *how* things happen. Much of the richness of a scenario is in the things that are not said. A scenario specifies its actors' goals and behaviors, and these can be arbitrarily detailed. Yet a scenario narrative is easily modified or elaborated, and can be made deliberately incomplete to help developers cope with uncertainty.

The concrete and flexible character of scenarios addresses the tension between wanting to make progress quickly but at the same time keeping the design space open for further change (Tradeoff 1.3). Designers can use scenarios to try out ideas and get feedback. But scenarios can be revised quickly and easily, helping to avoid premature commitment. Sharing and developing scenarios

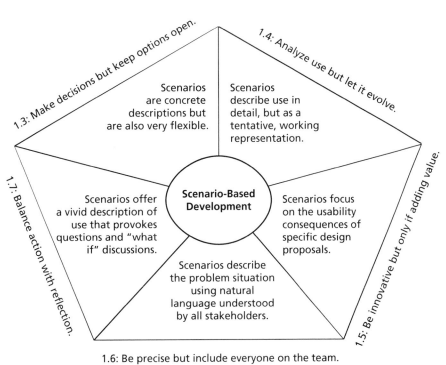

Scenarios are concrete descriptions but are also very flexible.

Scenarios describe use in detail, but as a tentative, working representation.

Scenario-Based Development

Scenarios offer a vivid description of use that provokes questions and "what if" discussions.

Scenarios focus on the usability consequences of specific design proposals.

Scenarios describe the problem situation using natural language understood by all stakeholders.

1.3: Make decisions but keep options open.

1.4: Analyze use but let it evolve.

1.7: Balance action with reflection.

1.5: Be innovative but only if adding value.

1.6: Be precise but include everyone on the team.

Figure 1.5 Tradeoffs in usability engineering addressed by scenarios. Numbers in figure correspond to the tradeoff numbers in the text.

helps to control the uncertainties of design work, while sharpening and strengthening design goals.

TRADEOFF 1.3

Designers are motivated to make progress quickly, BUT premature decisions and commitment can lead to poor solutions.

Another tradeoff in usability engineering is related to the observation that people's activities co-evolve with the technology they use: Designers must understand people's tasks to be able to support them with technology, but the new technology will change what people do (Tradeoff 1.4). For example, early spreadsheet programs revolutionized budget management. That success caused an increase in time spent using spreadsheet programs, which in turn caused spreadsheet users to develop new needs (Nielsen, et al. 1986). They wanted better support for budget projections, and better integration with other computer-based tasks, such as planning, communicating, and presenting information. Subsequent spreadsheet programs were designed to provide this support.

TRADEOFF 1.4

Analyzing users' current tasks is essential in designing useful and usable systems, BUT new designs change what people can do and how they choose to do it.

Scenarios help designers respond to current needs while also anticipating new needs. They offer insight into meaningful situations, but at the same time do not imply that things will stay the same. They describe systems in terms of the goals that people will be pursuing as they use the system. Scenarios focus designers on the needs and concerns of people in the real world.

Most designers hope to facilitate human activity with elegant and innovative systems. Everyone wants to invent the replacement to the spreadsheet or a better Web authoring language. However, not all elegant and innovative ideas will succeed like the spreadsheet or HTML; even elegant and innovative functionality can sometimes undermine usability (Tradeoff 1.5).

TRADEOFF 1.5

The rapidly evolving software market demands innovation and new features, BUT some functionality may actually undermine usability.

Sometimes good ideas are ahead of their time. In 1982, IBM produced the Audio Distribution System, a digital phone messaging system that even by today's standards had a very powerful set of file management and editing features. But the product did not do well in a marketplace oriented to analog phone answering technology—it was too advanced for the time. It required too much learning and too much conceptual change by users.

Software applications that are developed and refined over many versions often suffer from "creeping feature-itis." In searching for novel and elegant design ideas, developers can lose sight of people and their tasks. They push the technology envelope, but they do not create useful systems. Unfortunately, when functions do not contribute to the solution, they can become the problem: Unneeded functions create a learning burden for new users and continuing confusion for more experienced users.

Scenarios address this tradeoff by focusing software development on use, rather than on features that *might* enhance use. While it is certainly important for developers to push ahead with new technologies, pursuing them on a feature-by-feature basis invites side effects. Changing any individual user interface feature may impact the consistency of displays and controls throughout; it may even raise requirements for new functionality. Scenario-based analysis helps designers to steer between the twin risks of overconfidence (attempting to accomplish too much) and conservatism (attempting to do too little).

Yet another tradeoff concerns communication and collaboration in software projects. Programmers often use technical design representations (e.g., a data flow diagram) to express and share ideas; managers use their own specialized representations (e.g., a job specification) to describe their needs. These special-purpose representations increase the precision of communication. But they may also exclude participation by some individuals or groups who are important to successful development (Tradeoff 1.6). For example, end users are likely to have trouble following a data flow diagram; programmers may not understand the details or implications of a personnel description.

TRADEOFF 1.6

Technical design representations can increase the precision of communication, BUT may exclude participation by untrained team members.

Scenarios address this tradeoff by using a universally accessible language: All project members can "speak" the language of scenarios. Scenarios facilitate **participatory design**—design work that takes place as a collaboration between developers and the people who will use the system (Muller 1991, 1992). Scenarios help to integrate many different kinds of knowledge and experience by simplifying communication among different kinds of experts. Within a development team, scenarios assist in handoff and coordination, by maintaining a guiding vision of the project's goals.

A final usability engineering tradeoff comes in the conflict between thinking and doing. Developers want to take action and make progress quickly, but too great a focus on software construction can work against the reflection and analysis needed to discover and implement high-quality design solutions (Tradeoff 1.7). Developers naturally reflect on their activities as they work. However, as humans we take pride not only in what we know and learn, but in what we can show at the end of the day. It is impossible to predict or understand everything in advance, and long discussions of alternatives can be frustrating. People want to act, to make decisions, to see progress.

TRADEOFF 1.7

Software development provides concrete and rewarding evidence of progress, BUT can direct attention away from reflection and analysis.

Design review meetings are often used for reflection. In such meetings interim results are evaluated by working through objectives, progress reports, specifications, and so on. Such reviews can improve design work in many ways, by clarifying problems, alternatives, or decisions. However, a review meeting removes designers from the day-to-day context of their work; they must stop working to reflect.

The evocative nature of scenarios helps to address this. By telling a concrete story of user interaction, a scenario conveys a vivid image of what the system will do. It stimulates imagination and encourages "what-if" reasoning about alternatives. In a scenario it is easy to change the values of several variables at once and then think about the new states or events that might transpire. With scenarios designers can integrate their thinking about features that will or will not meet users' needs with the construction of situations that illustrate these thoughts.

Ultimately, the success of a design project depends on the care with which the problem is analyzed and solved. Scenarios are not a solution to a shoddy engineering process: If a team is unwilling or unable to take the time to analyze the needs of users, assess the available technology, and consider alternative solutions, only excellent design intuitions or simple luck will lead to good outcomes. However, scenarios are a lightweight usage-centered design representation that keeps designers focused on the overall goal of usability engineering—a useful and usable system.

1.5 Doing Scenario-Based Usability Engineering

This book shows how scenarios can be used to guide usability engineering—the scenario-based development (SBD) framework (Figure 1.6). The framework should not be understood as a waterfall, even though the diagram shows a "downward" flow from problem analysis to design and then to evaluation. At each step of the process, scenarios are analyzed and transformed in support of different development goals. We assume that all activities in SBD happen in an iterative and interleaved fashion, but for explanatory purposes we organize them into an idealized progression.

The chapters in the book motivate and illustrate the use of scenarios for addressing the many concerns of usability engineering. Together they demon-

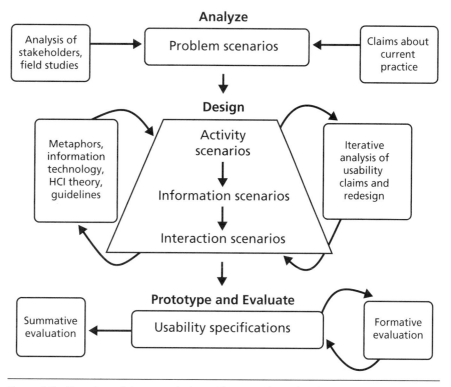

Figure 1.6 Overview of the scenario-based framework used in this book.

strate how scenarios can be constructed and analyzed for requirements analysis, to design a system's basic functionality, information layouts, interaction sequences, and documentation, and to develop prototypes and conduct usability evaluations. The penultimate chapter briefly surveys emerging interaction paradigms, and the final chapter discusses usability engineering in the context of related real-world constraints and pressures.

1.5.1 Analysis

The successive transformation of scenarios in SBD echoes the phases of software development—scenarios are used to analyze requirements, envision new designs, guide prototyping and implementation, and organize evaluation. In requirements analysis, the problem situation is studied through interviews with clients and other users (the stakeholders), field studies of the current situation, and

brainstorming among users and developers. This input is used to formulate problem scenarios that convey important characteristics of the users, the typical and
critical tasks they engage in, the tools they use, and their organizational context
(Chapter 2).

A key contribution of scenarios during requirements analysis is that they
evoke reflection and discussion. Writing down a narrative of one situation almost
immediately raises questions about other situations, about why this situation
(these users, these tasks) works the way it does, and how other situations might
work differently. The concrete and narrative character of scenarios also facilitates
mutual understanding and communication among the different groups who participate in requirements analysis.

In SBD, the analysis and refinement of scenarios is stimulated by claims,
statements that list important features of a situation and their impacts on users'
experiences. In requirements analysis, these features are elements in the current
situation; as the scenario content shifts from analysis to design, the claims call
out features of the proposed solution. Claims are related to the general notion
of tradeoffs in design, because they always analyze both positive and negative
usability impacts. The analysis of claims organizes and documents the "what-
if" discussions the design team carries out when considering and prioritizing
alternatives.

1.5.2   Design

The hub of any software development process is design—moving a project from
problem understanding to envisioned solutions. As a creative act, design often
seems mysterious. Requirements analysis can be overwhelming, but at least it is
anchored in the needs and possibilities of an observable situation. Evaluation can
also seem vast, but it too is anchored in the activities of real users working with
concrete design ideas or prototypes. Design stands between the two, vaguely indicating that a miracle occurs.

SBD organizes design into three substages with a rough ordering. First, developers envision activity scenarios—narratives of typical or critical services that
people will seek from the system (Chapter 3). These early scenarios provide a
concrete glimpse of the future that the designers are trying to enable through
their efforts. However, they deliberately focus on pure functionality, refraining
from specifying details about what the system will look like or how users will
manipulate it.

In the second design substage the team produces information scenarios.
These are elaborations of activity scenarios that provide details about the information that the system will provide to users. There are many complexities to

information scenarios. It is more than merely a matter of making it possible for people to see things on a computer display (Chapter 4).

The third substage involves the design of interaction scenarios. These scenarios describe the details of user action and feedback (Chapter 5). Each interaction scenario is a fully specified design vision: the users and task(s) being supported, the information needed to carry out the task, the actions the users take to interact with the task information, and the responses the system provides to users' actions.

System design does not happen in a vacuum. Although the designers using SBD methods begin with problem scenarios, they must actively search for new ideas to use in transforming the problem scenarios into design scenarios. They draw on many resources in this—analogies to real-world situations and objects, and their own knowledge of current information technology, along with their understanding of human abilities and preferences and relevant design guidelines. Throughout the design process, claims analysis is used to identify and discuss key features and usability tradeoffs.

As with requirements analysis, the reflection and discussion promoted by scenarios facilitate design at points where it is crucial to consider alternatives, and to work through the implications of design decisions. Scenarios are easy to write and change, so they support fluid and creative design reasoning. Again, as for requirements, the concrete and familiar form of scenarios enables input from many different interested parties.

1.5.3   Prototyping and Evaluation

SBD assumes that design ideas will be evaluated in a continuing fashion. This is often accomplished via a prototype that implements or demonstrates one or more pieces of the solution proposed in a scenario. Prototypes may be constructed at many points in design and with many different degrees of completeness or polish (Chapter 6).

A prototype can take many forms. For example, a very rough sketch could be used to prototype an activity scenario. Details of system interaction would not be specified, but people could evaluate the sketch in the context of the scenario, critique it, act out the scenario, explain it to peers, and so on. Potential users could read the scenario and look at the sketch, as an aid to considering whether the envisioned scenario meets their requirements, and how it might be elaborated to meet their information and interaction needs.

In SBD we distinguish between formative evaluation, which is carried out to guide redesign, and summative evaluation, which serves a system verification function (Chapter 7). Questions involved in the latter are: Have we actually built the system that was envisioned and specified? Did we meet or exceed the usability goals quantified in the usability specifications? In product development, summative evaluation is sometimes called the "go/no-go" test. If the product fails in summative evaluation, the process may start over (perhaps with a new product manager!).

In contrast, formative evaluation is aimed at improving a design prototype, not merely measuring overall quality. It asks questions such as: What is working poorly? Why? What changes might fix the problem? By the time the development process carries out a summative evaluation, it may be sufficient to know simply whether goals have been met. But earlier in the process, the development team needs information that can guide further development.

Scenarios guide evaluation through usability specifications—user tasks with specified usability outcomes that are evaluated repeatedly to guide redesign work. Scenario narratives describe the actors and their motivation, and other situation details that may influence people's ability to use or appreciate a prototype. Scenarios also predict the kinds of goals and reactions an evaluator will observe. As scenarios become more refined and concrete, they describe usability objectives more precisely, such as indicating how long a sequence of actions should take, or what reaction a piece of system feedback should provoke. In this sense, a scenario can be seen as a set of hypotheses about system use.

1.5.4   Other Approaches

All software development methods—and this includes all usability engineering methods—struggle with the tension between a waterfall with well-specified handoffs, and a flexible prototyping approach. Resolving the tradeoffs between these two perspectives will almost always lead to a linear development flow, accompanied by iterative feedback and reworking.

A good example is seen in Mayhew's (1999) usability lifecycle. This framework incorporates five major phases: requirements analysis, conceptual model design, screen design, detailed user interface design, and installation. Prototyping and iteration are integrated within a waterfall—all phases except requirements analysis include assessment activities that support iteration. The three central design phases (conceptual model design, screen design, and detailed user interface design) also include a combined assessment of whether all functionality has been addressed. If that assessment is not satisfactory, the process returns to requirements analysis.

Mayhew's usability lifecycle corresponds closely to the flow of analysis and development in SBD. One difference is in the role of scenarios in SBD as a unifying design representation. For Mayhew, the output of requirements analysis is a list of goals; the output of conceptual model design is a paper or computerized mock-up. In SBD the output of any phase includes user interaction scenarios. A secondary contrast is that SBD emphasizes the documentation and reasoning about tradeoffs throughout development.

Other general approaches to usability engineering include Nielsen's (1992) work on heuristic evaluation, Beyer and Holtzblatt's (1998) contextual design, and Constantine and Lockwood's (1999) essential use cases. As an eclectic framework, SBD shares features with all of these approaches: a mixture of analysis and design techniques, an emphasis on the detailed context of use, and an early emphasis on the basic functionality that users want. SBD differs from all of these other approaches in its central reliance on user interaction scenarios as an ongoing source of insight and reasoning about users' needs and experiences.

1.6 Example-Based Learning of SBD

Learning any method for software development is hard. Learning a usability method is especially hard, because human behavior is complex and unpredictable, and is influenced by so many interacting situation variables. Examples are very useful in presenting difficult material; a good example illustrates key concepts and can be used as a model for new problems (Gick & Holyoak 1980; Rissland 1984; VanLehn 1984). Thus, we present SBD methods by example through a case study of usability engineering. The example is cumulative; it develops scenarios progressively from requirements analysis through evaluation.

1.6.1 Case Study: A Virtual Science Fair in MOOsburg

Our example is drawn from a community network research project. HCI researchers at Virginia Tech are working with the town of Blacksburg, Virginia, on a community network system called MOOsburg (see *http://moosburg.cs.vt.edu*). MOOsburg is a **MOO**—a collaborative environment modeled on a geographic space, in this case the town of Blacksburg. People use MOOsburg to post or review community information (as they might also do using conventional Web sites; see *http://www.bev.net*). However, MOOsburg also provides a variety of shared interactive tools such as chat, electronic whiteboard and notebook, message board, calendar, simulations, and so on (Carroll, et al. 2001, 2001b). Co-present visitors can interact directly with these tools. Visitors can also create or modify objects for later use.

Figure 1.7   The MOOsburg system for community interaction in Blacksburg, Virginia.

Figure 1.7 shows three people visiting a local history museum in MOOsburg. The main view displays a panorama of the real-world museum; using the field-of-view control at the upper left, visitors can rotate the image to see the entire room. In front of the image are icons representing the three people online at this location. The visitors are using the text chat tool to discuss some of the exhibits. On the right is a toolbox from which they can create other objects for collaborative activities—for example, a shared whiteboard or a message board.

The map at the lower right is used to navigate to the virtual museum. The map corresponds to the real-world map of Blacksburg, and the virtual museum has been positioned at the real museum's street location in the town. MOOsburg users navigate by selecting dots on the map—each blue dot is an online site that can be visited; and places with other visitors are displayed in green. The map is zoomable, so that visitors can get an overview of the entire town (just the main roads show at the highest level) or zoom into a very detailed view (all roads, streets, and buildings are displayed). In this screen shot the user has zoomed in enough to see the building outlines.

MOOsburg has been explored and extended through the development of specific activities and tools within the general collaborative framework. We chart the development of one of these activities—a virtual science fair (VSF)—as the case study. The virtual science fair uses MOOsburg tools (e.g., email, online chat, discussion forums, and multimedia displays) to create a supplement to a traditional American science fair.

In a science fair, students develop individual projects. They exhibit their projects at the fair, where the exhibits are judged and awarded prizes. Although a science project is developed over many months, the fair itself takes place over a few hours. Science fairs are open to the public, but normally are attended by the participating students and their friends and families. The high-level concept for the virtual science fair is to extend the boundaries of a traditional science fair. Using MOOsburg, we hope to make the fair attractive and accessible to a larger group of community members, and to enrich the activities of exhibit construction, viewing, and judging.

The science fair case study will be presented in a cumulative fashion to illustrate the SBD process shown earlier in Figure 1.6. The central elements are covered in Chapters 2 through 8 (Table 1.3). Chapter 2 covers techniques for analyzing a problem situation (in this case a traditional science fair), and generating problem scenarios. Chapters 3 through 5 cover the three phases of design, first focusing on the activities that will be supported, then elaborating the scenarios to include the details of information representation and interaction techniques. Chapter 6 describes the creation of virtual science fair prototypes, and Chapter 7 illustrates how these prototypes can be used in usability evaluation. Chapter 8 illustrates the special design problem of creating effective learning and help materials.

Some of the case study materials presented in the book were developed in the MOOsburg project; others were created to serve the educational goals of this textbook. The result is a comprehensive model for students or practitioners who wish to apply scenario-based methods to usability engineering projects. At the same time, the science fair project has several domain-specific characteristics, including the following:

- there is no underlying business unit providing financial or organizational structure;

- it is relatively free of development schedules and similar external constraints;

Table 1.3 Scenario-based design techniques and methods illustrated by the virtual science fair case study.

Chapter	Techniques Illustrated	SBD Analysis and Design Products
Chapter 2: *Analyzing Requirements*	Stakeholder analysis, hierarchical task analysis, user profiles, interviews, artifact analysis, videotaping, field notes, theme analysis, stakeholder diagrams, participatory analysis	Problem scenarios Claims documenting tradeoffs in stakeholders' current practices
Chapter 3: *Activity Design*	Exploration of conceptual metaphors and MOOsburg services, reasoning from problem claims, participatory design	Activity design scenarios Claims documenting tradeoffs in the design of VSF activities
Chapter 4: *Information Design*	Exploration of presentation metaphors and MOOsburg information technology, reasoning from activity claims, screen and icon design, participatory design	Design scenarios elaborated to include information design details Claims documenting tradeoffs in VSF information design
Chapter 5: *Interaction Design*	Exploration of presentation metaphors and MOOsburg interaction technology, reasoning from activity and information claims, storyboards, participatory design	Design scenarios elaborated to include interaction design details Claims documenting tradeoffs in VSF interaction design
Chapter 6: *Prototyping Evaluation*	Key screens, scenario machine, evolutionary development	Mock-ups, screens, and other prototypes of the interaction design scenarios
Chapter 7: *Usability Evaluation*	Questionnaires, task instructions, data collection forms, verbal protocol and critical incident analysis, descriptive statistics	Usability specifications Usability test results
Chapter 8: *User Documentation*	Exploration of learning and help metaphors and MOOsburg help facilities, reasoning from activity, information, and interaction claims	Documentation design scenarios Claims documenting tradeoffs in VSF documentation design

- its target users are a population of diverse community residents whose participation will be entirely discretionary; and

- it has a strong emphasis on science education, communication, and collaboration.

Thus, while the methods illustrated are general, students will find that not all details will map directly to other usability engineering projects. Other examples can be found on the textbook's Web site (*www.mkp.com/ue-sbd*).

Summary and Review

This chapter has provided a brief review of the challenges and methods that have contributed to modern software engineering practices, and to the emergence of usability engineering as a concern within software development. It has also introduced the basic concepts and rationale for scenario-based development. Central points include:

- It is possible to combine prototyping with structured development—prototypes are used to evaluate, reconsider, and refine the specification documents produced during the different phases of development.

- Tradeoffs are a fundamental aspect of any design process and should be a central focus in design reasoning.

- Usability emerged as an issue when the population of end users and the situations in which computing was used expanded from specialty to general-purpose use.

- Usability can be seen as a union of three perspectives: the human factors of perception and performance, the cognitive interactions of humans and computers, and the groups and organizations that provide the context for personal computing.

- Usability engineering is supported by the specification and evaluation of measurable usability objectives throughout the system development lifecycle.

- Scenarios describe the setting, actor(s), and events of a user–computer interaction, but also include information about users' mental activities (goals, plans, and reactions).

- Scenarios are concrete descriptions of action that are rough and flexible in content and level of abstraction. These characteristics help usability engineers address a number of fundamental tradeoffs in the design and development of usable systems.

- Scenario-based development can be seen as a modified waterfall where the analysis of requirements leads to design, and ultimately to testing and deployment.

- Scenarios integrate the many tasks of system development by first organizing the analysis of user needs, and then serving as central representations of user needs that are developed in a systematic manner through design, evaluation, and documentation activities.

Exercises

1. Do you agree with Brooks's claim that there is no silver bullet? Why or why not?

2. Suppose you are involved in development of an online banking service. List the pros and cons of using only the waterfall model versus a process that includes rapid prototyping and iterative development.

3. Choose a common computer-based task domain (e.g., email, Web browsing, or word processing). Discuss one or two major tasks in this domain from the perspective of task and technology co-evolution. How have your tasks changed as a function of technology that has become available over the past few years? How have your own (or other users') needs influenced the technology?

4. Consider the design of your personal Web page. List some tradeoffs that you would consider (or did consider) in constructing this page.

5. Write a sample scenario that describes someone reading her email when she arrives at the office in the morning. Be sure to include all of the standard elements (Table 1.2).

6. Revise your scenario to consider the impact of different users, a different setting, or different goals or reactions.

Project Ideas

Organize into a small group (three to four students). Select a modern computing application domain that you are all familiar with, such as Internet shopping.

Analyze the problem from the three perspectives on usability discussed in the chapter (Figure 1.4). Answer these questions:

- What online shopping issues are suggested by each perspective?

- How might you address these issues if you were to develop a sample application in this domain?

- How might Tradeoffs 1.3 through 1.7 apply to the process of developing an Internet shopping application?

After your initial discussions, sketch out a scenario-based process you could follow to develop an Internet grocery store, working from the summary of SBD (Figure 1.6). Show how the general activities summarized for SBD would be translated into your problem domain of food shopping.

Recommended Reading

Brooks, F. 1995. *The Mythical Man-Month: Essays on Software Engineering.* Anniversary ed. Reading, MA: Addison-Wesley.

Carroll, J. M. 2000. *Making Use: Scenario-Based Design of Human-Computer Interactions.* Cambridge, MA: MIT Press.

Carroll, J. M., ed. 1995. *Scenario-Based Design: Envisioning Work and Technology in System Development.* New York: John Wiley & Sons.

Jacobson, I., M. Christersson, P. Jonsson, & G. Övergaard. 1992. *Object-Oriented Software Engineering: A Use Case Driven Approach.* Reading, MA: Addison-Wesley.

Mayhew, D. J. 1999. *The Usability Engineering Lifecycle: A Practitioner's Handbook for User Interface Design.* San Francisco: Morgan Kaufmann.

Sommerville, I. 1992. *Software Engineering.* 4th ed. Reading, MA: Addison-Wesley.

2

Analyzing
Requirements

Make work visible. This end goal of requirements analysis can be elusive when work is not understood in the same way by all participants. Blomberg, Suchman, and Trigg (1996) discuss this in their exploration of image-processing services for a law firm. Their studies of the firm's attorneys produced a rich analysis of document processing needs—for each legal proceeding, documents often numbering in the thousands are identified as "responsive" (relevant to the case) by junior attorneys, in order to be submitted for review by the opposing side. Every document page is given a unique number for retrieval purposes. An online retrieval index is created by litigation support workers; the index encodes document attributes such as date, sender, recipient, and type.

The attorneys told the analysis team that it would be easier to make the relevance decisions if the documents could be processed automatically to encode their objective attributes (e.g., date and sender). However, studies of human document processing revealed activities that were not objective at all, but rather relied on the informed judgment of the support staff. Something as simple as a document date was often ambiguous, because the index might display the date it was written, signed, and/or delivered; the date encoded required understanding the document's content and role in a case. Even determining what constituted a document required judgment, as papers came with attachments and no indication of beginning or end. Taking the perspective of the support staff revealed knowledge-based activities that were invisible to the attorneys, but that had critical limiting implications for the role of image-processing technologies (Blomberg 1995).

In this chapter we introduce the goals and methods of **requirements analysis**, the phase of software development in which the needs of clients with respect to a proposed project or technology are analyzed. Requirements analysis usually starts with a mission statement or orienting goals, then becomes more elaborate through studies and meetings with prospective clients. Under the waterfall model, the result is a **requirements specification**, a document that lists all functions and features that the proposed system must satisfy.

User-centered approaches to software development recognize that it is impossible to specify all requirements in advance. Clients cannot appreciate their real needs until they see what kinds of options are available; work practices naturally evolve as new technology is introduced. However, this does not mean that requirements analysis is impossible or unimportant, but simply that it must be seen as an ongoing process. Analysts must still develop a detailed understanding of clients, their current work practices, and their needs with respect to the technology under consideration. They must develop and convey a rich description of the problems and opportunities that could be addressed through software design and development.

In the legal office case described above, the mission was to find business applications of image processing. The requirements analysis team studied the processing of legal cases to understand how this activity might be enhanced by image processing. They discovered that different work groups (attorneys versus their data processing staff) had very different understandings of case processing. Thus, an important contribution of requirements analysis in this situation was to capture these different perspectives of the problem.

Usability engineers participate in requirements analysis by studying how work currently takes place to see if they can identify problems or opportunities that might be addressed by new technology. This analysis provides crucial input to the design of new computing systems: At a minimum, a project team hopes to enhance the current situation. Of course other input will be provided by analyses that look at concerns such as hardware platforms, cost, development schedule, or marketing strategies. But because this book is about understanding and responding to the needs of users, we limit our discussion to concepts and methods for analyzing usage concerns.

2.1   Analyzing Work Practices

What is work?[1] Try asking yourself or a friend this question. You will probably come up with the things you do during a typical day, the objects or tools you work with, and perhaps the people you talk to. A description of work involves three dimensions:

---

[1]In this discussion we use "work" to refer broadly to the goal-directed activities that take place in the problem domain. In some cases, this may involve leisure or educational activities, but in general the same methods can be applied to any situation with established practices.

- the **activities** of the workplace: What are the personal or organizational goals that individuals or groups pursue? What actions do they carry out to pursue these goals?

- the **artifacts** of the workplace: What information is retrieved or created in the course of carrying out work activities? What tools (computer based or not) are used to create and work with this information?

- the **social context** of the workplace: How are individuals and groups organized into larger structures? What roles are defined (implicitly or explicitly)? How do people depend on each other in achieving their goals?

Analyzing all of these aspects of work is complex. A popular approach for analyzing the first dimension (activities) is **hierarchical task analysis** (HTA): Individual tasks and subtasks are identified and organized into a hierarchy (Diaper 1989). For instance, in a bank the task of REVIEW-ACCOUNTS might be decomposed as RETRIEVE-ACCOUNT-LIST, FIND-RECENT-ACTIVITY, and REVIEW-ACTIVE-ACCOUNTS (Figure 2.1). Each subtask is also decomposed; for example, FIND-RECENT-ACTIVITY might break down into READ-LISTING and CHECK-DATE. If needed, an HTA can be elaborated to a very fine level of detail, perhaps including physical actions such as picking up or repositioning a document. HTA also indicates decision making, such as when a banker must decide whether or not to open up a specific account based on its level of activity.

A strength of HTA is the step-by-step transformation of a complex activity space into an organized set of successive choices and actions. The resulting hierarchy can be examined for completeness, complexity, inconsistencies, and so on. However, too much emphasis on task decomposition can be problematic (Trade-off 2.1). An analyst can become consumed by representing task elements, step sequences, and decision rules. Tasks and subtasks must always be understood

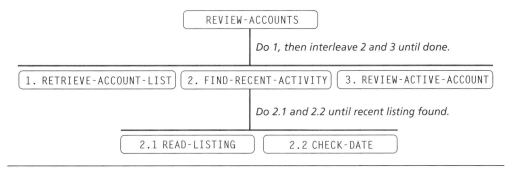

Figure 2.1 Hierarchical task analysis of a hypothetical account review task.

within the larger context of work; overemphasizing the steps of a task can cause one to miss the forest for the trees. Part of understanding what it means to review accounts at a bank is learning about the banking organization—who makes certain that accounts are up to date, who has access to various accounts, what happens once an account is reviewed, and so on.

TRADEOFF 2.1

Hierarchical task analysis documents the functional goals of a workplace, BUT may direct attention away from an organization's social relationships and goals.

The social context of work includes the physical, organizational, social, and cultural relationships that contribute to a work environment. Work activities do not take place in a vacuum. Tasks are motivated by personal goals; these in turn are motivated by the higher-level goals held by the organizations sponsoring the work (see "Activities of a Health Care Center" sidebar). A banker may report that she is reviewing accounts, but the bank may view this as "providing customer service" or perhaps "increasing return on investment."

Of course, the banker is not the only person working toward this high-level goal. Secretaries, data-entry personnel, database programmers, even the bank's executives, work with the banker to meet the bank's business goals. They collaborate by communicating with each other about their personal activites, as well as through shared tools and information. Their interactions are shaped not only by the tools they use, but also by their shared understanding of the bank's business practices—its goals, policies, and procedures.

Another aspect of work analysis is the study of workplace artifacts. The tools that people use to carry out their tasks can provide considerable insight into how they do their work (Carroll & Campbell 1989). An artifact is simply a designed object—typical office artifacts include the furniture, writing instruments and supplies of various sorts, forms and lists, folders, shelves and cabinets for storage, and computers and associated software packages (Figure 2.2). The features of each artifact encourage different kinds of actions and thoughts. For example, a pencil has a shape and weight compatible with the action of holding it between two or more fingers, sliding it across paper, and so on; the buttons on a phone have just the right size and resistance for human finger-presses; and a tape dispenser has a weight and sharp serrated edge to enable one-handed tearing of tape segments.

It is easy and fun to find artifacts and analyze their characteristics (Norman 1987, 1988). Returning to the example of a pencil, note that its shape suggests

Figure 2.2 Photograph of a receptionist's desk at Virginia Tech. The desk and its surroundings hold a huge set of artifacts used in the employee's day-to-day activities.

quite a bit about human hands, such as their size and grasping behavior. Pencil designers succeed to a great extent by giving new designs the physical characteristics of pencils that have been used for years. But the artifact is just part of the picture. Even an object as simple as a pencil must be analyzed with respect to its real-world use (Tradeoff 2.2). Different uses of pencils bring out different concerns—elementary school students need good erasers; very sharp points are important to architects or graphic artists; and preteens competing for social status may care only about name-brand visibility. In the photograph above, the receptionist positions a wide variety of writing instruments in a visible and accessible location so that visitors will find and use the tools as needed.

TRADEOFF 2.2

 Work artifacts reflect knowledge, roles, and procedures related to a task, BUT the actual meaning of an artifact is apparent only when observed in use.

Usability engineers have adapted some of anthropology's methods for analyzing the activities, artifacts, and social context of work. **Ethnography** is an

Activities of a Health Care Center

Activity theory offers a view of task analysis that emphasizes the goals and practices of a community (Bødker 1991; Nardi 1996). In this framework, an activity is comprised of three elements: a *subject* (the actor), the *community* in which he or she is operating, and the *object* of the activity (the goal). However, each of these elements is mediated by other features of the activity—the *tools* that support the work, the *rules of practice* that define the conventions and procedures to be followed, and the *division of labor* that positions the goal of this activity within the community in general.

Kuutti and Arvonen (1992) exemplify this framework for a health clinic. The organization wanted to evolve from a highly bureaucratic organization with strong separations between its various units (e.g., social work, clinics, and hospital) to a more service-oriented organization. A key assumption was that different units share a common object—enhancing the "life processes" of the town's citizens. This object was understood to be a complex goal requiring the integrated services of complementary health care units.

Activity theory provides an analysis of individuals acting within this community— for example, a physician. Although the entire community shares the goal of patient care, the physician works in a clinic, which is analyzed as a subcommunity. This clinic is geographically and functionally separated from other units, like the hospital and social work office. His day-to-day behavior is mediated by the tools and the rules of practice of his subcommunity.

As a result, the physician has no way to integrate his efforts with the work done by health care workers in the other subcommunities. For instance, he cannot benefit from the work on home life carried out by a social worker, or psychiatric treatments. There is a mismatch between the high-level shared goal and the physical working conditions. In activity theory, this mismatch is raised as a *contradiction* that must be resolved before the activity can be successful. In this case study, a more comprehensive analysis of "community" was needed. Email and telephone were used to foster a new virtual community, bringing together workers from different health units.

analytical technique used by anthropologists to gain insights into the life experiences of people whose everyday reality is vastly different from the analyst's (Blomberg 1995). An ethnographer becomes intensely involved in a group's culture and activities, sometimes even joining the group as a participant-observer.

In the HCI community, ethnography involves observations and interviews of work groups in their natural setting, as well as collection and analysis of work artifacts (see "Teamwork in Air Traffic Control" sidebar on pages 44–45). These studies are often carried out in an iterative fashion, where analysis of one set of data raises questions or possibilities that are pursued in follow-up observations and interviews. However, a full ethnographic study implies weeks or months of observation, and system development projects rarely have this luxurious a schedule. In practice HCI professionals often rely on "quick-and-dirty" ethnographies—these field studies are carried out in a more intensive and focused fashion, with the goal of learning just enough to guide subsequent design activities (Nardi 1997; Hughes, et al. 1996).

2.2 Getting Users Involved

Who are the users? This is obviously an important question in user-centered development. It is first raised during requirements analysis when a project team needs to decide whose activities to study. Managers or corporate executives are a good source of high-level needs (e.g., reduce data-processing errors, or integrate billing and accounting). These individuals may also have a coherent view of many workers' responsibilities and of the conditions under which tasks are completed. Because of the hierarchical nature of most organizations, these people are easy to identify and comprise a relatively small set. But if a requirements team stops there, they will miss the more detailed and situation-specific needs of the people who will be using the new system (Tradeoff 2.3).

TRADEOFF 2.3

Experienced workers have detailed knowledge about a task's context and operation, BUT people in related roles may have completely different understandings.

Requirements analysis must consider multiple **stakeholders**—the many different groups of people who will be impacted by the development of the system (Checkland 1981; Muller 1991). Managers authorize the purchase or development of a new computer system; workers with various job responsibilities use the system; and other employees may benefit or suffer indirectly. Each set of stakeholders has motivations and problems that a proposed system may address (e.g., productivity, satisfaction, or ease of learning). None of them can adequately communicate the perspectives of the others—as summarized in the law office sidebar, many details of a subordinate's work activities and concerns are simply invisible to those in supervisory roles. Requirements analysis must bring the full range of stakeholder groups into the observation and interviewing activities.

But do people even understand their own activities? We made the point earlier that too much focus on the steps of a task can cause analysts to miss important workplace context factors. A similar point holds with respect to interviews and discussions. People are remarkably good (and reliable) at "rationalizing" their behavior (Ericsson & Simon 1993). Thus, if asked, workers describe the prescribed

---

Teamwork in Air Traffic Control

An ethnographic study of British air traffic control rooms by Hughes, Randall, and Shapiro (1992) highlighted a central role for the paper strips used to chart the progress of individual flights. In this study the fieldworkers immersed themselves in the work of air traffic controllers for several months. They observed the activity in the control rooms and talked to the staff, and they also discussed with the staff the observations they were collecting and their interpretation of these data.

   The goal of the study was to analyze the social organization of the work in the air traffic control rooms. The researchers showed how the flight progress strips supported individuation—the controllers knew what their jobs were in any given situation, but also how their tasks were interdependent. This division of labor was accomplished smoothly because the controllers had shared knowledge of what the strips indicated; they were able to take on and hand off tasks as needed, and to recognize and address problems that arose.

   Each flight strip displays identifying information about an aircraft, its flight plan,

and its current status (see figure on facing page). However, these artifacts are more than just information displays. The strips are *work sites*, used to initiate and perform control tasks. Each strip is printed from the online database, but then annotated as flight events transpire. This creates a public history, so that any controller can reconstruct a "trajectory" of what happened with the flight. The strips are used along with radar data to spot exceptions or problems with standard ordering and arrangement of traffic. Individual strips get "messy" to the extent flights have deviated from the norm; thus, a set of strips serves as a sort of proxy for the orderliness of the skies.

   The team interacts through the strips. Once a strip is printed and its initial data verified, it is placed in a holder that is color coded for its direction. It may then be marked up by different controllers, each using a different ink color; problems or deviations are signaled by moving a strip out of alignment, so that visual scanning detects problem flights. This has important social consequences for the person responsible for a flight. This individual knows that other

---

or most typical version of a task. If a "procedures manual" or other policy document exists, task descriptions may mirror the official procedures and policies.

   However, this officially blessed knowledge is only part of the picture (Tradeoff 2.4). Experienced workers also possess much "unofficial" knowledge, learned when dealing with the specific needs of different situations, exceptions, particular coworkers, and so on. This expertise is often held as **tacit knowledge**— experts may not even realize what they "know" until confronted with their own behavior or interviewed with situation-specific probes. Tacit knowledge about work is often very valuable, because it may contain the "fixes" or "enhancements" that have developed informally to address the problems or opportunities of day-to-day work.

Teamwork in Air Traffic Control *(continued)*

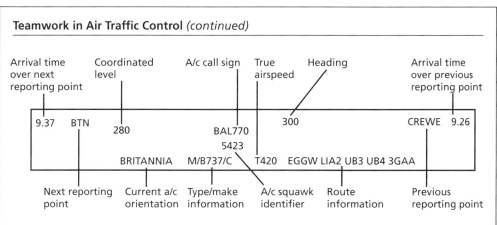

Diagram of the flight strip studied by Hughes, Randall, and Shapiro (1992, 117).

team members are aware of the flight's situation and can be consulted; who, if anyone, has noted specific issues with the flight; if a particularly difficult problem arises it can be passed on to the team leader without a lot of explanation; and so on.

The ethnographic analysis documented the complex tasks that rely on the flight control strips. At the same time it made clear the constraints of these manually created and maintained records. A particularly compelling observation was *trust* of

the strips. This was due not to the strips' physical characteristics, but rather to the social process they are part of—the strips are public; and staying on top of each other's problem flights, and discussing them informally while working or during breaks, is simply taken for granted. Any computerized replacement of the strips must support not just management of flight information, but also the social fabric of the work setting that makes the controllers confident of the information around them.

TRADEOFF 2.4

Documented standard procedures make work smooth and stress free, BUT much of an employee's value comes in the tacit recognition and resolution of exceptions.

Sachs (1993, 1995) suggests that organizations can understand themselves from two different perspectives—an "organizational, explicit" view and an "activity-oriented, tacit" view (Table 2.1). The organizational view is easy to reveal and document, because it is described in company policies and procedures. For example, a **workflow system** is a business support system that models explicit

Table 2.1 Contrasting an organizational, explicit knowledge view with an activity-oriented, tacit knowledge view (after Sachs 1995, 38).

Organizational Explicit View	Activity-Oriented Tacit View
Training	Learning
Tasks	Know-how
Position in hierarchy	Informal political systems, network of contacts
Procedures and techniques	Conceptual understanding
Work flow	Work practices
Methods and procedures	Rules of thumb, judgment
Teams	Communities

task knowledge of this sort. The business process model is then used to plan, coordinate, and track interrelated tasks. In contrast, understanding the second perspective requires the study of everyday work processes to see what employees actually do to make their organization function effectively. This often involves the analysis of informal and ad hoc communication and collaboration activities (see "Tacit Knowledge in Troubleshooting" sidebar).

One technique for probing workers' conscious and unconscious knowledge is **contextual inquiry** (Holtzblatt & Beyer 1993). In this method, people are observed as they carry out tasks in their normal work environment. Notes are made, but the observers are also free to interrupt the work if a problem arises, or to ask for elaboration or rationale for people's actions. For example, an analyst might see a secretary stop working on a memo to phone another secretary, and then ask her after the call to explain what happened between her and her co-worker. This creates a more elaborate record of the task (e.g., it may actually involve input from two employees). It also helps in identifying the *causes* of people's behavior, because they are prompted to reflect on their actions at the time that they take place.

A related approach is **participatory analysis**, where people are observed during normal work activities, and later engaged in discussion about these activities. During requirements analysis for the Virtual School (Chapter 1), we videotaped many hours of students conducting science experiments in their classrooms. Later on, we shared these videotapes with small groups of teachers

Tacit Knowledge in Troubleshooting

People often see their conversations with coworkers as a social aspect of work that is enjoyable but unrelated to work goals. Sachs (1995) discusses the implications of this in her case study of telephony workers in a phone company. The study analyzed the tasks of detecting, submitting, and resolving problems on telephone lines. The impetus for the study was the Trouble Ticketing System (TTS), a large database used to record telephone line problems, assign problems (tickets) to engineers for correction, and keep records of problems detected and resolved.

Sachs argues that this system embodies an organizational view of work, where individual tasks are modular and well defined: One worker finds a problem and submits it to the database; TTS assigns it to the engineer at the relevant site, and that engineer picks up the ticket, fixes the problem, and moves on. The original worker is done with problem analysis after submitting the ticket, the second can move on once the problem has been addressed, and so on. TTS replaced a manual system in which workers contacted each other directly over the phone, often working together to resolve a problem. The system was designed to make work more efficient by eliminating unnecessary phone conversations.

In her interviews with telephony veterans, Sachs found that the phone conversations were far from unnecessary. The initiation, conduct, and consequences of these conversations reflected a wealth of tacit knowledge held by the engineers—selecting the right person to call (with relevant expertise for the problem), the "filling in" on what the first worker had or had not determined or tried to this point, sharing of hypotheses and testing methods, iterating together through tests and results, and carrying the results of this informal analysis into other possibly related problem areas. In fact, TTS had made work *less* efficient in many cases, because in order to do a competent job, engineers developed "workarounds" wherein they used phone conversations as they had in the past, and then used TTS to document the process afterward.

Sachs noted that the telephony workers were not at first aware of how much troubleshooting knowledge they were using in their jobs. They described tasks as they understood them from company policy and procedures. Only after considerable data collection and discussion did they recognize that their jobs included the skills to navigate and draw upon a rich organizational network of colleagues. In further work, Sachs helped the phone company to develop a fix for the observed workarounds in the form of a new organizational role: a "turf coordinator," a senior engineer responsible for identifying and coordinating the temporary network of workers needed to collaborate on troubleshooting a problem. As a result of Sachs's analysis, work that had been tacit and informal was elevated to an explicit business responsibility.

and students. We asked them to suggest interesting features of the activities, and to help us understand why activities worked well or poorly, and what might be done to improve the learning outcomes (Chin, Rosson, & Carroll 1997).

2.3   Science Fair Case Study: Requirements Analysis

SBD starts with requirements analysis. Of course, we do not claim that requirements are analyzed all at once in waterfall fashion. However, some analysis
must happen early on to get the ball rolling. User interaction scenarios play an
important role in these early analysis activities. When you do a field study of a
workplace, you observe episodes of real work that may or may not involve technology. The usability engineering goal is to identify aspects of current activities
that might be improved or redesigned.

Figure 2.3 summarizes the activities of requirements analysis in SBD. The
fieldwork is guided by a root concept, a basic understanding of the project mission that is developed and shared by members of the project team. Field studies
examine the activities of various project stakeholders—customers or clients who
have an interest or "stake" in how the project turns out. The data from field studies is complex, so various summary representations are developed to organize key

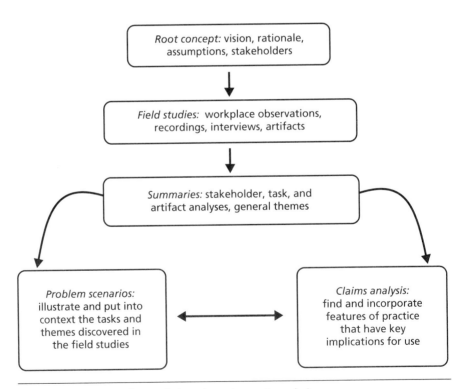

Figure 2.3   Overview of scenario-based requirements analysis.

ideas. These insights are then synthesized into problem scenarios, that is, narratives of activities in the current situation that reflect needs and opportunities for redesign. These scenarios are complemented by claims that analyze the features of the current situation that are most important in the usage experience. In the following we expand on each of these techniques and representations.

2.3.1 Root Concept

Before going into the field, the analysis team should develop a shared understanding of the project's high-level goals. In SBD we document this understanding as a root concept (Table 2.2). The root concept is multifaceted, including a statement of project vision and rationale, an initial analysis of project stakeholders, and an acknowledgment of starting assumptions that will constrain or otherwise guide the development process. The **root concept** is related to the stakeholder analyses of soft systems methodology (see Checkland 1981; Checkland & Scholes 1990).

A project's starting vision and rationale may come from many different sources. Sometimes a vision statement is handed down from management, a client, or a marketing division; at other times it will emerge from open-ended discussions about new technologies, or as a solution to specific known problems (e.g., inefficiency or dissatisfaction with a business process). The vision for the virtual science fair was prompted by the increasing access to network technologies on the one hand, and by theories of informal education on the other. The education rationale comes from evidence that rich and meaningful learning is enhanced when children work on authentic projects outside the normal boundaries of the classroom (Jeffs & Smith 1996).

Part of developing a shared vision is the identification of people who will have a vested interest (or stake) in the project outcome—the stakeholders. Notice that not all stakeholders will actually use the proposed system. For example, we expect that the online science fair will involve students, teachers, community members, and judges. But school administrators are also stakeholders, because the success or failure of the science fair reflects on their school system. The stakeholder analysis is refined by considering how the various stakeholders might benefit (or suffer) if the vision were to be implemented.

The final element of the root concept is a list of starting assumptions and how they may impact the project. It is important to consider these early in the project lifecycle, because they may have important effects on subsequent analysis and design work. The science fair project was carried out by university

Table 2.2   Root concept developed at the beginning of the virtual science fair project.

Component	Contributions to the Root Concept
High-level vision	Students exhibit science projects online in an ongoing fashion
Basic rationale	Online activities enable more community involvement in science education
	Digital media enhance potential quality of exhibits
Stakeholder group	
Student exhibitor	More options for building and exhibiting science projects; more interactions
Student visitors	Easy to visit and comment on friends' activities and progress
Teacher	More flexibility in coaching; sharing of this responsibility with community
Community member	Better access to science fair activities; more options for participation
Community judge	Greater flexibility in judging; more refined administrative support
School administrator	Greater visibility and recognition of education programs
Starting assumptions	Will be built using the services and infrastructure of MOOsburg
	Designers and implementors are university researchers
	Development will take place through participatory analysis and design efforts

researchers, so it is relatively unconstrained in many dimensions (e.g., schedule, cost, performance characteristics, etc.). But because the project will be implemented within MOOsburg, this community network system is a strong external constraint. At the same time, the development team decided in advance to collaborate with the many community stakeholders throughout the process (participatory design).

The stakeholders name the groups or individuals who should be consulted or observed in the fieldwork. The brief description of each group's vested interest points to questions or tasks that should be raised and observed in the workplace. For example, we should ask students about their project construction and exhibition activities, talk to community members about how and when they visit these fairs, and consult the school administrators about how a science fair is recognized and allotted resources.

2.3.2 Analysis of Current Practice

The root concept sets the scene for a field study of current practices. With a shared understanding of project stakeholders, goals, and assumptions, the team can start to analyze the activities that will be transformed by the system. Attention should be directed to the needs and concerns of all stakeholders. For the science fair, this includes students, teachers, community members, judges, and the school administration.

Preparing for the Field Study

As team members develop their root concept, questions will come up about the current situation the system is hoping to address. For example, in thinking about a science fair, we wondered about the projects students currently develop and exhibit, the resources they draw on for project development, how the projects are exhibited and judged, how and when parents or other community members contribute to project work, and so on.

A side effect of these initial discussions is that group members learn more about each other—personal background, interests, and biases about science fairs, as well as skills and aptitudes in fieldwork. This helps to organize the group. For example, one member may take on a leadership role, ensuring that decisions are made, a schedule is constructed, and that everyone understands his or her responsibilities. Other team members may take on the job of identifying and making contact with individuals willing to be observed or interviewed. Others may focus on creating and assembling an interviewing guide and data capture tools.

Figure 2.4 presents a guide for conducting our interviews with student exhibitors at a science fair; different guides were developed for each stakeholder group. Each guide should support—but not overconstrain—the questioning process. At the top there is a reminder about what the interviewer is trying to accomplish. The goal is to learn what the participants think about their own activities, so the guide should avoid specific and pointed questions early in the interview. Instead, begin with open-ended prompts that explore general background and how the interviewees think about their work ("tell me about what you do"). More specific questions are listed at the end, reminding the interviewer to address these issues if they have not yet been not raised in the earlier discussion.

In addition to preparing an interviewing guide, the team must decide how to document their field observations. If the work setting involves considerable physical manipulation of objects, a videotape may be helpful. Otherwise, a small tape recorder can be used to record conversations. In either case, plan in advance how you will use the recording equipment (i.e., where will you place the

Our goal is to understand both *how* and *why* students participate in the science fair. We want to know the things they do as part of the fair, and the sorts of resources (both physical and human) they use. We also want to learn something about the individuals we talk to—their history, and especially their use of or reactions to technology associated with science fairs.

Open-ended prompts about science fair involvement (remember to follow the interviewee's lead):

How long have you been in science fairs; have you exhibited before?

How did you get involved in this year's fair?

Tell me about your exhibit; can you show it to me? What did you do create it?

Did anyone else work with you on this project? How?

Tell me about the other people you have interacted with as part of the fair.

How will (or has) the judging take place?

What do you like about this science fair (or about your exhibit)? What are you unhappy with?

Specific things we want to know, including technology (ask directly if they've not yet been covered):

What technology (computer or otherwise) have you used in this project?

What technology would you have liked to use if it was available?

What background do you have in using computers?

How could an expert from the community contribute to your science project?

How could your parents contribute?

Can you imagine an online version of this science fair? What would it be like?

Figure 2.4 Interviewing guide for field study of science fairs.

camera[s] or the microphone, and how many tapes will you need), and be certain to gain participants' permission for any recordings in advance. It may also be useful to bring along a camera to make snapshots of work activities. Finally, one or more team members should take detailed written notes. In gaining permission for the visit and observations, be clear that all recordings, photos, or notes will be treated confidentially.

It is important in a workplace study to establish a comfortable relationship between yourself and the workplace participants. In some settings, workers may be selected by management and may resent spending time with you. In workplaces that rely on very little technology support, participants may be intimidated by developers or researchers who are experts in computer science or design. Your team must be sensitive to social factors like this one and focus first on establishing a friendly and nonjudgmental tone to the exchange.

Observations, Interviews, and Artifacts

The photo in Figure 2.5 was taken during a visit to a science fair. Even a single snapshot like this reveals many details about the work setting and activities. For example, we see that the student is using a computer as part of the exhibit, and is showing his project to several people at once. The visitors seem to be a family group ranging in age from a small child to an adult. Also in the room are non-computer artifacts, including posters on the walls and refreshments on a table. It isn't obvious what relation the posters have to the computer exhibits, but interviews with the students indicated that only some projects had computer-based content, whereas all projects had a physical poster display.

The posters on the wall are a good example of a science fair artifact. A workplace artifact is any resource that seems to play an important role in an activity;

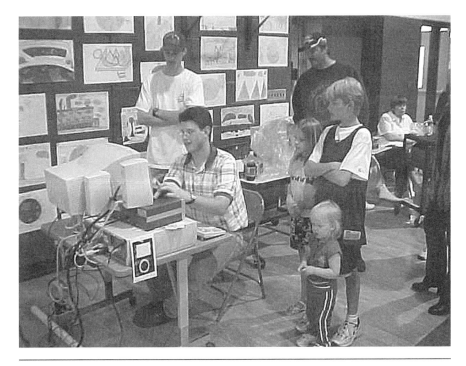

Figure 2.5   High school student demonstrating his exhibit at a science fair.

for example, this photo contains artifacts such as the computer with its software and data, posters on the wall, furniture, and even the room itself. Other artifacts from the field study included registration and evaluation forms and an advertisement poster. In some cases, these artifacts are documented by videotapes or photographs; in other cases, the observation team must ask specifically for copies of relevant documents or other tools, or may simply make notes that describe such objects.

In addition to taking photographs, we observed exhibit activities and interviewed students and visitors. In this case, our field study was opportunistic—we simply observed the participants and activities underway during our visit. If we had been studying a more structured workplace (e.g., a business office), we would have spent more time planning the visit, first finding out when key activities take place, and making sure that we visited during these times. Sometimes a team may need to simulate an important but infrequent real-world activity—for example, asking a retail store employee to act out the process of reporting a theft.

How much field data should you collect? How many visits are necessary, and to how many different sites? This depends on the project's scope and resources; large or innovative projects usually spend more time on requirements analysis. At the same time, some projects may have a tight schedule or other limited resources, so that extensive fieldwork is impractical. As a rule of thumb, we recommend at least one set of observations and/or interview for each stakeholder group. For the science fair, this meant talking to students, teachers, community members (including parents, judges, and visitors), and the school administrators.

2.3.3   Summarizing the Field Data

Fieldwork produces a wide variety of data (photos, videos, notes, etc.) that can be overwhelming. Here we discuss several summary representations that can be used to organize the findings about a project's stakeholders, their activities, and the tools or artifacts they use.

Stakeholders

The observations and interviews for each stakeholder group are organized into stakeholder profiles (Table 2.3). These profiles summarize the general characteristics of each group, and are based on the observations and interviews from the field study. On occasion they may include published research about the population (e.g., information about demographics, disabilities, or other special characteristics). We organize the summaries into background, expectations for the proposed system, and preferences regarding information technology. We will use

Table 2.3   Stakeholder profiles developed from the science fair field study.

Stakeholder	General Group Characteristics
Students	*Background*: Mixed experience with computing (from extensive use of computer games and several years of programming, to minimal keyboarding and basic office applications). Moderate to extensive experience with Web, email, and Internet chat. Only a small group of students participate in science fairs on a regular basis.
	Expectations: An online system should make exhibit construction easier and more fun. Will see the system as a variant of other (e.g., Web-based) hypermedia systems.
	Preferences: Most comfortable with PC-Windows, from school or home. Enjoy multimedia systems, even when slow over a phone line or other poor connection.
Community members	*Background*: Bimodal distribution with a few having extensive computing experience through work, and others with only modest (or no) exposure to email and Web. Many have visited their children's exhibits (though not always science) in the past. Few actually attend science fairs on a regular basis. A small group repeatedly volunteers to mentor or judge.
	Expectations: Many are unsure about how if at all they would contribute to creating a project, but able to imagine browsing exhibits online. No thoughts about encountering or talking to others while browsing the exhibits.
	Preferences: Those with background are comfortable with AOL and similar ISPs, generally PC-Windows. Less patient with "fancy" graphics or multimedia. Want guides or help to work through new applications; willing to read manuals.
Teachers	*Background*: Most are familiar with a range of applications, Web-based browsing and discussion, specialized courseware. A few have basic programming skills; most are able to author documents in HTML and other hypermedia systems such as PowerPoint. Most science teachers have extensive experience with science fair participation and advising.
	Expectations: An online system will draw in other experts to guide students in projects, decrease reliance on teachers, allow focus on special needs. Expect Web authoring and browsing, possibly email discussions with outside experts.
	Preferences: Mixture of PC and Mac users. Strong concerns about access rights and about ability to get overview information. Willing to work from online or written guides or reference material. Want example (starter) projects.

(continued)

Table 2.3 *(continued)*

School administrators	*Background*: Familiar with Web, email, and standard office applications, especially word-processing and spreadsheet functions. Science fair is managed largely through volunteers.
	Expectations: Increased visibility of science fair, better connections between school and community. Convey interesting things that students are doing. Like teachers, expect such a system to involve combination of Web and email.
	Preferences: Mixture of PC and Mac users. Concerned that system is state-of-the-art and attractive; will want to print colorful examples and summaries of the online materials to share with community groups and agencies.

these profiles later to generate hypothetical stakeholders who will play the role of actors in the problem scenarios.

A related summary is the **stakeholder diagram** showing the relations among different stakeholder groups (Figure 2.6). Students do not work on their projects in isolation; teachers advise them and community members may provide comments or serve as official judges. These sorts of relations are important to document and, like the profiles above, will be useful in developing the problem scenarios—scenarios often involve more than one actor, and the actor interactions will illustrate these general relations.

Notice how the relationships diagrammed in the figure show the interactions of the school administration with other stakeholders. A simplistic analysis of science fairs might ignore the influence of the school administration, but in fact these individuals have key responsibilities for recruiting and rewarding participation, as well as in gathering resources for such events.

Discussion of stakeholder relations helps a team understand the impacts that one group of participants may have on others. For instance, the number of students who participate affects the number of community members needed to judge the exhibits, as well as the resources needed from the school administration. Similarly, the background and interests of the community members who visit a student's exhibit will influence the ease and enjoyment of the exhibiting process.

Task Analysis

Another set of summaries is developed to document the tasks of each stakeholder group. Table 2.4 presents a simple list of tasks that were observed and discussed during the science fair. Although we do not yet know what aspects of the science

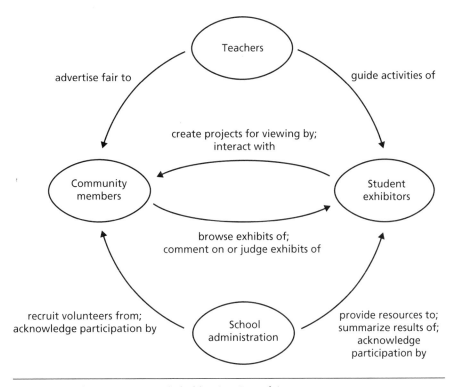

Figure 2.6 Relations among stakeholders in science fair.

fair will be addressed by the new project, we want to have as complete a list as possible of the contributing activities. Clearly, the students, visitors, and judges are most central to the science fair activity, but teachers and administrators have their own set of supporting tasks.

For tasks that have many steps, or that are particularly important in an activity, a hierarchical task analysis may be developed. As discussed earlier, this analysis decomposes complex tasks into subtasks. Figures 2.7 and 2.8 present a hierarchical task analysis for two central science fair tasks—exhibit preparation (2.7) and judging (2.8). We are confident that both of these tasks will be addressed in some way by the new system, so it is worthwhile to analyze in detail how they are currently accomplished.

Each box in the task analysis diagrams represents a task step. Vertical lines indicate decomposition of a step into two or more subtasks; the subtasks are gathered together under the horizontal lines. Numbering indicates how a task is decomposed, and the plans show the logical ordering or dependencies among subtasks. For example, in Figure 2.7, the plan for the project content analysis task

Table 2.4 Tasks carried out by stakeholders as part of the science fair activity.

VSF Stakeholder	Science Fair Tasks Observed or Discussed
Students	Reviewing participation requirements; proposing a project; carrying out the project; constructing an exhibit; demonstrating the project
Community members who visit exhibits	Finding out about the fair; traveling to the fair; browsing projects at a fair; interacting with students at their exhibits
Community members who serve as judges	Volunteering to be a judge; studying the evaluation form; evaluating a specific project; writing and submitting exhibit evaluations
Teachers	Helping a student refine a proposal project; providing pointers to resources and other information; critiquing a student's project in progress; helping a student create an exhibit
School administrators	Recruiting volunteers to judge projects; summarizing participation in fair; highlighting winning projects in annual report; specifying resources needed for next year's fair; acknowledging student and judge participation

says to first write down the project structure, and then summarize the content for each element.

Artifact Analysis

Figures 2.9 and 2.10 present two artifacts collected in the science fair study, an advertising poster (2.9) and a judging form (2.10). Workplace artifacts can be of many sorts—data files, forms, software, brochures, and so on—and help to document task information and procedures. The poster that advertises the fair shows which features the organizers believe are important to convey to potential visitors. The judging form reflects the value system applied to exhibit evaluation, which dimensions are important, how the dimensions should be weighed against one another, and so on. Other artifacts relevant to science fairs are the student registration form, newspaper notices recruiting volunteers to serve as judges and later announcing the winners, instructions provided to judges and to students, photographs of the exhibits, prize ribbons, and even the thank-you notes sent by fair organizers to the volunteers helping to set up and judge the exhibits.

Table 2.5 summarizes what was learned from the poster and the judging form, broken into the information and procedures implied by each artifact. The poster reflects what the organizers believe are the most important or interesting

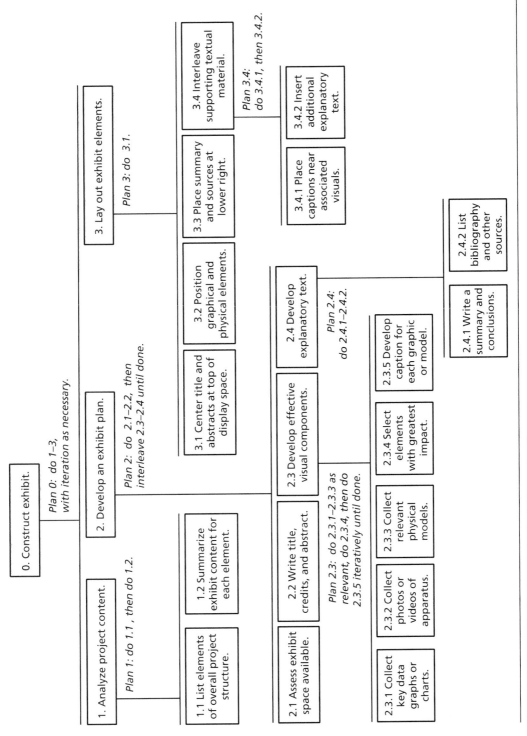

Figure 2.7 Hierarchical task analysis of exhibit construction.

59

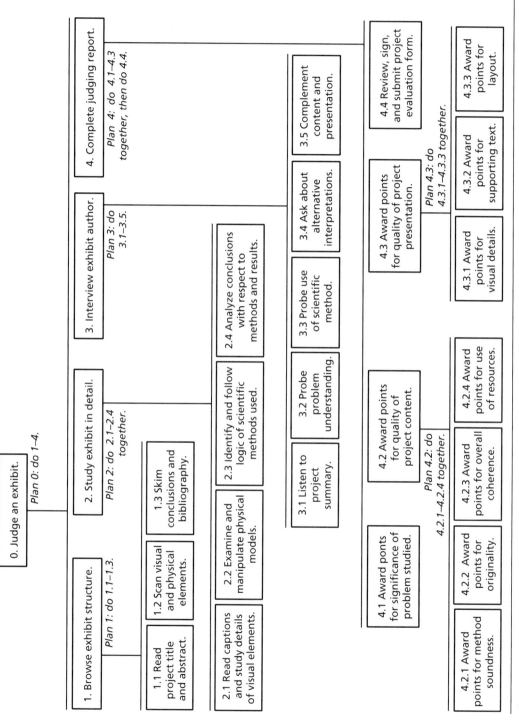

Figure 2.8 Hierarchical task analysis of exhibit judging.

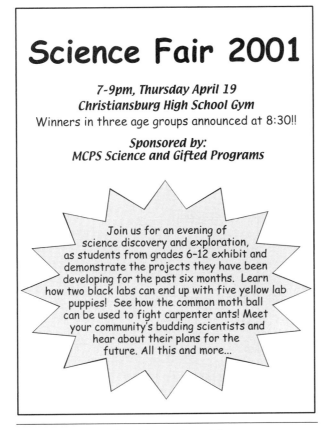

Figure 2.9 Poster advertising a science fair.

aspects of the fair. The judging form highlights characteristics related to the quality of exhibits. It is possible that an artifact will reflect information that conflicts with field observations (e.g., we might have found out that the organizers had changed, a sponsor had been added, etc.), so it is important not to accept without question the information or procedures that they imply. As we noted earlier, much of what people know or experience in a situation is based on tacit knowledge, or is the result of other stakeholders' views and concerns.

Workplace Themes

As the discussion of field data continues, the team should begin to identify and illustrate **workplace themes**. A workplace theme is simply a category that is proposed for related observations or discussion points. Different stakeholders will

MCPS SCIENCE FAIR 2001
Judges' Rating Form
Division I (Grades 6–8)

For each exhibit, begin with a brief overview, then study the project in detail. Interview the student to assess his/her understanding of the problem domain, methods used, interpretations provided, etc., before assessing points in the categories below. Plan to spend about 15 minutes at each station; this should allow you to judge the full set of exhibits you have been assigned. Submit your completed forms to Ms. Czerny.

_____ **Problem Significance (10)**

Quality of Project Content:

_____ Soundness of methods used (15)

_____ Originality of scientific approach (10)

_____ Overall logic and coherence (15)

_____ Use of outside resources (10)

Quality of Project Presentation:

_____ Visual or physical model details (15)

_____ Captions and explanatory text (10)

_____ Overall layout (15)

_____ **Total (100)**

Comments:

Figure 2.10   Rating form used to judge exhibits at a science fair.

Table 2.5   Information and procedures implied by the poster and the judging form.

Science Fair Artifact	Implied Information Needs and Procedures
Fair publicity poster	*Information*: when and where fair is held; sponsoring organization; time when winning exhibits announced; sample projects; contact information
	Procedures: fair lasts 2 hours; judging takes 1.5 hours; projects take up to 6 months to complete; exhibits entered and judged in three age-level groupings
Judging form	*Information*: judging is age-specific; exhibits judged on three dimensions; quality is complex judgment broken into subcategories; Ms. Czerny is head judge
	Procedures: interview addresses significance and quality; judging takes 15 minutes; forms submitted when all are done; head judge compiles results

focus on different aspects of the current situation (e.g., based on their personal motivations or backgrounds), but the analysts should search for underlying patterns in the problems observed or concerns raised.

A useful technique for identifying workplace themes is to write down on a post-it note any comments or observations that seem interesting. These notes are then arranged on a wall. The analysis team works together to rearrange related post-its into groups (Figure 2.11). As groupings are proposed, their usefulness is tested by trying to name them—if you find yourself with too many "Miscellaneous" or "Other Problems" groups, your work is not done yet! This is similar to the "affinity diagrams" used in contextual design (Beyer & Holtzblatt 1998; Wixon, Holtzblatt, & Knox 1990).

The thematic groupings are reviewed, discussed, reorganized, and renamed until a team is satisfied with their shared understanding of the data. The process can also be carried out in a participatory fashion with other project stakeholders. Sometimes a comment or discussion point may fall into more than one theme. This is fine; simply make some indication that multiple copies have been made.

As the number of themes becomes large, it may be useful to create a tabular representation like that in Table 2.6, which collects a number of science fair observations under six themes. Notice that we were careful to include both *good and bad* things about the current practice of science fairs. This is a key aspect of

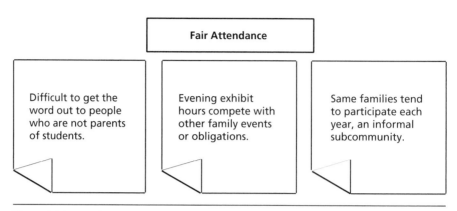

Figure 2.11   Post-it notes capturing comments under a "fair attendance" theme.

the SBD framework: Even though we are most interested in "fixing" problems, we want to make sure that we do not "break" things that are working well.

Workplace themes are a critical source of information for the problem scenarios and claims produced during the requirements phase. They make explicit a team's shared understanding of what is most interesting or important about the problem domain the team has been studying.

2.3.4   Problem Scenarios and Claims

Stakeholder profiles and diagrams, task and artifact analyses, and field data themes form a scaffolding from which problem scenarios are constructed. A **problem scenario** tells a story of current practice. These stories are carefully developed to reveal aspects of the stakeholders and their activities that have implications for design. Other members of the project team (e.g., managers, software engineers) should be able to read the problem scenarios and appreciate the work-related issues that the field study has uncovered.

We call these "problem scenarios" not because they emphasize problematic aspects of current practices, but rather because they describe activities in the problem domain. In SBD new activities are always grounded in current activities. It is just as important to understand what is working well already and to build on this as it is to find difficulties that must be addressed.

Scenario writing is a creative activity. The fieldwork uncovers key tasks and themes that should be illustrated. Real-world characters and context are created to help in generating the stories and in making them believable and evocative. Sometimes an observed episode will form the base for a scenario, but in most cases the stories will be entirely fictional.

Table 2.6 Summary of themes from the science fair field study.

Theme	Issues Contributing to the Theme
Fair attendance	Difficult to get the word out to people who are not parents of students
	Evening exhibit hours compete with other family events or obligations
	Same families tend to participate each year, an informal subcommunity
Student participation	Participants are usually experienced, know a good deal about projects and judging
	Enjoy feeling creative; highly motivated to innovate in methods and displays
	Very excited but also anxious during judging, proud if they or friends "win"
Community involvement	Parents are the most active supporters, often bring family of "cheerleaders"
	A few people involved year after year, often as mentors, organizers, or judges
	Those who do come enjoy themselves, talk to one another as well as browse
	Some visitors see posters in background, but never get around to examining them
	Some feel they might like to be involved but too busy doing other things
	Some may discover "results" through newspaper summaries or other institutions
Judging	Very demanding activity, sometimes hard to give each exhibit enough time
	Relies considerably on paper form to guide comments and ratings
	Usually assigned only a subset (e.g., by age or topic) to evaluate
	Often must deal with a broad range of quality and sophistication in exhibits
Exhibit construction	Takes place over long period of time through planning and iteration
	Constrained by available space and materials (e.g., 4'×6' poster boards)
	Follows a general structure, a top-to-bottom, left-to-right, flow of ideas
	Should provide an overview, as well as details on closer investigation
Resources	Usually scheduled in open multipurpose space such as a high school gymnasium
	Students sometimes get project materials from schools, often from home
	Technology support is minimal, often no power or equipment options
	Organized and judged by volunteers who are "rewarded" with recognition

A useful way to get started is to describe a few **hypothetical stakeholders**, imaginary people with characteristics you think are typical of a stakeholder group (similar to Alan Cooper's notion of a "persona"; Cooper 1999). These stakeholders will serve as actors in the problem scenarios, and the background and motivation for each helps us to imagine how a specific scenario might unfold from that person's perspective.

Figure 2.12 describes five hypothetical stakeholders for a science fair—a student exhibitor, her teacher, her next-door neighbor, a longtime science fair judge, and the fair organizer. For projects with a strong commitment for innovation, a related technique that involves the generation of "unusual" actors

---

Sally Harris	is a Blacksburg High School sophomore who has participated in the science fair for the past three years. She is very interested in science and often spends time looking into science phenomena on her own initiative. She is a good student in general, poised and articulate. She has extensive experience with computers, both at school and with her own Windows PC at home. She has been using word processors and graphics editors for many years, and in the past two years has started using spreadsheets and a few simple programming packages. She spends time on the Web almost every day, sending email to friends or just surfing around.
John King	is an experienced physics teacher at Blacksburg High School. He is often the one who recruits students to participate in the annual science fair; he participated himself for years as a kid and feels he gained a lot from the experience. John is a popular teacher, involved in extracurricular sports activities as well as his science teaching duties. Students frequently stop to chat or joke with him in the hall, and his office hours are always packed. He also has a wife and three children and is very involved in church and community activities. John regularly uses a networked Windows PC in support of his physics teaching, both for tracking down resources on the Web, and for demonstrating and analyzing physics experiments with his students.
Alicia Sampson	lives next door to Sally Harris. She owns a hardware store and has three children—Jeff, who is a junior in high school; Delia, a seventh grader; and Bobby, a fifth grader. Jeff is into music and art and has never been involved in science fairs. Lately, Delia has started to show some interest in science,

---

Figure 2.12 Hypothetical stakeholders who will be the actors in the problem scenarios.

	and Alicia is eager to encourage this however she can. She helped Delia search the Web for information on bumblebees recently, and she was impressed with how fluent Delia has become with their home computer and the Internet. Alicia knows there is a science fair every year, because Sally's mom mentioned it last year, but she has never considered going. Between Jeff's practices and performances, Bobby's basketball and soccer, and Delia's dance and gymnastics, Alicia is not sure she has time for more activities.
Ralph Morton	is a retired civil engineer who used to work for the town of Blacksburg. He is a longtime Blacksburg resident with many friends and activities. For the past five years he has served as a judge in the local science fair. He is happy to serve because he enjoys seeing and contrasting the individual creativity in the various student projects. The organizers know they can count on his experience in judging and often give him the most advanced projects to evaluate. Ralph is friendly with a number of other judges; they keep in touch over email and occasionally organize guest lectures or field trips for the schools.
Rachel Berris	directs the gifted program for Blacksburg schools. She is a longtime advocate for the regional science fair, because she believes that it offers an important enrichment opportunity for talented science students. She works on organizing the fair off and on throughout the entire year, petitioning for resources from the school administration, scheduling a time and location, recruiting judges and teachers, encouraging past participants to register again, and in general talking up the activity. She has been working with the fair for over 10 years now and knows many of the individuals and families who are involved year after year. She knows that the school district relies on her to make the fair happen and is proud to have this responsibility.

(e.g., a neighborhood gang leader) might be used as a complement to envisioning more typical characters (Djajadiningrat, Gaver, & Frens 2000).

Figure 2.13 presents five problem scenarios that use one or more of the hypothetical stakeholders as actors. We used the tasks listed in Table 2.4 as a starting point for these stories, but there is no strict 1:1 mapping. The goal is always to tell a story about the current situation that is meaningful to the actors, and that brings out some of the issues identified during analysis. This sometimes involves a combination of two or more tasks. For example, the story about Alicia and Delia touches on three of the tasks listed for community visitors—finding out about the fair, browsing an exhibit, and interacting with a student.

1) Sally plans her exhibit on black holes.

Sally Harris is a high school sophomore who has been researching black holes for the past three months. This is a topic that has fascinated her for years, and her biology teacher encouraged her to research it for the science fair this year, even though Sally won't be taking physics until next year. She has been in the science fair for the past three years, so she knows a lot about the kind of projects students select, how they organize their exhibits, and what the judges look for.

She is a bit worried about the space and materials provided to everyone—a standard 4x6 poster board, with a two-foot shelf underneath for supporting physical materials or models. This year she has explored some new methods—for example, an Authorware simulation that illustrates her theory of black hole formation. But she knows from past years that there are few electrical outlets in the gym, and she doesn't have a laptop to use in the exhibit anyway. She checks with the organizer, Rachel Berris, just in case, but Rachel confirms that the school district has no money for special resources such as laptops, and that she will be able to use only battery-powered equipment.

As she studies her simulation, Sally thinks of a way to turn the lack of computer support into a "feature": She will create a sequence of visualizations that can be flipped like a deck of cards to show the animation. In fact, as she works, she gets into it and decides to create several variations, so that visitors can guess which one matches her project data and conclusions. She will then chart people's guesses as a dynamic element in her exhibit. She knows from experience that this is just the sort of thing judges will notice and award points for. Now she just has to figure out how to fit everything into the space she will have.

2) Mr. King coaches Sally on her project.

Mr. King worked during his lunch hour so that he could save some time to come to the lab and work with Sally on her exhibit. He knows that Sally has already done a lot of work researching black holes, but he wants to make sure she comes up with an effective layout and that she covers all the standard project areas well. When she signed up, Sally told him she has done this several times, so he figures the session will go pretty smoothly.

When he gets to the lab, Sally is already there and has begun to collect stacks of materials on a lab table, which happens to be the same 4×6 size as the bulletin board she will have at the fair. John cannot tell what is in the piles, but a quick look suggests that they hold materials related to the standard sections, Introduction at the top left, and so on. Sally shows Mr. King some photos of galaxies she has downloaded from the Web; she is very

Figure 2.13   Problem scenarios illustrating how science fairs currently take place.

careful when handling these because they were printed in high resolution on expensive glossy paper.

Mr. King notes that Sally already has the standard sections well covered in her piles but thinks that she has too much content. Sally agrees and asks him to help her select the best pieces. He reminds her that both the judges and the visitors will be very influenced by first impressions as they walk up to the exhibit, so they first look for example materials that will look good from a distance. They use the table to lay these out, then choose supporting materials that provide the logical connections and explanations. Sally makes notes about figures and other documents that she still needs to create. She also talks to Mr. King about her idea for the interactive element, and he agrees that the judges will love it. But he's worried that the exhibit will get too complex and messy, and suggests a decorated hanging container for visitors' experiments and comments.

3) Alicia and Delia go to the science fair.

Alicia Sampson owns a hardware store. Her neighbor, Sally Harris, is participating in the science fair for the third year in a row, and Sally's mom has mentioned it several times. She wants to go to show support for Sally, but also wants to encourage her daughter Delia's interest in science. However, she also feels a little awkward about going—she knows the fair is in the high school gym, and she has not been inside the school since she was a student there. Five years ago she even signed a petition asking the school board to tighten budgets in high school science. But she saw a science fair poster at Krogers today, and wonders if her husband can take Bobby to his basketball game. He's free, so she and Delia go on their own.

When Alicia and Delia walk into the gym, Alicia smiles, sharing briefly with Delia some pleasant memories of high school basketball games. After quickly scanning the open area, Alicia is amazed at the variety in projects. Some have just a few diagrams, others have complex physical models. She and Delia head for a project that has attracted a big crowd, but then she spies Marge (a former bridge partner) across the gym, so she and Delia go over to join Marge instead.

Marge is at Sally Harris's exhibit on black holes, and Sally is showing her a flip-card animation of black hole formation. Alicia and Delia pause to listen, and Alicia is happy to see Delia try out the animation. As they move on, Alicia is surprised to realize how much she has learned about black holes, a topic she's heard mentioned many times, but never really thought much about. Delia seems interested too; she tracks down one of her own friends and brings her back to meet Sally. Remembering Sally's poise and verbal skills, Alicia decides to follow up with her about a summer vacancy at her hardware store. As Alicia and Delia leave, they are talking about how they might get involved in next year's fair.

(continued)

Figure 2.13 *(continued)*

4) Ralph judges the high school physics projects at the science fair.

For the last three years, Ralph—a retired civil engineer—has been a judge at the Blacksburg science fair, so he is not surprised to be asked again; he agrees because he knows that the organizer, Rachel Berris, counts on his experience on the judging team. In past years, he was occasionally able to get advance information about the exhibits, but this year could find out only the student names in advance. He is given the task of judging the high school physics projects; given prior years, he knows he will have to work quickly to get all five evaluated in the 90 minutes allotted. On the night of the fair, Ralph arrives promptly at 7 P.M., picks up his forms, and begins the process of studying the exhibits and interviewing the students. His previous experience helps him to assign ratings in the specified categories, but as usual he finds it difficult, especially when trying to compare across projects. At one point, he needs to evaluate two very nice projects in parallel, and finds himself running back and forth comparing details, annotating the scores with explanatory comments. Finally he is done; he signs the forms and submits them. Rachel and her assistant are already compiling a large stack of forms. Ralph is relieved to finish on time, and is eager to see how his evaluations will compare with those of the other judges.

5) Rachel organizes a presentation for the superintendent.

Rachel was proud of the science fair projects that were exhibited this year, so she is delighted when Superintendent Mark Carlisle tells her he wants to show highlights from the fair at next month's school board meeting. She hopes that if he can impress the school board with some of the best exhibits, he will be able to make a case for increasing the resources available for next year's fair. Carlisle wasn't able to attend the fair himself, so Rachel briefly describes some highlights. She is careful to tell him about the problems with Sally's exhibit, mainly that she was unable to demonstrate her black hole simulation because of lack of equipment and power sources.

Carlisle asks Rachel to collect sample materials for a 15-minute PowerPoint presentation. She spends a good part of the next week tracking down the winning authors and getting copies of their best poster elements. Some of the material is provided in digital form, but she has to use a scanner to digitize about half of it. After she has a good set of visuals, she browses them, looking for the most impressive and self-explanatory examples, adding a few notes here and there to help Carlisle summarize the source projects. When she is done, she emails the PowerPoint presentation to Carlisle. She also decides to sends him Sally's simulation file, just in case he has time to show it. Unfortunately, she later discovers that Carlisle's presentation backfires: The school board thought that the winning projects were of such high quality that there was no apparent need to increase resources for next year's event.

Although the field studies provide an understanding of the current situation, it is up to the scenario writers to decide what tasks to illustrate, how to weave in the themes and stakeholder relations, and what other details about the character or situation to include. In Figure 2.14 we diagram how we came up with the first scenario: We took one of Sally's most important tasks (planning her exhibit), then imagined how she would approach this task. We gave her a plausible topic, and considered what her goals would be and what actions and reactions might take place as she worked on her exhibit ideas. We continually referred to the themes to see if we could incorporate anything relevant to the themes in this situation.

Scenarios often involve more than one stakeholder. For example, Alicia and Delia encounter Sally during their visit. Indeed one contribution of this scenario is to explore the stakeholder relationship between visitors and students at the fair (Figure 2.6). As suggested here, the stakeholder diagram can also be a guide when generating scenarios—as a story unfolds, consider whether interactions with other stakeholders could make the scenario more realistic or raise issues that the team has uncovered.

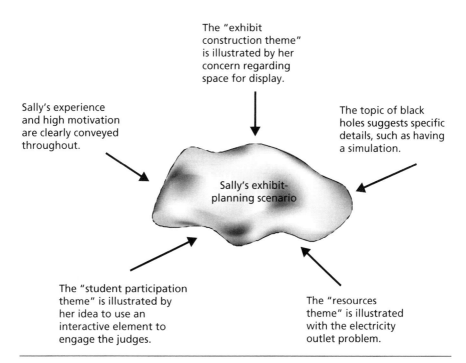

Figure 2.14 Ideas and concerns that contributed to the exhibit-planning scenario.

A scenario should convey what its actors are like, and what forces are influencing their behavior. Both Sally and her teacher are busy people; this is typical though not part of the science fair itself. Alicia Sampson's family life has no direct bearing on the fair or its operation. However, these details provide concrete bits of context that allow the reader to empathize with the actors' motivations and experience. The details also evoke thoughts about contrasting situations where other factors are in play, such as a case where Sally's neighbor lives alone and has no other obligations. This "what-if" thinking is an important benefit of writing and sharing scenarios in requirements analysis.

The five scenarios in Figure 2.13 deliberately reuse actors and artifacts (most notably Sally and her exhibit). This adds to the overall coherence of a scenario set: The description of Sally's project during construction has to make sense in the context of coaching, visiting, judging, and archiving. Such reuse encourages a broader analysis of the people and artifacts in the problem domain, because impacts on more than one activity are considered. Of course, this comes with a cost of not generating descriptions of other people and artifacts—for example, an inexperienced judge who is unable to complete the forms in the time allotted. A set of problem scenarios serves only as an illustrative set of "stakes in the ground." They are suggestive, not exhaustive.

In SBD, scenario writing is always interleaved with **claims analysis**, where the features of a situation that have important effects on the actors are identified. Each such feature is written down with its hypothesized good and bad effects. Claims analysis is related to the tradeoffs identified in each chapter of this textbook. Claims can be seen as examples of tradeoffs, where the tradeoffs are reflected in the claim's upsides and downsides. The difference is that claims are tied to specific artifacts and activities, while the chapter tradeoffs are general statements of competing concerns. Claims can often be seen as instances of these more general tradeoffs. Claims analysis plays several important roles in SBD:

- Claims elaborate a set of scenarios, explaining how and why a particular feature is having a range of impacts on the actors.

- A claims analysis documents why one or more scenarios were written, by isolating the most important features of the narratives.

- The claims extend the scenarios, pointing to possible effects a feature might have in other scenarios (i.e., without writing out a new scenario).

- Claims analysis promotes a balanced view of a situation. Each feature is analyzed to consider both positive impacts (prefaced with plus signs in Table 2.7) and negative impacts (prefaced with minus signs).

- The claims motivate design reasoning—designers will try to increase positive impacts while decreasing negative impacts (Chapters 3 through 5).

Table 2.7   Claims analyzed while developing the problem scenarios. The consequences preceded with plus signs are referred to as "pros" or "upsides" of a feature; those with minus signs are the "cons" or "downsides" of a feature. As a group they illustrate the tradeoffs associated with the feature.

Situation Feature	Possible Pros (+) or Cons (−) of the Feature
Exhibits composed of physical elements	+ leverages existing skills at grasping, moving, and constructing things in the world
	+ encourages direct engagement and involvement by visitors
	− but each element consumes a fixed amount of physical space
	− but some pieces may be expensive or difficult to produce or copy
Repeated involvement by the same students	+ increases student familiarity and competence from year to year
	+ encourages formation of a "science fair community"
	− but inexperienced students may find it hard to "break in"
Holding the fair in the high school gym	+ reinforces the feeling of community and school interaction
	+ may bring back memories of other school events held in this place
	− but the organizers may need to coordinate with other school events (e.g., sports)
	− but the gym may not be set up with fair-specific resources (e.g., electricity)
Organizing the exhibits into poster boards	+ simplifies construction by providing a generic rectangular layout
	+ provides a convenient visual overview for visitors as they approach
	− but some exhibit elements may be difficult to attach to such a board
	− but the uniform size may be too big or too small for some exhibits
Competition among students for prizes	+ rewards students who have contributed high-quality time and effort
	+ increases the excitement and engagement of event attendees
	− but students who try hard but don't win may be frustrated
	− but the diverse exhibits may be difficult to compare systematically
Judging forms or checklists	+ are familiar and convenient objects for taking notes while walking around
	+ organize and guide the judging procedure
	− but may be difficult to modify in exceptional cases
	− but will lead to considerable document processing if the fair is large

(continued)

Table 2.7 *(continued)*

A summary of the winning projects	+ gives explicit credit to the students who do the finest work
	+ emphasizes that the event has an important outcome
	− but nonwinners may feel left out or slighted if they are not mentioned
	− but such a summary may give a biased view of general project quality

How did we come up with the claims in Table 2.7? We first identified the "interesting features" of a scenario. During requirements analysis, a **claims feature** is anything in the situation that has notable effects on an actor's experience—an object, a procedure, even another person. (During design, we use claims to analyze features of the new design.) Some features may emerge during theme analysis (physical exhibits, the high school gym as an exhibit space; see Table 2.6). The search for features is also influenced by the technology you are likely to apply. For instance, we knew in advance that digital storage and display are very different than their physical counterparts, so we tried to analyze the impacts of physical project elements.

Once an interesting feature was identified, we considered its consequences for the actors in the science fair scenarios. A consequence is simply some impact on a person's ability to carry out or enjoy an activity. For instance, does the physical character of Sally's materials make it easier to plan and construct her exhibit? Harder? More or less pleasant or satisfying? Often a scenario will convey just one consequence of a feature, but most features have more than one possible effect, both positive and negative. In cases where the analysis team is relatively unfamiliar with the problem domain, discussions with stakeholders about features and consequences may be essential (Chin, Rosson, & Carroll 1997).

A claim can be extended by thinking about the impact of the same feature in other situations. Sometimes this means considering a slight variant of an existing scenario (e.g., what if Sally had a two-foot poster board to work with?). A feature may have different consequences for different stakeholders, so it is important to consider effects that might be occurring in other scenarios (e.g., the physical flip cards were attractive to Delia). Sometimes a consequence found during discussion leads to additions or revisions to a scenario. For example, we added the comment about Sally's handling of her photos only after first proposing that reproduction cost is a negative consequence of physical exhibits.

As we indicated above, claims are often related to the more general trade-offs that are discussed in this textbook. For example, thinking about poster boards directed our attention to the general structure of exhibits (typical elements and layouts), but we also recognize that students have strong feelings of creativity and personal ownership (Tradeoff 2.1). The judging form presents task-oriented information (the evaluation dimensions and their relative weights), but seeing the forms in use reveals that they are not always used as intended (Tradeoff 2.2). Holding the science fair in the gym is a good use of community resources, but individual students may find the large multipurpose space hard to use (Tradeoff 2.3).

Analysts and designers often ask how many scenarios and claims are enough, and how to tell if they have come up with the "right" ones. There is no simple answer to these concerns. SBD is an **inquiry method**—it raises questions that promote rich discussions and understandings of people and activities. Thus, one answer is that you are not done until there are no more questions. Obviously this is not a practical response, so we also offer a few rules of thumb:

- Write at least one scenario for every stakeholder.

- Analyze at least one or two claims from each scenario.

- For stakeholders with many tasks or with tasks that are complex, write multiple scenarios.

- Beyond these guidelines, if an exhaustive analysis is demanded, more systematic methods such as hierarchical task analyses or use cases should be developed as a complement to the problem scenarios.

2.3.5   Scenarios and Claims as Requirements

Are problem scenarios and claims a requirements specification? No. A problem scenario does not specify what a new system should do; it presents insights gleaned about the current situation. Subsequent design reasoning will respond to these problem scenarios and claims by creating and refining a design vision that will be implemented as a software system. In this sense, problem scenarios and claims express requirements only implicitly by describing the needs and opportunities in the current situation.

Problem scenarios relate how particular features of the world are believed to impact people's activities and experiences; claims provide a more explicit analysis of these impacts. A design process must then respond to these needs and possibilities, maintaining or improving on the positive characteristics while diminishing or removing the negative.

Remember that this textbook presents a simplified view of SBD. In practice, analysis and design are tightly interleaved. As soon as usage concerns or opportunities are discovered in the problem situation, potential design solutions will be proposed and considered. Indeed, we can see this in the science fair example: Our requirements analysis focused almost immediately on the usage issues that are most likely to be influenced by networks and digital media (e.g., scheduling and space constraints). At the same time, because the entire process is iterative, we know that these scenarios and claims are only a first pass at understanding the problem situation. Our analysis of users' requirements will continue to develop as design ideas emerge and are explored in new scenarios and claims.

Summary and Review

This chapter summarized some of the important issues in analyzing the needs of the situation a system will transform. The virtual science-fair case study was introduced and used to illustrate requirements analysis activities in SBD. Central points include:

- A work setting must be analyzed from the perspective of diverse stakeholders, and work activities must be observed in their real-world context, to be fully understood.

- The objects and materials (artifacts) of a workplace can provide insights into work processes that are often only understood tacitly by individual workers, or that are distributed across many elements of a work setting.

- To gain the most from field studies, it is critical to plan in advance the questions to be asked, what and how data will be collected, and how a comfortable exchange between analysts and work participants will be ensured.

- Field notes, workplace artifacts, and videotapes or other interview records should be examined for general patterns (themes) in stakeholder characteristics, task or procedure structure, and the information required or assumed by tasks.

- Problem scenarios synthesize a range of workplace needs and opportunities, with an emphasis on typical or critical issues uncovered through stakeholder, artifact, and theme analysis.

- A claim hypothesizes a relation between a feature of a situation and the likely positive or negative consequences for actors in the situation; claims document tradeoffs that may be addressed by future design work.

Exercises

1. Analyze the task of writing a memo to your boss requesting a raise. Develop a hierarchical task analysis (presented graphically as in Figures 2.7 and 2.8, or textually using an indented list) for this task. Be sure to include the logic needed to order or choose among steps at each level.

2. Examine a calendar currently in use by you or an acquaintance. What does it tell you about the tasks of scheduling or finding out about events? What specific information does it tell you about the individual(s) using it?

3. Analyze the problem of adding or dropping a course from your class schedule in the first week of classes. What exception conditions might arise? How are they handled? Who (or what) holds the information about how to handle each exception? Create a stakeholder diagram to show the relations and dependencies among different organizational units.

4. Generate a sixth problem scenario (or extend one of the sample scenarios) for the science fair. Experiment with actors who have different characteristics (e.g., a student with no prior science fair experience, or a judge who also has a child participating in the fair).

5. Propose one or two additional claims based on the problem scenarios presented in Figure 2.13.

Project Ideas

Conduct a requirements analysis for the online grocery store problem:

- As a team, develop a root concept.

- Collect field data by observing activities at a local grocery store and interviewing members of different stakeholder groups. (Be sure to get people's permission before you photograph or videotape them.) Gather or photograph shopping artifacts.

- Analyze your field data, creating stakeholder profiles and diagrams, task analyses, and workplace themes.

- Use your field data results to develop a set of hypothetical stakeholders and problem scenarios. Use claims analysis to document features of grocery shopping that have interesting tradeoffs for one or more stakeholder groups.

Recommended Reading

Beyer, H., & K. Holtzblatt. 1998. *Contextual Design: Defining Customer-Centered Systems*. San Francisco: Morgan Kaufmann.

Cooper, A. 1999. *The Inmates Are Running the Asylum: Why High-Tech Products Drive Us Crazy and How to Restore the Sanity*. Indianapolis: Sams Press.

Nardi, B. A., ed. 1996. *Context and Consciousness: Activity Theory and Human-Computer Interaction*. Cambridge, MA: MIT Press.

Wixon, D., & J. Ramey, eds. 1996. *Field Methods Casebook for Software Design*. New York: John Wiley & Sons.

3

Activity
Design

Sometimes even an obvious idea is a bad idea. Take the case of automatic meeting schedulers (Grudin 1990). Everyone knows that setting up a meeting can be tedious and frustrating, typically involving proposals, counterproposals, iterative checking, and confirming. This is just the sort of troublesome activity that computers should be able to help with—let the computer discover and solve the constraints imposed by conflicting schedules. But for such a system to work, it is important that all prospective attendees enter and maintain their personal schedules.

To the contrary, early studies of office work showed that electronic calendars are used largely by managers or executives as a communication tool for keeping their staff informed and oriented (Ehrlich 1987a, 1987b). Meetings are scheduled by secretaries on behalf of their bosses. This means that automating the scheduling task has clear payoffs for bosses and their secretaries. But for other employees, the payoff is that they are more easily summoned to meetings! Unless electronic calendars provide attractive services for the individual user—sufficient to warrant the data entry and modification needed to maintain an online calendar—the evident need for automated scheduling will remain a vexing problem.

—≈≈≈—

This chapter introduces the concepts and methods of **activity design**. This is the first phase of design reasoning, in which the problems and opportunities of current practice are transformed into new ways of behaving. The emphasis is on the basic concepts and services of the new system; subsequent chapters will discuss more detailed issues such as the how to present and interact with these basic services.

The goal of activity design is to specify **system functionality**. This can be seen as the "back end" of an application: what information it holds or accesses, the kinds of operations that are permitted based on this information, and the results that are returned by these operations. Although the system functionality determines what is possible, the concrete experience of the user is determined by

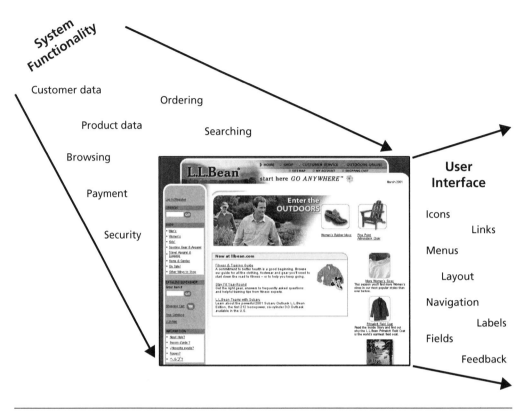

Figure 3.1   A user's experience with a system is a combination of the underlying system functionality and the user interface provided for interacting with these functions.

the **user interface**, the physical representations and procedures that are provided for viewing and interacting with the system functionality.

Figure 3.1 diagrams this distinction for a popular online shopping system (the Web site is available at *http://www.llbean.com*; this particular screen shot was taken in March 2001). The choice of products to offer, the information stored about the products and the customers, the ordering and payment process—these are decisions made in the design of the system functionality. Choosing how to display a product, how images and descriptions will be composed into screens, how users will navigate among screens—these are questions for user interface design.

Both aspects of system design will influence the user's experience. System functionality determines what is possible, while the user interface determines what users must do to experience these possibilities. If a catolog offers poor products, or if inadequate information about products is provided, shoppers will not find the system useful or satisfying. The system functionality is the essence of an interactive system; it must address genuine goals and concerns. But the user interface is equally important, acting as a sort of "gatekeeper" to the underlying functions. If people cannot recognize or interpret the information provided, or cannot anticipate or deduce what steps to take, they will not be able to benefit from even the highest-quality services.

This chapter focuses on the design of system functionality. Other authors refer to this as conceptual design or task-level design (Johnson 2000; Hackos & Redish 1998). We prefer the phrase "activity design" because it emphasizes the broad scope of what is being designed: people carrying out activities with the support of computer software. It is essential to design software systems *in a usage context,* always considering whether and how they will support human goals and activities.

We postpone user interface design not because the details of information and interaction are unimportant, but because they are complex. By considering system functionality first, designers can make progress more quickly—they can focus on *what* a system will do, and not worry about how at the same time (Constantine & Lockwood 1999). It is hard to analyze user interface needs and choose appropriate displays and interaction techniques when you do not yet know what a system will do (and why). Ultimately, even small user interaction difficulties can destroy a system's usability. Designers are most likely to make these mistakes early, when they are still learning about the users, their tasks, and their concerns.

Focusing first on activities also creates a natural boundary between the system functionality and its user interface software. This makes it easier to construct alternative user interfaces for a system (e.g., for users with differing abilities). But most importantly, it reinforces the central goal of designing activities that users will find effective, comprehensible, and satisfying. We turn now to issues that impact these design goals.

3.1   Designing Effective Activities

Effectiveness is a tricky concept. It is tempting to equate effectiveness with efficiency—in other words, with productivity, the cost of achieving something with respect to time or space. But, in fact, effectiveness is a more general concept. Simply put, a design is effective to the degree that it satisfies the needs it is intended to meet. If efficiency is important in the problem situation, then efficiency will be one aspect of effectiveness. But the real question is how to make sure your solution has the "right" services.

Designers begin with their own beliefs—explicit and implicit—about technology. Coming up with novel ideas is intrinsically rewarding; this is often what leads people to be designers in the first place. Innovation can lead to radical transformations in how we view tasks, and even in what goals are reasonable.

Unfortunately, technology for its own sake often gets in the way of effective design (Tradeoff 3.1). For example, **technological determinism** is a school of thought wherein technology is seen as the most important factor influencing success of an organization (Woodward 1965). Under this view, tracking and applying leading-edge computer technology become driving organizational goals. But clearly not all innovations are useful in all situations. The World Wide Web is full of useless sites where interactive hypermedia systems have been created simply because being on the Web is the "in" thing; the infamous paper clip in Microsoft Office is another generally recognized example of technology overstepping its usefulness.

TRADEOFF 3.1

Technological innovation can transform tasks in exciting and satisfying ways, BUT incremental changes to existing practice are easier to understand and adopt.

Sometimes the most effective designs introduce only minor changes to a situation. Small changes are easier for people to understand and appreciate, as well as easier to implement. But there is clearly a dilemma here: If designers focus too much on users' current practices, they may miss important opportunities for innovation. Most users will not be familiar with novel technology options. A user-centered development team wants to be solicitous of and responsive to users' needs and preferences, but in general these users will have a limited ability to apply new technology to their tasks. Of course, this is a major motivation for iterative development, where users are exposed to technology at many different phases of the development process.

In **cooperative design** (sometimes also called participatory design), an interactive system emerges through a direct collaboration between designers and prospective users. The overall process is one of mutual learning: Software developers interact with user representatives to learn more about the work setting and vice versa (Kyng 1995; Carroll, Chin, et al. 2000). Changes are made and incorporated into work practices in an incremental and iterative fashion. Through direct contributions to design, the user participants come to identify with the new technology, which also aids in acceptance and adoption of the system once it is complete (Greenbaum & Kyng 1991). Cooperative design is a whole lifecycle approach—user participation starts during requirements analysis and continues throughout design, prototyping, and implementation.

When envisioning new applications of software technology, it is important to remember that a person's experience depends on much more than just a piece of software. It is easy to become consumed with software production. After all, this is what software developers are trained to do—analyze requirements, produce design specifications, and build software. Design documents and prototypes are concrete indications of progress; they can be tested to find out what to do next. However, as discussed in Chapter 2, people's activities are very much influenced by the social or organizational context of work (Eason & Harker 1989). The scope of design must encompass the entire situation.

The implicit goal of design is to provide computer support for people's tasks, but putting one task or subtask "online" may make related activities difficult or impossible (Tradeoff 3.2). For instance, shoppers often bring lists along on their expeditions. A designer might note this and plan to include computerized support for shopping lists: If lists are created and maintained online, it becomes easy to keep records, request auto-fulfillment, repeat orders, and so on. But would online shopping lists contribute to an effective design in general? Most shopping lists are created at many different times in the midst of other activities that evoke shopping needs. Often multiple people contribute to a list over a period of time. Unless these interrelated activities can be integrated within a single system, moving the lists online may disrupt the social context of shopping.

TRADEOFF 3.2

The goal of software design is to provide computer-based support for tasks, BUT some needs are better supported by physical or social features of the situation.

Analyzing the role of shopping lists in shopping activities is an example of **distributed cognition** (Hutchins 1995). Distributed cognition is concerned with how task-relevant information is distributed throughout a situation in many different forms—the knowledge and skills of the people involved, the state of the tools or other artifacts in use, and the recent or long-term memories of specific events. This framework has been applied to the detailed analysis of complex tasks such as flying an airplane (Hutchins & Klausen 1996). However, the general concepts apply just as well to more mundane activities such as shopping, where the contents of a cupboard or a closet represent information that may play a critical role in one or more shopping tasks.

Scenarios help to reason about which aspects of an activity are best supported by computer software. By thinking through a hypothetical situation, designers "try out" new ideas about technology in a realistic setting. The possibilities already present in the real-world are highlighted, providing a balance against the tendency to identify and computerize as many task elements as possible. Scenarios emphasize the context in which activities take place, so they help to recognize how the many different aspects of a situation (including other people and tools) can be combined into an effective activity design.

A third tradeoff in designing for effectiveness is choosing an appropriate level of generality. Designers normally seek solutions that cover as many cases as possible. For example, given the job of designing an online product database, most designers would develop a scheme for classifying, organizing, and retrieving all products in the same way. Such generality has obvious benefits—the database is simple to build and maintain, and browsing and selection work the same for every product. This makes the design quite effective from the perspectives of ease of learning and software maintenance.

The problem is that designing a general solution can diminish effectiveness for specific tasks (Tradeoff 3.3). For instance, suppose specific products are tightly linked in people's buying activities—when shoppers buy one, they virtually always want the other. A common example is computer hardware and peripherals; a new printer cannot be used until the connecting cable is also purchased. The general-purpose solution treats each product the same, so shoppers would be forced to go through two seemingly independent selection procedures, first browsing and selecting from the printer category, then doing the same for cables. The result is likely to be irritation and uncertainty (how to be certain you have the right cable?). For scenarios like these, a database that supports special-case "bundling" is a better solution, even though it complicates creation and maintenance of the database. Scenario-based reasoning of this sort helps designers find an effective combination of general and task-specific functionality.

TRADEOFF 3.3

General-purpose design solutions increase reuse and consistency in a system, BUT any given task may be best supported with specialized functionality.

3.2 Designing Comprehensible Activities

Designing for effectiveness is not enough—the new activity design must also be understandable. As people work with a computer system, they must be able to tell what goals are possible and whether they are making progress on these goals.

They will use whatever knowledge they possess to figure out what is happening; this lets them choose and carry out appropriate actions. Someone who cannot make sense of events will have difficulty planning further action, and is likely to give up in frustration.

In the end, it is a system's user interface—the information presentation and interaction techniques that are the topics of Chapters 4 and 5—that makes the system more or less comprehensible to users. But during the early phases of activity design, the **designer's model** of the system begins to form—his or her own understanding of the information and tasks that will constitute the system. This model will be elaborated and refined through the development process; it guides the development of concrete design artifacts such as scenarios, user actions, and screen displays.

Figure 3.2 contrasts a designer's model of an online shopping system with how a user might understand the same system. The designer's model is depicted as an abstract network, implying that it is a systematic and relatively complete

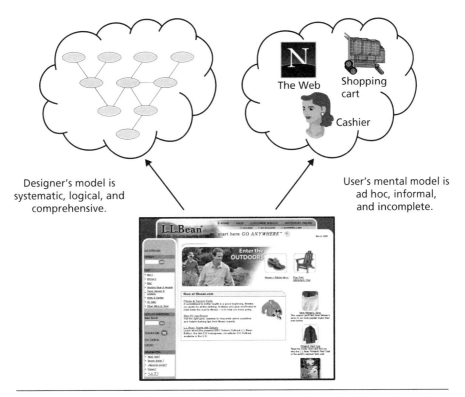

Figure 3.2 A user's mental model of a software system may be quite different from the designer's model.

body of knowledge. Although a designer's model is also a mental representation, designers often use technical representations such as feature lists, task analyses, data-flow diagrams, or object-action tables to express these models (van Harmelen 2001). In SBD, designers write scenarios and claims to document and share their design models.

A user's understanding of a system is likely to be less well formed. We use the term **mental model** to mean a loosely organized body of concepts and procedures used to select relevant goals, choose and execute appropriate actions, and understand what happens (Carroll & Olson 1988). The diagram depicts the case of a new user who has not yet interacted with the online shopping system—at this point the model consists largely of knowledge about shopping in general (a cashier, a shopping cart) and about other Web systems (e.g., how Web browsers work).

Early in use, a mental model is very much influenced by knowledge of related systems and activities (e.g., shopping in the real world). As experience increases, the user's mental model becomes more detailed and specific to the system in use. For example, an experienced online shopper may possess very well-defined mental scripts for frequent tasks such as retrieving and browsing sale items. However, mental models are always incomplete and are constantly updated through use.

Designers naturally want to anticipate and facilitate construction of useful mental models. Unfortunately, the psychological processes that create users' mental states are not directly observable; designers can only guess at mental models based on users' behavior or comments (Tradeoff 3.4). Different users begin with differing backgrounds, or will have goals that lead them to interpret the same system behaviors in different ways. Thus, despite the strong requirement to design concepts and services that are intuitive and easy to comprehend, designers are simply unable to observe many of the factors that will influence users' understanding.

TRADEOFF 3.4

Designers must anticipate and support mental model construction by users, BUT the psychological processes that create mental models are not observable.

One thing we do know is that users find it easier to understand new ideas when they are similar to familiar concepts (Holyoak & Thagard 1995). Users often learn to interact with systems by applying metaphors—a **metaphor** is a known concept used to understand a new concept by analogy (Carroll & Thomas

1982). In Figure 3.2, the user is relying on pieces of a store metaphor (cashier, shopping cart) to understand online shopping.

Designers often use metaphors deliberately as an aid to comprehension and planning (Erickson 1990; Madsen 1994). For example, most online catalogs have incorporated some version of the shopping cart metaphor, and many advertise sales or provide coupons that can be applied to obtain special prices. The hope is that if a metaphor is followed faithfully, even users with little computing expertise will be able to understand how that part of the system works.

Building a new system by analogy to an existing system simplifies initial comprehension and use. Unfortunately, metaphors can also have a narrowing influence on mental models, because they may limit the kinds of activities users will expect or seek out (Tradeoff 3.5; see also Halasz & Moran 1982). For example, researchers noted that the early users of word processors made extensive reference to a typewriter metaphor (Carroll & Mack 1985; Mack, Lewis, & Carroll 1983). But while this metaphor was helpful in thinking about text input and printing, it led to an overly "physical" view of digital documents. Learners had difficulty understanding editing features such as insert mode, or special characters that turn formatting controls on and off.

TRADEOFF 3.5

People seek to understand the world in familiar terms, BUT they must go beyond the familiar in order to develop new (and improved) ways of acting.

Although metaphor breakdowns may lead to errors initially, they also encourage revision and updating of mental models (Carroll, Mack, & Kellogg 1988). For example, Amazon.com provides a shopper review service; people who browse or purchase a product are invited to write a review for others to use in the future. Note, though, that this concept breaks the store metaphor; in the real world, shoppers do not (at least not by convention!) leave personal notes among the shelved goods. But digital views of products are flexible: They can exist many places at once, and may include different views for different tasks. Recognizing why it is okay to "write on" digital versus physical products enriches the user's mental model of online shopping.

Metaphors are also useful in design brainstorming, when people seek to generate completely novel ideas (see "Of Warehouses and Meeting Places" sidebar). Often there are one or two obvious metaphors, or real-world domains, that share many features with the new functionality. A physical store is an obvious metaphor for online shopping, a town library for a digital library. But in addition

Of Warehouses and Meeting Places

Madsen (1994) describes how different metaphors were used to stimulate discussion about computer support in libraries. The metaphors were chosen to promote contrasting conceptions of what a library "is" and thus suggest different sets of library features and tasks. Two of these metaphors were a *warehouse* and *meeting place*:

1. The warehouse metaphor connotes a place where books and other materials are stored and supplied. The staff in a warehouse are concerned with the stock currently available, goods (i.e., books) on order, purchase and loss of goods, and delivery of goods to customers (i.e., lending). The key tasks become finding and tracking goods, optimizing purchases, and avoiding loss. Database and information retrieval software are a good starting point for computerized support for such tasks.
2. In contrast, the meeting place metaphor shifts the focus to conversations and dis-

cussions about books or other library materials. These conversations may involve various combinations of people—for example, the staff talking among themselves or to staff at different libraries, the staff talking to library patrons, and patrons talking to each other. Ideas of this sort suggest an entirely different range of software support, including, for example, an event or meetings calendar, online book requests or reviews, and so on.

The metaphors are useful not because they are direct and accurate descriptions of a library, but because they promote a deliberately biased view of library activities. Designers can then ask how they can make a library a better warehouse but at the same time improve it as a meeting place. Metaphorical thinking pushes on the boundaries of a mental model that we might otherwise take for granted.

to these very similar domains, a designer might explore more unusual analogies to see if new ideas are provoked. Suppose you imagined that an online catalog is like a storybook. This might lead to novel ideas about how to present the company's products (e.g., via narratives that have actors, motivations, and a plot line). In SBD, metaphorical brainstorming is a key technique for expanding the space of ideas.

3.3   Designing Satisfying Activities

In business settings, computer use is often mandatory. Once an employee is hired, he or she is expected to use the information technology already in place. But even when an organization's tools appear to be useful and comprehensible, work will suffer if the employee finds them irritating, depressing, or otherwise unpleasant. Such cases may "simply" lead to poor employee morale. But when use is discretionary, tools that fail to satisfy their intended users will simply be discarded.

One way to satisfy users is by automating tedious or error-prone tasks (e.g., retrieving addresses from an alphabetized list of client records). Indeed, many software development projects take task automation as a prime objective, with the general intention of saving time or money. But lurking behind this objective is an important tradeoff: Automating unrewarding work makes people happy, but it is possible to remove so much responsibility from the human that he or she feels unimportant (Tradeoff 3.6). An extreme case is a worker who ends up in front of a computer console, pushing buttons at the appropriate time so that a computer can carry out what was formerly his or her job.

TRADEOFF 3.6

Automating tedious and error-prone steps improves job satisfaction, BUT automation of some activities may undermine motivation and self-esteem.

Knowing what to automate requires careful study of the employee's respon-sibilities and sources of reward. Most jobs involve some degree of **knowledge work**—workers apply personal expertise and knowledge to collect the right infor-mation and make the right decisions (Muller et al. 1995). Contrast the knowl-edge work of a reference librarian who works with clients to find useful materials to that of a catalog librarian who indexes and organizes new materials. Giving the reference librarian an online database that automates reference retrieval saves time that can be spent instead on the knowledge-intensive tasks of resource analysis and recommendation. But giving the catalog librarian an automatic clas-sification system (e.g., via keywords) might remove job responsibilities that are crucial to his or her feelings of personal accomplishment.

To find the right balance between automation and personal control, designers must carefully consider all organizational implications of redesigning a business procedure. It is not enough to determine whether a particular job will be faster or easier to complete. In **sociotechnical systems theory**, technology and the surrounding organization are analyzed, designed, and iterated as a single co-evolving system (Eason 1988; Mumford 1987). This paradigm assumes from the start that successful systems will be those where technology and the social system evolve together over time, each adapting to the other.

Another important question is "satisfying for whom?" Most computer soft-ware is used by a single person at a workstation. Individuals create documents in a word processor or debug financial models in a spreadsheet. Ease of use and satisfaction are defined in terms of an individual user's reactions. But as networks and collaborative systems have become more pervasive, this view has become too simplistic (Tradeoff 3.7). Virtually all work now has collaborative elements. Even the most private and creative activities (e.g., writing a research paper) are shared, displayed, or evaluated by others at some point.

TRADEOFF 3.7

The people who use systems are motivated by personal goals and needs, BUT software must also be designed to support collaborators' goals and needs.

When designing for satisfaction, the increasingly collaborative nature of computer use creates a dilemma: Activities that benefit a group may be experienced as tedious or frustrating for individual group members (Grudin 1994). The analysis of shared calendars at the beginning of this chapter is illustrative—a shared database succeeds to the extent that an entire workgroup cooperates. But if some individuals are expected to do extra work so that others benefit, the perceived inequity will lead to dissatisfaction.

There is no easy answer to this dilemma. It always takes extra effort to share and coordinate activities (Bannon & Schmidt 1991). Information that otherwise might have been left informal and tacit must be made explicit and archived. Policies and decisions about shared resources, access, control, reporting, and so on, must now be developed, communicated, and implemented. The challenge is to design activities that support these group processes, but that are pleasurable or otherwise satisfying for individuals as well.[1]

Activity scenarios help to reason about shared work. The real-world usage context contains clues about other stakeholders in an activity. Even if a scenario focuses on the goals and experiences of one individual, it contains information about the setting and about the actor's motivations and responsibilities. These details lead designers to question and analyze related impacts on coworkers and on the group.

---

[1]With respect to shared calendars, the increasing popularity of products such as Microsoft Scheduler provides evidence that group members in general are benefiting from computer-aided coordination. This is likely due to the trend toward less hierarchical organizations (Rousseau 1997) and to increased integration with time-management tasks (e.g., to-do lists, reminders, and links to task-related resources).

3.4   Science Fair Case Study: Activity Design

Moving from problem scenarios to activity design scenarios represents a crucial move in SBD: This is where the design team first introduces concrete ideas about new functionality, and new ways of thinking about users' needs and how to meet them. Although the overall development process is iterative and highly responsive to feedback, the ideas introduced now will have an especially significant impact, because they will scope and organize much of the detailed design work that follows.

During activity design, scenarios and claims serve as a flexible and inexpensive medium for imagination and discussion. The focus on realistic situations helps designers to generate specific ideas, as well as to think through the implications that these ideas have for the scenario actors. The combination of problem scenarios and claims allows designers to conduct a deliberate and systematic investigation of design possibilities.

Figure 3.3 summarizes the major components of activity design. Problem scenarios are transformed into activity design scenarios through a combined process of brainstorming about design ideas, reasoning from previous claims, and working through the general concerns of activity design (e.g., as discussed in the first half of this chapter). Throughout, the scenarios are evaluated and

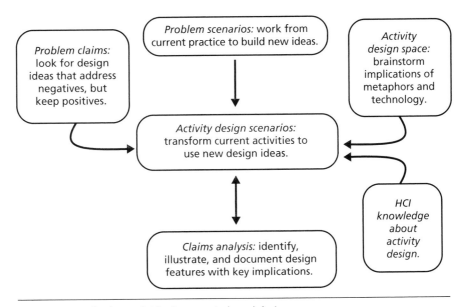

Figure 3.3   Designing activities in scenario-based design.

refined by identifying key features and their consequences for use (via claims analysis). The general design goal is to maintain or enhance positive consequences while removing or minimizing negative consequences (Carroll & Rosson 1992).

Exploration of ideas (divergent thinking) is a key element of any design process. Although many effective designs make only small changes to current practice (Tradeoff 3.1), it is always important to push on the boundaries of how things are currently done. Detailed problem analysis should be complemented with "out of the box" thinking aimed at opening up the space of possibilities. In SBD we do this by brainstorming about metaphors and technology options.

3.4.1   Exploring the Activity Design Space

A strong metaphor for the virtual science fair comes from MOOsburg itself—a virtual world, presenting a familiar spatial structure (the town of Blacksburg, Virginia) with streets, buildings, rooms, people, and objects. People can move around within the structure, interact with people and other objects, and so on. This virtual-world metaphor provides a general backdrop to the design of the system throughout the next few chapters.

However, we also explored other metaphors in search of less obvious features. Table 3.1 shows how we took each problem scenario in turn, and considered metaphors for central objects like the exhibit, or for activities like visiting the fair. For example, we thought about exhibits as if they were lab journals or documentaries. A lab journal is quite informal and personal, a sort of working document; it suggested to us that exhibits might be more than a final "formal" presentation, such as being available as an informal work in progress. The documentary metaphor suggested that there might be a time line or story of how the project was researched and the exhibit constructed.

Different metaphors can often be mixed or composed into a single coherent concept. An exhibit can be a formal display for judging, but might also contain informal information, or a story of how it came to be. A teacher may play the role of a peer with experienced science fair participants, but a director with less experienced students. Of course, not all metaphors combine well. It is difficult to think about the fair summary as both a sales pitch and a thank-you note, because the two concepts have very different goals.

Information technology is another source of design ideas. For our project, the MOOsburg system already provides a range of information and communication services (Table 3.2). For example, there is a shared multimedia notebook that can be used to hold or edit text and graphics; the electronic whiteboard supports

Table 3.1   Metaphors for objects and activities at a virtual science fair.

VSF Activity	Real-World Metaphor	Implications for VSF Activities
Constructing an exhibit is like writing a . . .	Lab journal	Informal and personal notes, raw data, work in progress
	Documentary	Carefully constructed "story" of how the project happened
Coaching a student is like being a . . .	Peer (colleague)	Social support, reactions to ideas, suggestions
	Director	Specific directions about exhibit content or layout
Visiting the fair is like going to a . . .	Study room	Quiet and focused attention to pieces of information
	Public lecture	Receiving preorganized information as part of a group
	Cocktail party	Informal discussions, moving from one group to another
Judging exhibits is like making a . . .	Balance sheet	Mathematical model of data, equations, results
	Discussion	Extended conversations about reactions, values, criteria
Summarizing the fair is like creating a . . .	Report card	Assessment on well-established categories of achievement
	Guided tour	Interactive visit of best sites with helpful commentary
	Thank-you note	Personal recognition of participants, mentors, judges, etc.

informal drawing or picture display. Users can also post or browse Web pages within the system. These familiar technologies serve as a sort of metaphor themselves, leading to specific ideas about exhibit content and structure.

The type and amount of technology exploration a team does will depend on its starting assumptions (recall the root concept from Chapter 2). If a design must fit into an existing system infrastructure (like MOOsburg), the natural focus is on options provided by that infrastructure. In practice, many development settings will be of this sort—consider, for example, the assumptions inherent in building a Web or Windows-PC application. On occasion, though, a team will have few existing constraints, such as being tasked with finding and exploring uses of an emerging technology. In such cases, this exploratory phase may be quite extended and varied.

Table 3.2   Ideas about activity design suggested by current MOOsburg tools.

VSF Activity	MOOsburg Technology	Implications for VSF Activities
Constructing an exhibit is like using a . . .	Multimedia notebook	Project reports may have graphics, sounds, etc.
	Electronic whiteboard	Informal drawings and annotations will be simple to add
	Web pages	The exhibit may have hyperlinks (internal or external)
Coaching a student is like using a . . .	Email	Familiar, asynchronous communication with attachments
	Threaded discussion	Comments and replies organized by topic
	Chat	Real-time conversation among co-present people.
Visiting the fair is like using a . . .	Room panorama	Exhibits, tables, etc., are distributed around the space
	Slide show	Exhibitors present while visitors make notes, ask questions
Judging exhibits is like using a . . .	Voting booth	Input from multiple judges on a set of questions
	Threaded discussion	All judges contribute to a single structured evaluation
Summarizing the fair is like using a . . .	Charting package	Numerical coding and summaries of outcomes
	Multimedia notebook	Diverse exhibit elements collected in sequential order
	Interactive map	Predefined path through interesting exhibits

3.4.2   Activity Design Scenarios and Claims

After exploring metaphors and technology, the design team begins to transform current practice, envisioning new ways to meet the needs of the stakeholders in the problem scenarios. Just as we did when generating problem scenarios, we use a tightly interleaved process of scenario writing and claims analysis.

It is hard to say how to "do design" because so many things contribute at once. Begin by considering a problem scenario, using the claims to identify features of the situation that might be changed by introducing technology. Use the ideas from the metaphors and technology to come up with possible changes. Try out the changes in the scenario to see how it would now transpire, thinking through how the actors would react, what they would want to do next, and so on. At the same time, think about other situations that the feature might impact, or other consequences that it might have. In other words, try to think through the many possible side effects of introducing a design feature into a scenario.

Let's take as an example one central transformation—putting the science exhibits online. Looking back at Sally's exhibit-planning scenario, we can think concretely about how such a change might impact her goals and activities (Figure 3.4): Sally thinks the virtual exhibits might give her more options for presenting her work, as well as making the exhibit more interactive. She also understands that the physical constraints of a physical board are no longer in place. At the same time, Sally is concerned about the physical models she has created, wondering how she can share them in an online system. Overall, the positives outweigh the negatives, so we incorporate this feature. We document our analysis of the pros and cons as a claim (the first entry in Table 3.3 on page 100).

This activity scenario incorporates less obvious ideas as well. The claims analysis of the original scenario documented how the lab table supported Sally's planning activities, and we wanted to provide similar support in the new design. The solution proposed is a template, offered as a guide to the layout process. Again, we used claims analysis to think through the pros and cons of a template (second claim in Table 3.3): It might be seen as too heavy handed or restrictive by experienced students. We conveyed this as a concern of Sally's, also noting that a template must have sufficient flexibility for her creative ideas.

We applied similar reasoning to the other scenarios, looking for opportunities to apply new metaphors or insert new technology. The results appear in Figure 3.5. To simplify the case study content, the figure presents abbreviated scenarios that describe just the new design features. Readers may want to refer to the actors described in Figure 2.12 and the problem scenarios in Figure 2.13 to recreate a more complete setting and context for the envisioned activities.

Some of the activity design ideas can be traced to specific metaphors or technology exploration. For instance, the idea to make the judging forms editable came from our thinking about judging as a discussion, which is a more open-ended activity than filling out a form. As we tried this out in the judging scenario, we recognized that providing Ralph with an editable form would give him a greater sense of control, and might encourage him to take action on special cases. This led us to envision a situation in which he has difficulty comparing Sally's and Jeff's exhibits, and how he edits the form to deal with this problem. At

Example Problem Scenario ⇨	Transformed into Activity Design Scenario
1) Sally plans her exhibit on black holes.	*1) Sally plans her exhibit on black holes.*

Background on Sally, her motivations, . . .

Sally is a bit worried about the space and materials that are provided to everyone— a standard 4′×6′ posterboard, with a two-foot shelf underneath for supporting physical materials or models. This year she has explored some new methods, for example, an Authorware simulation that illustrates her theory of black hole formation. But she knows from past years that there are few electrical outlets in the gym, and she doesn't have a laptop to use in the exhibit anyway. She checks with the organizer, Rachel Berris, just in case, but Rachel confirms that the school district has no money for special resources such as laptops, and that she will be able to use only battery-powered equipment.

As she studies her simulation, Sally thinks of a way to turn the lack of computer support into a "feature": She will create a sequence of visualizations that can be flipped like a deck of cards to show the animation. In fact, as she works, she gets into it and decides to create several variations, so that visitors can guess which one matches her project data and conclusions. She will then chart people's guesses as a dynamic element in her exhibit. She knows from experience that this is just the sort of thing judges will notice and award points for. Now she just has to figure out how to fit everything into the space she will have.

Background on Sally, her motivations, . . .

Sally is curious about how creating a virtual exhibit will be different from the ones she has created in the past. She hopes that she will have more flexibility in presenting her ideas, and thinks she might be able to come up with some interactive elements that she knows the judges will like. In fact, she has already developed an Authorware simulation that illustrates her theory of black hole formation, and she wants to include this in her virtual exhibit.

When Sally goes to the exhibit construction area, she finds a template with a suggested layout—title page, abstract, slide show, detailed results, project report, and bibliography. At first she is worried that this will not fit the materials she has already created. But when she starts adding material, she can see that there is also still a lot of flexibility—for example, she can add a new component to hold her simulation. But she is not yet sure how she can share her physical star models.

Sally knows that judges and visitors really like interactive components, so instead of just presenting her simulation in "demo" mode, she decides to build in some interactive parameters, so that people can see her conclusions but also experiment with their own ideas. This makes her realize she will need some way to collect and share these experiments.

Figure 3.4 A problem scenario is transformed into an activity scenario.

2) Mr. King coaches Sally on her project.

Mr. King had a busy day, so he arranges to work with Sally on her project from home this evening.

Given Sally's science fair background, he is curious about how she will take advantage of the opportunities provided by the virtual exhibits.

He logs on and can see that Sally has already arrived. He joins her and positions himself to share her view.

Sally sees him arrive, greets him, and shows him the template she is working with. Mr. King can see that she is bringing in files that she must have created earlier on her PC; he recognizes Word files, Excel graphs, and some JPEG images.

Intrigued, he wonders whether these files will be read-only or if they will invoke the corresponding editors. He double-clicks on a chart object and is impressed when it opens Excel. At the same time, he wonders to himself whether visitors might accidentally change some of Sally's content.

Mr. King is concerned that Sally is bringing in too many files. He reminds her that even though this is an unlimited space, visitors and judges have limited time and will be very influenced by first impressions. Sally agrees and they start browsing her elements and choosing ones that are most revealing at first glance.

Sally shows him her simulation and describes her idea for making it more interactive. He likes the idea but is worried that the visitor-contributed experiments will make her display too messy. While she continues to work, he explores the exhibit construction tools and finds a way to create nested layers. He proposes that a layer might be used to hold the experiments, as well as other supplementary materials.

3) Alicia and Delia go to the science fair.

When Alicia's daughter Delia shows her an email invitation to a virtual science fair, the two of them decide to follow the link right then and there. They are curious about how this will be different than a regular fair.

On arrival, they see an overview of the virtual science fair. They notice that some exhibits are still "under construction," so they figure that one difference may be that this fair is ongoing. The welcome note confirms this, indicating that all virtual exhibits will be complete by next Thursday, when the judging will take place.

(continued)

Figure 3.5   Activity scenarios for the virtual science fair (in summary form).

Figure 3.5 *(continued)*

They decide to look around anyway since they have time, and Delia suggests that they visit the exhibit that already has several people at it, thinking it must be interesting. But then Alicia notices that her friend Marge is also here, so they join her instead. She is talking to Sally Harris about her exhibit on black holes.

Sally and Marge see them arrive, and pause briefly to say hi. But Alicia and Delia don't want to interrupt, so they look around at other parts of the exhibit. Delia finds a stored discussion about red dwarfs and she and her mom browse it. Delia adds a comment to this discussion and is pleased when Sally notices and elaborates on her point.

Alicia asks Sally about an unfamiliar object, a simulation. Sally shows her how it demonstrates her current theory of black hole formation, and asks them whether they want to try out some variations. Alicia is surprised and pleased at how quickly Delia understands how to change the model and get new results.

4) Ralph judges the high school physics projects at the science fair.

Ralph is intrigued when Rachel recruits him to judge the virtual science fair, wondering how this will be different than the normal fair judging he has done for the past three years.

When he first visits the virtual fair, he is surprised at the variation in progress, and wonders how some of the students will finish in time for the judging next Thursday.

He is happy to see that he can do his judging any time on Thursday, as long as he is done by 8:30 PM.

On Thursday, he starts in the morning, first scanning each of the five high school physics projects assigned to him, making some notes in the form provided. He recognizes the form from previous years and figures that as usual he will need to make annotations explaining the numerical judgements it requests.

Later, when he examines the projects in more detail, this is just what he finds himself doing: Jeff Smith has emphasized solid research methods at the expense of innovation, while Sally Harris has done the reverse in her black hole project.

He wonders if he can weight the categories differently in the two cases, and finds that he can edit the forms, as long as he also provides his rationale as a comment.

As he starts to submit the forms, he is at first annoyed when he must authenticate each one with his password, but then reminds himself that these prizes mean a lot to the students.

After submitting all five forms, he is shown the results thus far, and is not surprised to see that Jeff and Sally are tied for first place.

5) Rachel organizes a presentation for the superintendent.

When Superintendent Carlisle asks Rachel to put together a presentation of winning projects, she first takes him on a personal tour of the fair, to set the context for the summary she will prepare.

She shows him Sally's exhibit with the simulation, and Jeff's exhibit with the systematic methods, and pulls up Ralph's judging form that used different weightings. She wants to make sure he understands that having the forms online made the judging more interesting but also more complicated.

After the quick tour, Rachel goes through the saved exhibits more slowly, opening the more visual elements (Excel charts, JPEG images) and making copies onto her own workstation. She notes that each time she makes a copy, a "recognition" notice is sent to the student.

Later, she creates a PowerPoint file and imports the visuals, adding a few notes that will help Carlisle speak to each example. When she emails Carlisle the PowerPoint file, she includes Sally's simulation, just in case he has time to show a more in-depth example of student work.

---

the same time, we noted a negative consequence—a set of forms may become inconsistent and difficult to merge.

Other design ideas can be traced to general tradeoffs in designing interactive systems. The idea to build exhibits out of existing desktop documents (e.g., Word, Excel; see the first three scenarios) was motivated by the general belief that building from existing practice is a good idea. But the claim documenting this reasoning in Table 3.3 also points to a negative impact—students may be disappointed when they are not offered special-purpose tools with flashy graphics or other user interaction novelties (Tradeoff 3.1).

It is important to remember that the claims in Table 3.3 were generated *in parallel* with the activity scenarios. Each claim documents a design feature that was considered and debated with respect to its pros and cons. Other features were considered but rejected because the cons outweighed the pros. For example, we considered that form editing could be a collaborative activity involving all judges, but decided that this would require too much inter-judge coordination and was not realistic for volunteers at a science fair.

In addition to documenting key design decisions, claims bring out issues for future design work. For instance, one claim raises a flag about the potential complexity of an unlimited presentation space. In response, we have proposed the general idea of exhibit layers, but this needs further design work. Similarly, we have suggested that conversations at an exhibit can be stored, but future

Table 3.3   Claims analyzing the key features of the activity design.

Proposed Activity Design Feature	Hypothesized Pros (+) or Cons (−) of the Feature
Putting exhibits online	+ remove many constraints regarding space and diversity in layout + facilitates an iterative process of design, construction, and editing + simplifies access to the exhibits by people separated in space and time − but may lead to a decreased emphasis or interest in physical components − but exhibitors may try to include too much, making exhibits complex
An exhibit template with traditional science project components	+ simplifies and guides the exhibit planning process + builds on prior exhibiting experience of fair participants + enhances consistency and comparability of exhibits for viewers and judges − but may discourage more inventive and creative exhibit structures
Integrating the products of common tools into the online exhibits	+ builds on exhibitors' existing skills and preferences + extends the apparent diversity of the fair and its services − but visitors may be confused about what is and is not "part" of the fair − but students may wish that flashy new tools had been provided
Email notices of the virtual science fair	+ can be directed specifically to individuals expected to be interested + may include a direct link to the online activity, simplifying access − but people without email accounts may feel excluded or slighted
Exhibiting projects that are not yet completed	+ emphasizes the extended and ongoing nature of science projects + encourages future visits for purposes of checking progress − but students may be embarrassed about showing a project that is not yet done
Archiving discussions at an exhibit	+ enables less redundancy in question answering by exhibitors + offers visitors more options, for a richer browsing experience + emphasizes the ongoing and community-oriented nature of the fair − but visitors may feel obliged to read all archives before asking anything

Editable judging forms	+ acknowledges that judging is never completely objective or predictable
	+ increases judges' feeling of control and contribution to the rating process
	− but may lead to evaluations that are difficult to interpret or compare
Authentication of the judging forms	+ reminds judges that their evaluations are valuable and confidential
	− but may be annoying if the number of forms is large
Preserving exhibits after the fair is over	+ simplifies access and review of example projects
	+ emphasizes a view of the fair as an ongoing event, extended in time
	− but isolated exhibits (e.g., without students or other visitors) provide only a partial and perhaps misleading picture of the overall fair activity

design work should consider how to convey that the implied task of reviewing these archives is optional.

Later on, we will build design prototypes to test our claims, so that we can see if the analyzed pros and cons match users' actual experience (Chapter 6). But right now, the scenarios serve as a flexible and inexpensive medium for trying out the new ideas. Each proposal is elaborated and given substance as the actors' actions and experiences are specified. The scenario context helps us to consider whether and how a feature is meeting the actors' needs, what the actors might be thinking as a feature is encountered, and whether they will understand what has happened when the task has been completed.

These scenarios and claims address system functionality only; they explore people's general goals and activities, not the details of information presentation or physical interaction. The exhibit planning scenario describes Sally's concerns and plans, but says nothing about how she interacts with the science fair or its tools. The judging scenario assumes that the form can be edited, but offers no details about form appearance or editing procedures. These user interface details will be the topic of Chapters 4 and 5.

3.4.3 Refining the Activity Design

SBD assumes constant iteration. As soon as design ideas emerge, they are tried out, elaborated, and refined through scenarios and claims analysis. We now turn to two techniques that are useful in this iterative process: taking a computational perspective on a scenario, and engaging stakeholders in participatory design discussions.

Taking a System Object's Point of View

Scenarios emphasize people and their activities. But it can sometimes be helpful to consider the software implied by a scenario—in other words, to take a computational perspective on the emerging design. An analysis of software design issues can uncover key feasibility issues (e.g., how will an exhibit template be implemented?). But a software perspective can also suggest new ideas for system functionality (e.g., perhaps different exhibit elements should have customized behaviors).

SBD adapts the methods of responsibility-driven design, a popular approach to object-oriented software development (Wirfs-Brock, Wilkerson, & Weiner 1990; Wirfs-Brock 1995; Wirfs-Brock & Wilkerson 1989). Designers identify objects that play an important role in a scenario, and then construct a **point of view** for each object (POV; Rosson 1999b). Each POV is created by doing a scenario walk-through from the perspective of a hypothetical software object.[2] In this sense, the scenario is elaborated by writing "scenarios within scenarios." Each POV envisions the activities of one software object over the course of the scenario.

Three POVs from the exhibit-planning scenario are presented in Table 3.4. They were created with the aid of **anthropomorphism**: We imagined a question of the form "If I was Sally's exhibit in the planning scenario, what could I do to be useful?" (Rosson & Gold 1989; Robertson et al. 1994). Answering such a question may prompt design ideas in which a software entity takes initiative or is responsive to a person's actions. In this sense, POV analysis is a special form of metaphorical thinking, in which software objects are viewed as intelligent agents.

The POV analysis presented here is quite modest, providing a software perspective for just a few of the exhibit-related objects. However, even this degree of analysis moves the exhibit-planning scenario to a more concrete level. In order to write the POVs, we had to step through Sally's interactions regarding her exhibit, and imagine how these interactions would translate into requests sent to

---

[2]Of course, the POV concept could be applied to any perspective. When we write scenarios from two different stakeholders' perspectives, we are also manipulating point of view. Our more narrow use of the term is consistent with previously published discussions (Rosson 1999b; Rosson & Carroll 2001).

Table 3.4   Points of view (POVs) developed for three software objects that might be used to implement the exhibit-planning scenario.

Scenario Object	Point of View for the Object
Sally's exhibit	I was created when Sally registered for the fair. When she first opened me, I used my template to create a set of default elements, and labeled myself "Under Construction." As Sally gave me actual elements to hold, I made sure that they were connected to the right default. When she gave me a simulation object, I worked with it to set up a new kind of element. Whenever I was asked to display myself, I made sure all my elements did the right thing.
The VSF template	I was defined by the fair organizer. When Sally created her exhibit, I worked with it to get it set up right. The exhibit asked me what elements it should contain, so I gave it my list of objects (Title, Abstract, etc.), along with their normal organization. When the exhibit asked me if it was okay for Sally to add new kinds of content, I checked my edit policy and said yes.
The simulation	Sally created me before she put the exhibit together. When she added me to the exhibit, the exhibit created a new kind of component, and asked me what it should be called. I said "Star Model" because that is the name Sally had given me. The exhibit also asked me for an image to use in my control, so I created a thumbnail of my first screen. The exhibit asked me what application to use if I was opened, and I told it I was an Authorware simulation.

objects, what result each request would produce, and so on. Although we are not yet proposing specific user-interaction techniques, we are modeling user behavior at a rather detailed level.

Several usability issues are raised by these POVs. The exhibit object contains and manages its elements; each element is responsible for its own display procedures. This is a sound architecture for extensibility, but it might raise issues later on for display quality and consistency. The template object is defined externally; it is then in charge of deciding whether new types of components can be added. This implies that we can have *non*editable templates, a possibility we have not yet considered. Are there new activity scenarios where this option would make sense? One example might be a young or first-time exhibitor where the template should play a stronger guiding role.

Note that POV analysis also moves the project in the direction of software design. The relationship between an exhibit and its elements indicates that the elements have common characteristics and behavior—they can display themselves, and they know their source application. In an object-oriented language this common behavior is modeled as **inheritance**, where an abstract class (e.g., ExhibitElement) defines the shared behavior, and each subclass (e.g., Title, Abstract) defines a specialization of the general concept. Even a very informal and preliminary analysis such as the one in Table 3.4 can open channels of discussion between usability and software personnel at a very early point in the project lifecycle (Rosson & Carroll 1995, 2001).

3.4.4   Participatory Design

Activity design scenarios and claims can be elaborated and refined in cooperation with stakeholders. Because the design at this point describes only the system's functionality, such interactions will be quite informal. For example, a design team might revisit the individuals or groups observed during the field study. They can present the activity design scenarios and gather reactions and suggestions for change. Some stakeholders may even enjoy using claims analysis or the point-of-view technique to come up with new ideas about their task objects.

The use of participatory development methods was an important starting assumption for the virtual science fair (as documented in our root concept; see Table 2.2). Thus very early in the project, we conducted participatory sessions with stakeholders (community members, students, and teachers). We asked them to imagine system tools that could be active and helpful agents in the task. We gave them index cards labeled "Object name" and "Object responsibilities" as prompts for these ideas. A sample result appears in Figure 3.6, summarizing how a calendar tool could help out in an exhibit.

Of course, inviting users to work with a computational metaphor is just one technique for expanding their views of current activities with computing support. Any form of metaphorical thinking can help users think "outside the box." For example, we could have asked users to discuss and expand the metaphors in Table 3.1. In participatory design work, we have collaborated with users to develop claims analysis of their current practices, and then together generate design ideas that addressed the issues raised by the shared analysis (Chin, Rosson, & Carroll 1997).

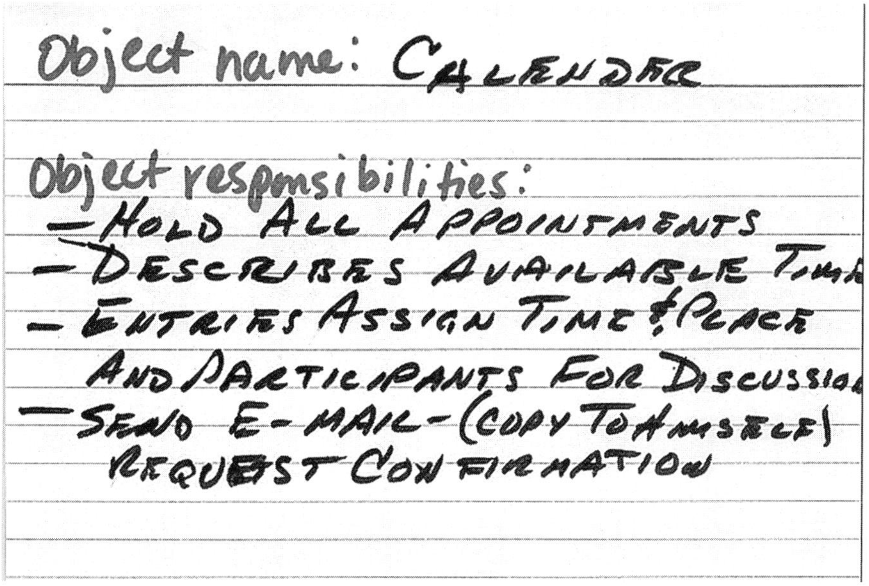
Object name: CALENDAR

Object responsibilities:
—HOLD ALL APPOINTMENTS
—DESCRIBES AVAILABLE TIME
—ENTRIES ASSIGN TIME & PLACE
AND PARTICIPANTS FOR DISCUSSION
—SEND E-MAIL—(COPY TO HIMSELF)
REQUEST CONFIRMATION

Figure 3.6 Card describing possible contributions of a "helpful" calendar in a science fair scenario.

3.4.5 Coherence and Completeness

A general concern for any scenario-based method is the coherence of the design result. This can be a problem if designers respond too much to the needs of the specific situations desccribed in scenarios (Tradeoff 3.2). It is possible to envision a set of scenarios where each one is wonderfully effective, comprehensible, and satisfying, but the set as a whole contains contradictions or inconsistencies.

Coherence will be improved if the same designers work on all scenarios—people naturally combine and synthesize situations, and this reduces the likelihood of incompatible visions. We have also found that it helps to reuse actors and task information across scenarios. Inserting the same design features into different settings and activities helps to ensure that the ideas fit together into a coherent whole. A more systematic analysis of system concepts—for example, a matrix of major task objects and the actions supported for each—may also be developed as a check on coherence concerns.

A related issue is completeness. Clearly, it is impossible to write down all user scenarios. Even writing down a large number quickly becomes cumbersome.

There is also the worry that serious attention to users' current activities will lead to missed opportunities for entirely new functionality (Tradeoff 3.1). One recourse is to think more generally about users and tasks, looking for task needs that were not raised in requirements analysis, but which are now reasonable to consider.

As a simple example, we might propose that people use computers to create, modify, share, store, and access task-relevant information. We might then ask ourselves whether this general view of computer-based activities suggests goals not yet considered in the virtual science fair activities. Might Sally's parents want to add comments to her exhibit? Might Sally share her exhibit with Delia as a model for next year's fair? If a team decides that these are genuine possibilities for the system, new scenarios might be written to explore these goals, even though the original analysis failed to uncover an existing need.

Concerns about coherence and completeness are also addressed by participatory design activities. Presenting activity design scenarios to groups of stakeholders is a good way to evoke a concrete discussion about the pros and cons of the new ideas. This discussion will inevitably bring to light mismatches among features (coherence problems), as well as help to uncover new needs not yet realized (completeness problems).

Summary and Review

This chapter has introduced activity design and discussed some of the fundamental tradeoffs in introducing computer technology into existing situations. The virtual science fair was used to illustrate how to transform problem scenarios into activity design scenarios, using metaphor and technology exploration as a source of new ideas. Central points to remember are:

- Designing activities first helps to simplify and modularize design, and at the same time reinforces the centrality of users' needs and goals in the design of interactive systems.

- The scope of activity design is the entire situation, including the physical and social characteristics of the environment.

- Metaphors help users understand new technology, but often limit people's grasp of new ideas. At the same time, the ways in which metaphors mismatch a situation can suggest new ways of thinking.

- Reducing tedium and the physical steps of a task can increase user satisfaction, but designers must take care to respect and enhance (not remove) the aspects of work that are personally rewarding.

- Envisionment of activity scenarios is tightly interleaved with the analysis of tradeoffs implied by the new design features under consideration.

- Taking a computational perspective on scenario objects may improve communication and cross-fertilization between usability and software engineers.

Exercises

1. Suppose you were designing an online banking system (e.g., personal finance over the Web). Discuss the implications of Tradeoffs 3.1 through 3.3 for this design problem.

2. Analyze the shopping cart used by your favorite online shopping system. In what ways does it mismatch the behavior of real-world shopping carts? Do these mismatches help or hurt the activities of selecting and ordering products?

3. One effect of exhibit templates on exhibit construction is that the first steps are automated—standard components are predefined and serve as a guide for the student importing his or her own content. Use Tradeoff 3.6 to critique this proposal. To what extent does a student exhibitor engage in "knowledge work"? How does the template affect this?

4. Suppose that the virtual science fair was being developed as a standalone Web application (i.e., rather than part of MOOsburg). Create new versions of the metaphor and technology exploration tables that you could use to explore this alternative design space.

5. Write an alternative version of each scenario in Figures 3.4 and 3.5—take the same general task, but bring in actors with different backgrounds and goals, or objects such as the exhibit with different content or organization. Discuss the impact of these variations on your understanding (designer's model) of the activity design.

Project Ideas

Continue to work on your online shopping problem, using the problem scenarios as a basis for a new set of activity designs:

- Discuss metaphors and technology that suggest new ideas about online shopping activities; write down and elaborate the ideas you brainstorm as a group.

- Transform the problem scenarios into activity scenarios. For each new feature, think about the impact it will have on the actors in the scenario. Include this experience as part of the narration.

- Refine the activity scenarios and document your design rationale with claims analysis and participatory design.

Recommended Reading

Collins, D. 1995. *Designing Object-Oriented User Interfaces*. Redwood City, CA: Benjamin Cummings.

Constantine, L. L., & L. A. D. Lockwood. 1999. *Software for Use: A Practical Guide to the Models and Methods of Usage-Centered Design*. Reading, MA: Addison-Wesley.

Nardi, B. A., & V. L. O'Day. 1999. *Information Ecologies: Using Technology with Heart*. Cambridge, MA: MIT Press.

Van Harmelen, M., ed. 2001. *Object Modeling and User Interface Design*. London: Addison-Wesley Longman.

4

Information Design

David Siegel, author of *Creating Killer Web Sites* (1997, 22), discusses a design project he carried out for a leading publisher of children's books. Siegel wanted to encourage exploration of the information model behind this Web site, and at the same time to suggest that reading books can be fun. In the original design, he included a long "entry tunnel" (an animated, sometimes interactive, presentation used to set a theme and tone for a Web site). Visitors needed to solve a problem, switching on the lights in this entry tunnel, in order to arrive at a room with book displays they could browse. The result was that the content of any book was 14 clicks from the site's front door. People enjoyed the site, but rarely reached the book display.

In the revised design, visitors arrive at the site and are whisked through a very short entry tunnel—an animated GIF of the front door opens, and the user enters. Without clicking at all, the user sees a book display, showing the table of contents of a randomly selected book. Selecting a chapter—the user's first click in the site—displays that content.

This chapter introduces the concepts and techniques of **information design**. During information design, the objects and actions possible in a system are represented and arranged in a way that facilitates perception and understanding. Information design includes the design of application screens, World Wide Web pages, menus, dialog boxes, and icons. The content of information design may also include spoken language and other sensory information such as three-dimensional displays or pressure, but discussion of these less common techniques is postponed until Chapter 9.

There are many standard pitfalls in information design. Consider the millions of Java applets producing small animations in Web pages throughout the world. Possibly one in a hundred of these is truly useful. Consider command buttons that appear with brushed-aluminum finish, or spectral reflections. Such visual effects catch our attention, but people quickly tire of them. At best, they do not contribute to communication; worse, they can undermine it—many of these special effects reduce the legibility of button labels. Graphical decoration that does not serve a communicative purpose is a hallmark of poor information design.

Some experts assert that information design is best left to graphical design specialists. Graphic designer David Siegel (1997, 8) concurs with hypermedia pioneer Ted Nelson's comment: "Multimedia must be controlled by dictatorial artists with full say on the final cut." We disagree. Traditional graphical design addresses problems that are far simpler (e.g., posters, maps) than those of interactive information design. Visual design principles are important to interactive system design; this is eloquently demonstrated in Edward Tufte's classic books on visual displays (Tufte 1983, 1990, 1997). But the problems of posters and maps take us only part of the way. Information design succeeds if it makes people's activities easier or more pleasant, and fails otherwise.

4.1 Stages of Action in Human-Computer Interaction

We have organized our discussion of information design (and the next chapter on interaction design) by the stages of action proposed by Donald Norman (1986) as a framework for studying human-computer interaction. Norman was an early pioneer in HCI; he is a cognitive psychologist who has written extensively about the mental planning and interpretation processes associated with human-computer interaction.

Norman describes two gaps between users' understanding of their tasks on the one hand, and a computer system's support of these tasks on the other. The **Gulf of Evaluation** refers to the "cognitive distance" between what is displayed on a computer screen and the user's mental representation of task objects and goals (top half of Figure 4.1). In contrast, the **Gulf of Execution** refers to the distance between a user's current task goals and the procedures and actions that the system provides for pursuing these goals. We will discuss issues related to this second gulf in Chapter 5.

Figure 4.1 shows a hypothetical accountant working on a problem with last month's budget. In order to use the computer for this task, he must perceive what is displayed on the computer screen—a group of pixels is seen as a line or other figure, brightness and color are experienced, and so on. He must then interpret these simple perceptions as objects that play a role in the computer software—for example, an icon, a button, or a highlighted column in a spreadsheet. Finally, he must make sense of what he has seen with respect to his task goals,

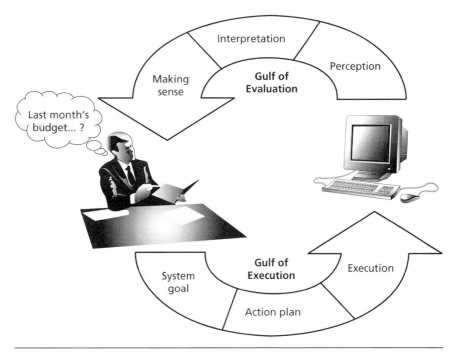

Figure 4.1 The Gulf of Evaluation in human-computer interaction (after Norman 1986). (The Gulf of Execution is discussed in Chapter 5.)

perhaps realizing that he has successfully updated a spreadsheet total, or that he has mistakenly selected the wrong column of numbers.

Norman's framework emphasizes that people's interactions with a computer are not simply a matter of looking at the display and deciding what to do. Many years of research in cognitive psychology have demonstrated that our understanding of information in the world is constructed through an active process of perception and interpretation (Shaw & Bransford 1977). The goal of information design is to support the perception, interpretation, and comprehension of computer-based information. In the rest of this chapter we discuss a number of concerns and tradeoffs in achieving this goal.

4.2 Perceiving Information

At the heart of information design is guiding viewers to see the structure(s) in an information display. The colors, pixels, or tones that a display device can present are the designer's palette. These features are created and arranged to suggest a

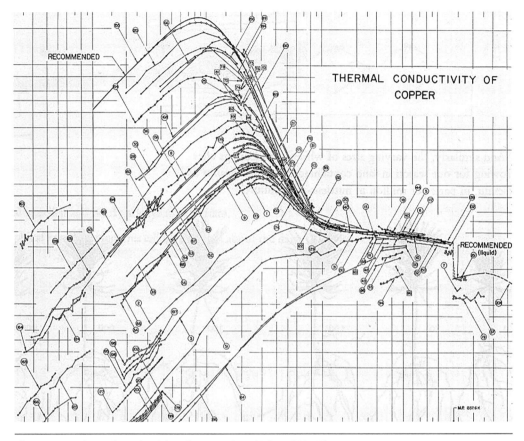

Figure 4.2 Thermal conductivity of copper data (Tufte 1983, 49).

higher-level structure. For example, Figure 4.2 demonstrates how a refined information design can elegantly reveal complexity. The image is taken from one of
Tufte's (1983) books on visual design; it shows over 200 research papers that
reported a relationship between temperature and the thermal conductivity of
copper.

Tufte's example is simple and economical. Each data set (each study's data
points/results) is represented as a connected set of points, forming a curved line
segment. This groups the individual points into higher-level structures, reducing
the number of graphical entities by more than an order of magnitude. Graphing
multiple curves on the same coordinate system creates even more structure, coming from their relative shapes and convergence. Tufte uses this example to show

how it is possible to present a complete data set—in this case thousands of data points—while also conveying emergent summary information.

4.2.1 Gestalt Perception

In the 1920s, a group of German psychologists described the **Gestalt principles** of perceptual organization (Gestalt comes from the German word for "whole"). These principles describe the configural properties of visual information—how individual bits of information are grouped together, what elements will be seen as a coherent figure, and what elements will appear as background. These principles became one of the foundations of perceptual psychology, and have many applications to the design of computer information displays (Table 4.1).

Gestalt principles do not tell you how to represent information entities (e.g., what icon to use); rather they are concerned with the consequences of

Table 4.1 Gestalt principles of perceptual organization that aid perception of user interface visual elements.

Gestalt Principle	User Interface Examples
Proximity: elements near each other tend to be seen as a group	Words on a menu bar, columns in a tabular display, text in a paragraph
Similarity: elements that share visual characteristics (shape, color, etc.) tend to be seen as a group	Toolbar icons (proximity operates here as well), data visualization
Closure: there is a tendency to organize elements into complete, closed figures	Overlapping windows, menus, dialog boxes and other user interface controls
Area: there is a tendency to group elements in a way that creates the smallest possible figure	Icons on a workstation screen, pop-up menu on top of a document display
Symmetry: there is a tendency to see symmetric elements as part of the same figures	Window manipulation controls (e.g., scroll bar, selection handles)
Continuity: there is a tendency to group elements into continuous contours or repeating patterns	A page of paragraphs, a grid of spreadsheet cells, a left-justified list of selections or parameters

low-level perceptual details such as shape, size, position, and color. More than one principle may operate at once, such as in a menu bar or tool palette, where items are positioned next to each other, are of the same size and general shape, and are lined up to form a contour. The use of multiple cues like these is sometimes referred to as **redundant coding** of perceptual cues. Redundancy of this type increases the speed and accuracy of perceptual processing.

The principles of Gestalt perception direct attention to the many relationships among information elements in a complex display. These relationships interact and combine to create groups and subgroups, forming the basic structure of an information display. When designers talk about a display's "gestalt," they are referring to the viewer's immediate perception of figure, background, and form, as in Tufte's example of copper thermal conductivity–temperature relationships.

4.2.2   Organization in User Interface Displays

User interface displays contain many levels of perceptual structure. The basic display elements—the pixels, contours, and characters—are grouped into higher-order structures such as paragraphs, icons, file lists, check boxes, and menu bars. These in turn are grouped into even higher-order structures. For example, Figure 4.3 shows a dialog box used to set page borders in Microsoft Word. This structure (which appears on top of an open document) includes radio buttons for choosing the kind of border; a scrollable list of line styles; pull-down menus for color, width, decoration, and scope; and a special area for previewing the effects of new settings.

Tufte's goal for graphical data display—to make each data point and the overall interpretation immediately accessible—cannot be applied directly to user interface design. In Figure 4.2, it is enough to convey a cloud of points, because the details of any particular point are not interesting. In contrast, most elements of a user interface display convey functional information about the system. In a dialog box, each control makes a specific task-related contribution. The radio buttons for settings are interpreted and operated differently than the pull-down menu for style.

Nevertheless, user interface design should be guided by the same Gestalt principles that are operating in the graph analyzed by Tufte. Viewers should perceive an immediate sense of organization, but at the same time see the individual control elements. Unfortunately, this leads to an inescapable tradeoff: Presenting information about all current options helps people understand what is possible,

Figure 4.3 Dialog box used to set and preview page borders in Microsoft Word.

and supports flexible interaction. But every piece of information or control that is presented increases the complexity of the visual display (Tradeoff 4.1). The designer must make hard decisions about what is essential. There is just too much information to present.

TRADEOFF 4.1

Displaying all active task entities enhances understanding and feelings of control, BUT each display element adds to the complexity of the user interface design.

One way to reduce complexity is to decompose and link related information. For example, a control in one dialog box may open a secondary dialog. The dialog box in Table 4.3 is one of three "tabbed" dialog boxes accessed through the `Borders and Shading…` item on the `Format` menu. These three dialog boxes organize and link a huge amount of information: two groups of 5 radio buttons, one of 32 radio buttons, two scrolling menus, 10 pull-down menus, five preview widgets, 15 commands, two groups of four input fields with scrollable preset values, and two groups of four check boxes; a grand total of 90 elements. And this is for a rather small portion of word processing functionality!

Designers must limit what is displayed to what is essential, and structure what is displayed such that the most essential information is most easily perceived. For example, `Borders and Shading…` opens the border-setting dialog box by default, suggesting that these settings are more likely to be changed than `Shading` or `Page Borders`. The `Options…` button opens a subdialog box for border offsets; again this implies that border offsets are not changed as often as style, color, or width.

The impact of Gestalt principles can be seen in the shape, contrast, and layout of many information displays. For example, the dialog box in Figure 4.3 includes command buttons that are rounded rectangles with single line labels. Similarity and proximity combine to help viewers see these display objects as a group.

Just as the use of similar visual characteristics promotes the grouping of items, the use of contrasting features causes elements to fall into different groups. The radio buttons in the left column of Figure 4.3 are of a different shape and size than the scrollable list or the pull-down menus in the center of the dialog box. The pull-down menus have a similar shape to the command buttons, but are distinguished by the two arrowheads on the right.

The use of multiple contrasting cues to create structure in a display leads to another fundamental design tradeoff (Tradeoff 4.2). Perceptual distinctions such as size, shape, and color can be used to organize complex displays. But each visual cue adds complexity and clutter to a display. As more distinctions are built into a display, any one feature will become less noticeable and valuable in guiding perception.

TRADEOFF 4.2

Perceptual distinctions highlight and group user interface elements, BUT the more distinctions a display uses, the less noticeable and useful any individual cue will be.

A common example comes in the use of color as a perceptual cue. Color can be an effective way to create contrasts and promote grouping. But if the design introduces too many color values (e.g., 12 different shades), this visual characteristic would become confusing. People cannot distinguish and group many color values at once. In such a case color would become a nondistinct, decorative attribute that might actually interfere with other visual distinctions. Color distinctions are effective when they are few in number and consist of relatively muted shades.

User interface structures can also be reinforced with the careful use of **white space**, the parts of the display that contain no graphical elements. For example, the space between columns in a text display causes them to align vertically and form a subgroup structure. In Figure 4.3, the white space between the button at the lower left and the two buttons at the lower right segregates them. The similarity of shape groups them together relative to other display elements, but the use of white space suggests that there is also a task-relevant subgrouping (opening a toolbar versus canceling or accepting the changes).

Mullet and Sano (1995, 75) offer a simple **squint test** to check user interface design groupings. They suggest that designers examine their work with one eye closed and the other squinted. If the display organization is not apparent in these circumstances, it is unlikely to be immediately perceived by users.

A more direct way to create perceptual groupings is to add explicit graphical separators or bounding boxes. For instance, the three columns in Figure 4.3 are separated by faint lines, and the entire subdialog has a bounding box that separates it from the general-purpose command buttons.

Borders and bounding boxes are a popular structural cue; after all, a set of nested lines or boxes represents an intended decomposition very directly. However, as with other visual cues, these borders add clutter to the design, decreasing the effectiveness of other visual cues. In Figure 4.3, the separator lines are relatively subtle and restrained, taking up minimal space. Unfortunately, it is not uncommon to find bold (e.g., four-pixel) lines, or bounding boxes that are nested three deep. In such designs, the separators can become the most noticeable element in the design (see Johnson 2000, 149–58).

The most common design errors with respect to perceptual organization come from trying to do too much. Packing in too much information makes the structure of a display difficult to perceive. Including too many distinctions in shape, font, color, and so forth makes a display cluttered. Heavy-handed remedies, such as bold separators, nested bounding boxes, and bright colors, only make matters worse. The best advice, of course, is to understand people's tasks well enough to make the hard choices about what to present. Then, use restraint: Design a small number of display elements that contrast clearly and meaningfully; that are simple and subtle in color and shape; and that are grouped chiefly by proximity, symmetry, similarity, and continuity.

Grids for Information Design

To some extent, designing a well-organized and balanced information display is a matter of art. Indeed it is, in the sense that a visually balanced design is more pleasant to look at and use. It is also a matter of human performance: A balanced design is easier to decompose, understand, and use. Moreover, in designing a series of user interface displays, it is important to achieve visual balance in a similar manner throughout the related screens. Many designers—even experts—would like a procedural strategy to help ensure that they achieve balance and that they do so in a consistent manner throughout the user interface design.

A standard recommendation is **grid-based design**. It is surprisingly simple. The most basic grid consists of six vertical columns of equal width, exactly spanning the width of the display area (usually leaving some border on both right and left). This provides a layout structure with considerable flexibility, but ensures that all elements will align, and makes it very easy to verify that the display is symmetrically balanced across its central vertical axis (Mullet & Sano 1995).

The figure below shows a grid-based design developed by Aaron Marcus and Associates for Kaiser Permanente. The smallest unit of the grid defines the vertical height of the font and the input fields. Larger display elements are constructed as multiples of this smallest unit, and related display elements (e.g., the lower row of buttons) are sized and positioned similarly. The entire set of elements is symmetrical around the center axis. Even the Kaiser logo has been sized to fit into the grid layout scheme. Subsequent screens in this series use very different visual elements, but follow the same grid size and layout conventions. The result is that when viewers move from screen to screen, the immediate perception is of a regular and predictable information structure.

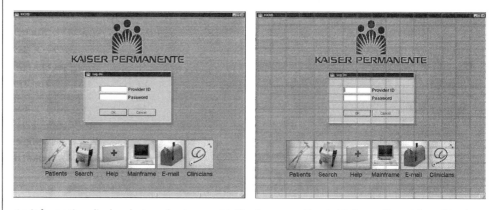

An information display designed using a grid. The image on the right shows the grid used to size and position the elements in a regular and pleasing fashion.

4.3 Interpreting Information

Perceiving an information display as a set of objects and groups enables the **interpretation** process. During interpretation, the contents of the rectangle in the center of the figure in the previous sidebar are recognized as input fields used for logging into the system. Perceptual processing identifies the major structures in the display—rectangles of various sizes, text strings, and so on. But in order to act on this information, the user must interpret what these display elements mean in the context of this particular software system.

Returning to the dialog box in Figure 4.3, we can see that the Microsoft Word designers use a **visual language** to aid interpretation. The visual language consists of the shapes, terms, and groupings that are used in a regular and consistent fashion to express system features. When experienced users see the rounded rectangle labeled "OK," they interpret it as a command that will apply the selected border settings. At the same time, they do not interpret the rounded rectangle labeled "Auto" as a command; in this vocabulary, the label on a pull-down menu is recognized as a command parameter.

In a good visual design, the vocabulary of shapes, terms, and layout techniques stands on its own. The need to reinforce the meaning of an element with explicit structures (e.g., bounding boxes) or explanatory text indicates a gap or ambiguity in the design vocabulary and adds clutter. Thus, a high-level goal of information design is to build a visual language in which each distinction communicates something significant to users. Unsystematic or unmotivated variation is distracting.

To support the interpretation process, designers need to anticipate and support users' reactions to user interface elements. In this section we focus on three strategies for doing this: choosing images, symbols, or words that are already familiar to users; refining a set of design elements through successive abstraction; and selecting images or words that suggest task actions implicitly.

4.3.1 Familiarity

People learning and using computers already possess a good deal of relevant knowledge. For example, we all know one or more natural languages. This means that labeling a user interface button as `Find` or `Search` can take advantage of the meanings people already know for these words. The terms do not convey precisely what the button will do, but they do suggest the function in a generic way that people can recognize and remember, and that is good enough for most circumstances.

GUI Bloopers

Jeff Johnson's book *GUI Bloopers* (Johnson 2000) is a rich source of user interface problems, observations, and advice that he has collected over many years as a design consultant. He organizes the chapters into numbered "bloopers" that capture the most common mistakes he has observed in the design of screens, terminology, dialog boxes, and so on. For example, Chapter 4 of his book discusses 10 textual bloopers summarized below (Johnson, 2000, 187–245).

Johnson's book of user interface do's and don'ts provides many examples of how the quality of a user interface can be destroyed by poorly conceived details. Fortunately, Johnson also offers many strategies for avoiding these common mistakes. Each blooper is followed by one or more design rules; these can be applied as blooper-avoidance guidelines. For example, Johnson suggests that we can guard against the "Unclear terminology" blooper by avoiding similar terms, avoiding concepts that differ in subtle ways, avoiding ambiguous terms, and testing the terminology on prospective users.

Textual Blooper	**Variations and Examples**
Inconsistent terminology	Different terms for the same concept (`results` and `output`); same term for different concepts (`view`)
Unclear terminology	Concepts too similar (`membership` vs. `subscription`); ambiguous terms (`file`, `load`, `object`)
Speaking Geek	Using programmer jargon (`ROM`, `macro`, `download`); turning common words into programmer jargon (`resources`, `dialog`); turning verbs into nouns (`compile`, `compare`); exposing terms from the code (`string`, "`error 347`"); assigning arbitrary meanings to short, nondesccriptive terms (`cat`, `awk`)

In contrast, consider a command button labeled `grep` (this is a search command in the UNIX operating system). This particular command returns all lines of a set of files that match a specified regular expression; `grep` is an acronym for "global regular expression print." But knowing the rationale for the name does not help much; people tend to learn names like `grep` by brute-force association (Norman 1981b).

TRADEOFF 4.3

 A familiar vocabulary eases interpretation, BUT familiar terms are usually less distinctive and precise, and what is familiar for one person may not be familiar for another.

GUI Bloopers *(continued)*	
Careless writing	Inconsistent writing style (mixing nouns and verbs); poor grammar, spelling, and punctuation
Clueless error messages	Message determined by low-level code (`Cannot delete cached page`); reason for error not passed up to higher-level code (`Error parsing datafile. Data not parsed.`); generic message components (`Name contains invalid characters`)
Misuse (or nonuse) of "..."	Omitting "..."; overusing"..."
Inconsistent use of colons on setting labels	Blank space alone versus colon followed by blank space
Tooltips that say the same thing as label	Button labeled `Print` also provides tooltip that says `Print`
Same title on different windows	Window title bars don't identify specific windows; programmer copied window code but forgot to change title; programmer didn't know title was in use elsewhere; programmer thought title fit both
Window title doesn't match invoking command	Selection of a command (`New Employee`) results in window with nonmatching title (`Add Record`)

Categories and examples of common mistakes in the design of user interface terminology and messages.

One might conclude from this that designers should use familiar terms and symbols as much as possible, but making design decisions about familiarity is not always simple. Familiar terms often have multiple meanings. For example, "view" and "update" can be either nouns or verbs. Even if a system vocabulary uses "view" only as a noun, there are many possible interpretations—a data presentation, a partial view of a virtual space, one of several problem analyses, and so on. "Enter" is a common user interface term, but depending on the context it may mean either "submit these data" or "come into this space." (Try interpreting this message: "Select and enter data file." See "GUI Bloopers" sidebar.)

Another problem in choosing familiar terms is a variant of the concern discussed earlier in designing for satisfaction—what is familiar to one user may not be familiar to another. Not all users are native speakers of English. A user interface developed in one country or culture cannot simply be translated to achieve the same level of familiarity in another. One outcome of requirements analysis should be an understanding of the user populations who will use the system, so that the information designers can focus on the languages and symbols most likely to be familiar.

A common belief among designers is that graphical elements will produce a more universal interpretation because we all live in the same physical (visual) world. This is true to some extent. Red traffic lights mean stop all over the world. A schematic human figure without a skirt means a man, and with a skirt means a woman. In user interface displays, a question mark means a help command; an icon of a folder means a container for data files. Many of these elements are low level and have become so familiar that it is easy to forget that they are part of a nearly universal user interface language.

However, symbols and icons do not always address the concern of "familiar to whom?" A traditional rural American mailbox (a cylinder with a hinged door, mounted on a pole) is often used to represent email services. But few Americans have ever used such a mailbox, and many have never even seen one. Their familiarity with this design comes from books or pictures. In other countries mailboxes have an entirely different look; mailboxes—and mailbox icons—are often square rather than cylindrical. In fact, the mailbox icon common in Italy is similar to the trashcan icon in American user interfaces. An American mailbox icon would be unfamiliar for Italian users; an Italian mailbox icon could actually mislead American users.

4.3.2 Realism and Refinement

Abstract imagery is often effective in visual design. Road signs are a good example. The figure in a "pedestrian crossing" sign does not mean that a human oriented and sized in exactly this way is just ahead (Figure 4.4). Drivers know that the sign is simply indicating there is a right-of-way for pedestrians coming up. People perceive and classify the simple shapes in road signs very rapidly, even when the shapes are only briefly glimpsed. These images are good examples of

Figure 4.4 Road signs are highly refined visual images, because they include only the most critical visual features.

visual refinement, because they include only the most critical visual features (Mullet & Sano 1995).

At the same time, psychologists have demonstrated remarkable capabilities for people to recognize images that are realistic. In a classic experiment, people were shown thousands of photographs just once; several weeks later they were asked to recognize these photographs from a mix of thousands of similar images they had never seen. Recognition accuracy was above 95% (Shepard 1967). How can user interface designers decide when to use realistic images and when to develop more refined shapes?

It is important to consider not just the accuracy with which a user can recognize an item, but also the process of recognition. A photograph or realistic drawing is usually more complex than an abstract symbol (Tradeoff 4.4). This means that even though people may recognize what a realistic item portrays, the perception and interpretation process may take longer. Learning to recognize the meaning of a simpler and more abstract image will lead to better performance in the long term. Realistic images also tend to suggest instances of a concept (e.g., the printer down the hall) rather than the abstract concept often intended (e.g., printing).

TRADEOFF 4.4

People's recognition memory for realistic images is accurate and long-lasting, BUT realistic images are often complex, and suggest instances rather than concepts.

Mullet and Sano (1995) emphasize that the best level of abstraction for an image depends on the user's task and on the display technology available. However, they suggest that in most cases, developing relatively refined images will improve a visual design. They advise removing all but the most distinctive and characteristic features. For instance, an effective icon for a calculator might include only the squares for the number keys, with larger rectangles at the lower right and top to show the calculate key and the display. Numbers and labels on the keys could be eliminated, producing a simpler and more immediate interpretation of the image as a calculator.

The interpretation of abstract images is enhanced when an entire set or family of icons is refined together. A good example is the four text alignment controls on the Formatting Toolbar of Microsoft Word (Figure 4.5). These buttons show an abstract representation of the task goal—lines aligned left, centered, aligned right, or justified—but as a group are a very effective indicator of text alignment functionality.

Figure 4.5 The text alignment controls from the Microsoft Word Formatting toolbar.

4.3.3   Recognizing Affordances

One result of interpreting a user interface element is knowing what you can do
with it. This is sometimes called recognizing the element's affordances. An **affordance** is an aspect of an object that makes it obvious how the object is to be
used. In user interface displays, the features that create affordances are usually
visual, but user interface designers have explored auditory and tactile features as
well (Gaver 1986, 1989; Gaver, Smith, & O'Shea 1991).

Recognizing an affordance is an immediate consequence of perception. A
button affords pushing; a check box affords checking; an input field affords
entering text. The affordances of current display elements serve as input to the
planning process in which users decide what to do next (Chapter 5). For example, the "type here" affordance of a blinking cursor may be used as input to a
plan for how to insert a word in a text field.

A common-sense way to think about affordances is that they are features of
a display element that suggest things to do. The title bar at the top of a window
looks like a bar that you can grab and drag around, a notebook tab looks like a
section separator that can be pressed, and the lever on a gauge invites you to drag
it to a new position.

In interactive systems, affordances are sometimes tightly coupled with
actions. For example, the hyperlinks in a Web page are typically underlined and
colored blue, but as the pointer passes over a link, the pointer may also change
shape (e.g., into a hand). The new pointer image emphasizes that this text affords
highlighting. In this case, the user interface offers both persistent display information (the blue underline) and dynamic, use-sensitive information to communicate the affordance of a link. Similarly, the "handles" provided for moving or
sizing windows may appear only when the pointer is in position.

Affordances must be visible to aid interpretation (Tradeoff 4.5). This means
more competition for screen space and more complexity. Scroll bars, guides and
rulers, handles, or other format controls are visible and ready for interpretation
during editing tasks. Fortunately, people are practiced at focusing or narrowing
their attention; a person focused on a task is usually able to ignore irrelevant

affordances. But a visual element that is part of the area in focus may be distracting, particularly if it is visually distinctive.

TRADEOFF 4.5

Dynamic hiding of controls that are not in use conserves space and simplifies the
display, BUT also conceals the controls' affordances from the user.

One solution is to make the affordances dynamic. For example, some windowing systems show scrollbars only when the pointer moves to the side of the
relevant window. In graphic editors, the handles for resizing objects appear only
when an object is selected. This leads to a less cluttered display, but means that
users must know that the controls are available and must learn the procedures for
activating them.

4.4 Making Sense of Information

The last step in crossing the Gulf of Evaluation is making sense of the information that has been perceived and interpreted. Users do this by relating the information to what they currently understand about their task, and evaluating
whether and how it addresses their active goals and interests. They try to determine whether what they have seen (or heard, or felt) is connected somehow to
objects or events in the world. If they cannot make sense of the information,
they may try out new interpretations. They may also be willing to put things "on
hold" for a bit, gathering more information to better grasp the big picture. But a
continued failure to make sense of system information leads to confusion, an
inability to plan further action, and frustration.

Minard's (time-series visualization of Napoleon's Russian campaign is a classic example of a visual design that aids comprehension (Figure 4.6). The width of
the upper light-gray band shows the changing size of Napoleon's army as it
moved from the Polish frontier to Moscow. The diagram indicates that the army
had more than 400,000 men as they crossed the Niemen River in June, but only
100,000 in Moscow a few months later. The lower dark band shows the army's
retreat, annotated with links to the increasingly frigid temperatures graphed at
the bottom. The combined visual representations are an extremely rich but com-
pact description of this disastrous military campaign.

Minard's tableau produces a strong separation between the light and
dark bands. To make sense of it, viewers must integrate the display with their
knowledge of maps in general, with maps of Eastern Europe in particular (e.g.,

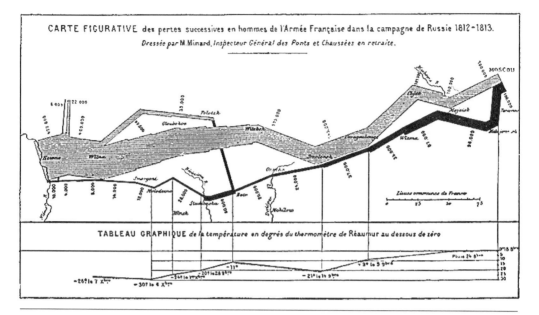

Figure 4.6   Minard's visualization of Napoleon's Russian campaign.

recognizing the rivers as landmarks), and with general knowledge of the Russian campaign (e.g., that many men were lost). The bands are then easily understood as travel paths plotted on the map, with the size of the paths indicating the size of the marching army.

As this example suggests, making sense of information requires information integration. Viewers connect new information with whatever knowledge they have available, ranging from long-term personal knowledge or domain expertise, to events or opportunities that happened a split second ago. Often a user must integrate several different display states. For example, a user opening a new document in Microsoft Word first sees a `File` menu drop down. Then the menu choice `Open` is highlighted, the `File` menu disappears, and a dialog box with a scrollable list and the prompt `Select a document:` appears. By integrating this sequence of visual display, the user understands that the system is now ready for identification of the needed document.

The process of making sense relies on people's abilities to detect patterns and relationships across different information presentations and to relate these patterns to knowledge of the world and of the task underway. In this section we discuss the ways in which consistency, visual metaphors, information models, and dynamic displays can facilitate users' ability to make sense of user interface displays.

4.4.1 Consistency

One thing that helps people make sense of information displays is consistency. If similar elements are presented in similar ways across different displays, users are better able to integrate across screens and make the necessary connections. A **visual design program** is a set of visual design features that are used to create consistent displays. These features may be of many sorts—some may be decorative or artistic, such as a logo or a subtle color scheme. More obvious features are the elements defining the visual vocabulary, the shapes and sizes of controls, font types and sizes, and the character of the icons used. Information layout is also part of the design program—for instance, always positioning the OK button at the lower right of a dialog box.

Consistency in design lets people create and benefit from expectations. When things look and act as expected, it is easier to make sense of what is happening. But as is true for any general advice, focusing on consistency will not lead to the best overall design (Tradeoff 4.6). There are often other task-specific factors that outweigh the benefits of consistency (Grudin 1989). An oft-cited example is the positioning of standard command buttons (e.g., Cancel, OK) in dialog boxes. These usually appear in the bottom right corner of a dialog box. Users expect them to be there, and know what to do with them when they see them. But for some dialog boxes, there may be additional buttons in the grouping, or other aspects of the visual design may be compromised by insisting on a bottom row of buttons.

TRADEOFF 4.6

 Consistent use of shapes, sizes, colors, and position sets up expectations that help users make sense of information, BUT in some cases consistency may actually impair user performance or satisfaction.

Terminology should also be used consistently. "Move backward," "Backward," and "Reverse" are all possible terms for a command that moves an object backward. But in the context of a second "Move forward" command, only one is consistent; only one expresses a coherent design program. A user who knows the command syntax <action> <specifier> as well as the specific command "Move forward" can infer the command "Move backward," along with several other similar commands. The ability to make inferences of this sort shows **transfer of learning**: What is learned once can be transferred to a new case. Command language consistency has significant effects on the ease of learning and using sets of command (Carroll 1985).

Consistent use of language and visual characteristics within an application is called **internal consistency**. Designers also must worry about **external consistency**, which refers to the use of design programs across different systems or applications. The similar user interface styles found in Macintosh or PC-Windows applications are examples of external consistency. Like internal consistency, this commonality supports transfer of learning, in this case from one application to another.

4.4.2   Visual Metaphors

The scope of consistency can be extended one step further: An information display can be consistent with objects and actions in the real world. When a visual element looks like an object in the real world, people will often use the visual metaphor implied by the similarity as an aid in making sense of the information.

In Chapter 3 we discussed how conceptual metaphors (a store or a library) can be useful in understanding how new concepts and services work. A concrete technique for evoking metaphoric thinking is with visual or auditory displays. For example, Minard's representation of Napoleon's Russian campaign (Figure 4.6) evokes the metaphor of a European map. The diagram is not literally a map; an authentic map would have provided a poorer design base for his overall purposes, and no real map incorporates graphical elements such as the representation of Napoleon's army. But the viewer's familiarity with maps and with Eastern European geography are critical in making this an effective information design.

Visual metaphors are pervasive in user interface design. The "messy desktop" is often cited as an example; it captures the notion that tools and task objects can be scattered, grouped, and piled on a surface, and are available for interaction by pointing, grabbing, and dragging. Spreadsheet programs exploit a "ledger" metaphor. Word processing applications present documents as sheets of "electronic paper." Electronic mail builds from metaphors of mailboxes, address lists, signatures, and other elements of postal services. Information systems often use the metaphor of "digital libraries." Immersive virtual environments use the entire physical world as a metaphor.

The most useful design metaphors are a balance of consistency and familiarity with inconsistency and innovation. Metaphors provide overall organizing concepts, but should not be taken too literally (Tradeoff 4.7). The intent of technology is to enhance the physical world, so by definition consistency with the world must break down at some point. The messy-desktop metaphor must not be taken too literally or the design will replicate the familiar problems of real desks and offices: incoherent piles of documents, time wasted searching for tools and data, valuable documents accidentally thrown away, and so forth. Instead, most desktop systems have tools that address these problems; some simply stretch the metaphor (e.g., `Arrange`, `Clean Up`, `Find`), and others are plainly inconsistent (e.g., `Alias`, `View-as-list`).

TRADEOFF 4.7

Visual metaphors leverage real-world knowledge of objects, BUT metaphors that are very literal may introduce information that is irrelevant or misleading to a task.

Figure 4.7 shows a good metaphor that was applied without enough thought. The desktop calculator is clearly a useful appliance, and typically it is presented with a strong physical metaphor. Extending the calculator to have scientific functions is ambitious, with strong implications for complexity. The example has a one-line output display, widely spaced "buttons," and shifted functions. These constraints are necessary for physical calculators, but can be addressed in virtual appliances in various ways: a toggle could be used to change

Figure 4.7 Overly literal user of a metaphor (from Mullet & Sano 1995).

labels and functions on keys, and the keys could be positioned more closely, reducing unnecessary pointer travel and allowing space for more keys. A multi-line (scrollable) output display could be provided. The space constraints for the online calculator are just not that compelling; the designers were captured by their visual metaphor (Mullet and Sano 1995, 33).

4.4.3   Information Models

A great challenge in contemporary user interface design is the richness of the information presented to users. As computing power increases and becomes more accessible, interactive systems incorporate ever more data and functions. People navigate vast spaces of information, analyzing and interacting with it at varying levels of detail. It is common to hear of people who "got lost" in these spaces—and not only new users. An **information model** is a set of concepts, relationships, and representations that are developed to help users make sense of large data sets and complex functionality.

The most common information model is the **hierarchy**, where every node (except the root) has a unique parent node, but any parent node may have multiple child nodes. Hierarchies are simple and efficient. They map well to information that can be organized by levels of abstraction: Intermediate nodes are used to represent categories at increasing levels of detail. A hierarchy decomposes and organizes navigation through a complex space (with an average of n branches at each nonterminal node, the space is reduced by a factor of n at each step).

Not surprisingly, hierarchies are a pervasive information model. Conventional menu interfaces are hierarchies. The Dewey decimal system and other standard library classification systems are hierarchies. Many Web sites rely on large information hierarchies; it is relatively easy to convert a hierarchy into a **site map** that provides an overview of a complex set of pages. Clearly, though, the success of a hierarchy depends on how well it decomposes the information space it presents (Tradeoff 4.8).

TRADEOFF 4.8

Hierarchy is an intuitive and powerful structuring device, BUT heavily nested hierarchies with artificial relationships are confusing and difficult to navigate.

A hierarchy that uses unfamiliar concepts as intermediate nodes will confuse users rather than help them in making sense of the information space. Imagine an online shopping system that uses item part numbers as a basis for a browsing hierarchy. The part numbers may mean something to the employees of the company but are likely to be seen as arbitrary, unhelpful, and confusing to users. Another common problem is when a lower-level concept is grouped under an inappropriate parent node.

A related concern is the tradeoff between **breadth** and **depth** in a hierarchy. Offering many choices at each level (high breadth) reduces the number of levels that the user must navigate and integrate. However, perceiving, interpreting, and making sense of many choices at each level (high depth) is difficult. This issue has been studied extensively for menu hierarchies. In most cases, user interface designers have found that broad and shallow menu systems lead to better performance and greater user satisfaction than ones that are narrow and deep (Shneiderman 1998, 249).

A strict use of hierarchical decomposition can lead to inflexible designs. Complex information spaces are sometimes more appropriately modeled by general networks. For example, a Web page is often referenced by more than one other Web page; users may want to access a generic service such as email from multiple points in a menu system. Relations among items may be bidirectional, as when two Web pages refer to each other. Particularly with the advent of the World Wide Web, these more general network models are becoming more common (see "Web Design" sidebar on pages 136–137).

When an information model is complex, it is often desirable to visualize the underlying data model in a single display (Andrews 1995; Hendley, et al. 1995). **Information visualization** is a user interface technique in which visual features are used to code different attributes of the data. For example, a set of interconnected Web pages can be visualized as a network of nodes and arcs, where the arcs are used to show connections to other units.

Many of these projects combine related sets of information in two- or three-dimensional spatial displays—for example, long-distance telephone traffic that is shown overlaying a map of the calling area. Color often plays a key role in information visualization, as shown in Figure 4.8, where color is used to show cancer statistics as a function of geographic area. As in Minard's visualization of Napoleon's campaign, the map provides an organizing scheme for the information model, while taking advantage of viewers' familiarity with spatial representations of this sort.

4.4.4   Dynamic Displays

A major advantage that user interface displays have over traditional displays such as maps is the possibility for dynamic redisplay or animation. Computer-based

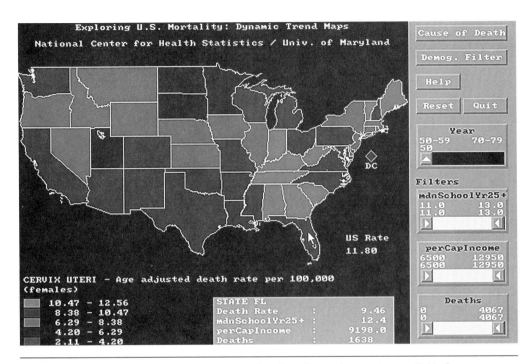

Figure 4.8 Visualizing U.S. cancer statistics as a function of state (screen shot available from *ftp://ftp.cs.umd.edu/pub/hcil/Screen-dumps/DQcancerstats/cervix.gif*).

displays can be dynamically restructured, changed in size, filtered, and animated. People are good at making sense of motion and depth variations, so including dynamic features such as these can provide powerful cues to the overall structure of an information model.

A popular example of a dynamic display is the **fish-eye view** (Furnas 1986). This technique combines a large overview of an information model with local expansion of the portion of the model currently in focus. In order to fit more information into the overview, the more peripheral information may be "squeezed" or distorted in some way, just as one might see when looking through an optical fish-eye lens.

The fish-eye technique has been generalized and explored in a number of **focus+context** visualizations by Stuart Card and colleagues at Xerox PARC (Card, Robertson, & Mackinlay 1991). In the simplest examples, the overview of the information model might be in outline form, perhaps a program listing. Each module might then be selectable for in-line expansion. But the concept can also be applied to more complex situations, such as a viewer that provides a three-

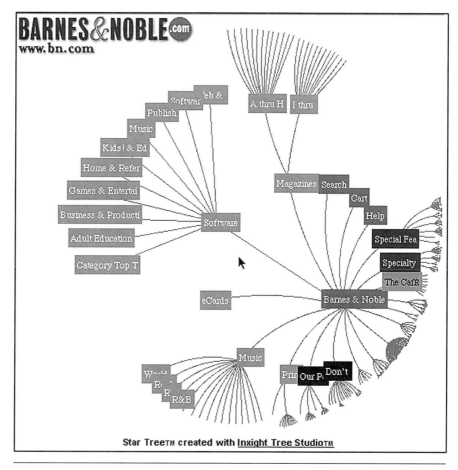

Figure 4.9 A hyperbolic browser (Inxight Tree Studio) used to visualize Web pages from Barnes & Noble (*http://www.inxight.com*).

dimensional view of a hierarchical file structure (Robertson, Card, & Mackinlay 1991).

Figure 4.9 shows a hierarchy visualization that uses a hyperbolic transformation to condense the information in the periphery (Lamping, Rao, & Pirolli 1995). The visualization updates when users click on a node, using a smooth animation to shift the focus to the new node. Because of the degree of distortion in the periphery (e.g., see the subtrees at the lower right), this particular visualization allows a very large amount of data to be presented at once.

Displaying an overview of large information structures provides an orienting context, but competes for screen space. Visualizations of large data sets may also be so complex that the underlying structure is hard to detect (Tradeoff 4.9). An alternative is to reduce the amount of information displayed at any one time, and let the user request more information as needed. In the Pad++ system, users zoom in and out of a hierarchical structure; at any given point, the context includes only what is in the neighborhood at the current level. Users "pull back" to get a broader view (Bederson & Hollan 1994).

TRADEOFF 4.9

 Visualization of complex data sets helps to grasp the underlying structure of the information, BUT for large data sets the visualization may be too large and complex to be useful.

This technique is interesting because it provides no persistent overview; the overall structure is understood by integrating across screens. The argument is that if users can move rapidly and continuously among views with more or less detail, then perhaps there is less need for a persistent high-level view. Figure 4.10 shows how the MOOsburg map uses this technique; users orient to major roads, and then zoom in to find specific streets or buildings.

Another approach to balancing information needs with screen space is **semantic filtering**. In this technique, the semantic attributes of each data point determine its visual representation—whether it is visible, what its coordinates are, its shape and color, and so on. Williamson and Shneiderman (1992) demon-

Figure 4.10   Three views of the map used to access locations in MOOsburg. On the left, the map is zoomed out to the coarsest level of detail. In the middle, an intermediate view is provided, and on the right the user has zoomed in close enough to see building outlines. This tool leverages community residents' familiarity with the streets and buildings in the town. When the mouse is moved to a street or defined site (a dot), its name will appear in a status area.

strate this with HomeFinder, a map-based example. HomeFinder displays a schematic map of Washington, D.C., with a dot representing every home currently for sale. Sliders for price range, number of bedrooms, cost, and distance, and check boxes for features such as garage and fireplace are set as a filter on the query. The display is updated in real time; as the user moves a slider, houses appear or disappear from the map, conveying very precisely how each parameter affects the information in the display.

Multiple coordinated views of an information structure can also help in grasping the underlying model. For example, the View Matcher—a tool for learning to program in Smalltalk (Carroll, Singer, et al. 1990)—presents five complementary views of an example application (Figure 4.11). The application view itself is linked to the Smalltalk source code, the execution stack, an object

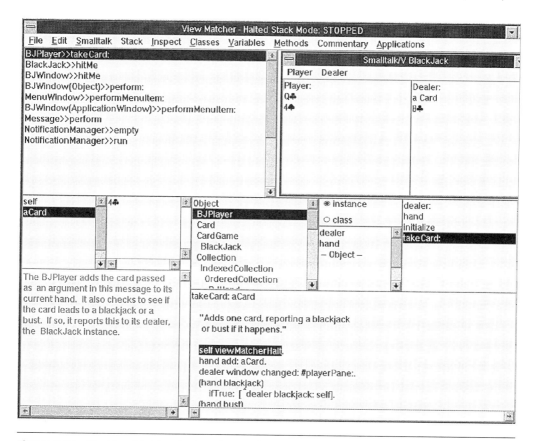

Figure 4.11 The View Matcher for learning Smalltalk coordinates five different views of an example application: the application view (upper right), the code view (lower right), the explanation view (lower left), the object inspector view (middle left), and the message stack view (upper left).

Web Design

During the past decade, the World Wide Web has become a major focus for user interface design. The growth of the Web and of its importance to information access, communication, and electronic commerce has been awesome. There are two aspects to Web design: designing individual page layouts, and designing the linking structures that connect information within and between pages.

Designing Web pages was initially a step backward in user interface technology. Early versions of HTML had no tag for centering and did not support tables. User interaction with Web page forms processed by CGI scripts involved round-trip server communication reminiscent of mainframe applications of the 1970s. Early Web pages were often just lists of directories and file names—pretty similar to the FTP and gopher directories they replaced. Indeed, there were strong practical incentives *not* to employ images in page layouts, because they increased download times and con-

tributed to the already-halting rhythm of early Web-based interactions.

The use of links in Web pages quickly evolved from somewhat boring mimicry of hierarchical file structures to utter chaos, with everything linked to everything else. Many de facto standards emerged, such as presenting home or site-map links throughout a given Web site, and explicitly indicating layering and chunking of Web pages within a site.

As larger sets of information became available, designers began to focus on the challenges of structuring and presenting them in usable ways. There are now a multitude of Web stylebooks written by consultants and other practitioners (Horton 1994; Nielsen 1999). Most of these books rely on personal opinion rather than user studies, but several general issues overlap with the information design concerns of this chapter.

Page size: The richness and uneven quality of Web information has made users

inspector, and software documentation. As a programmer interacts with the application, each of the five views is updated. In Figure 4.11, the Blackjack game provides an overview, while the other four views provide detailed information about what is happening in the overview. This general technique is common on the Web, with one frame presenting an overview or index, and details presented in other frames (see "Web Design" sidebar).

Techniques for dynamic display are emerging very rapidly, but it is important to keep in mind that the ultimate success of any information visualization will depend on its ability to support sense-making with respect to task goals. As Plaisant et al. (1996) emphasize, different techniques are appropriate for different tasks. Open-ended exploration has very different needs than data monitoring or diagnostic activities. The computing resources, screen space, and perceptual processing entailed by sophisticated graphical techniques can be quite large, and it is important to weigh these against users' actual information needs. This general

---

Web Design *(continued)*

---

impatient. Only a small proportion are willing to scroll down to view nonpresented parts of a Web page. The advice is to design a Web site with pages that fit in a single screen. From this perspective, the need to include within-page links is a sign of poor design.

Writing style: People do not want to read a Web page; they want to quickly scan so that they can decide where to go next. HTML offers good support for text formatting and presentation, but authors must take a "scan-friendly" approach to writing. A quick overview of a page's content should be apparent in the first few lines; the first line of a paragraph should convey its contents.

Frames: The use of frames to coordinate different substructures in a Web site is quite common—for example, an index frame that is used as a top-level menu. But many experts caution against the use of frames, because they can cause unpredictable problems for peripheral tasks such as reloading of pages or printing.

Multimedia: HTML is touted as a framework for "hypermedia," because it supports the presentation of diverse kinds of content, including graphics, audio, and video, as well as text. But richer media such as images and video bring a huge cost in the time it takes to load a page. Authors are advised to present a thumbnail or other placeholder, and let users choose whether they want to separately download the full contents.

The Web is a fast-changing infrastructure for technology and application development. New technologies such as Java have enabled client-based interactivity. Many elegant Web page and Web site designs can be found, as well as some pretty awful ones. Each site reflects the sensibilities and quirks of individual designers: The graphical conventions and structure of the page you are viewing may be quite different from those of the next page you see.

---

dependency on task goals is a key motivation for a design process that is founded on specific use situations.

4.5   Science Fair Case Study: Information Design

The goal of information design is to specify representations of a task's objects and actions that will help users perceive, interpret, and make sense of what is happening. Users must be able to determine the status of their current activity, and what they can do to pursue their goals. In SBD, we carry out information design by elaborating the activity design scenarios with presentation details (Figure 4.12): Individual user interface elements are developed and combined to convey an overall information model. During the elaboration process, the pros and cons of information design features are considered and documented through claims analysis.

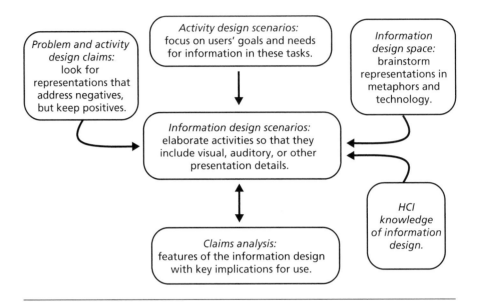

Figure 4.12   Developing information scenarios in scenario-based design.

4.5.1   Exploring the Information Design Space

Earlier we looked for new ideas about virtual science-fair activities by thinking about real-world activities, and about the general tools and services available in MOOsburg. During information design, we also carry out this sort of brainstorming, but the emphasis is on the ideas a metaphor or technology suggests about information presentation.

Our understanding of physical science fairs again provides an overarching visual metaphor. For example, we can envision that when Alicia and Delia visit the fair, they walk into a high school gym and see poster boards positioned in groups on the floor; the exhibits look like pages tacked up on bulletin boards; student authors are standing next to their exhibits; groups of visitors cluster around exhibits; and judges can be recognized by their badges. This is a powerful and useful metaphor, but we do not want to constrain ourselves to this or apply it too literally (Tradeoff 4.7).

In Table 4.2, we have reused the metaphors presented earlier to brainstorm about science fair activities, but focus on implications for information design. In most cases, the design ideas are visual in character, although some metaphors point to a role for auditory information (e.g., oral commentary as part of a documentary, or a "buzz" of conversation at a cocktail party). Although it is quite natural to consider new metaphors at this point, for the sake of simplicity we have

Table 4.2 Metaphors for a virtual science fair, with emphasis on information design.

VSF Information	Real-World Metaphor	Ideas about VSF Information Design
An exhibit looks like a . . .	Lab journal	Loosely organized pages with handwriting, sketches
	Documentary	Movie or animated sequence of screens and audio
A teacher-coach looks like a . . .	Peer (colleague)	Friendly face of same age, character as student
	Director	Professional-looking image with specific tools, agenda
The fair looks like a . . .	Study room	Empty work area with a place to write, materials to read
	Public lecture	Uninterrupted single presenter in focal view
	Cocktail party	Groups of people, auditory cues to conversation, activity
A judging form looks like a . . .	Balance sheet	Grid with cells displaying labels, values, equations
	Discussion	Questions, answers, comments in sequential order
A fair summary looks like a . . .	Report card	Check marks, letters, or numbers marking assessment scales
	Guided tour	A sequence of exhibits with annotations or comments
	Thank-you note	Form letter with personal salutation, thanks, signature

restricted ourselves to this familiar set. As always, there are no right or wrong answers. The goal of metaphor brainstorming is to expand the understanding of design possibilities.

The metaphors for central science fair objects such as the exhibit space and the exhibits serve an important orienting function in brainstorming. For example, the physical science fair metaphor emphasizes spatial relations and containment structures; the cocktail party metaphor suggests that we visualize people and their communication; and the lecture metaphor suggests the presentation of slide shows or other multimedia materials. Again, we are not looking for the "right" metaphor, but for a range of ideas.

A high-level metaphor may also evoke ideas for how to present specific task objects. For example, the physical science-fair metaphor suggests a display of tables, poster boards, and so on. Under this metaphor, an exhibit looks like a set of documents arrayed in a two-dimensional space (i.e., the poster board). In contrast, the cocktail party metaphor suggests a display that is filled with visitors; in this metaphor, the exhibits might be in the background (e.g., on the "walls") or they might be objects that people pull out and display on demand (e.g., from their "pockets" or "briefcases").

A natural complement to descriptions of different metaphors is a sketch. Even a quick hand-drawn sketch can be a great aid to group discussion, especially if these discussions include stakeholders from the work setting. Figure 4.13 contains rough sketches of three metaphors for the main screen of the virtual science fair.

In parallel with discussions of visual metaphors, we explored the information-design possibilities suggested by MOOsburg tools. (Novel technology should also be considered at this point if relevant or feasible.) Because our goal at this phase is to organize and present information, the relevant technologies are more specific than those discussed in Chapter 3 (Table 3.2). Table 4.3 lists information design ideas that came from thinking about MOOsburg tools.

Many of the ideas in the two tables can be combined. For example, a multimedia notebook might be used to edit and present a lab journal; a Web browser might be used as a presentation device for a documentary (e.g., as a sort of slide show). A room panorama could be used to present a traditional fair (the main objects are exhibits), a cocktail party (the main objects are people), or a lecture (the main objects are a presenter and his/her materials).

Metaphor and technology discussions will inevitably raise other more pragmatic concerns—hardware and software platforms, implementation or delivery costs, team expertise, and so on. Although discussion and resolution of these nonusability issues are beyond the scope of this book, tabular summaries like

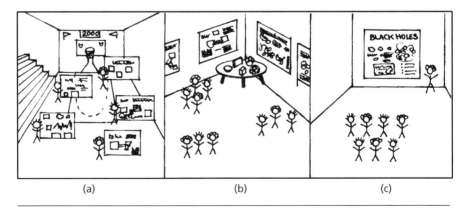

| (a) | (b) | (c) |

Figure 4.13   Three views of a virtual exhibit space suggested by the metaphors of (a) a high school gymnasium; (b) a cocktail party; and (c) a classroom lecture.

Table 4.3 Ideas about information design suggested by current MOOsburg tools.

VSF Information	MOOsburg Technology	Ideas about VSF Information Design
An exhibit looks like a . . .	Multimedia notebook	A video and audio presentation organized into pages
	Electronic whiteboard	Rectangular white space with colored lines and text
	Web pages	Netscape-like browser with underlined hot links
A teacher-coach looks like a . . .	Email	A list of messages organized by date or sender
	Threaded discussion	A list of comments indented to show replies/responses
	Chat	Sequential log of messages prefaced with sender name
The fair looks like a . . .	Room panorama	Panorama of walls, floor, maybe doors and windows
	Interactive map	Geographic coordinates showing landmarks, paths
A judging form looks like a . . .	Voting booth	Privacy curtain with levers or buttons labeled with choices
	Threaded discussion	Exhibits at top level, evaluative comments/replies indented
A fair summary looks like a . . .	Charting package	Labeled X and Y axes with lines, histograms, etc.
	Multimedia notebook	A video and audio presentation organized into pages
	Interactive map	Path traced out on a map, showing notable places to visit

those shown here, complemented with sketches like those in Figure 4.13, should provide a good starting point for identifying and discussing these other categories of concerns.

4.5.2 Information Scenarios and Claims

Activity scenarios illustrate the functionality proposed for a system in the context of specific uses. During information design we insert details of what the user sees (or hears or feels, depending on the application). As we do this, we also elaborate how the actors will perceive, interpret, and make sense of the information they encounter.

A key resource at this phase of design is the claims analysis of the activity design scenarios (see Table 3.3 in Chapter 3). Many of these include pros or cons related to the perception or comprehension of science fair information. For example, one concern about providing an unlimited virtual exhibit space was that students may end up producing overly large or complex exhibits. This concern should be addressed by the information design. Another example is the embarrassment some students might feel in having their incomplete projects advertised. As always, the design heuristic is to address the negative impacts while maintaining or enhancing the positive ones.

We focused first on one scenario, the visit of Alicia and Delia. The information needed in this activity is central to the entire project—they first see the fair itself and then an individual exhibit. This scenario is also a good example of our primary goal to increase community involvement, so we wanted to be sure that the information design was particularly appropriate and engaging in this situation.

Figure 4.14 shows how the visit activity was elaborated to include details about information presentation. On the left is the activity design scenario; on the right are additions that illustrate our information design ideas. Some of the new material describes information displays, while other material describes the actors' perceptions and reactions to these displays. In the course of the scenario, details are provided about a number of important elements in the information design—the initial view of the fair, the other visitors, the exhibits as a group, as well as the content of Sally's exhibit.

One important design decision concerned the representation of student exhibits. Like other MOOsburg activities, the virtual science fair is created as a "space" within the existing town structure. But we considered two alternative designs for the exhibits:

- represent each exhibit as a nested subspace, each with a room panorama and interactive map for navigating within the space; or

- represent the exhibits as independent objects, with their own representations and user interface.

The subspace alternative extends and reinforces the general spatial metaphor of MOOsburg; exhibitors could post materials on multiple walls and bring in many diverse supporting objects. This design emphasizes creativity and richness in exhibits. However, it complicates the information design for visitors—conceptually a visitor must "jump into" the fair space to get to each exhibit subspace. It also makes exhibit construction more complex—each subspace

Example Activity Design Scenario	⇨	Transformed into Information Design Scenario

3) Alicia and Delia go to the science fair.

Background on Alicia, Delia, and their motivations, . . .

When Delia shows Alicia an email invitation to a virtual science fair (VSF), the two of them decide to follow the link right then and there. They are curious about how this will be different from a regular fair.

When they arrive at the VSF, they are able to get an overview of what and who is there and the current activites taking place. They can see that some exhibits are still "under construction," so they figure that one difference may be that this fair is ongoing. A welcome note confirms this, indicating that all virtual exhibits will be complete by next Thursday, when the judging will take place.

They decide to look around anyway since they have time, and Delia suggests that they visit the exhibit that already has several people viewing it, thinking it must be interesting. But then Alicia notices that her friend Marge is also here, so they join her instead. She is talking to Sally Harris about her exhibit on black holes.

Sally and Marge see them arrive, and pause briefly to say hi. But Alicia and Delia don't want to interrupt, so they look around at other parts of the exhibit. Delia finds a stored discussion about red dwarfs and she and her mom browse it. Delia adds a comment to this discussion and is pleased when Sally notices and elaborates on her point.

3) Alicia and Delia go to the science fair.

The email includes a string that Delia recognizes as a URL in MOOsburg.

At the VSF they recognize the standard MOOsburg layout—panorama view of the fair, brief list of objects to work with, chat tool, and interactive map.

Alicia recognizes the map as a high-school floor plan. She shows Delia where she worked in the office as a peer counselor. They see a green dot in the gym, blue dots in other rooms. Alicia infers they are "in" the gym; she plans to check out the rest later.

The main view is crowded. At the back is a large Welcome sign, with thanks to organizers, and other announcements.

Exhibits are arrayed around the room, each with a student name attached. Some are covered with a black and yellow banner; Delia suggests that these must be "under construction."

People are in the room. Some are small photos, others smiley faces or simple line drawings. Because they logged in under Delia's school ID, they appear as her school photo.

They are attracted to an exhibit with lots of people around, but then Alicia notices her friend Marge, so they join her instead at Sally's exhibit.

The exhibit appears in a separate window. Like in the welcome area, there is a main

(continued)

Figure 4.14   Elaborating an activity scenario to include information design details.

Figure 4.14 *(continued)*

Alicia asks Sally about an unfamiliar object, a simulation. Sally shows her how it demonstrates her current theory of black hole formation, and asks them whether they want to try out some variations. Alicia is surprised and pleased at how quickly Delia understands how to change the model and get new results.

view. It displays what looks to them like a title page.

Near the main view are what appear to be several miniaturized windows. There is also a list of visitors and a text chat window.

Sally and Marge's conversation is being displayed in the chat log; they pause briefly to say hi.

Alicia is impressed with how much Delia knows about how to use PowerPoint and Excel. Delia explains she has been using these in science. They watch the slide show for an overview, as Sally's voice-over explains key points.

Delia sees a discussion board with an indented list of questions and answers. Alicia enjoys seeing her study the questions and pose one of her own.

The simulation is unfamiliar to Alicia, so she asks Sally. She demos it and invites them to change it, showing them the "Visitor Experiments" folder to use for their results.

owner (student) would need to develop a customized map. Because our root concept emphasized broad community and student interaction, we chose to adopt the second, simpler model.

At the same time, the presentation of exhibits should be rich and flexible enough to suit the needs of many different exhibitors. We carried over the MOOsburg concept of a main view, but surrounded it with information displays that represent the many contributing elements of each exhibit. This idea was combined with the earlier concept of a template, so that new projects are given a default layout. The elements themselves were inspired partly by our analysis of physical science projects and partly by the metaphors of slide shows and lab journals. We used similar reasoning to elaborate the other activity design scenarios; the information design elaborations are summarized in Figure 4.15.

1) Sally plans her exhibit on black holes.

Sally's new exhibit opens as a separate window next to the view of the VSF.

She sees that it already has a predefined structure, with placeholders for what seem to be exhibit components. There is a main view with a number of smaller views surrounding it.

The main view shows "Title page image" in a fancy graphical font. She infers she should import an image file to use as her title page. She also infers that this view is displayed when the small "title" window is selected.

When she explores the other miniatures she sees other prompts—for example, "PowerPoint slide show" and "Project report." She doesn't see anything about simulations, so worries whether she can include hers.

She sees a list of visitors—currently only herself—and some exhibit tools, consisting of a project calendar and discussion board. Will she have to add her simulation as a new exhibit tool?

She adds the image file from her PC that she created as a title page. As she does this, she notices menu options for renaming, deleting, and adding exhibit components. Relieved, she realizes that the standard layout is just a starting point. She now is confident that she can add her simulation as a component.

2) Mr. King coaches Sally on her project.

Mr. King checks Sally's project calendar, and he sees from the grayed-out sections that she is busy all day. So he adds an appointment to work with her tonight.

He sees that Sally is already working when he arrives. He joins her and sees that she has added a title page and is reviewing her project slide show. He opens the slide show to watch along with her, using the chat tool to make occasional comments.

When they finish, she tells him she will now bring in some other files from her PC. He watches while she adds a project notebook and a set of data analyses.

In the miniature, the data analysis looks like an Excel spreadsheet, and he wonders if it is read-only or if it will invoke Excel. He tries a double-click, and it opens the data in Excel in a separate window. He worries that visitors might tamper with Sally's data, but she explains that he can make changes but not save them.

Mr. King is concerned that Sally is bringing in too many components. He reminds her that even though this is an unlimited space, visitors and judges do not have unlimited time and will be biased by first impressions. Sally agrees and they start removing components that do not reveal much at first glance.

(continued)

Figure 4.15   Elaborations to the science fair scenarios that describe the features and reactions to information design.

Figure 4.15 *(continued)*

When Sally shows her idea about the interactive simulation, he worries that visitor-contributed results will make her display too messy. He explores the exhibit construction menu and finds a way to create nested components. He suggests using layers to hold visitor-created content and other less central materials.

4) Ralph judges the high-school physics projects at the science fair.

When he first visits, he sees a panorama with many exhibits around the room. He is surprised at how many still show "under construction" and worries whether they can all be done in time for judging on Thursday.

On Thursday, he logs in using the special judging ID provided by Rachel. He appreciates how this gives him a custom view of the VSF, showing just the five projects he has been assigned, along with the judging forms.

The judging form looks a lot like the paper forms he has used for years. He does notice that the numerical ratings look like input fields, and hopes this means the final calculations will be done for him.

He wants a quick overview, and is delighted to find that he can open all five exhibits at once, even though the display becomes complex when he also opens all of the forms to take notes.

Later, he comes back to examine the projects in more detail, and as in the past finds the form inadequate.

He wonders if he can weight the categories in the two forms. He sees that the final score is a formula and he is allowed to edit it, weighting Jeff's and Sally's ratings differently. But his change cannot be saved until he adds a note explaining his rationale for the modifications.

After submitting all five forms, a new object appears in the VSF panorama, labeled "Judging results." He opens it and sees a set of histograms charting results in each age group. Sally and Jeff are tied!

5) Rachel organizes a presentation for the superintendent.

During Rachel's virtual tour of the VSF archive, Superintendent Carlisle's display shows only what Rachel chooses to open. This makes it easy to show Ralph's judging forms and the issues in comparing exhibits.

To create her presentation, Rachel goes back through the winning exhibits, which are easy to find because of the blue/red/yellow ribbons attached to them.

Opening each one, she looks over the components to choose the more visual elements, and then opens them and makes copies of interesting displays.

When she makes a copy, a message box reminds her that a copy notice was sent to the author.

Where did the many details of the information scenarios come from? As for activity design, the answer is difficult to provide, because so many factors contribute to the overall design. Many of the details follow from MOOsburg's virtual-world metaphor. But we have also tried to address potential usability problems noted in earlier claims. And, of course, we were influenced by the general HCI concerns discussed in the first half of this chapter.

Table 4.4 lists the information design claims analyzed in parallel with scenario development. Like the scenarios, the claims become more extensive and detailed as visual representations are proposed and their usability implications are examined. These claims list a number of important features in the information scenarios, pointing to each feature's likely impacts on users' ability to perceive, interpret, and make sense of what is happening in the online science fair. At the same time, they document how that design was influenced by a combination of metaphors, technology options, and general tradeoffs in information design. For example:

- Some of the detailed exhibit content is nested in layers in hopes of simplifying initial perception (Tradeoff 4.1).

- Exhibits under construction are flagged, even though this adds visual complexity and continues our concern about student embarrassment (Tradeoff 4.2).

- The exhibits are organized into bounded views. This helps to separate the elements, but the boundary lines add clutter (Tradeoff 4.3).

- We use task-specific "science-project" terms in the template, even though they may not be familiar to all viewers (Tradeoff 4.4).

- We use both thumbnail images and more abstract icons, depending on the concept being conveyed (Tradeoff 4.5).

- The judging form hides its "editability," because form modification is secondary to judging exhibits (Tradeoff 4.6).

- The custom interface for judges is a specialized view of a complex information model (Tradeoff 4.9).

As in all scenario-writing efforts, the development of the science fair information-design scenarios was a creative process involving analysis and synthesis of many factors. The activity design scenarios provided the initial situation and goal constraints; metaphors and technology helped to generate possibilities; the general tradeoffs in information design assisted in selecting among and synthesizing ideas and constraints.

The scenarios and claims are not a complete representation of the information design. It is impractical and probably impossible to describe every detail of a

Table 4.4   Claims analysis used to guide and document information-design reasoning.

Design Feature	Possible Pros (+) or Cons (−) of the Feature
The main viewing window for each exhibit	+ directs viewers' attention to the selected component + builds on the visual structure of the overall fair and of MOOsburg − but makes it impossible to view multiple components together − but may lead to a decreased emphasis or interest in physical components
Labeling template structures with project subsections	+ reminds students of the science content expected in their exhibits − but may confuse visitors without science-fair backgrounds − but may discourage innovative exhibit content
Embedded examples of expected components	+ gives concrete and direct insight into what can be included as an element − but students may worry if they do not have these component types
Nested exhibit components	+ simplifies browsing and comprehension of top-level components − but viewers may not realize that these layers exist
Separate "windows" for the various exhibit components	+ aids perception and comprehension of the different activities − but may be confusing for exhibits with many components
Using a room panorama for laying out exhibits	+ leverages visitors' familiarity with real-world buildings and layouts + produces a convenient (spatial) overview of exhibits at the fair − but visitors may wonder if they must "walk" to reach exhibits
Yellow and black flags over incomplete exhibits	+ builds on common experience with sites "under construction" + emphasizes that the fair activity is extended, dynamic, and ongoing − but these bright color cues make the display more complex
Listing all visitors to an exhibit	+ emphasizes the group- and community-oriented nature of this event + aids awareness of and access to co-present participants − but some visitors may object to having their "presence" advertised
Exhibit components shown as miniaturized windows	+ suggests that they may contain interactive content − but viewers may misinterpret them as independent applications

Customized VSF interfaces for judges	+ implies that judges are recognized and that their task is appreciated
	+ simplifies access to judging relevant information
	− but may reduce judges' connections to other activities in the fair
Hiding the calculations used to tally ratings	+ simplifies the form, directing attention to the main job of judging
	− but judges may not realize that these formulas can be edited

visual display, or to narrate every aspect of a person's perception and reaction to a display. The choice of which and how much presentation detail to include is left to the design team developing the vision. For systems that envision novel or complex information designs, the number and detail of the information scenarios are likely to be greater. For a system involving more conventional WIMP (windows, icons, menus, and pointers) interface designs, it should be sufficient to work through a few scenarios such as those shown here.

4.5.3 Refining the Information Scenarios

Although textual scenarios and claims are important SBD design products, there is much truth to the old saying that a picture is worth a thousand words. The visual details of a design can be crucial in conveying exactly what is being proposed. Even at this very early point in design, a team should explore the "look and feel" of user interface proposals. This can be done quickly and inexpensively by sketching important views described by the scenarios (Figures 4.16 and 4.17; some usability engineers refer to these as "key screens," e.g., Kreitzberg 1996).

These science fair sketches show what the system might look like at two points during Alicia and Delia's visit. The welcome screen is clearly important, because it orients and motivates the actions of all visitors; this view must convey what the fair is "all about." The view of an individual exhibit is also important; much of the detailed activity of the fair takes place using this representation.

As sketches like these are discussed and refined, the individual visual elements also become an important topic of design. For example, the scenario mentions a generic icon that will represent exhibits in the overall exhibit space; we need to design the image for this icon. The scenarios also mention various controls and menu items that are interpreted and used by the actors; we need to design the details of these controls. Elements such as these comprise the visual vocabulary that plays a critical role in the perception and interpretation of task information (Mullet & Sano 1995).

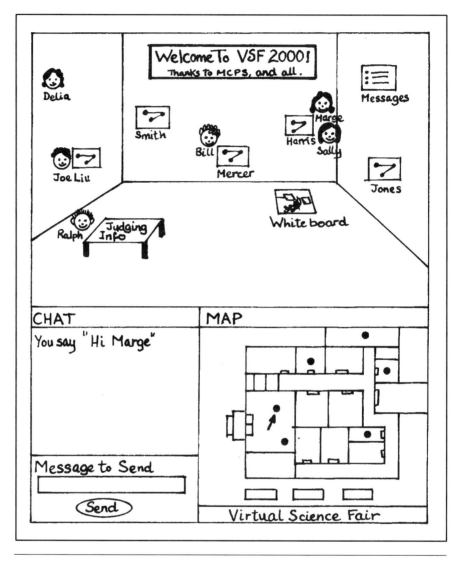

Figure 4.16   Sketch of the overall exhibit space.

Detailed Design

Some detailed design elements are inherited from MOOsburg. This is common—most user interface programming platforms have predefined visual objects and control elements (often called "widgets"). For example, all objects in MOOsburg have menu options for being locked down in a place, picked up, and so on. Thus,

Figure 4.17   Sketch of Sally's exhibit on black holes.

we focused our design work on the new menu options needed by the science fair. We worked first with the scenario in which Mr. King works with Sally, because he uses the menu system to discover and implement nested layers in her exhibit.

This scenario mentions several exhibit construction tools; we decided to put these in a Construction menu, so that the menu name would imply what services it contains. Although the content of the menu is not specified in the scenario, we assume that it will enable Sally and other authors to link their project files to the exhibit. We postpone the details of this interaction until Chapter 5. However, we note that it must contain an option for creating a nested layer.

Thinking about this menu caused us to consider other aspects of menu design. For example, Rachel needs a menu option for making copies of exhibit elements. But rather than create a new menu just to hold this option (thereby cluttering the display), we choose for now to reuse the pervasive `Save as...` dialog available through the operating system's `File` menu.

The design of the `Construction` menu led to a related design issue. This menu will support exhibit creation, so we considered the possibility that it appears only for users who are students or coaches. That is, when Alicia and Delia (or other visitors) view Sally's exhibit, the `Construction` menu will simply be absent. This simplifies the information design for visitors while supporting the specific needs of students. At the same time, there are costs to making this choice: Truly helpful contributions by visitors are now impossible, and there may at times be confusion about menu options (Table 4.5).

Our design of exhibit icons considered the tradeoff of realism and complexity (Tradeoff 4.5). We debated the use of project-specific images for exhibit icons (e.g., a thumbnail image of the title page). We ultimately decided against

Table 4.5 Claims associated with features proposed during detailed information design.

Design Feature	Possible Pros (+) or Cons (−) of the Feature
Hiding the `Construction` menu from visitors	+ reduces the number of controls that visitors must interpret
	− but prevents well-intentioned, helpful contributions by visitors
	− but students and visitors may be confused when logged on together
Generic icons representing all exhibits in the VSF	+ simplifies and speeds perception of the overall science fair display
	− but implies a degree of similarity among exhibits that may be inaccurate
	− but students may be unhappy with the lack of individual expression
Thumbnail views of an exhibit element's content	+ previews the entire exhibit, attracting viewers to interesting elements
	− but increases the visual detail and complexity of the exhibit display

this because we believed that it would not scale well—the overall scene would quickly become complex, and details of individual exhibits would be hard to perceive. Furthermore, the visit scenario emphasizes the importance of social context (i.e., other visitors) rather than exhibit content. Thus, we designed a generic exhibit icon, while recognizing the negative consequences of doing this as a claim for information design (Table 4.5).

In contrast, our reasoning about the icons representing the different components of Sally's exhibit recognized their dual role: They provide an overview of the exhibit, but also serve as view-access controls. Here we concluded that the interpretation benefits of a preview outweigh the complexity costs of a set of thumbnail images (Table 4.5).

In addition to providing an overview of the exhibit, the scenarios describe how the different elements convey the type of media they contain (Word, Excel, etc.). One possibility is to make this an implicit effect of the thumbnail images (i.e., a text document looks like text even in miniature). But we also considered various icon "decorations" that could indicate more directly which application was used to create the element.

When discussing these alternatives, we created the sketches in Figure 4.18: the sketches contrast an unadorned thumbnail of a Microsoft Excel chart with two other possibilities that include information about the source application. These visual details (the name in the middle, the familiar graphical "X" on the right) make the icon more complex, but may better convey the nature of the document it represents. Eventually, we decided that even a simple miniaturized window provides sufficient affordances to suggest the Excel opening behavior (e.g., as Mr. King did in the second scenario).

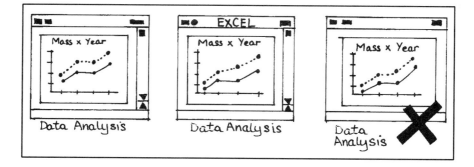

Figure 4.18   Rough sketches of ideas for control icons for the exhibits.

Participatory Design

End users can also help to develop or refine an information design. In a project developing educational software to support remote collaboration in science projects, Chin and colleagues (Chin, Rosson, & Carroll 1997; Chin & Rosson 1998) carried out sessions with teachers and students, to develop rough sketches of what the system might look like. Muller and colleagues (1995) describe similar experiences for software supporting telephone operators; many other examples have been reported by projects exploring and developing methods for cooperative design (Greenbaum & Kyng 1991).

Figure 4.19 shows a felt board and other simple office supplies used in participatory design of the science fair screens. Small groups of teachers, students, and community members were given activity design scenarios and asked to mock up screens illustrating the activities. Notice that the felt board resembles a Netscape browser; we added this constraint to simplify the design problem. As expected, people's Web experience influenced their design ideas (e.g., they used

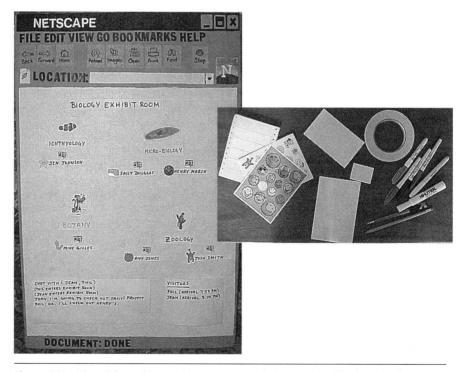

Figure 4.19   Materials used in participatory screen design sessions for the virtual science fair.

frames to organize the display and changes in color to show when an item had been viewed). The Web browser constraint seemed to help these participants get started more quickly, but probably discouraged more radical presentation ideas (see Chapter 6).

4.6 Consistency and Coherence

As we discussed earlier, a design can be assessed with respect to both internal and external consistency. At the least, the individual display elements and the overall design program should be internally consistent. For example, the two sketches in Figures 4.16 and 4.17 reserve different areas of the screen for similar functions—the main object "in view" is in the upper part of the screen, a chat tool for communcation is in the lower left, and controls for navigation are in the lower right. At the same time, we need to consider the consistency of the individual elements in a display. Do all buttons (e.g., Send) have the same look, and do they use the same font in the label? Do scrollbars appear in the same place and with the same look?

Notice that the current information design reflects a compromise between consistency and task-specific creativity. We provide an exhibit template that controls the displays that students generate to some extent (e.g., as compared to a custom Web page). This means that the overall fair should gain some coherence, because as viewers move from one exhibit to another, the general layout will stay the same. At the same time, by allowing individual students to edit the template, the design leaves open many of the details that will be presented at each exhibit.

Summary and Review

This chapter has discussed many of the issues that must be considered when designing the representation and organization of the information a system will use. Norman's (1986) stages of human-computer interaction were used as a framework to consider these issues. The virtual science-fair scenarios were elaborated to include proposals for an overall information design as well as detailed design of individual elements. Central points to remember include:

- Norman's analysis of stages of action in HCI is a useful framework for issues related to user interface design. The Gulf of Evaluation (perception, interpretation, and making sense) emphasizes the perceptual and cognitive issues associated with information design.

- Gestalt principles of perceptual organization offer useful guidance in thinking about how to select and arrange the elements of a visual display.

- Making images and words familiar and realistic can aid interpretation, but too much familiarity can dilute important distinctions, and too much realism can lead to interpretations that are too tied to concrete instances.

- The design of affordances—what an interface element suggests about its use and manipulation—is a key technique for supporting information interpretation.

- It is the overall information model—how it maps to users' mental model of the task, the extent to which it is self-consistent, and so on—that determines how well users will be able to integrate and make sense of their actions as they progress through a task.

- Rough sketches of screen layout or of individual screen elements can be very useful in making information scenarios more concrete, especially if the team decides to share these with user representatives.

Exercises

1. Use the Gulf of Evaluation to analyze the information that you process when you check your email for the first time each day. What happens during perception? Interpretation? Making sense?

2. Make a screen dump of your online course schedule. Analyze the display from the perspective of the Gestalt principles in Table 4.1. Can you see any examples of these principles in action? If so, are they helping or hurting perception? Can you see any opportunities for improvement?

3. Design a new command vocabulary for your university's course registration system. For simplicity, assume an entirely text-based user interface. Develop two contrasting vocabularies, including one that emphasizes familiarity and another that emphasizes flexiblity and generality. Which one would you prefer to use? Why?

4. Browse your personal file system. Design two different visualizations for the files (e.g., a hierarchy or other network; include dynamic behavior as relevant). Sketch samples of the two designs, and discuss how each design supports the common file-system tasks of file management, retrieval, and version control.

5. Surf the Web to find one Web page that easily passes the "squint test," and another that definitely fails. Analyze the visual features and graphical layouts. Why does one succeed while the other one fails?

Project Ideas

Continue your work on the online shopping project, elaborating the activity scenarios to include information design.

- Discuss metaphors again, but now from the perspective of information presentation.

- Reason from the claims analyzed from the scenarios developed thus far.

- Write one scenario as a complete narrative; for the others, just list the new details of presentation and user experience.

- Write claims to document tradeoffs that you addressed in the information design.

- Develop at least one sketch in support of each scenario.

- Discuss how your design reflects a coherent visual design program.

Recommended Reading

Card, S. K., J. D. Mackinlay, & B. Shneiderman, eds. 1999. *Readings in Information Visualization*. San Francisco: Morgan Kaufmann.

Howlett, V. 1996. *Visual Interface Design for Windows*. New York: John Wiley & Sons.

Johnson, J. 2000. *GUI Bloopers: Don'ts and Do's for Sofware Developers and Web Designers*. San Francisco: Morgan Kaufmann.

Mullet, K., & D. Sano. 1995. *Designing Visual Interfaces: Communication Oriented Techniques*. Englewood Cliffs, NJ: Sunsoft Press.

Nielsen, J. 1999. *Designing Web Usability: The Practice of Simplicity*. Indianapolis: New Riders.

Ware, C. 1999. *Information Visualization: Perception for Design*. San Francisco: Morgan Kaufmann.

5

Interaction Design

Doors let people into spaces. That's what people are looking for when they come up to a door, whether it's made of wood, metal, glass, or some unknown material: Where is the handle, and how do I use it to unlatch and push open the door? As Don Norman has pointed out in his book *The Design of Everyday Things* (1988), even such an obvious and simple user need is easily defeated by poor design.

Norman (1988, 3–4) illustrates his point with an amusing anecdote of a friend "trapped" in the doorway of a European post office. The door in question was part of an outside entryway (a row of six glass doors), with an identical internal entrance beyond. As the man entered through the leftmost pair of doors, he was briefly distracted and turned around. The rotation caused him to slightly shift his position to the right. When he moved forward and pushed a door in the next row, it didn't move. He assumed it must be locked, so he moved to the next pair of doors. He pushed another door; it also refused to move. Beginning to feel confused, he decided to go outside and try again. But now when he pushed the door leading back outside, it also didn't move. His confusion turned to mild panic . . . he was trapped! Just then a group of people entered at the other end of the doorways. Norman's friend hurried over and followed them, and was successful this time.

The problem was a simple one and would have been easy to avoid. Swinging doors come in pairs, one side containing a supporting pillar and hinge, the other one free to swing. To get through, you must push against the swinging side. For these doors, the designers went for elegance and beauty. Each panel was identical, so there were no visual clues as to which side was movable. When Norman's friend accidentally changed his position, he became out of sync with the "functional" panels within the row of glass. The result was an entryway that looked nice but provided poor support for use.

The goal of **interaction design** is to specify the mechanisms for accessing and manipulating task information. Whereas information design focuses on determining which task objects and actions to show and how to represent them, an interaction design tries to make sure that people can *do the right things at the right* *time*. The scope of possible action is broad—for instance, from selecting and opening a spreadsheet, to pressing and holding a mouse button while dragging it, to specifying a range of cells in the spreadsheet.

Interaction design focuses on the Gulf of Execution in Norman's (1986) analysis of human-computer interaction (Figure 5.1). The user begins with a task goal, such as the desire to investigate an irregularity in last month's budget. To pursue this goal, the real-world objective is translated into an appropriate system goal—a computer-based task such as examining an Excel spreadsheet. The system goal is elaborated as an action plan that specifies the steps needed to achieve the system goal: point at an Excel icon, double-click to open it, point at the first cell containing a sum, and so on. Finally, the plan is executed: The mouse is grasped and moved until the cursor is over the icon, a double-click is performed to launch Excel, and the pointer is moved to the bottom of the first column.

The example in the figure continues through the cycle to emphasize the important role of system feedback. While the execution takes place, some visual changes appear; for instance, when the file is opened, a new figure (the window) is seen. These changes are interpreted with respect to the spreadsheet context, and ultimately with respect to the budget question.

This is a deliberately simple example, but even a trivial interaction such as opening a spreadsheet can be undermined by usability problems. Suppose that

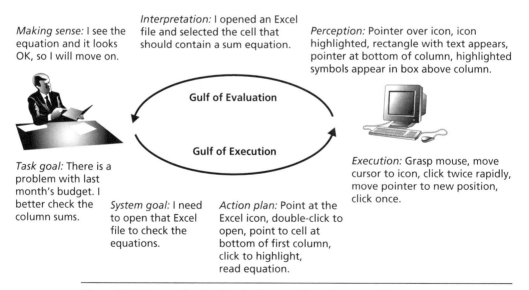

Figure 5.1 Stages of action in a budget problem: choosing, planning, and executing an action, and then perceiving, interpreting, and making sense of the computer's response.

the spreadsheet is very large and only a portion of it shows when it is opened, making it difficult to determine its status; or suppose that it is has links to other files that are not present, resulting in warning or error messages. And, of course, opening the spreadsheet is just the beginning. As the task progresses, the computer responds with changing information displays that must be perceived, interpreted, and understood in order to plan and carry out the next set of steps.

As in Chapter 4, we have used Norman's (1986) framework to organize our discussion of interaction design. Here we are concerned with the three stages making up the Gulf of Execution—selecting a system goal, creating an action plan, and executing the action plan. For the sake of simplicity, we limit our discussion to standard user interaction techniques—the **WIMP** user interface style (windows, icons, menus, pointers), the default on most PCs and workstations.

As in all aspects of system development, designers have many options to choose from in designing a user interaction. Their goal is to compose and sequence user-system exchanges in a way that is intuitive, fluid, and pleasant for the task at hand. Doing this depends on understanding the details of the usage situation. There are no simple right or wrong answers; as usual, interaction design is peppered with tradeoffs.

5.1   Selecting a System Goal

To pursue a task with computer support, a user must first translate his or her real-world goal into a software-oriented goal, also known as a **system goal**. The simplest case is one where the system object or action is identical to the real-world concept—perhaps in our example above, the accountant sees an object named "last month's budget." This is a very close match to what is wanted; deciding to open it is trivial. The system goal in this case has high **semantic directness**, in that the user's task goal is mapped very easily onto an appropriate system feature. Of course, the names or pictures of system objects and actions do not usually match task goals exactly, so some amount of processing and inference is required. One goal of interaction design is to minimize this cognitive effort as much as possible.

5.1.1   Interaction Style

A powerful technique for helping people translate their task goals into system goals is **direct manipulation** (Shneiderman 1983). A direct-manipulation user interface is built from objects and actions that are direct analogs of objects and actions in the real world: User interface controls look like buttons that can be pressed; and data containers look like folders that are grabbed, dragged, or stacked. An active application looks like a window that has been opened for the user to see inside. Choices are shown as menus to be opened and browsed so that items can be selected.

User interface controls that look or sound like familiar objects in the real world simplify the problem of choosing a system goal (Hutchins, Hollan, & Norman 1986). If a user wants to put something away, there are folders waiting to be used. When a user wants to organize information, the objects are on the screen waiting for action. Of course, direct-manipulation techniques require that the right objects and controls are present at the right time—displaying a large set of folders on a screen will be of little help if the goal involves navigation to a Web page.

Even this simple example makes it clear that direct manipulation is not a universal interaction technique (Tradeoff 5.1). Persistent visibility of objects and actions is essential, but a large number of display elements will lead to visual clutter. People must decide which of their many tasks are frequent or important enough to "leave out in the open."

TRADEOFF 5.1

 Visible user interface controls that are analogs to real-world objects simplify the mapping from task to system goals, BUT not all task goals have visual analogs.

Direct manipulation also requires that objects can be represented visually, and that the operations on these visual entities are analogs to physical actions (e.g., pointing, selecting, and dragging). But there are many system concepts that have no obvious visual representation. In the accountant example, how could a system visually represent "the two managers who did not yet turn in their budget numbers"?

Direct-manipulation user interfaces are often complemented with some form of a **command language**. A command language consists of a vocabulary and composition rules (syntax) used to identify and manipulate task objects indirectly. Instead of pointing at a file or a piece of data, a user types or says its name, or specifies it through a logical expression, a mathematical equation, or some other symbolic description. In these cases, the distance from a task goal to a system goal can be substantial—the user must remember and produce the right vocabulary words in the right order.

Expressing system goals with commands is economical and flexible. Text requires minimal display space, and simple commands can often be combined to create more complex expressions. This makes it possible to satisfy many different system goals with a relatively small vocabulary. But even for small vocabularies, learning the rules for specifying and ordering commands (the command syntax) can be difficult (Tradeoff 5.2). Many common objects and actions have multiple names in natural language (e.g., copy/ duplicate, move/relocate, and table/ matrix). If these concepts represent possible system goals, users must remember which of the synonyms to use.

TRADEOFF 5.2

Expressing system goals indirectly with names or symbols is flexible and economical, BUT learning a command vocabulary can be difficult or tedious.

Buttons and menus offer an interesting compromise between direct manipulation and command-based interaction. They are persistent visible objects that users can point at and select. But the content that they represent is usually a command. In a menu system, complex command expressions may be constructed through a sequence of choices. For example, the procedure for opening a new browser in Netscape might be summarized as "Execute the File command New with an argument of Navigator." Indeed, one reason that menus are so pervasive in WIMP user interfaces is that they have a flexibility and economy similar to command languages, while offering the advantage of recognition over recall.

5.1.2 Opportunistic Goals

Sometimes a person has no particular task goal in mind. For instance, someone first starting up a computer in the morning may have no specific agenda, and instead relies on the computer display to remember what needs doing. In such situations, attractive or convenient system goals may be adopted in an opportunistic fashion.

Opportunistic behavior is evoked by perceptually salient or engaging elements in the user interface display. An interesting possibility is detected, which causes the user to remember a task or to adopt a new goal. A familiar example is the response often exhibited on arrival of new mail, where users drop whatever task they are engaged in to check out a new message. Opportunism is also common when novice users are confused or distracted, and seek guidance from the system about what to do next. In these cases, any object or control that looks intriguing or helpful may be accepted as the right thing to do.

TRADEOFF 5.3

Intriguing task options encourage flexible goal switching, BUT opportunism may lead to inappropriate, confusing, or frustrating experiences.

In most cases, opportunism is not a serious usability problem. Setting aside one task to pursue another can enhance feelings of flexibility and increase the spontaneity of one's activities. However, designers should analyze sources of opportunism in their user interfaces, and seek ways to minimize it when it would interfere with task goals (Tradeoff 5.3). Novices become seriously derailed when they are drawn into complex or exotic functionality (Carroll 1990). People may want to know when new email arrives, but they should be able to deactivate such alerts when concentration is important.

5.2   Planning an Action Sequence

The steps needed to achieve a system goal comprise an **action plan**. With experience, many such plans will be learned and automated, such that they require little conscious thought (Anderson 1983). Most users do not consciously plan the steps for accessing and making a selection from the bookmark list in their Web browser; opening a spreadsheet may well happen without conscious attention. However, for more complex tasks, or for people working with a new application, the user interface is a critical resource in determining what steps to take (Payne 1991).

The concept of a plan is related to the task analysis techniques discussed in Chapter 2. Task analysis specifies the steps and decision rules needed to carry out a task; this can be seen as an idealized action plan for the analyzed task. Plans can be decomposed and analyzed at many levels of detail, depending on the interaction concern in focus (e.g., making a selection from a list box versus constructing a piechart). First-time or occasional users may need to think about the details of selecting or manipulating individual user interface controls, but experienced users will operate at a much higher task-oriented level of abstraction.

Action planning is an active process. People retrieve what they know about a system from their mental models. They use the system information available and make inferences to fill the gaps, often relying on experiences with other systems. As a result, the plan guiding the behavior of any one user may overlap only partially with the action plan intended by the designer. People are not machines. Even if we could somehow be taught every possible plan for every possible contingency, we would be unable (or unwilling!) to ceaselessly retrieve and execute these plans in rote fashion.

5.2.1   Making Actions Obvious

How do users know what to do at all? To a great extent, they learn by experience. Users rely on their current mental models and on their reasoning ability to decide what to do. As execution takes place, system feedback may lead them to revise or elaborate their action plan (i.e., through perception, interpretation, and making sense). The success and failure of such episodes results in learning about what works and what does not work; mental models are updated and plans are reinforced or revised.

One way to help users learn what to do is to make it easy to predict, by trying to emulate real-world tasks (Moran 1983). For example, people editing a report will circle or underline a piece of text, and then write an editing mark or comment near it. A word processor that follows this scheme will be easier to understand than one that expects users to first enter their comment and then point to the text it describes. Thus, one design strategy is to document existing procedures, and then define action plans that build on these procedures. The problem with this is that most software projects seek to enhance or improve current tasks. This means that there will always be computer-based tasks that have no real-world analogs (Tradeoff 5.4).

TRADEOFF 5.4

 Action plans that correspond to real-world tasks and manipulations are intuitive and easy to learn, BUT many computer functions extend real-world tasks.

An effective direct-manipulation interface can also simplify action planning. The same physical analogies that aid selection of system goals (recognizing a folder as a place to put things) also help to suggest what actions to take (grab and open the folder). This effect on action planning is related to the concept of affordances discussed in Chapter 4. People need not memorize "press a button to activate it"; a screen button affords pressing because it looks like a real-world button. Dimming choices on a menu makes the grayed-out items look inactive, discouraging inappropriate selections; even a relatively subtle affordance like this can be important in ensuring smooth interaction.

As pointed out earlier, it is impossible to support all user tasks with direct manipulation interfaces. Physical analogies work well for simple actions, such as identification, selection, movement, interconnection, and duplication operations. But how do you carry out a search by direct manipulation or apply a global substitution? Researchers working with programming languages have spent decades exploring direct-manipulation techniques for writing programs, but support for logic, abstraction, and reuse continue to challenge these efforts (Cypher 1983; Lieberman 2001; Rosson & Seals 2001).

5.2.2   Simplifying Complex Plans

In WIMP user interfaces, people rely on icons, buttons, dialog boxes, or other user interface controls to guide them through action sequences. The user looks at a menu bar, and one set of choices is offered; he or she opens the menu and another set appears. A menu item is selected, and another set of more specific choices is presented via a dialog box. And so on. This simplifies planning, because users only need to know the next step. What would otherwise be learned as the command words and parameters of a command language is implicit in a sequence of menus, or in the input fields, check boxes, and other controls of a dialog box.

Nonetheless, plan complexity is still a major design concern. People are always trying new things, and as applications become more powerful, the usage possibilities become more complex. Problems are likely to arise when users attempt tasks with many steps—for example, many levels of nested menus, several interconnected dialog boxes, or many links leading to a Web page. A long sequence of interdependent actions is hard to keep in mind, and users can lose track of where they are. This can lead to omission or duplication of steps, or other errors (see "Designing for Errors" sidebar).

Studies of human memory have shown that people have a limited capacity to hold information in mind (Miller 1956). We can hold more information if it is possible to **chunk** it—that is, organize several interrelated bits of information into a single unit. Chunking often is a natural consequence of use; the more times certain bits of information occur together, the more likely they are to become a chunk. Information that naturally occurs together may be chunked even without previous exposure. Common examples of information chunking are people's names, phone numbers, dates, and so on.

User interface controls help to chunk interaction sequences. Figure 5.2 illustrates this for the task of using Microsoft Word to indent a paragraph. From the perspective of the system software, this task requires seven inputs from the user: specification of beginning and end points identifying the text, selection of the `Format` menu, and of the `Paragraph` option within that menu, selection of the `First line` indentation option, typing an indentation amount, and selecting `OK`. But from the user perspective, the plan includes three chunks: paragraph selection, accessing the paragraph settings, and setting the indentation.

Defining the chunks of an action plan is a critical aspect of interaction design, but chunking that is arbitrary or that ignores implicit task boundaries is

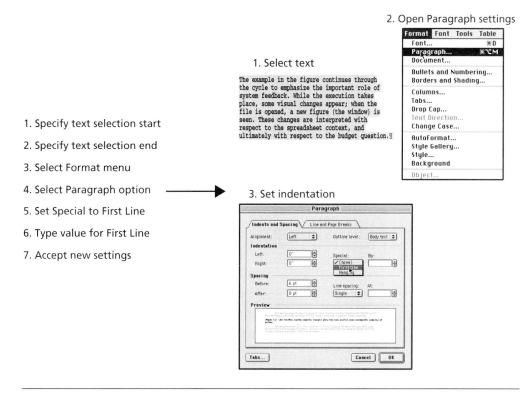

1. Specify text selection start

2. Specify text selection end

3. Select Format menu

4. Select Paragraph option

5. Set Special to First Line

6. Type value for First Line

7. Accept new settings

Figure 5.2 User interface controls organize complex plans into smaller, more manageable sequences of actions.

worse than no chunks at all (Tradeoff 5.5). Steps that naturally go together should not be placed in separate chunks. And steps that are very different should not be squeezed into the same chunk. Suppose that in the indentation example above, the line to be indented is identified by pointing at the text (step #5). This would disrupt the third chunk, resulting in a disjointed and awkward interaction.

TRADEOFF 5.5

Decomposing complex plans into chunks aids learning and application of action plans, BUT the sequence may create arbitrary or unnatural step boundaries.

Action planning is also simplified by internal and external consistency (Chapter 4). For example, if some tasks require users to first identify an action and then indicate the object to which it applies, while others require the opposite order, people will almost certainly make errors in learning these procedures.

Designing for Errors

Problematic interactions with computer software are usually reported as errors, but this term may not really reflect what is happening in most cases. The term "error" implies that someone is to blame. But most user interaction errors arise without any intent, and so should be analyzed as misunderstandings or confusions (Lewis & Norman 1986). But regardless of terminology, such problems are inevitable and designing for error is an important piece of interaction design.

Norman (1981a) makes a basic distinction between **mistakes** and **slips**. If an inappropriate intention is established and pursued, a mistake is made; if the right thing is intended but a problem comes up along the way, a slip occurs. In HCI, mistakes are common for novice users, because their mental models are relatively incomplete. Slips are common among experts, who have many overlearned action sequences and who often execute plans with little or no attention. Lewis and Norman (1986) expand on this analysis, giving examples and design approaches for minimizing errors. The table

on the facing page names and exemplifies several error types, along with general design advice for minimizing them.

Lewis and Norman also discuss techniques for helping users detect or recover from errors (see also Carroll 1990). A general technique is to provide a forcing function that prevents the user from continuing down an error path. Specific examples include:

- gags (e.g., locking the keyboard);
- warning (e.g., an alert explaining that you cannot copy a file to a locked diskette);
- do nothing (e.g., simply ignoring a request to change the color of an imported graphic);
- auto-correct (also sometimes called DWIM or do-what-I-mean, e.g., the auto-formatting and spelling correction common in modern word processors);
- let's talk about it (initiating a dialog, e.g., as when a file name is not recognized); and
- teach me (e.g., letting the user add words to a spelling dictionary).

The memory phenomenon responsible for conflicts of this sort is **interference**. Interference is the inverse of transfer of learning; in these cases prior knowledge leads users to do the *wrong* thing.

5.2.3 Flexibility

People are good at multithreaded activities, that is, pursuing multiple goals at once. We often interrupt ourselves, set aside our current goals, and take on new goals (see Section 5.1.2 on opportunistic goals). This makes us responsive to our environment; we can rearrange task priorities as a function of new information, or even as a function of what seems more or less rewarding at the moment. It also increases our feelings of control—we see ourselves as people who make decisions about and manage our own behavior.

Designing for Errors *(continued)*

Type of Error	Example Situation	Design Approach
Mistake: asking for nonexistent function or object	Mistyping the name of a command so that its function cannot be executed	Represent (e.g., in lists, icons) what is available
Mistake: over-generalizing an earlier experience	In a listserve, using "reply" when intending to reply only to the sender of a message	Present through training or documentation a more complete set of examples
Slip: doing something that is appropriate, but not for the current interaction mode	Trying to input text into a document while the Font dialog box is open	Minimize modes and when necessary mark well with status and feedback cues
Slip: making a request that is interpreted as something else	Using a keyboard shortcut to turn off underline before adding a space (in Microsoft PowerPoint this reverses the existing underline)	Improve consistency of low-level controls within and across applications
Slip: completing an automated (but inappropriate) action	Deleting a text selection before the selection has been correctly specified	Predict locus of such errors and increase the amount of feedback (or alerts) provided

As the power and sophistication of personal computers has increased, multithreaded interaction has become pervasive. Most machines can easily run three or four different applications simultaneously with little or no impact on processing speed. The implications for interaction design are strong: People must keep track of where they are in one plan while they pick up on another; when they return to a deferred plan, they need to remember where they were, so that they can resume. For complex plans with many embedded activities, people will put a plan on hold but expect to maintain the current task context. A user filling out a complex Web order form should be able to leave the form temporarily (e.g., to investigate another product) and return to it later without losing the data already entered.

Multiple overlapping windows are commonly provided to increase the flexibility and control of user interactions. Each window holds the status and data relevant to an ongoing plan. **Property sheets** are special cases of this general technique; they are opened to investigate or set task-relevant characteristics such as the preferences defined for a Web browser or email program. Users can put aside one task and continue another simply by clicking on a window to bring it (along with its status information) into focus.

An obvious cost of multiple windows is an increase in plan complexity (Tradeoff 5.6). When multiple tasks are underway, people often are forced to take on an extra task—finding and activating windows. They may end up spending valuable time on housekeeping chores such as minimizing, resizing, or rearranging windows. They may also be drawn into tasks that have low priority (opportunism). Providing clear indications of task identity and status (e.g., title bars, the current state of contained data or processes) can help to address this problem.

TRADEOFF 5.6

Allowing plan interruption and resumption enhances feelings of control, BUT management of simultaneous plans is demanding and may increase errors.

A variant of multiple windows is a **tiled display**. This style can now be seen in the many Web applications that use frames. Different categories of information are presented in persistent subareas of the display. An important difference between overlapping and tiled window displays is that users see all of the tiled presentations all the time. In fact, this is a key design consideration: If a task involves multiple related goals and information sets, designing a coordinated tiled display can encourage dynamic construction and switching among plans. Our work on programming tools for Smalltalk demonstrates this—a tiled display supports simultaneous interaction with complementary views of an example application (Carroll, Singer, et al. 1990; Carroll & Rosson 1991).

In order to work on two tasks at once, individual plans must be interruptible. User interaction **modes** work against flexible task-switching and activity management. A mode is a restricted interaction state, where only certain actions are possible. Common examples are an "insert mode" that only accepts text input; an alert box that must be dismissed in order to continue work; or a dialog box whose settings must be accepted or canceled before returning to the main window.

Modes are sometimes necessary—for example, when an urgent system event has taken place and the user must acknowledge this or take some action before continuing. However, in general, designers should avoid putting users into situations where they are forced to complete a plan before continuing. The ever-present `Cancel` button on dialog boxes is a compromise solution—users may not be able to continue work on their data while a dialog box is open, but at least they can quickly leave the mode.

5.3 Executing an Action Sequence

The final phase of an action cycle is execution of plan steps. In some sense, execution is an inconvenience—what users really want is to accomplish their goals directly, but they must do this by carrying out a sequence of physical actions. On occasion, though, the execution process itself may be rewarding. Video game experts probably feel a sense of accomplishment and reward when they push a joystick just the right amount. In either case, the design of simple and fluid action sequences will greatly impact people's competence and satisfaction in plan execution.

The most important actions to get right are those that are repeated over and over: pervasive actions such as selection, opening, moving, control keys, menu navigation, and so on. Not surprisingly, these are the sorts of interactions addressed by many user interface style guides (Apple Computer 1992; IBM 1991; Sun Microsystems 1990). From a design perspective, pervasive controls are also the elements that developers have least control over; the look and feel of these controls is usually inherited or highly constrained by a windowing system and associated code libraries. Nonetheless, careful examination of these primitive operations can be important in selecting user interface software tools.

5.3.1 Directness

The choice of input device for a task should consider how well it meets the task's performance requirements. The mapping of a physical movement with a device to a task's input requirements is referred to as **articulatory directness**. Twisting a device is a direct technique for adjusting rotation, and typing a number to specify rotation angle is an indirect mechanism for providing this input. Pressing a mouse button while dragging corresponds closely to grabbing and holding on to something as it is relocated; clicking on an object, and then moving the mouse and clicking again to reposition it, is less direct. Table 5.1 lists a number of common input devices, along with their physical characteristics and likely applications.

The term **pragmatics** is sometimes used to refer to the physical behaviors required by a user interface (Buxton 1983). User interface pragmatics is a concern for user engineering and refinement in the same way that the perceptual and

Table 5.1 Example input devices with different operational characteristics.

Device	Input Characteristics	Sample Applications
Button	Simple discrete input	Command execution or attribute specification
Keyboard	Spatial array, small-finger movement, allows combination key presses, discrete	Open-ended, continuous symbolic input
Mouse	Grasped with hand, one or more buttons, large arm movement, analog	Pointing and selecting in a 2D-space
Trackball	Grasped and rolled with hand, constrained movement in horizontal plane, one or more buttons, analog	Panning (rolling over) large maps or other 2D surfaces
Joystick	Grasped with hand, pushed or twisted, one or more buttons, constrained movement in three dimensions, analog	Setting direction of movement in virtual space, continuous zooming
Data glove	Tracking of finger and hand position in three dimensions	Grabbing and positioning objects in virtual space

cognitive characteristics of a user interface are analyzed and refined. Physical actions have an underlying structure or "phrasing" that should correspond to the conceptual task they implement. For example, in the paragraph indentation example shown earlier (Figure 5.2), the first two chunks in the plan have been mapped into two distinct gestural phrases:

1. Pressing the mouse down to specify the start of the selection, and then holding it down while dragging, creates a tension that is relaxed when the mouse button is released. When the button is finally released, the event is used to specify the end point of the selection.

2. Similarly, pressing the mouse down on the `Format` menu title, and then holding it down while navigating to the `Paragraph` menu choice, defines another gestural phrase. In fact, early versions of pull-down menus did not operate this way; menu access and choice were independent actions. A better understanding of user interface pragmatics led to the convention of "spring-loaded" menus.

As Table 5.1 suggests, input devices vary in their pragmatics, and this in turn interacts with task requirements. Buxton (1986) makes this point by contrasting a trackball with a joystick (Figure 5.3): The trackball affords a rolling movement over an input area, somewhat like a mouse. This makes it good for "panning" a two-dimensional information structure (think of panning as multidirectional scrolling). Thus, a designer might choose a trackball for interacting with maps, circuit diagrams, or other spatial representations.

In contrast, a joystick is optimized for directional pointing; movement occurs in the indicated direction, perhaps with acceleration or intensity determined by gesture force. This means that joysticks work well for tasks where you want to control the orientation or angle of a movement or data, such as tracking a target, or avoiding obstacles while moving through an environment.

These analyses of individual devices are useful for simple tasks, but complications arise when a task requires a combination of input (Tradeoff 5.7). For example, Buxton (1986) describes a task that requires control of three dimensions—changing depth or point of view while moving around in a map. This more complex task involves two simultaneous inputs—one that specifies horizontal position and another for depth. The combined input is quite challenging with a trackball; rolling and twisting a ball at the same time is quite difficult to

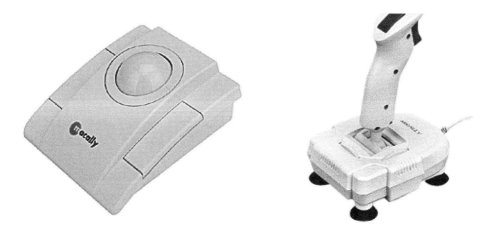

Figure 5.3 Two pointing devices with very different pragmatics. A trackball affords rolling in multiple directions; a joystick affords pushing in a desired direction with varying degrees of force.

execute. The joystick is a better choice for the more complex task, because pushing and twisting motions are easy to combine.

TRADEOFF 5.7

Physical movements that reinforce task goals enhance ease and pleasure, BUT
actions most natural for individual task goals may combine poorly or conflict.

5.3.2 Feedback and Undo

One of the most crucial elements of interaction design is **feedback**—the system-
generated information that lets users know that their input is being processed or
that a result has been produced. If people cannot see how fast they are moving
in a space, they cannot adjust their speed to increase accuracy. If they cannot
see that a target has been selected, they will not know to manipulate it. If they
cannot see what text they have typed, they will not be able to detect and correct
mistakes.

The need for feedback is obvious, yet from a software construction perspective, it is easy to ignore: Tracking and reacting to low-level actions require significant testing and code development, so user interface developers may be tempted
to minimize their attention to such details. One important responsibility of
usability engineers is to make sure that this does not happen.

Of course, constant and complete feedback is an idealization. Every bit of
feedback requires computation; input events must be handled, and display
updates calculated and rendered (Tradeoff 5.8). As feedback events become more
frequent, or as the updates become more complex, system responsiveness will
deteriorate. Thus, a challenge for interaction design is determining which aspects
of an action sequence are most dependent on feedback, and what level of accuracy is adequate at these points (Johnson 2000).

TRADEOFF 5.8

Immediate and continuing feedback during execution helps to track progress and
adjust behavior, BUT frequent or elaborate updates can introduce irritating delays.

An example is window manipulation—early systems animated the movement or resizing of the entire window contents as feedback. However, this made
the interactions sluggish. Modern windowing systems demonstrate that a sim-

ple frame is sufficient in most cases to convey size or location changes. (As an exercise, see if you can think of cases where this would not be a good solution.)

Designing task-appropriate feedback requires a careful analysis of a task's physical demands. Speed and accuracy trade off in motor behavior: A task that must be done quickly will be done less accurately (Fitts & Posner 1967). Thus, dynamic feedback is important for a sequence of actions that must be carried out rapidly. Similarly, if accuracy has high priority (e.g., positioning a medical instrument under computer control, or deleting a data archive), extensive and accurate feedback should be provided.

Even with high-quality feedback, execution errors will be made. Frequent action sequences will be overlearned and automated; automated sequences may then intrude on less frequent but similar behaviors. Time and accuracy of pointing depend on target size and distance (**Fitts's Law**; Fitts 1954; Fitts & Peterson 1964). Thus, from a performance perspective, an information design should make objects as large as possible and as close as possible to the current pointer location. But this is not always feasible, and pointing latency and accuracy will suffer. Users also make anticipatory errors—for example, pressing `Delete` before verifying that the right object is selected. And, of course, many execution errors have nothing to do with motor performance, but rather result from distraction or lapses of concentration, as when a user mistakenly presses `Cancel` instead of `Save` at the end of an extensive editing session (see "Designing for Errors" sidebar).

Sometimes execution errors are easy to correct. A mistyped character is easily deleted and replaced with another. In a direct-manipulation system, a mouse that overshoots its target can quickly be adjusted and clicked again. But when errors result in substantial changes to task data, the opportunity to reverse the action—i.e., to undo—is essential. Indeed, this is a key advantage afforded by work within a digital (versus real world) task environment: If the system is designed correctly, we can say "oops, that isn't what I meant to do," with very little cost in time or energy.

Although some degree of reversibility is needed in interactive systems, many issues arise in the design of undo schemes (Tradeoff 5.9). It is not always possible to anticipate which goal a user wants to reverse—for example, during paragraph editing, do users want to undo the last character typed, the last menu command, or all revisions to the paragraph so far? Another concern is undo history, the length of the sequence that can be reversed. A third is the status of the `Undo` command: Can it also be undone and, if so, how is this interpreted? Most interactive systems support a restricted undo; users can reverse simple events involving data input (i.e., typing or menu choices) but not more significant events (e.g., saving or copying a file). Undo is often paired with Redo, a special function provided just for reversing undo events.

TRADEOFF 5.9

Easy reversibility of actions aids confidence and encourages speed, BUT users will come to rely on undo and be frustrated when it "undoes" the wrong thing.

Of course, even simple undo schemes will do the wrong thing at times. In Microsoft Word the AutoFormat feature can be used to correct keyboard input as it is typed, such as changing straight quotes to curly quotes. But unbeknownst to most users, these automatic corrections are also added to the undo stack—typing a quote mark causes *two* user actions to be stacked, including the ASCII key code for the straight quote, plus its automatic correction. A request for undo first reverts to a straight quote, a character the user will have never seen while typing!

Feedback and undo are broad issues in user interface design. Although our focus here is on their role in plan execution, feedback contributes to all levels of planning and action. The order summary in an online store helps the buyer make sense of the transaction thus far. Being allowed to go back a step and fix just one problem with the order data will have a big impact on satisfaction. Reminding a user that he or she is about to commit $450 to the order on submission may be irritating at the time, but it forces the important step of verifying an action with important (perhaps not undoable) consequences in the real world.

5.3.3   Optimizing Performance

An obvious design goal for execution is efficiency. Users asked to input long or clumsy sequences of events will make errors, they will take longer, and they will be unhappy. For routine and frequent interactions, time lost to inefficient action sequences may be estimated and valued in hundreds of thousands of dollars (Gray, John, & Atwood 1992). Thus, it should come as no surprise that much work on user interface design and evaluation techniques has focused on performance optimization (Card, Moran, & Newell 1983).

Perhaps the biggest challenge in optimizing performance is the inherent tradeoff between power and ease of learning. In most cases, a command language is more efficient than a graphical user interface (GUI), simply because users can keep their hands in one position (on the keyboard) and refer indirectly to everything in the system. An experienced UNIX system administrator is a classic image of a power user. In a GUI, users point and click to access objects and actions; this takes considerable time and effort, especially when objects or actions are deeply nested. However, a GUI is much easier to learn—users recognize rather than recall the available objects and actions, and careful visual design can create affordances to guide goal selection and plan execution.

Most user interfaces support a combination of graphical and text-based interaction. System objects and actions are presented visually as window contents, buttons and menus, icons, and so on. At the same time, frequent functions may be accessed via **keyboard shortcuts**—keyboard equivalents for one or more levels of menu navigation. Particularly for text-intensive activities such as word processing, such shortcuts have substantial impacts on input efficiency and on satisfaction. Comparable techniques using keystroke+mouse combinations can be equally effective in drawing or other graphics-intensive applications. Simple **macros** that chunk and execute frequent action combinations provide a customizable fast-path mechanism.

Whether or not a user interface includes special actions for optimizing performance, careful attention to a sequence of actions can improve execution efficiency. Consider the design of a menu system. The time to make a menu selection depends on where the menu is relative to the selection pointer, how long it takes to reveal the menu, and how long it takes to find and drag the pointer down to the desired item. A design optimized for efficiency would seek to minimize execution time at all these points (while still maintaining accuracy). For example, a context-sensitive, pop-up menu reduces time to point at and open a menu. Dialog boxes that are organized by usage patterns optimize time to interact with the controls. (See Sears [1993] for detailed discussions of layout appropriateness.)

Providing good **defaults** (choices or input suggested by the system) is another valuable technique for optimizing performance. Dialog boxes display the current values of required settings, but if a setting is optional or has not been specified yet, a most-likely value should be offered. It may not always be possible to guess at a good default (e.g., when users enter personal information for the first time), but even if a partial guess can be made (e.g., that they live in the U.S., or that their travel will take place this month), people will appreciate the input assistance, as long as it is not difficult to reset or replace suggestions that do not match task needs. Defaults also help in planning, by suggesting what is normal behavior at this point in a task.

The problem with optimizing an interface for frequent action sequences is that it is difficult to optimize one execution path without interfering with others (Tradeoff 5.10). More conceptual issues arise as well. For example, ordering menu items by frequency of selection may compete with a task-based rationale (e.g., editing operations versus file manipulation). If a frequently used button on a dialog box is positioned near the starting position of the pointer, the resulting layout may be inconsistent with the visual design program in place. If some menu functions are accessed directly via a cascaded menu tree, while others are accessed by opening and interacting with dialog boxes, inconsistencies in the overall dialog structure can result (e.g., compare `Insert Picture` versus `Insert Object` in Microsoft Word.)

TRADEOFF 5.10

Optimized action paths and good defaults for frequent tasks improve task efficiency, BUT may introduce inconsistencies or intrusion errors into less frequent tasks.

There is no easy solution to these tradeoffs, but working through detailed use scenarios can uncover possible performance issues. For example, the keystrokes of alternate action sequences can be modeled mathematically to compare their efficiency (see, e.g., the keystroke-level model of Card, Moran, & Newell 1980). Current research is aimed at automating this sort of low-level modeling and comparison. For example, Hudson et al. (1999) describe a user interface tool kit in which user input events are recorded by the user interface controls that handle them (e.g., a menu that is opened, or text that is entered into a field). When a usability engineer demonstrates a task, an automatic record of user input can be created and used as the basis of performance modeling.

An important application of performance optimization techniques is users with special needs. A blind user can use a screen reader to hear descriptions of items in a visual display, but careful attention to where and how task objects are displayed can have significant impacts on how long it takes to describe them. Users with motor disabilities can benefit immensely from customization facilities supporting the flexible definition of keyboard macros, speech commands, or other substitutes for tedious pointer-based navigation and selection.

5.4 Science Fair Case Study: Interaction Design

Interaction design continues the design of user interaction details. A fully elaborated interaction scenario should describe user input and system responses in enough detail that it can serve as a partial specification for software design. Interaction design is sometimes referred to as **dialog design**, because it is concerned with the step-by-step exchange between humans and the system. Whereas information design concentrates on what users see and understand, interaction design considers how users will select or manipulate system information.

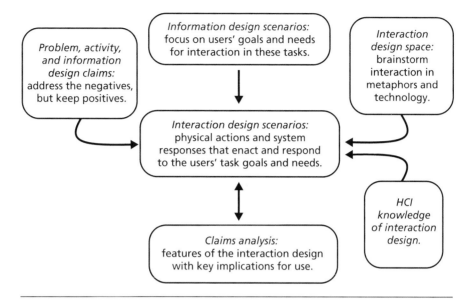

Figure 5.4   Interaction design in scenario-based development.

The activities of interaction design are very similar to those of activity and information design (Figure 5.4). The interaction design space is explored, knowledge of HCI interaction principles and tradeoffs is applied, and the information design scenarios are elaborated to specify the details of user interaction. Throughout, the analysis and discussion of claims guides designers' attention to particularly important aspects of the user experience.

As we move on to interaction design, remember that in real-world projects this phase of design would be tightly interleaved with activity and information design. Designers explore functionality in activity scenarios, and then refine and test their ideas by generating information and interaction scenarios. Information and interaction design are necessarily interdependent—the interactions possible with a system are determined by the information the design presents.

5.4.1   Exploring the Interaction Design Space

Earlier we considered metaphors for basic functionality and for information design; now we turn to the design of interaction techniques for accessing and manipulating science fair objects and actions. Our general metaphor of a physical science fair leads to a direct manipulation style of interaction: Students constructing exhibits might work with "piles" of materials; they "grab" and "tack up" the documents to their exhibit. People visiting an exhibit first "scan" the room and then "walk over" to an exhibit; when they want to see details, they "lean in" to an exhibit.

Other metaphors suggest different ideas about the interaction design space (again for simplicity we limit ourselves to the metaphors already explored in Chapters 3 and 4; see Table 5.2). The metaphors for viewing exhibits suggest a virtual-book style of interaction on the one hand (open to and turning pages, reading one page at a time), and a movie or slide show on the other. The visit metaphors point to a range of interaction possibilities—handwriting recognition for notes, auditory or video stream output, and gesture recognition for greetings or other social behaviors.

Table 5.2 Metaphors for a virtual science fair, with emphasis on interaction design.

VSF Interaction	Real-World Metaphor	Ideas about VSF Interaction Design
Viewing an exhibit is like . . .	Lab journal	Open to a page, read whole page, turn page to continue
	Documentary	Buttons to start/stop play; pause or replay if desired
Coaching a student is like . . .	Peer (colleague)	Video or audio for two-way conversation, face-to-face
	Director	One-way commentary, seizing control of the interaction
Visiting the fair is like . . .	Study room	Gesture or character recognition as notes are written by hand
	Public lecture	Constant stream of auditory and/or visual output
	Cocktail party	Walking in a door, waving at friends, shaking hands
Filling out judging form is like . . .	Balance sheet	Type into fields, add up numbers for tallies
	Discussion	Raise hand, add comment in place, take turns commenting
Creating a fair summary is like . . .	Report card	Select category, enter numeric or symbolic value
	Guided tour	Point at objects, type or speak related comment, move on
	Thank-you note	Add recipient and address to default content, write signature

Once more we complement the exploration of real-world metaphors with ideas suggested by the current set of MOOsburg tools (Table 5.3). Often the two sources are complementary—for example, it is easy to imagine using an electronic blackboard to take informal notes encoded through handwriting recognition. This pairing leads to further ideas about input devices: A mouse is a poor device for drawing gestures or characters, so if we choose this style of interaction we may want to support a pen or stylus. Raising hands or waving an arm implies that users will have input sensors on their hands or arms; we might instead consider a more symbolic alternative, perhaps a schematized "wiggle" or vibration

Table 5.3 Ideas about interaction design suggested by current MOOsburg tools.

VSF Interaction	MOOsburg Technology	Ideas about VSF Interaction Design
Viewing an exhibit is like . . .	Multimedia notebook	Chose a page, scroll up and down to view elements
	Electronic whiteboard	View entire board or magnify portions by zooming
	Web pages	View one page at a time, click on links to see related pages
Coaching a student is like . . .	Email	Identify recipient and address, then type message
	Threaded discussion	Select comment, then choose "reply" and type response
	Chat	Type characters at any time, press "send" to submit
Visiting the fair is like . . .	Room panorama	Rotate to view all, approach and grab objects, post notes
	Interactive map	Find locations of interest, click to move to new location
Filling out a judging form is like . . .	Voting booth	Select and read question, click on button to enter vote
	Threaded discussion	Go to student thread, read, reply to comments, enter new comment
Creating a fair summary is like . . .	Charting package	Enter and select categories and numbers, choose chart type
	Multimedia notebook	Create a page, type characters, use menus to import images
	Interactive map	Click at location on map, add summary object, repeat

made by the visual representation of participants in a room. As always, the intent here is not to settle on the right or wrong techniques but to explore a space of possibilities.

5.4.2   Interaction Scenarios and Claims

The information scenarios in Chapter 4 described how task objects and actions might be presented in the science fair, and how these elements could be organized into groups and higher-level information models. Design issues revolved around how users would perceive, interpret, and make sense of what they saw in the online displays (the Gulf of Evaluation). We turn now to questions of action: how do users choose a goal to pursue? How do they pursue their goals? How do the system's user interface controls influence the success and satisfaction of their efforts?

At this point in the usability engineering process, we have deliberately narrowed our coverage of the case study. Figures 5.5 and 5.6 show just two interaction scenarios—Mr. King coaching Sally, and Alicia and Delia visiting the fair. These two scenarios cover several central stakeholders and activities; between them they touch on a large portion of the overall design. They are complex enough to illustrate the techniques we use for interaction design. And, by restricting the example in this way, we are able to present a full scenario narrative. Remember that narratives such as this are a cumulative end product of the three design subphases; along with the claims, screen designs, and other supporting documents, they serve as the design specification used for prototyping and usability testing (Chapters 6 and 7).

It is impossible to account for every idea in a design; sometimes features are introduced because someone on the design team wants it that way, or everyone agrees that it seems the right thing to do. As we developed specific ideas about user actions and science fair responses, we analyzed the usability implications as claims. Not surprisingly, many of the interaction concerns are related to issues raised during activity and information design (see Table 3.3 and Figure 4.14). Several of these open issues included:

- dealing with the potential complexity and diversity of individual exhibits;
- helping visitors feel welcome and comfortable as they join ongoing activities; and
- encouraging more intensive, interactive exploration of exhibit contents.

By the time interaction design takes place, many constraints are in place. For example, we decided earlier to address the complexity of Sally's exhibit with nested components. When we thought through people's interaction with such

2) Mr. King coaches Sally on her project.

(Background on Mr. King, his experience and expectations about working with Sally) During his lunch period, Mr. King logs onto the VSF. Sally's project opens automatically, because that is how he last left MOOsburg. He opens her calendar by selecting Calendar in the Construction menu. It displays the current week, and he can see that she grayed out all the afternoon hours. He presses the Request button and types a brief message: "Can we work starting at 8 PM?" A feedback message confirms that an appointment request has been emailed to Sally Harris. When he checks at home after dinner, he has email from Sally agreeing to the request, so he goes back to the VSF.

Mr. King can see that Sally is already there when he arrives: The Current Visitors list shows her name. When he arrives, his name is added and flashes briefly in red, so Sally notices him arrive and greets him with a chat message. He quickly notes that she has already added several new items—a title page (which is displayed by default in the main view) and a slide show. He selects her name in the Visitors list, and then uses Control+I to see what she is viewing. The miniature window titled Slide Show flashes in red, so he figures she must be working on her slides. Leaving her name selected in the list, he uses Control+F to synchronize his view with hers. His main viewing area updates to display the message, "Slide show being modified." PowerPoint then opens to the side, positioned at the slide she is working on. Mr. King's view of the slides is now controlled by Sally; when she moves to a new slide, so does he. He watches and makes suggestions as she refines the slides, using the text chat.

Sally tells Mr. King that several elements in the template are still empty, but that she has developed most of her material and is about to upload it. Because he is still synchronized with her, he is able to watch this process. She selects a template icon, then selects Get File from the Construction menu. A familiar file-browsing dialog box appears, and he watches as she selects the files from her PC and then presses the Upload button. After each upload, the miniaturized window updates and flashes in red briefly.

Mr. King recognizes the Data Analysis file as an Excel document. Curious, he wonders if he can get to the actual data or if this is just a results presentation. He is unable to open it and is confused for a minute, but then realizes that he is still synchronized with Sally. He quickly presses Control+F to leave this mode, and then double-clicks the Excel icon. As he expected, Excel opens to the side, and he can edit the charted data. He plays with it a bit and is relieved to see that while he can edit the chart inside Excel, he is not allowed to Save changes to Sally's exhibit.

As they work, Mr. King begins to get concerned that Sally is bringing in too much material. She has filled in all the template elements, and added several unique ones of her own,

(continued)

Figure 5.5   Fully detailed interaction scenario describing the coaching activity.

Figure 5.5 *(continued)*

including an Authorware star-model simulation. He types a message reminding her that visitors and judges do not have unlimited time, and need a good first impression. She agrees and they chat for a bit about which of the extra icons really work as part of the overview.

He tries out the simulation. When he selects the icon, he is shown an animated demo in the main view. But then he opens it with a double-click and plays around with it. This time he sees that Sally has allowed him to save his work as a new file. He advises Sally that this could be bad for the exhibit, crowding the display. She agrees, but thinks the visitor experimentation is one of her innovations and will win points with the judges.

Mr. King wants to help with this, so while Sally goes back to refine her title page, he explores the Construction menu; Nested Components looks promising. It is grayed out until he selects an exhibit component, but then he sees a dialog box that prompts uploading of material into a "back layer" of the selected component. He tells Sally about this, and they decide to create and nest a Visitor Experiments folder to hold visitors' contributions.

---

3) Alicia and Delia go to the science fair.

(Background on Alicia, her attitudes about science fairs, motivations regarding Delia, and so on.) Delia calls her mom over to see an email reminder about the virtual science fair. She points to the underlined text and says that it's a URL and they can go right now if she wants. So they do.

When they arrive, Alicia sees that they are in MOOsburg (she has recently worked with some Tech grad students to create a site for her store). She recognizes the layout—a main view in the top, a map in the lower right with a green dot indicating their position, various icons placed around in the view, and a chat tool in the lower left. But the map is not of Blacksburg as usual; after looking for a moment, she recognizes the floor plan of the high school, and shows Delia the main office where she worked for a while. She can see by the green dot that the VSF is located in the high school gym; the panorama photo in the main view reinforces this, and she even sees the bleachers to the side.

There are lots of objects in the main view. A banner on the back wall welcomes them, thanks the organizers, and announces that judging will be on Thursday. They see other visitors—Alicia explains to Delia that some of them have custom icons because they have edited their personal profiles. Delia and she show up as the default "middle-school girl"

Figure 5.6   Fully detailed interaction scenario describing the visiting activity.

icon because Delia has never changed this part of her profile. Their icon flashes red briefly, which Delia finds a bit embarrassing; she hates to be noticed in a crowd.

There are also a number of objects that Alicia and Delia infer are exhibits: They all have the same icon, a miniature board with graphics; Alicia sees her neighbor Jeff Smith's name underneath one. Delia points to some black and yellow flags across some of the exhibits, suggesting that these must be "under construction."

Delia starts to open an exhibit in the middle with lots of people around it, but then Alicia notices her friend Marge. She tries the technique she has used elsewhere in MOOsburg, selecting Marge's icon and then using "Control+I" to see if she is working with anything. An exhibit with the label "Sally Harris" flashes briefly in red, so they decide to open this one instead.

The exhibit appears in a separate window. Like the VSF itself, it has a main view that is currently showing Sally's title page, "Black Holes: Magnets of the Universe!" In place of the map in the lower left, Alicia sees a group of what appear to be miniature windows. The one labeled "Title Page" is currently selected, and when she selects "Abstract," the main view updates its content to show a brief paragraph introducing the exhibit. There is a list of visitors to the left, a list of exhibit tools, and a chat window. As before, Delia's name flashes in red for a few seconds when they arrive, and Marge and Sally pause their conversation to say hi.

Alicia and Delia don't want to interrupt, so they explore the other exhibit elements. Alicia is impressed when Delia recognizes the Excel file, opens it, and starts playing around with Sally's data; she didn't realize until now how much computer software Delia has been learning about in science classes. When they start up the slide show, they hear Sally's voice-over explaining key points.

Delia notices an FAQ board as part of the exhibit. By now she is very comfortable with the little windows, so she double-clicks to open it on the side. She sees that questions have people's names attached; in fact she discovers a question left by her friend Martin. She elaborates on his question and is a bit surprised when the VSF tells her that he has been sent a notice of the updated discussion—now he is sure to tease her in school tomorrow!

Alicia is curious about something labeled "Star Model." When she clicks on it, they see an animation of a black hole gradually sucking in surrounding stars. They wonder whether this element is also interactive like the Excel file, so they double-click. Sure enough, a separate window opens to the side, displaying Sally's simulation model, along with suggestions about experiments, and a folder of earlier experiments. When they select one created by Martin, yet another window opens and shows Martin's animation. They don't have time to make their own right now. But Delia thinks this is neat, so she plans to come back later with her friend Heather.

material, we considered the idea of showing the nested element in the main view, effectively replacing the context provided by the parent. But because this would remove the task context provided by the parent window, we decided to use secondary windows for nested elements. We documented the negative impacts of this decision (increased complexity in window management) in a claim (Table 5.4).

Table 5.4   Claims analyzing important features of science fair interaction.

Scenario Feature	Possible Pros (+) or Cons (–) of the Feature
Using Control+I to find out what a co-present user is working with	+ ties information about people directly to their representation on the display + simplifies the screen display by hiding activity information cues − but this conflicts with the real-world strategy of just looking around − but not all users will know how to find out about others' activities − but it may be difficult to integrate awareness information about multiple people
Using Control+F to link and unlink user views	+ ties person following directly to his/her representation on the display + sets up a symmetrical on-off following "mode" + minimizes the likelihood of accidentally entering the linked mode − but not all users will know about this special Control key command
Highlighting and flashing a new arrival's name	+ encourages current participants to notice and welcome arrivals + suggests to the arrivals that their presence and participation are desired − but some arrivals may be embarrassed by the personal attention − but current participants may be distracted from ongoing activities
File-browsing dialog boxes for uploading of material from the workstation	+ builds on familiarity with conventional client-server applications + emphasizes a view of exhibits as an integration of other work − but the status of these personal files within the VSF may be unclear
Double-clicking to open the application associated with an exhibit component	+ builds on people's familiarity with conventional desktop applications − but people may be confused about the status of the opened application

The title page as the default view on opening an exhibit	+ encourages students to develop a flashy, engaging overview graphic
	+ gives casual visitors an engaging view with low cognitive demand
	− but may orient exhibitors and visitors too much to a single graphical view
	− but it may be hard to create an engaging but simple view for some projects
Viewing exhibit elements by selecting its miniature view	+ leverages experience with radio-button selection mechanisms
	+ simplifies a quick browse by "poking" one icon after another
	− but requires viewers to alternate attention from main window to controls
Viewing nested material by opening and making selections from its parent object	+ emphasizes that this is a secondary component
	+ ensures that users will create a context for interpreting the nested material
	− but conflicts with the normal "poke-and-view" mechanism
	− but requires several extra keystrokes to access this material
Opening nested exhibit elements as separate windows	+ maintains the initial activity context as background
	+ increases flexibility and pursuit of parallel activities
	− but requires more attention to window management

Visitors arriving at the science fair are welcomed implicitly by the appearance of their personal icon (their **avatar**) in the main view. Our elaboration of this reinforces the connection to MOOsburg, suggesting that some visitors appear with custom photos as icons, while others arrive in a more generic form. This gives special recognition to people who have more regular involvement. At the same time, we were inspired by the cocktail party metaphor, and wanted to provide a more visible welcoming event. We decided to briefly flash an arriving visitor's icon (or name at an exhibit), thinking that this would attract attention and prompt hellos from other visitors. We added this feature despite its obvious tradeoffs (distraction or possible embarrassment), because it is consistent with our root concept of increasing community interaction.

At the same time, we wanted to promote awareness of other people's activity. We learned from the science fair studies that visitors often treat the science fair as a social event; indeed, the visit scenario was designed to explore this. As an example of this opportunistic goal, Alicia wants to find out what Marge is doing. The science fair display is already crowded with people and object icons, and we did not want to make it even more complex by adding person-specific activity cues. We decided instead to implement this as a query, even though this departs from the real-world metaphor of looking around to see what is happening.

Adding this special key command prompted us to look for other opportunities with similar needs. For example, we elected to support a view-synchronization function (allowing Mr. King to watch Sally work) with a similar technique. An important piece of the rationale for both of these cases is that these services are not required for basic interaction at the VSF, so it is less costly to "hide" them in special Control key commands.

To explore the issue of increased interaction with the science exhibits, we described detailed interaction with the miniature windows. We considered both simple selection, where the miniatures work somewhat like radio buttons, and activation, where they open the source application for further exploration. We imagined how a young student like Delia might react to Sally's Excel analysis, persuading ourselves that she might have enough computer background to benefit from a live spreadsheet. At the same time, we addressed Mr. King's concern about data protection by specifying that there will be a read-only mode.

As in previous chapters, many of the interaction design claims are related to the general tradeoffs discussed in the first half of this chapter. For example, we addressed issues related to pursuit of opportunistic goals (Tradeoff 5.3), decomposition of complex activities (Tradeoff 5.5), opening related activities as independent execution threads (Tradeoff 5.6), and choosing default displays and selections (Tradeoff 5.10). These tradeoffs were not applied directly to generate the design ideas or the claims, but rather they helped us to direct our attention to common HCI concerns.

5.4.3   Refining the Interaction Scenarios

Adding interaction details to the design scenarios gives them a more concrete feeling. It is almost possible to imagine the actors stepping through the activities. Of course, it is still necessary to infer some of the very specific details (e.g., what it feels like to double-click on an icon, or what it means to make selections in a dialog box), but these primitive actions are easy to imagine for anyone who has a general familiarity with interactive computer systems.

However, even though these scenarios in Figures 5.5 and 5.6 are quite elaborate, the low-level details about selection techniques and input events must still be decided. Many of these details will not be addressed until an interactive prototype is constructed (Chapter 6); the software platform or user interface toolkit will predetermine many such decisions. But in parallel with development of the interaction design narratives, careful consideration should be directed to the available options for input and output devices and user interface controls.

Detailed Design

To implement an interaction scenario, the system's input and output devices must be specified. It is not enough to say that Alicia clicks on a map; this clicking action must be mapped to a particular device, cursor image, and so on. Different devices have different implications for physical behavior (recall Table 5.1). The interaction designers should carefully examine the devices supported by the selected development platform (indeed, sometimes such concerns will help determine the appropriate platform). For the virtual science fair, we simply adopted the default input and output mechanisms used in MOOsburg—a mouse for pointing and selection, keyboard for text input, and a single screen for output—although we may eventually support speech input and output.

Another aspect of detailed design addresses the user interface controls (often called **widgets**). In the science fair project, many of these details were fixed by the Java user interface libraries used by MOOsburg (Isenhour, Rosson, & Carroll, in press). However, we ask the questions in Table 5.5 to think about user actions and feedback. For example, MOOsburg displays generic system menus (e.g.,File) in a fixed menu bar, but context-specific menus (e.g., for moving or opening an exhibit) appear as pop-up menus near the selected object. This emphasizes the connection between selected objects and their behaviors, and reduces the execution time for evoking the object-specific functions. However, the technique hides initial view of the options, and requires the infrequent behavior of clicking the right mouse button. Because of this we reversed the "right click for options" convention and displayed the options in response to the left click normally used for object selection.

Interaction Storyboards

SBD adapts Wirfs-Brock's notion of **user-system conversations** (Wirfs-Brock 1995) to examine short interaction sequences in depth. Wirfs-Brock uses this technique to elaborate use cases in object-oriented design—a user interaction is modeled as a two-sided conversation, with the user's input events making up one side, and the system response the other. A point-by-point analysis of this sort can help to force out otherwise hidden issues.

Wirfs-Brock generates textual descriptions for each side of the conversation. We used instead a simple sketch of the screen at each point during the dialog, annotated with information about what the user sees and does. The result is a

Table 5.5   Questions used to raise user action and feedback concerns about user-interface input devices and controls.

UI Control	Sample Questions about Specific Interaction Mechanisms
Pointing/selection	How many pointer shapes are available? What is the relation between pointer and insertion point? What keys can be used to position the pointer and how? What selection shortcuts are available, and how do these vary across tasks?
Menus	How are they opened? Where do they appear? How are submenus accessed? How are inappropriate items indicated? What shortcuts or fast paths are supported?
Text input field	How is the insertion pointer positioned? How is unacceptable input signaled? How are defaults initialized and removed?
Undo	What is the unit of change? How does it vary across tasks? How far back can you go? What is the undo/redo relationship?
Buttons	How is pressing signaled? How are active and inactive buttons distinguished? What happens when a window is resized?
Icons	How is selection indicated? How does the icon draw itself when its referent is moved or copied? Are multiple images supported and, if so, how?
Dialog boxes	Are they modal or not (or either)? How are they positioned? Can they be repositioned? How is embedding indicated? How is navigation among fields supported? How are defaults set and reset?
Alerts	Where do they appear? Do they include sound? Are they modal? Do they have a time-out mechanism?
Windows	How are they opened and positioned? How are they moved and resized? How are hidden (but active) windows surfaced? What window relationships can be signaled?

rough **storyboard**, a graphical event-by-event enactment of a complex or crucial sequence of user-system interactions. (A storyboard is an example of a low-fidelity prototype; see Chapter 6. Note that we have developed this one in a graphical editor to make it more legible, but often a rough sketch would be sufficient.)

Figure 5.7 shows a storyboard developed during the detailed design of the visit scenario. It does not represent the full narrative, but focuses on a portion of the episode that raised special interaction concerns—the actions on miniature windows that either update the main view or open a separate window to the side

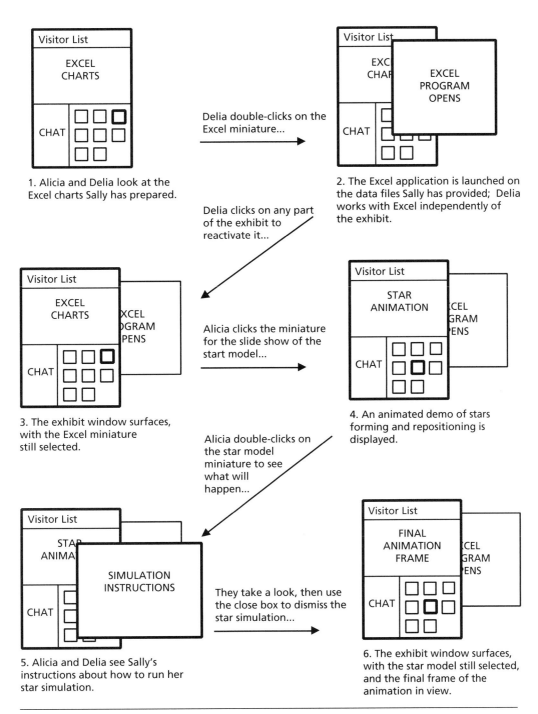

1. Alicia and Delia look at the Excel charts Sally has prepared.

Delia double-clicks on the Excel miniature...

2. The Excel application is launched on the data files Sally has provided; Delia works with Excel independently of the exhibit.

Delia clicks on any part of the exhibit to reactivate it...

3. The exhibit window surfaces, with the Excel miniature still selected.

Alicia clicks the miniature for the slide show of the start model...

4. An animated demo of stars forming and repositioning is displayed.

Alicia double-clicks on the star model miniature to see what will happen...

5. Alicia and Delia see Sally's instructions about how to run her star simulation.

They take a look, then use the close box to dismiss the star simulation...

6. The exhibit window surfaces, with the star model still selected, and the final frame of the animation in view.

Figure 5.7   A simple storyboard sketching interactions with the miniature windows.

of the exhibit. We took the case where there is already an Excel window open to the side and Alicia and Delia go on to explore the star simulation. This level of interaction seemed reasonable in a visit situation, and we wanted to see if the general scheme of view selection and application launching would work.

In Figure 5.7, the dark borders signify the currently active window and controls. The brief episode shows how Alicia and Delia open first the Excel application, work with it overlaid on the exhibit, and then go back to the exhibit and open another source application. At this point, there are three windows on the display: the overall exhibit view, and the two source applications (in fact, there would also be the original science fair view, which we have ignored in this storyboard for simplicity; it would be a second complex window in the background). The complexity would multiply even more if visitors opened more source applications. By walking through the details of this interaction sequence, we obtained a more concrete feel of what it would be like to click on a control to view its content, and to double-click for more extensive interaction. We persuaded ourselves that the two forms of interaction would be distinct for users (single-click versus double-click) and that they offered a natural mapping to the task goals (the more intense action of double-clicking produces a more intense result of activation).

This storyboarding activity also had a pervasive side effect: We decided that clicking on any window that was part of a set (e.g., an exhibit with several secondary windows open) would cause all of the windows in the set to surface together. The related windows provide a context for interpretation, and so they should be managed as a group.

The virtual science fair envisioned to this point has raised many questions that are best addressed through prototyping and user testing. It is not enough for us to convince ourselves that we have made the right decisions—ultimately, the users will decide. For instance, the techniques just described for exhibit viewing and application launching are in need of empirical evaluation; the creation and access of nested components is another good example. In Chapters 6 and 7 we will show how design scenarios and claims are used in prototyping and usability evaluation.

Summary and Review

This chapter has discussed issues relevant in designing interaction sequences for interactive systems. We elaborated the science fair design to demonstrate how interaction issues can be envisioned and discussed. The use of storyboards as a detailed analysis technique was also illustrated. Central points to remember include:

- Norman's Gulf of Execution provides an overarching framework for understanding the planning and execution of interaction sequences.

- Direct-manipulation user interfaces can make system goals and actions obvious, but may do so at the cost of complex visual displays or tedious execution sequences.

- Task decomposition through menu selection is a powerful technique for simplifying and guiding plan development, but can backfire if the decomposition does not match the user's mental model of the task.

- Some user interface errors are true errors (mistakes); others are best understood as slips. Mistakes and slips are unavoidable in user interaction, so designers should anticipate and design for them.

- Giving the user control is important in interaction design, but this may come with an increase in task management (e.g., multiple windows).

- Common interaction sequences should be amenable to optimization through good defaults, fast paths, or custom creation of macros.

- Input devices can vary significantly in their physical affordances (e.g., contrast a mouse to a joystick); understanding and respecting these affordances should be a key aspect of interaction design.

- All systems should support undo sequences, but an effective undo scheme requires an analysis of how users think about their behavior, so that it reverses actions in predictable ways.

- During interaction design, many details will be predetermined by the software packages supporting a development team. These packages should be carefully examined for interaction options and associated effects on planning and execution.

Exercises

1. Use the Gulf of Evaluation and the Gulf of Execution to analyze the task of deleting the oldest three messages in your email list. Start with your Inbox open, then describe:
   - Initial perception, interpretation, and making sense of the display. How does this understanding help you choose a system goal that will achieve your task goal?
   - Your action plan. What steps must you take to achieve the system goal?

- The execution steps. How is the plan implemented?
- System feedback. What responses does the system provide during plan execution that are perceived, interpreted, and understood in terms of progress on the task?

2. Invent two menu systems that you could use to support the tasks of writing a check, determining current balance, and making a deposit into an online checking account. Design one set of menus to match your understanding of these tasks as well as possible, and make the other depart from this understanding in significant ways. Discuss the implications of each set of menus for system use.

3. Step through two different email tasks (e.g., writing a new email, and transferring an email to a folder). For each one, analyze the support for the undo process provided by your email client. Does it reverse your actions in a predictable and natural way? Discuss why or why not.

4. Analyze your computer's file manager with respect to facilitites for optimizing frequent tasks. What techniques does it support? Which of these have you incorporated into your own use? Why or why not? What other techniques should be added?

Project Ideas

Continue your work on the online shopping project by adding interaction details to the information scenarios:

- Discuss the interaction implications of different metaphors, and consider the implications that different input devices might have for your system (it's fine to include devices that don't really exist yet!).

- Elaborate your information scenarios. Choose at least one scenario to present in fully detailed form; for the others, describe the interaction techniques you have envisioned and their effects on goal selection, planning, or execution.

- Select one or two low-level sequences about which you have particular concerns. Analyze these concerns through a more detailed storyboard.

- Document important user interaction tradeoffs in your design through claims analysis.

Recommended Reading

Carroll, J. M., ed. 1991. *Designing Interaction: Psychology at the Human-Computer Interface*. New York: Cambridge University Press.

Greenstein, J. S. 1997. Pointing devices. In *Handbook of Human-Computer Interaction*, 2d ed., eds. M. G. Helander, T. K. Landauer, & P. V. Pradhu, 1317–48. Amsterdam: North-Holland.

Norman, D. A. 1988. *The Psychology of Everyday Things*. New York: Basic Books.

Norman, D. A., & S. W. Draper, eds. 1986. *User Centered System Design: New Perspectives on Human-Computer Interaction*. Hillsdale, NJ: Lawrence Erlbaum Associates.

Shneiderman, B. 1998. *Designing the User Interface: Strategies for Effective Human-Computer Interaction*. 3d ed. Reading, MA: Addison-Wesley.

Prototyping

Two large corporations—a computer company hoping to develop technical expertise in new areas, and a publisher seeking new markets—formed a partnership to develop a multimedia system for university engineering education. The project team was diverse. Most of its members came from the computer company, but they consisted of scientists, programmers, and engineers from many specialty areas, including information retrieval, multimedia systems, human-computer interaction, and artificial intelligence. The team also included one representative from the publishing company and two university professors who served as education consultants.

The envisioned system would make it easy for professors to create multimedia case studies for class activities in which students worked with case study content—individually and in groups—in an open-ended manner, analyzing them and preparing multimedia reports. All communication regarding the assignments (distribution, questions, submission, and evaluation) would take place over a network. The system must be accessible to both teachers and students, although the concrete activities of the two user groups would be quite distinct. A set of instructional modules would be built to demonstrate and test the capabilities of the system. The project required digitization of substantial content—video, text, sound, and images—in support of the example course modules.

The first few months culminated in an all-hands meeting, during which a prototype was to be demonstrated. In fact, two prototypes were demonstrated at this meeting, with rather different objectives. The core team built a rapid prototype in Smalltalk, showing a very basic user interface but including a skeleton for underlying system services. The consultants used an interface scripting language to enact user scenarios. The core team's prototype looked less finished, but was a concrete beginning on an actual implementation, whereas the consultants' prototype looked very finished, but was only designed to focus goals and issues. The project team could not escape the obvious, albeit superficial, competition between the prototypes; the representative from the publishing company (the least technically sophisticated member of the entire team) was clearly beguiled by the consultants' prototype. Tension between the two early visions emerged, with long-lasting impacts on the project (see Carroll 2000 for more discussion).

—⁙—

A logical entailment of iterative design is that prototypes are constructed and evaluated to guide redesign and refinement. A **prototype** is a concrete but partial implementation of a system design. Prototypes may be created to explore many questions during system development—for example, system reliability, bandwidth consumption, or hardware compatibility (Sommerville 1992). A **user interface prototype** is a prototype built to explore usability issues (Wasserman & Shewmake 1982).

Prototypes can be developed in service of many goals—to discover or refine user requirements, inspire or explore design ideas, share or co-develop designs with user participants, make a precise test of specific open issues, and share or deploy early implementation efforts. The most common use of prototypes in usability engineering is to collect usability test data. But as illustrated in the sidebar on page 203, the goals of prototyping are not always clear even within a highly motivated team of experts. The common-sense understanding of prototyping as a way to try out ideas can lead to quite different interpretations and efforts in the minds of different project stakeholders.

There are many options for building user interface prototypes. These techniques vary a great deal in terms of (1) the cost and effort of producing the prototype and (2) the fidelity and generality of the resulting artifact. Table 6.1 lists some of the most common prototyping techniques used in usability engineering practice, ordered roughly by these two dimensions. For example, a team can sketch a series of screens in just a few minutes, but creating a computer-based animation may take days or weeks. On the other hand, the animation will seem more realistic and more impressive.

An important responsibility for usability engineers is choosing an appropriate and cost-effective prototyping technique. This requires a thorough understanding of the goals of the prototype and the resources available for building and then evaluating the prototype.

6.1 Exploring User Requirements

In the early stages of system development, prototypes may be built to explore ideas about new technology, document or analyze current tasks, or share visions of what the future may hold. A prototype is created to illustrate some aspect of

Table 6.1   Common approaches to prototyping in usability engineering.

Type of Prototype	Description
Storyboard	Sketches or screen shots illustrating key points in a usage narrative
Paper or cardboard mock-up	Fabricated devices with simulated controls or display elements
Wizard of Oz	Workstation connected to invisible human assistant who simulates input, output, or processing functionality not yet available
Video prototype	Video recording of persons enacting one or more envisioned tasks
Computer animation	Screen transitions that illustrate a series of input and output events
Scenario machine	Interactive system implementing a specific scenario's event stream
Rapid prototype	Interactive system created with special-purpose prototyping tools
Working partial system	Executable version of a system with a subset of intended functionality

current or future use, and is shared with a group of potential users or other stake-holders. Questions, reactions, and ideas for changes are recorded and used to better understand problems or opportunities.

The fact that a project is in its early stages does not mean that only modest or rough prototypes can be constructed. A company that wants to encourage its clients or employees to "think out of the box" may use high-quality multimedia simulations, or actors role playing a situation to present a vision that is dramatically removed from current practice. One famous example is the *Knowledge Navigator* video created by Apple Computer (Dubberly & Mitch 1987; see "Video Prototyping" sidebar). In this sense, a science fiction movie often includes video prototypes of future interactive system designs.

However, most projects do not have the resources to build a polished vision of future human-computer interactions. Fortunately, less expensive techniques work well for many goals. In the science fair project, we used informal screen sketches to explore information layout possibilities (Figures 4.16 and 4.17). We mocked up a felt board to use in participatory design sessions (Figure 4.19). We also developed summary views of a series of screens, to examine a user interaction sequence that was of particular concern (Figure 5.7). These can all be seen as variants of the **storyboard** technique, where one or more sketched or computer-drawn pictures are used to explore a specific scenario.

The choice of prototyping technique must take into account the goals and resources of the project team, the audience, and the manner in which it will be presented. On the one hand, a business audience of managers, salespeople, or marketing professionals is accustomed to high-quality graphics, so hand-drawn sketches may evoke a poor response. On the other hand, a single sketch or storyboard that is accompanied by a vivid and compelling scenario narration may capture the imagination of such an audience just as well as an expensively produced video or computer animation (Erickson 2000).

The presentation context of the prototype is also a key factor. If the team offers little orienting information, assuming that a prototype will be self-evident, viewers will rely on their own backgrounds and expectations to make sense of it. Someone who is not familiar with technology or prototyping techniques may interpret a simulation of the future as reality, or at least as a feasible project outcome. Unless this is the intended goal, the prototyping team must carefully describe just what the prototype represents and why it is being demonstrated.

Even when sufficient context is provided, a high-quality prototype can have unintended effects (Tradeoff 6.1). A futuristic vision is exciting and can provoke intense discussions of what the system is all about. But it can also cause premature commitment to the details of the vision. To create a convincing vision, the prototyping team must choose and simulate specific user goals, system displays, and input and output episodes. If the result is attractive and persuasive, decision makers may simply conclude that they want what they have seen, and refuse to support the more iterative analysis and design process needed to develop a usable system. Premature commitment can be especially troublesome when the prototype is computer based, because the team may have difficulty explaining how little has really been implemented.

TRADEOFF 6.1

 High-quality graphics and animation can be used to create convincing and exciting prototypes, BUT may also lead to premature commitment.

As a result, usability professionals point to an important role of "roughness" in early analysis and design activities (e.g., sketches or mock-ups; Erickson

1995). A rough prototype is not polished; it is deliberately incomplete and sketchy. As a result, the process of presenting the prototype becomes more central—a hand-drawn sketch or storyboard is too unfinished and ambiguous to stand on its own, so its envisioned use must be conveyed with narratives, role playing, or some other experiential activity. The roughness naturally encourages question and discussion, as viewers notice and attempt to fill in the missing details. The outcome of such activities may depend more on the theatrical or facilitation abilities of the prototype presenter(s) than on its physical qualities.

For projects using participatory design methods, it is even more important to present rough prototypes. Generally, a system's target users or other stakeholders will not have as much computing background as the development team; working from a paper-and-pencil prototype minimizes differences in computer experience and emphasizes instead the importance of domain expertise. Because such prototypes are typically created with common office materials, a broad range of individuals can contribute design ideas directly. This elicits greater participation and increases stakeholders' feeling of ownership and commitment to the project (Muller 1991, 1992; Muller, Wildman, & White 1993).

In the **PICTIVE** method (Plastic Interfaces of Collaborative Technology Initiatives through Video Exploration; Figure 6.1), users and developers work together with concrete design objects that include both general-purpose office materials (post-it notes, paper, highlighters, tape, etc.) and pre-drawn user interface images and controls (menu bars, icons, etc.; Muller 1991). The shared construction of displays from these elements is videotaped for later presentation and discussion of the design results.

A rather different approach is "off-the-shelf" prototyping, where new computer-user situations are approximated with combinations of existing technology (Carroll, Rosson, et al. 1998). For example, a telephone might be used to simulate audio conferencing over the Web, or email folders might be used to simulate a discussion forum. Future users can try out the existing technology to see what it enables in terms of goals and activities; their experiences with these related systems helps them to imagine what a more complete system might provide. Off-the-shelf prototypes can be a relatively inexpensive way to explore usability issues that are hard to appreciate with static materials such as paper and pencil.

6.2 Choosing Among Alternatives

Throughout a project, usability issues that cannot be resolved by discussion or analysis will crop up. If the issue is important, one or more user interface prototypes may be developed to compare alternative solutions. For example, a team designing an online shopping system may be uncertain whether to use

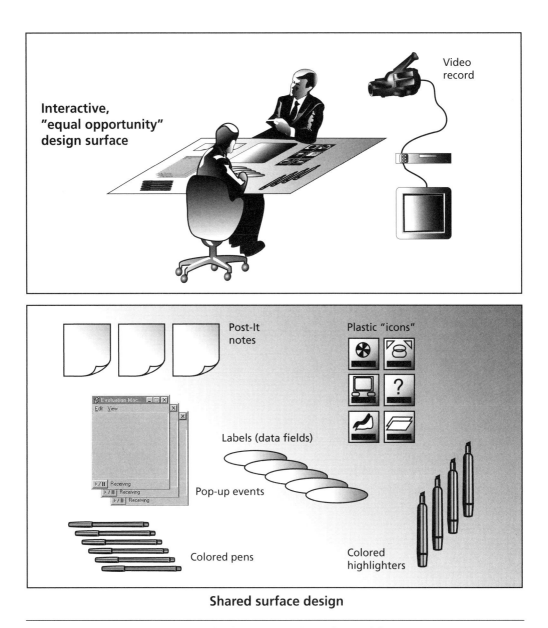

Shared surface design

Figure 6.1   Collaborative work setting (top) and design objects (bottom) for the PICTIVE participatory design method (Muller 1991).

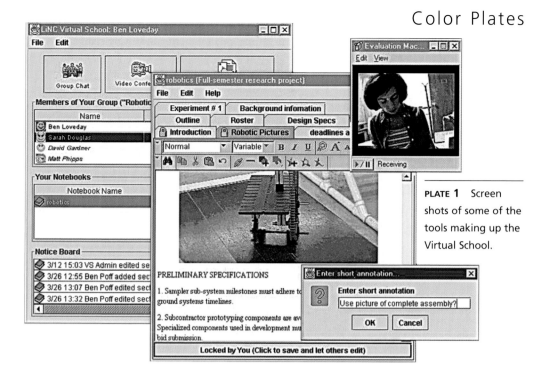

PLATE 1 Screen shots of some of the tools making up the Virtual School.

PLATE 2 The MOOsburg system for community interaction in Blacksburg, Virginia.

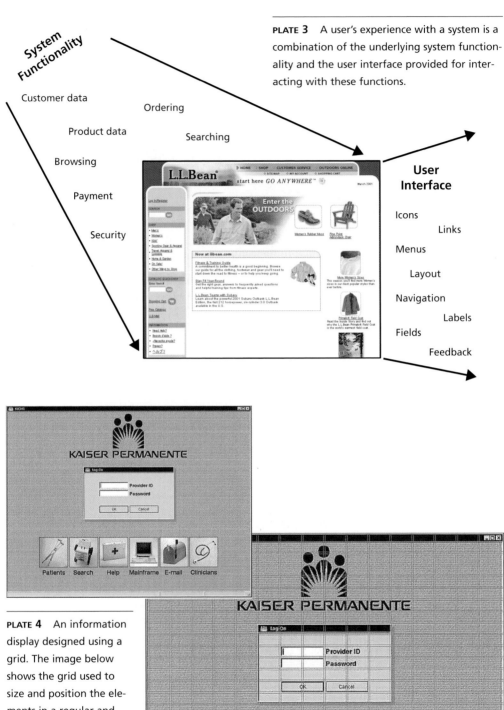

System Functionality

System Functionality

Customer data

Ordering

Product data

Searching

Browsing

Payment

Security

PLATE 3 A user's experience with a system is a combination of the underlying system functionality and the user interface provided for interacting with these functions.

User Interface

Icons

Links

Menus

Layout

Navigation

Labels

Fields

Feedback

PLATE 4 An information display designed using a grid. The image below shows the grid used to size and position the elements in a regular and pleasing fashion.

KAISER PERMANENTE

Provider ID

Password

OK   Cancel

Patients   Search   Help   Mainframe   E-mail   Clinicians

KAISER PERMANENTE

LogOn

Provider ID

Password

OK   Cancel

Patients   Search   Help   Mainframe   E-mail   Clinicians

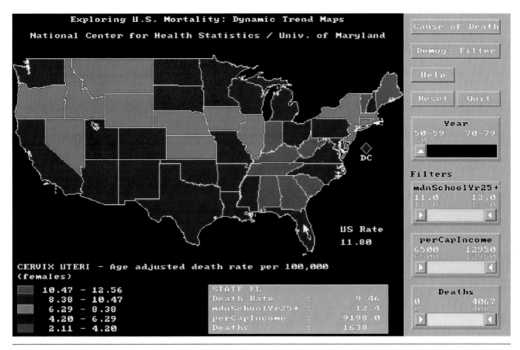

PLATE 5   Visualizing U.S. cancer statistics as a function of state.

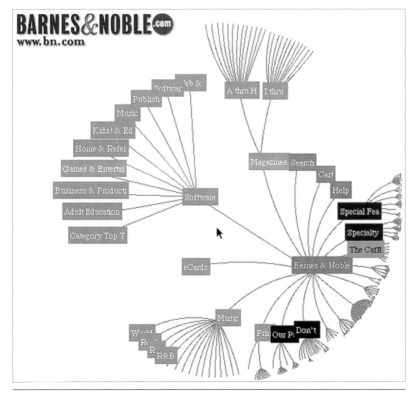

PLATE 6   A hyperbolic browswer (Inxight Tree Studio) used to visualize Web pages from Barnes & Noble (*http://www.inxight.com*).

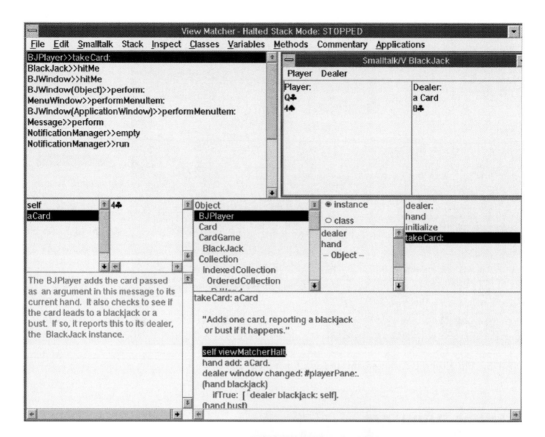

PLATE 7 The View Matcher for learning Smalltalk coordinates five different views of an example application: The application view (upper right), the code view (lower right), the explanation view (lower left), the object inspector view (middle left), and the message stack view (upper left).

PLATE 8 A scenario mock-up developed by a professional artist. The source scenario for this mock-up comes from the Virtual School project described in Chapter 1.

PLATE 9 Screen from scenario mock-up used in participatory design.

PLATE 10 Some of the major tools used in prototyping a user interface with Macromedia Director.

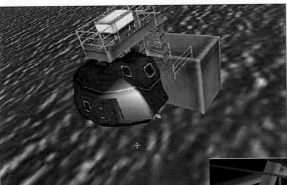

PLATE 11 Sample virtual reality applications: (top) VRML model of a space capsule floating on water, and (right) a molecular structure inside a CAVE.

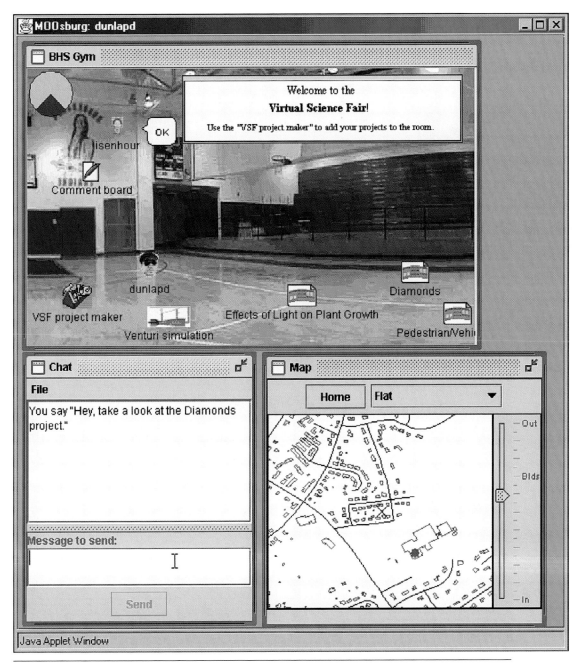

PLATE 12   One prototype of the science fair exhibit space, where each visitor or object is merely presented "in front" of the background.

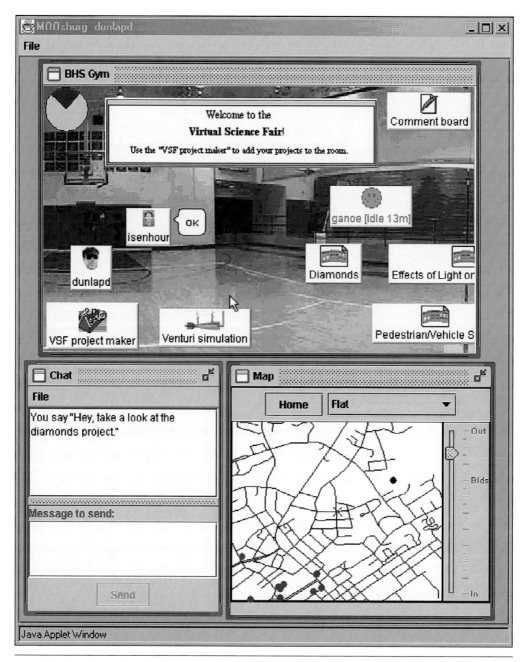

PLATE 13 An alternative prototype of the science fair exhibit space, presenting each icon with a white bounding box.

Video Prototyping

A SunSoft team exploring new-generation user interfaces chose to use video prototyping techniques, because the film medium removes all of the real-world constraints of physical devices, and of input and output processing. At the same time, the team wanted to create a *believable* 10-year vision. The result was the *Starfire* video (Tognazzini 1994): Julie, a product manager for an automobile company, must develop a multimedia presentation for an emergency meeting with her CEO. She has five hours to put together a presentation that would normally take a week to prepare. With the help of technology, the report is constructed and delivered smoothly, including a rapid retrieval of just the right information needed to neutralize an attack by a rival product manager.

Tognazzini reflects on seven guidelines his team followed to make this video prototype visionary but at the same believable:

1. Carefully question how realistic the interaction techniques will appear (e.g., just pointing at something to retrieve it), and be willing to skim over details that would require too much of a leap into the future.

2. Ensure that the vision works, that is, that the actors' goals are achieved. This means being willing to spend the cash to get things right, or to iterate as much as needed.

3. Be sure that something goes *wrong* in the story, because this is what happens in real life (Julie's competing manager has a surprise rebuttal).

4. Avoid impossible hardware designs, especially for input and output devices.

5. Do not eliminate or finesse interaction with computers simply to save money (i.e., it is cheaper to film a video where the actor just talks). Design a believable user interface and then simulate the parts of the interaction that you can afford.

6. Emphasize visibility of the simulated user interactions; a scripted video can reveal more about user interaction than normal observation allows.

7. Include or explore social as well as technical issues; they are an important part of real life and make the vision more engaging.

---

conventional Web pages with interactive forms, or a Java applet with a direct-manipulation interface. A direct-manipulation interface is likely to be more engaging and may promote sales. However, a Java-based solution will take longer to develop. Special-purpose prototypes illustrating the two styles could be tested with users to see how much of a difference the user interface makes.

Not all user interface prototypes are built for usability testing. Suppose the online shopping team is also debating what feedback to provide during the purchase transaction. They want to include enough that buyers can track their progress through the transaction, but not so much that they are slowed down or irritated (Chapter 5). The problem in this case is that network delays will introduce timing uncertainties into the user interaction, making it hard to predict the response-time effects. To better understand the problem, a prototype could execute a scripted interaction over and over, in many different network contexts. The resulting timing data could then be used to predict the delays users would experience.

Prototypes developed to answer specific questions help to set constraints or boundary conditions on a design solution—a user interface designer decides to use Java instead of HTML, or to provide feedback only after a `Submit` request, not during the request construction. However, in order to be confident of test results, the prototype and associated test must be realistic (Tradeoff 6.2): If the Java versus HTML prototypes cannot be used for actual tasks, or if they are evaluated by people more sophisticated than the average Web user, the results will be difficult to interpret. If feedback delays are measured in a limited range of network conditions, or if the simulated dialogs are too simplistic, the timing runs will not be representative. As a result, constructing and testing special-purpose prototypes can be quite expensive, taking resources away from other project activities.

TRADEOFF 6.2

Detailed special-purpose prototypes help to answer specific questions about a design, BUT building a meaningful prototype for each issue is expensive.

Scenario-based reasoning and claims analysis can help in deciding what and when to prototype. Scenarios describe representative users engaged in useful or satisfying activities, so they are an implicit source of information about meaningful test conditions. The associated claims analysis points to open issues in the design; discussing the pros and cons may suggest alternatives that should be evaluated.

6.3   Usability Testing

Usability testing is the core of usability engineering practice: Representative users are asked to interact with system prototypes, and their behavior and subjective reactions are studied (Chapter 7). Prototypes can be used to test all aspects of usability for a system—what users will expect when they encounter parts of the system, how they will go about pursuing their goals, how they will respond to system feedback, and what subjective reactions they will have.

The most convenient prototype for usability testing is an early working version of the system. A working system brings a sense of realism to test tasks—the system has sufficient functionality and user interface features that test participants can behave in a relatively natural and unhindered fashion. Task instructions can be minimal, because evaluators can rely on the system to guide users through the test tasks. Issues associated with overall complexity or internal consistency can be examined, and the measures of satisfaction or irritation that are collected will be much more meaningful.

Unfortunately, waiting for a running version of a system may mean that usability testing must be postponed well into the development process (Tradeoff 6.3). A popular alternative is to build a realistic simulation with rapid prototyping tools (e.g., Visual Basic or Macromedia Director), with the understanding that the prototype is temporary and will be replaced eventually by the real system. A discardable prototype can be an excellent option if the usability professionals already have expertise with an appropriate tool, but if not, building the prototype may become a major implementation effort itself. There is also the risk that a prototype will exhibit enough functionality that the team (or its management) comes to believe that what began as a prototype *is* the final system.

TRADEOFF 6.3

Realistic prototypes increase the validity of user test data, BUT may postpone testing, or require construction of customized (throw-away) prototypes.

Significant user feedback can be collected without an operational system. For example, very early in the design process, a test participant can be given a hypothetical task context, asked to describe his or her initial goal, shown a single display screen, asked for an immediate reaction or interpretation, asked to indicate what action should be taken to pursue the goal, and so on (Carroll & Rosson 1985). The prototype in this case is just a few screens (or even pieces of paper), but it supports collection of valuable information about whether and how the design matches people's expectations and goals (see "Low-Fidelity Prototyping" sidebar). A **scenario machine** prototype is similar, but includes enough programming logic to move participants through a predefined sequence of displays (Carroll & Kay 1985).

More complex arrangements may be necessary when the user interface involves novel input and output, or the system provides computational services that are hard to convey with displays or printed materials. In a **Wizard of Oz** simulation, one or more team members hides in another room. This person

Low-Fidelity Prototyping

Usability engineers often worry that usability tests conducted on special-purpose prototypes will not provide realistic usability evaluation data. As a result, they may choose to delay their evaluation activities until a running version of the system is available. The problem with this is that the test results may come too late in the overall development cycle to have an impact on design.

Virzi, Sokolov, & Karis (1996) argue that usability evaluation of even very rough (what they term low-fidelity) prototypes can provide useful input to redesign activities. For example, during development of an electronic encyclopedia, these researhers compared test users' experiences with a low-fidelity prototype and a high-fidelity prototype.

In this case, the low-fidelity prototype was simply a deck of index cards corresponding to screens in the encyclopedia. In contrast, the high-fidelity prototype was a functional electronic book. The interesting result was that test users detected problems of the same sort (e.g., item selection was difficult and function key positioning was inconsistent) and at the same frequency for both prototypes. Although it is impossible to "prove" a hypothesis of no difference, experiments such as this hold great hope for evaluators seeking inexpensive prototyping methods.

At the same time, Virzi, Sokolov, and Karis emphasize that low-fidelity prototypes are not appropriate for all usability testing needs. For example, if a team has usability concerns related to system performance or the aesthetic characteristics of a visual design, a more realistic prototype is necessary for a meaningful test. The following table lists some of the strengths and weaknesses of low-fidelity prototyping discussed by these researchers.

Advantages and disadvantages of low-fidelity prototypes in usability testing

Advantages	Disadvantages
Faster to create and iterate	Cannot test performance issues
Costs less, smaller impact on resource planning	Cannot assess detailed aesthetic or flow issues
Smaller investment, minimizes resistance to change	Will not engage client or marketing personnel
Demands fewer special skills, increases participation	Cannot be used to guide documentation team
Flexible format, can be customized to situation	Developers may be dismissive or confused
Can be constructed at any point in the process	Scales poorly to large or complex issues

observes a user's input and simulates appropriate output; the simulated output is then displayed as if the computer had generated it (Carroll & Aaronson 1988).

A challenge for Wizard of Oz prototyping is that the "wizard" must behave according to rules that match the actual capabilities, accuracy, and errors of the computer. For example, in Maulsby, Greenberg, and Mander (1993), the wizard attended only to natural language segments that were part of a predefined language model. Depending on the complexity of the service being simulated, considerable preparation and training may be required. The speed with which humans can process and generate information is also an issue—a Wizard of Oz prototype will not be effective for tasks where response time and accuracy are crucial to perceived usability.

Other options include prototypes that present all of the intended functionality of a system, but only at the top level (sometimes called a **horizontal prototype**). For example, a participant may be able to initiate an online shopping order, but not complete it. This can be useful in studying people's high-level goals and action plans. Alternatively, the prototype may implement one or two tasks in full detail (sometimes called a **vertical prototype**); this is most useful when a few tasks are seen as particularly complex or central to the design. If a system has considerable functionality, but little or no error detection, it might be evaluated as a **chauffered prototype**—a well-trained assistant accepts and executes requests on behalf of the actual test participant.

6.4   Evolutionary Development

In some projects, user interface prototypes are a natural byproduct of the overall development process. **Evolutionary development** is an approach to software design and development that moves through analysis, design, development, and testing in a tightly interleaved and incremental fashion. Working prototypes are built as soon as possible in the project, evaluated in some fashion, and the results immediately applied to guide changes. A working version of the system is always available, but is also always being updated to reflect the most recent set of tests and design enhancements.

An evolutionary development process is particularly suitable for exploratory projects, where a team has an open-ended mission and few if any business or pragmatic constraints. In such projects, the first prototype is likely to be small in scope, as the team searches for direction. As ideas are explored and accepted, more functionality is added in an incremental fashion.

Evolutionary methods can be used in more structured projects as well, as long as a series of incremental steps is planned in advance. For example, an e-commerce project plan may include services for buyers, sales personnel, and management. But the team may decide to first prototype the buying functionality, and then add in separate services for the other stakeholders. This simplifies the software development process and enables evaluation of the most business-critical services (i.e., purchasing) first.

The incremental and evolutionary approach to system development has become very popular in recent years, due partially to the explosion of Web-based information services and the accompanying pragmatics of developing systems in "Web time" (Chapter 10). Now that virtually anyone can prototype and publish a flashy Web page over a weekend, the pressure to quickly develop new and intriguing network applications, or to add new features to existing services, is a strong nonfunctional requirement. High-level software technology such as HTML and XML support rapid development; software engineers are developing methods designed to produce systems quickly but also with a high degree of accuracy (Beck 1999).

If a prototype is built as soon as an idea is proposed, feedback about its usefulness and feasibility can be obtained immediately. However, there are disadvantages to doing this (Tradeoff 6.4). If the idea is a good one (and sometimes even if it is not!), the team will accept it and proceed to refine and elaborate. In so doing, they discard other possibilities, or fail to even take the time to search for other ideas. This is the problem of local optimization. Refining an acceptable idea may produce a satisfactory solution, but it may eliminate the analysis, reconceptualization, and radical transformation that could produce an excellent solution.

TRADEOFF 6.4

 Iterative refinement of an implementation enables continual testing and feedback, BUT may discourage consideration of radical transformations.

A related problem is the implicit impact of the code developed during evolutionary development. Suppose a prototype is found to be unacceptable from a user interface perspective (the shopping interactions are extended and awkward), but its basic services are working (the customer does eventually end up with a purchase). If considerable effort has been spent on developing a prototype, it may be very difficult to discard it and redesign the problematic interaction sequences. Teams working under time pressure will find it very painful to follow Fred Brooks's advice to "plan to throw one away," even if they have built a deliberately small and incomplete version.

The decision to discard or radically transform an evolutionary prototype depends to a great extent on the culture and mission of the development group. A team with flexible resources and a commitment to excellence is much more likely make major changes. But such decisions also depend on the software technology in use. For example, a dynamic language such as Smalltalk is designed for rapid iteration and change. Program code can be modified while software is executing; features are typically implemented in a modular fashion so that the rest of the system continues to work as before.

Constant change and iteration are not appropriate for all evolutionary development projects, however. In large and complex projects, it may be necessary to decompose a system into components that are developed by different groups and later integrated. Safety- or security-critical applications typically require careful documentation and monitoring throughout development. Development settings such as these should use a staged process, with each incremental refinement planned and agreed to in advance.

Even for exploratory development projects, constant iteration and change can be dangerous. If there is no overall software architecture in place that constrains the changes made to the code, the software system can quickly become complex, hard to understand, and thus difficult to maintain (Tradeoff 6.5). For systems built to serve a short-term purpose, this may be acceptable, but software that will be maintained and enhanced over time needs a coherent and extensible design (Meyer 1988).

TRADEOFF 6.5

 Dynamic environments encourage experimentation and change, BUT many small design changes may lead to complex software that is difficult to maintain.

6.5   Science Fair Case Study: Prototyping

User interface prototypes are developed for many different purposes throughout system development. Prototyping is a key element of **iterative design**—design ideas are made concrete in a prototype, evaluated (Chapter 7), and modified through redesign.

In SBD, prototypes are built in parallel with writing scenarios. A scenario describes how features of a system contribute to the users' experience; a prototype is a preliminary implementation of a system or its features. However, this does not imply a 1:1 correspondence between scenarios and prototypes. Often only a few features in a scenario are prototyped. Or a prototype may implement features from multiple scenarios; indeed, it may demonstrate features not yet described in a narrative. In general, a prototype is more refined than a scenario, simply because a prototype must take a position on physical details (shape, color, positioning, and so on) that need not be specified in a narrative.

In the science fair project, we created prototypes for a number of purposes. Early in the project, prototypes were used to explore individual design scenarios. The goal was to illustrate what the system might look like at a point in time, or during a short sequence of events. At various points in design, special-purpose prototypes were built to investigate specific usability concerns. Throughout the project, the system itself was developed in an evolutionary fashion within the MOOsburg software framework.

6.5.1   Scenario Mock-ups

The VSF project is a case study in participatory development, in which students, teachers, and community members contributed to activity and interaction design. Many of the participatory sessions used **scenario mock-ups**, which are sketches or drawings created to illustrate the functionality of one or more scenarios. In many cases, these were hand-drawn sketches (Figures 4.16 and 4.17) shared and discussed as we stepped through the actions of a scenario. The felt board used in the participatory design sessions (Figure 4.19) is another example of a scenario mock-up. Mock-ups are often created for novel input or output devices (e.g., a camera, a large wall display), or even for an entire work setting (e.g., an assembly line or a newspaper layout room). The roughness of these prototypes conveys that the design ideas are tentative and that wide-ranging input is needed.

On occasion, mock-ups were created to illustrate a graphic design in a more refined fashion. Figure 6.2 is a science fair screen mocked up in Microsoft Power-Point; it was built to suggest what Sally's exhibit looked like when first opened by Alicia and Delia. A mock-up like this requires more effort to create than the sketches in Chapter 4, and is used to support more detailed evaluation goals. When we created this, we had already developed an activity design for the scenario and were beginning to work out the details of information and interaction design. Our discussions focused on issues such as the miniaturized windows in the lower right, whether the function of these icons would be recognizable, whether the visitor list and chat log were in effective positions, whether color coding participants would be helpful in following the text chat, and so on.

Figure 6.3 presents yet another scenario mock-up; this one was developed by a professional artist using Adobe Photoshop. This is not a scenario from the science fair project; it represents the "Marissa" design scenario written for the Virtual School project described in Chapter 1 (Carroll, Chin, et al. 2000). In this case, the mock-up was created for marketing purposes (we needed to convey a

Figure 6.2 Screen from scenario mock-up used in participatory design.

Figure 6.3   A scenario mock-up developed by a professional artist. The source scenario for this mock-up comes from the Virtual School project described in Chapter 1 (Figure 1.2).

vision for project investors), and thus, visual refinement and appeal were high priorities.

6.5.2   Scenario Machines

A set of screen drawings or images can be used to simulate the flow of a scenario—the evaluators simply step through a series of screen images much like children use flip cards to animate a cartoon. But this can be quite tedious and requires manual intervention. Thus, interaction design issues are often demonstrated or explored with a scenario machine, a software prototype that implements one or more scenarios.

A scenario machine gives a sense of how the overall system will work by demonstrating one or more activities in depth. This approach is sometimes called a vertical prototype, because it builds a relatively complete version of just one part of a system. It can be contrasted with a horizontal prototype, which would include screens for all (or many) functions in a system but elaborate none of the details.

Like any prototype, scenario machines can be built at many levels of quality, with a corresponding variation in production cost. Table 6.2 lists some of the

Table 6.2 Several common user interface prototyping tools, with contrasting strengths and weaknesses.

Sample Tool	Strengths	Weaknesses
Hypertext Markup Language	Declarative tag-based code Many examples available over the Web Runs on different platforms using common Web browsers Graphical editors such as Dreamweaver	Limited user interface display elements and layout options User input restricted to link navigation and text input Processing of text input requires programming in Perl or similar language
Macromedia Director	Flexible support for many visual effects, animation, etc. Easy to simulate mouse-based direct manipulation Simple frame-by-frame script controls temporal behavior	Can be tedious to create and position many individual elements Emphasis is on display and animation rather than on user input and data processing
Microsoft Visual Basic	Extensive library of user interface display and control widgets Drag-and-drop visual editor to create and position visual elements and attach event handlers Good interface with databases and other programming tools	Constrained by existing widgets unless willing to develop new components Code quickly becomes complex and difficult to maintain Requires programming skills

tools commonly used to build user interface prototypes, along with a brief indication of strengths and weaknesses. The simplest approach is to create a computerized version of the cartoonist's flip cards—a sequential set of screens where pressing a button or link on one screen leads to the next. This effect is easy to do in a language like HTML, especially when graphical editing tools such as Macromedia Dreamweaver are available for constructing the pages and links. One problem is that realistic interactions (e.g., processing and responding to a user's input) are difficult to simulate in this paradigm. HTML is also quite limited in its support of display elements and layout procedures.

An alternative is to use a multimedia animation environment such as Macromedia Director. This environment offers much more flexibility and support in defining, positioning, and controlling visual and auditory elements. However, tools such as this are designed to convey a visual impression, not to accept, process, and respond to user input. A visual programming environment (e.g., Microsoft Visual Basic) raises many more possibilities for accepting and processing user input, while simplifying some aspects of prototype development (e.g., creating and positioning user interface controls). But despite the graphical development environment, a language like Visual Basic requires programming skills for effective use.

Figure 6.4 shows a prototype from a science-fair visit scenario, built early in the project in Hypertext Markup Language (HTML). In this scenario, Lucas arrives at the fair, greets Nancy who is already there, and goes with her to the exhibit area in the GYM. If a user clicks on the circle in the GYM area of the floor plan, the upper right frame updates to show a view of the exhibits. If a tool in the objects list is clicked, a second browser is launched to show the tool, and so on. In other words, this "prototype" consists simply of a series of HTML screens organized into frames, with links that can be used to play out a scenario script.

The increasing use of the Web for business, home, and leisure applications has made HTML a popular prototyping language. As a declarative tag language, it is simple to learn; a number of graphical editors are also available for creating HTML code automatically. Another attractive feature is that an HTML prototype can be put on a server and demonstrated virtually anywhere in the world. This was important to us because many of our participatory design sessions took place out in the community (e.g., at the schools and the senior center). However, the user interaction in HTML prototypes is restricted to the simple logic of hyperlinks. Creating dynamic Web pages (e.g., pages that respond in a situation-specific fashion based on user input) requires more conventional programming tools.

Later in the project, we built more sophisticated scenario machines using the Macromedia Director environment. This required somewhat more effort than writing and interconnecting HTML pages, but it also gave us many more

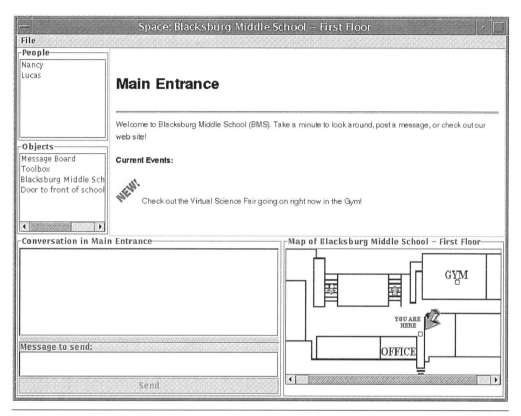

Figure 6.4 A screen from an early HTML-based scenario machine of the visiting scenario.

options for visual effects, such as dynamic feedback that was based on mouse activity. It is also relatively easy to work with individual user interface controls in this environment. Text, images, or other user interface objects can simply be dragged to any position, whereas in HTML it can take significant effort to set up a table as a grid for positioning elements, particularly when they are sized or shaped differently.

Macromedia Director was originally designed for graphical artists and film industry professionals, but has been adopted by many usability engineers as a prototyping tool for visual direct-manipulation interfaces. Nilson Neuschotz (2000) provides an excellent introduction to this tool, using a simple online store as an example.

The tool provides a visual construction environment built around a film metaphor (Figure 6.5). A multimedia system is composed of "cast members" (upper left window). Cast members may be visual objects (e.g., icons or buttons)

Figure 6.5 Some of the major tools used in prototyping a user interface with Macromedia Director.

or they may be behaviors that are assigned to visual objects (e.g., change appearance when the mouse pointer is on top of an icon). Visual cast members are often created with external graphical editors and imported; behaviors are composed from a set of common events and actions (middle left window). For example, an icon might change to one shape when the mouse pointer moves over it, to another when the mouse button is clicked, and so on.

The resulting prototype (called a "movie") is organized into "scenes," which take place on a "stage" (the large window on the right). The scene is enacted under the control of a "script" (lower left), which is simply a time-ordered set of frames. Any logic needed for moving among scenes must be defined as behaviors. The center window in Figure 6.5 shows a behavior that causes the prototype to jump from the "Start" scene to the "Star Model" scene if the mouse is clicked on the miniature of the star model.

Figure 6.5 shows just a small portion of the cast members and behaviors needed to implement an entire scenario (this one is based on Alicia and Delia's visit). For example, only one behavior for the Star Model miniature is visible, and only a few scenes have been created. But even this abbreviated view shows how the number of elements and relationships can quickly become complex.

Code development per se is minimal, which makes Macromedia Director attractive to nonprogrammers wanting to build visual prototypes with some degree of interactivity. The current version includes support for downloading information from Web pages; this means that a prototype can retrieve and respond to data created and maintained by other systems. However, this highly visual programming paradigm does not scale well for systems that use a large set of interactive elements. In the science fair project, most of our prototyping was done in the Java framework built to support MOOsburg (Isenhour, Rosson, & Carroll, in press).

We used scenario machines primarily as visual aids for participatory design discussions. The goal was to illustrate and envision the hypothetical actors' experiences. Note, though, that a prototype of this sort can also be used for more conventional usability evaluation: Instead of bringing a group of stakeholders together to view and discuss a prototype, we could have asked them to enact a specific scenario, and then observed their expectations, actions, and reactions. These findings could then have been used to refine the scenarios and prototypes (Chapter 7).

6.5.3 Prototyping Alternatives

Because the science fair is an application within MOOsburg, we already had a functioning software system that we could use to prototype alternative design proposals. This does not mean that it is easy to build multiple versions of the entire science fair design, but rather that we can easily construct simple prototypes that contrast two or three specific design ideas. Indeed, the philosophy behind MOOsburg is that its users should be able to design and implement their own places in the community network.

One of the tools MOOsburg provides for this is a background editor. This is a specialized version of an electronic whiteboard that is used to create and refine the image used as "wallpaper" at a MOOsburg location. Figure 6.6 shows the background editor being used to create a background for the main view of the science fair. A panoramic image was created by taking a number of exposures at different angles from the center of the high school gymnasium; the set of exposures was then stitched together with a digital camera utility program. The result was imported into the background editor, where we could manipulate its size and add additional information (e.g., the Welcome sign).

The next two screen shots illustrate a simple experiment we then carried out with this science fair view. During information design, we became concerned

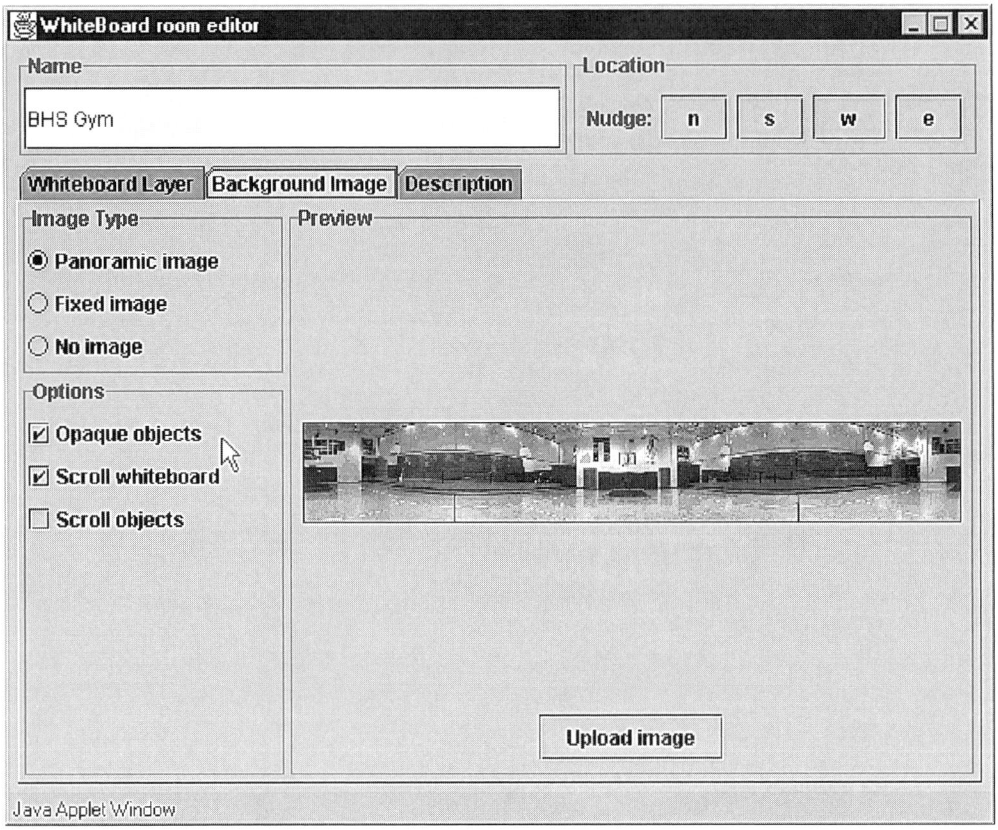

Figure 6.6   The background editor tool built into MOOsburg supports the importing of JPEG or GIF files in combination with simple graphical editing functions. The option "Opaque objects" is selected if the room designer wishes objects held in this room to have a white bounding box around them (see Figure 6.8).

about users' ability to perceive other visitors and objects "in front" of a background. Depending on the background and on the number of objects, the overall view can become crowded and visually complex.

We explored two alternative presentations. The first alternative (Figure 6.7) places each image directly on the background. In the second presentation (Figure 6.8), the objects are "opaque" (the bounding box around the object is filled with white). The two screen shots bring out the design tradeoff between simplifying perception (the opaque objects are easier to detect and interpret) and improving

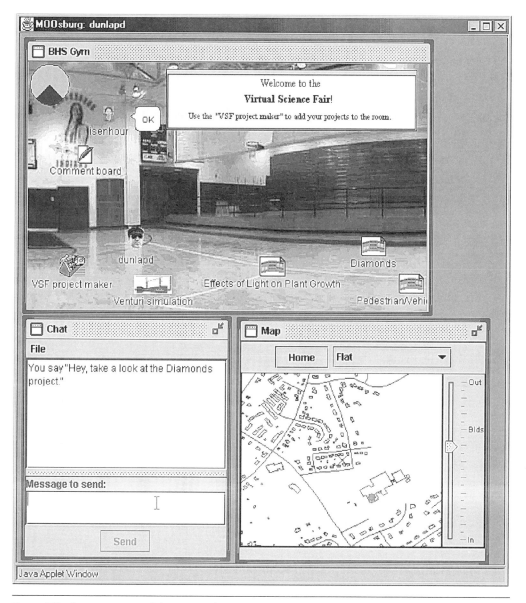

Figure 6.7 One prototype of the science fair exhibit space, where each visitor or object is merely presented "in front" of the background.

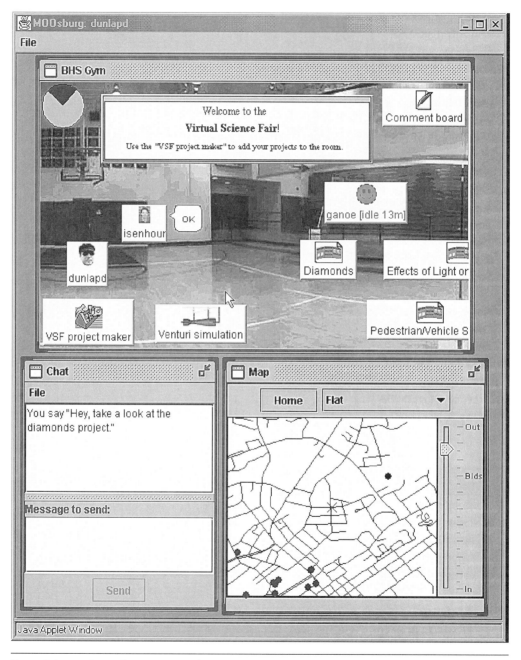

Figure 6.8   An alternative prototype of the science fair exhibit space, presenting each icon with a white bounding box.

visual appearance (they look awkward and unrealistic). Based on a small amount of usability testing, the MOOsburg developers decided that people building rooms should be allowed to choose either of these two display options. The choice of option seems to depends on several variables, such as the number of items in the room, the darkness of the background image, and the likely goals of the visitors.

6.5.4 Evolutionary Development

MOOsburg is a distributed client-server system built in Java (Figure 6.9). It consists of an object database holding a persistent software representation of every place, person, or object in the system. The database is stored on a central server,

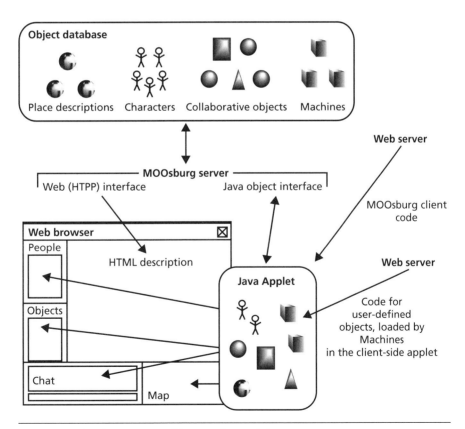

Figure 6.9 The client-server architecture for MOOsburg.

a networked machine that provides copies or descriptions of these objects on request. The server also applies and broadcasts updates to the objects so that all users in MOOsburg interact with the same objects. Requests to the server are made by client software that is executed on each user's workstation. When MOOsburg developers define a new object (e.g., a special message board), they make it available to others through a "machine" that creates instances of the new object.

The MOOsburg user interface is supported by a toolkit written in Java (the Content Object Replication Kit, or CORK; Isenhour, Rosson, & Carroll, in press). Java is an object-oriented language, and the MOOsburg software takes advantage of the abstraction and inheritance capabilities of the Java language. All science fair objects (the exhibit space, individual exhibits, and visitors) are implemented as subclasses (specializations) of a general-purpose class called `BasicObject`. This general-purpose class defines the behavior shared by all objects in the virtual environment: what it means to be created, named, positioned, moved, and so on. Objects that are used collaboratively (e.g., two people at an exhibit) are subclasses of a second abstract class that can process multiple input streams and broadcast resulting updates. Abstract classes such as these simplify the creation of new object types and user interface controls.

The object-oriented architecture of MOOsburg has been a critical enabler of evolutionary development in the science fair project. We can make small changes or enhancements with little effort, and can retract or revise these modifications without a major software redesign. If we did not have a coherent and extensible software framework, changes to the database or to the user interface would be made in an ad hoc fashion, producing unexpected side effects and making it difficult for new developers to understand or maintain the code.

Figure 6.10 demonstrates how MOOsburg classes were used to implement the opaque-object experiment. The figure lists the three central classes used in presenting the view of a place: a `Landmark` is a content object that simply holds the view of the object (its `WhiteBoardContent`) and a list of things currently there (people and other objects). A `WhiteBoardContent` includes a pointer to an image file (if relevant), a list of graphical shapes created, and two Boolean variables that can be either `True` or `False`. This is where the opaqueness option was inserted; the second Boolean variable specifies whether the image is panoramic.

An `InteractiveViewer` manages the actual display and manipulation of a background view. But it delegates much of the work to its `Landmark`, which in turn delegates the work to its own `WhiteBoardContent`. Similarly, the display of the people and objects in the room is delegated to the components responsible for each type of object. This sort of decomposition and delegation is standard in

```
Landmark                                  // Object that defines a place

  WhiteBoardContent content               // Background view of the place

  Thing[] things                          // List of things at the place. This

                                          // includes both objects and characters.

WhiteBoardContent

  URL image                               // The image shown on the background

  WhiteBoardItem[] shapes                 // Shapes drawn using whiteboard tools

  boolean opaqueObjects                   // True if objects should be opaque

  boolean panorama                        // True if image is a panorama photograph

InteractiveViewer                         // GUI component for displaying landmark

  Landmark landmark                       // The place the viewer is displaying

  ThingComponent[] thingComponents        // List of components that display

                                          // Views of Things at the landmark
```

Figure 6.10   Central classes used to implement the view of a location in MOOsburg.

object-oriented design, and provides the flexibility to modify and extend one class without revising code in associated classes.

At the same time, an evolutionary prototyping approach to software development has its own costs. The MOOsburg team has now invested considerable effort in the client-server architecture diagrammed in Figure 6.9, and in building classes such as those summarized in Figure 6.10. Radical changes or extensions to science fair functionality (e.g., objects that are indexed by age or category as well as place) would require a relatively large redevelopment effort. As a result, major refinements of this sort are likely to be ignored, or at best explored in a more limited way with special-purpose prototypes.

Summary and Review

This chapter has explored goals and techniques for building user interface prototypes. An important responsibility of usability engineers is choosing the right approach as a function of the goals and resources of the prototyping effort. Prototyping activities in the science fair project were used to exemplify different approaches to and goals for creating user interface prototypes. Central points to remember include:

- Even very early in a project, sophisticated prototypes can be built using video or computer animations. These create excitement for a project, but if not presented carefully may cause misinterpretation or premature commitment.

- Very rough prototypes (e.g., paper and pencil) can be quite effective in opening up the design space, encouraging analysis and design ideas by diverse stakeholders.

- When used to choose among design alternatives, a prototype should be as realistic as possible, to ensure that the data on which the decision is based will be a valid indicator of what would happen in the real world.

- Usability testing can begin very early in project development, as soon as ideas can be sketched on paper or using a graphics editor.

- The types of usability data that are meaningful depend on the fidelity of the prototype. With low-fidelity prototypes, users can react to screens and make predictions about functionality or controls, but data such as performance times and aesthetic judgments should be obtained with working system prototypes.

- An incremental development process yields ongoing access to prototypes. But because each prototype is a working system version, significant changes to function or user interface may be costly.

Exercises

1. Reread the vignette at the beginning of the chapter. How could a better outcome have been produced? Offer at least two specific suggestions that you believe would have improved the situation. Provide a rationale for each one.

2. Look over the scenario describing Alicia and Delia's visit in Chapter 5 (Figure 5.6). Compare it to the scenario mock-up in Figure 6.2. Make a list of the things that the scenario conveys, but that the screen image does not convey, and vice versa.

3. Develop a set of index cards that could serve as a storyboard for the scenario of Mr. King coaching Sally. On each card, sketch a state of the screen, and then on the back indicate what Mr. King does that moves it to

the next state. When you are done, step through the cards with a friend not familiar with the scenario. Is your friend able to follow what is happening? Discuss what you might do to enrich the experience.

4. The mock-up in Figure 6.2 was created in Microsoft PowerPoint. Create a similar mock-up using an HTML editor. After you are done, discuss the construction process—what was hard to do; what was easy; whether you think this is a good tool for a mock-up of this sort; and why or why not.

Project Ideas

Develop a prototype of your online shopping scenarios:

- Discuss the use of different prototyping methods and what each would contribute to your project; write a prototyping proposal that includes the rationale for the approach you decide to take.

- Implement the prototype.

- Discuss what you have learned by creating the prototype, how your design has been elaborated, and what feedback you are now in a position to obtain.

Recommended Readings

Boutkin, P., D. Poremsky, K. Slovak, & J. Bock. 2000. *Beginning Visual Basic 6 and Application Development*. Birmingham, UK: Wrox Press.

Guzdial, M. 2001. *Squeak: Object-Oriented Design with Multimedia Applications*. Upper Saddle River, NJ: Prentice-Hall.

Lowery, J. 2000. *Dreamweaver 3: Gold Edition*. Indianapolis: Hungry Minds.

Neuschotz, N. 2000. *Introduction to Director and Lingo: Multimedia and Internet Applications*. Upper Saddle River, NJ: Prentice-Hall.

7

Usability
Evaluation

In the mid-1980s, Digital Equipment Corporation was among the first software companies to define methods for usability engineering. During development of the MicroVMS Workstation Software for the VAXstation I, the usability professionals on the team defined a set of measurable user performance objectives to guide the development process. A central benchmark task was designed in which representative users created, manipulated, and printed the contents of windows. The usability objective was to reduce performance time on the benchmark task by 20% between version 1 and version 2 of the system. As development proceeded, measurements of users' performance on several related subtasks were made to identify areas of greatest usability concern in the design of version 1. The usability problems having the largest impacts on performance were used to prioritize changes and guide the redesign of version 2. In the end the team exceeded their objective, improving performance time on the benchmark task by 37%, while staying within the originally allocated development resources. Interestingly, however, measured user satisfaction for version 2 declined by 25% relative to version 1. (See Good, et al. 1986).

⸛⸛⸛

A **usability evaluation** is any analysis or empirical study of the usability of a prototype or system. The goal of the evaluation is to provide feedback in software development, supporting an iterative development process (Carroll & Rosson 1985; Gould & Lewis 1985). Insightful requirements and inspired designs create new possibilities for humans and for their organizations. But there are many ways that goals and plans for new technology can go awry. Despite best efforts and sound practices, the original goals for the system may not in fact be achieved. The system may not be sufficiently useful, it may be too difficult to use or to learn, or using it may not be satisfying. More profoundly, the original project goals may have been successfully achieved, but they may turn out to be the wrong goals. Usability evaluation helps designers recognize that there is a problem, understand the problem and its underlying causes in the software, and plan changes to correct the problem.

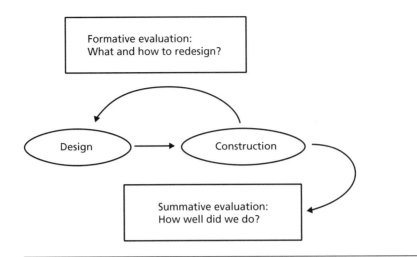

Figure 7.1   Formative and summative evaluation.

Scriven (1967) distinguishes between formative evaluation and summative evaluation (Figure 7.1). **Formative evaluation** takes place *during* the design process. At various points in the development process, prototypes or system versions are produced and evaluated. As discussed in Chapter 6, prototyping can be as simple as sketching out a few screens or as elaborate as defining and implementing a general software architecture. But the goal of formative evaluation is always the same—to identify aspects of a design that can be improved, to set priorities, and in general to provide guidance in *how* to make changes to a design. A typical formative evaluation would be to ask a user to think out loud as he or she attempts a series of realistic tasks with a prototype system.

In contrast, **summative evaluation** is aimed at measures of quality; it is done to assess a design result. A summative evaluation answers questions such as, "Does this system meet its specified goals?" or "Is this system better than its predecessors and competitors?" Summative evaluation is most likely to happen at the end of a development process when the system is tested to see if it has met its usability objectives. However, summative evaluations can also take place at critical points during development to determine how close the system is to meeting its objectives, or to decide whether and how much additional resources to assign to a project. A typical summative evaluation would be to measure performance times and error rates for standard user tasks.

Scriven (1967, p. 54) also describes two general classes of evaluation methods—analytic and empirical (he actually uses the terms "intrinsic" and "payoff"). He makes this distinction with an example:

If you want to evaluate a tool, say an axe, you might study the design of the bit, the weight distribution, the steel alloy used, the grade of hickory in the handle, etc., or you might just study the kind and speed of the cuts it makes in the hands of a good axeman.

In Scriven's example, evaluation of the axe characteristics is an **analytic method**, while studying a good axeman as he uses the tool is an **empirical method**. This distinction is important because analytic and empirical methods are complementary to formative and summative goals. Empirical evaluation produces solid facts, but the facts alone may difficult to interpret. If the axe does not cut well, should we change the bit or the handle? We need to know how and why the axe is supposed to work in order to decide whether its creators failed to implement a good design, or succeeded in implementing a bad design. Analytic evaluation of the axe identifies the characteristics that influence the axeman's performance.

Empirical methods are popular in usability engineering because they involve studies of actual users. The methods can be relatively informal such as observing people while they explore a prototype, or they can be quite formal and systematic, such as a tightly controlled laboratory study of performance times and errors or a comprehensive survey of many users (Table 7.1). But regardless of the care with which the data are collected, the interpretation of empirical results depends on having a good understanding of the system being evaluated.

Analytic methods have their own weaknesses; they produce many interpretations, but no solid facts. A claims analysis identifies features and tradeoffs, and may be used to argue about and assign value judgments. A user model can be built to represent and simulate the mental model a user might build in using an interactive system. A usability inspection considers the extent to which a set of guidelines or design principles have been followed. But the outcomes of analytic work depend very much on the analytic skills and biases of the analyst. Given a user interface to support direct manipulation, a usability inspection may uncover concerns with how direct manipulation has been implemented. The evaluator and the designer can argue about the approach that was taken, but the argument may be difficult to resolve without empirical testing.

How do you choose between analytic and empirical evaluation methods? Scriven (1967) proposes a mixed approach called **mediated evaluation**: Analytic evaluation occurs early and throughout the design process, but the resulting analyses are also used to motivate and develop materials for empirical evaluations. For example, a usability inspection may examine use of guidelines in a product. The potential problem areas discovered by the analysis could then become the focus of a follow-up empirical study. The analytic work both sets up and helps to interpret the empirical evaluation that studies actual use.

Table 7.1 Examples of empirical and analytic usability methods.

Type of Method	Example Methods
Analytic evaluation: Investigations that involve modeling and analysis of a system's features and their implications for use	Claims analysis: system features are analyzed with respect to positive and negative impacts
	Usability inspection: a set of guidelines or an expert's general knowledge is used as a basis for identifying or predicting usability problems
	User models: a representation of the mental structures and activities assumed during use is developed and analyzed for complexity, consistency, and so on.
Empirical evaluation: Investigations that involve observation or other data collection from system users	Controlled experiment: one or more system features are manipulated to see effects on use
	Think-aloud experiment: users think out loud about their goals, plans, and reactions as they work with a system
	Field study: surveys or other types of user feedback are collected from real-world usage settings

7.1   Usability Specifications for Evaluation

Mediated evaluation is a key idea behind **usability specifications** (Carroll & Rosson 1985; Whiteside, Bennett, & Holtzblatt 1988), which are precise and testable statements of the usability characteristics required of a system. The intention is to specify and manage usability goals in parallel with the functional goals for the system. Thus, at every step in the development process, as system functions are designed and specified, their consequences for users and their activities are also analyzed and specified. This parallel specification process ensures that usability concerns will always be considered and assessed as new features are proposed and incorporated into the design. In scenario-based development, the usability specifications are derived directly from design scenarios.

Usability specifications rely on a task analysis similar to the methods of hierarchical task analysis described in Chapter 2. A user interaction scenario describes work activities that are typical, critical, or novel. Task analysis breaks these activities into subtasks that provide a more precise specification of what users are expected to do. For example, a scenario in which a user "searches a digital library for Scriven's article on evaluation" might be analyzed into subtasks such as "accessing the digital library," "initiating the search function," and "specifying search keys for Scriven's article." Decomposing a scenario in this way allows the evaluator to state exactly what a given user should be able to do, and what level of performance and/or satisfaction is expected for each subtask (Table 7.2). The DEC project described in the initial vignette provides concrete evidence that such an approach can guide development (Good, et al. 1986).

A third idea behind usability specifications is that evaluation is iterative. Evaluation is not an isolated stage in the development cycle, but rather an ongoing process. Repeated analytic evaluations determine how the software will support users' needs; they also structure and guide empirical testing. As scenarios become more elaborate during design, so do the subtasks comprising them, and the behavior expected from users carrying out these subtasks.

Table 7.2 Sample usability specifications built to track usability of a scenario involving search for a reference in a digital library.

Digital Library Search Subtask	Usability Outcomes Expected
Accessing the digital library	A user with at least one hour of previous usage experience should be able to access the main page of the digital library in 20 seconds or less, with no errors, and should rate "ease of access" no less than 4 on a 5-point rating scale.
Initiating the search function	A user with at least one hour of previous usage experience should be able to initiate the search dialog from the main page of the digital library in 5 seconds or less, with no errors, and should rate "search availability" no less than 4 on a 5-point rating scale.
Specifying search keys for Scriven's article	A user with at least one hour of previous usage experience should be able to specify search terms that will successfully retrieve the Scriven reference in 30 seconds or less, with one error, and should rate "usefulness of search" no less than 4 on a 5-point rating scale.

As a mediated evaluation technique, usability specifications allow evaluators to address both formative and summative goals. Precise specification of a subtask along with user performance and satisfaction measures enable a test of "how well did we do?" But at the same time, the fact that the subtasks portray an analysis of a design scenario means that evaluators can also determine which features and outcomes are more or less problematic, thus guiding redesign. A test of the subtasks in Table 7.2 might reveal that the first subtask is performed within the time specified, but that users do not consider access to be "easy." This would direct evaluators to explore in more detail how users think about the access process to determine the source of dissatisfaction.

During usability evaluation, new test tasks—derived from scenarios exploring new goals, actors, and settings—are introduced to ensure that the evaluation is as general as possible. Evaluating a system with respect to a single set of design scenarios can lead to local optimization. Similarly, relying on a single evaluation approach can lead usability engineers to miss entire categories of information. Different usability concerns are addressed by different evaluation methods; choices among methods involve tradeoffs in resources required and in the precision and interpretability of evaluation results. In the rest of this chapter, we briefly survey different approaches to analytic and empirical evaluation.

7.2   Analytic Methods

It is not necessary to observe or interview users to evaluate an interactive application. Claims analysis is an analytic method that has been described and illustrated extensively in this book. In this method, the usability engineer identifies significant features in a design and generates hypotheses about the consequences these features might have for users engaged in activities (scenarios). A claims analysis is most often implemented for formative goals to better understand and guide a system's redesign. However, a refined set of claims can be also be used for summative goals—the design rationale provides one view of how well a system meets users' needs.

An important motivation for analytic methods is that they can be used early in a development process, well before there are users or prototypes available for empirical tests. Another motivation is cost: It is often less expensive to analyze a system than to design and carry out an empirical study. As we have seen, analytic evaluation also guides empirical studies by identifying controversial or novel design features. It helps evaluators know what to attend to, what to measure, and what hypotheses to test.

A hazard of analytic evaluation is that designers may feel that *they* are being evaluated. Presumably, the design they produce is their best effort, given organizational constraints. Every problem identified or every downside can be heard as criticism. While such a personal reaction is understandable, it is unprofessional. Colleagues, especially usability engineers, can help designers by promoting a cooperative atmosphere in which the development team as a group explores and refines the design.

7.2.1 Usability Inspection

Usability guidelines have a long tradition in software development. Smith and Mosier (1986) is one classic reference; the book lists many recommendations, examples, and exceptions. For example, one guideline is to "locate and display information and commands consistently." An example of this guideline in use is the predictable set of functions grouped under the `File` menu in Microsoft Windows applications. Traditional user interface guidelines were intended to be used by designers, although they are often criticized as being too general to provide useful design guidance (Grudin 1989; Newell & Card 1985).

More recently, guidelines have become popular as the basis of **usability inspection**, in which usability experts examine or work with a system in an effort to detect potential usability problems. Modern inspection methods differ from more traditional use of guidelines in two respects: First, the guidelines are used to guide evaluation, not design. They are used to prompt questions about a design, rather than to specify a solution approach. Second, they are deliberately open ended and incomplete. They are not used to consider all possible design features and potential problems, but rather as a help in finding key issues.

Nielsen (1994) describes an inspection method called **heuristic evaluation**, in which usability experts review a system against the 10 general guidelines listed below.

- Use simple and natural dialog
- Speak the users' language
- Minimize memory load
- Be consistent
- Provide feedback
- Provide clearly marked exits
- Provide shortcuts
- Provide good error messages
- Prevent errors
- Include good help and documentation

Nielson recommends that independent heuristic evaluations should be conducted by multiple usability experts; each evaluator identifies as many usability problems as possible. Bias (1991) describes **pluralistic walk-through**, a similar method in which developers, users, and usability engineers collaborate to analyze a system; Bias argues that a range of perspectives helps to find a larger set of problems. Polson, et al. (1992) describe the use of **cognitive walk-through** to analyze in detail a user's goals, expectations, and reactions during individual tasks. Inspection methods are extremely popular in industry, because they generate large numbers of potential usability problems at a relatively modest cost (Bias & Mayhew 1994; Nielsen & Mack 1994).

Inspection methods raise several tradeoffs for evaluation efforts. One is the nature of the analysis produced through inspection (Tradeoff 7.1). Usability inspection is aimed at finding and counting problems, rather than on understanding the implications of a problem. Furthermore, inspection alone does not reveal the **validity** of the findings. Validity is a crucial concern for any usability evaluation; it refers to the degree to which the findings correspond to what would be found in the actual use. For example, a usability expert might point out 100 potential problems, but only seven of these might ever occur in actual use. And of these seven, it may be that none is particularly serious for users.

TRADEOFF 7.1

 Usability checklists and inspections can produce rapid feedback, BUT may call attention to problems that are infrequent or atypical in real-world use.

Many usability inspections include a phase in which the expert classifies each problem on a scale of severity (e.g., from "a minor annoyance" to "would completely disrupt the user's task"). In this sense, the experts are providing their own assessment of validity, by providing implicit claims about how important a problem will be in real-world usage situations. This provides more guidance to designers, because they can better prioritize the attention they direct toward each problem.

A related question is the usage context provided for an inspection. In some discussions, Nielsen (1995) endorses the use of scenarios as a basis for heuristic evaluation, but in general he argues that scenario contexts may overconstrain how experts will think about system features. But as we have seen, design tradeoffs vary across scenarios. What may seem quite effective for one task (e.g., a context-sensitive menu choice that appears only when needed) may be cumbersome for another (e.g., an expert who wants to get to this option frequently and quickly). Such tradeoffs are difficult to discover and reason about in simple fea-tured-oriented inspections.

A third question concerns the more long-term contributions to the disci-pline of usability engineering. Heuristic evaluation is very lightweight and relies entirely on the creativity and experience of the evaluators—this is what makes it so popular and easy to do. But there is no mechanism for saving and reusing the insights developed in one evaluation process for use in future projects. Whatever is learned simply ends up as part of the evaluators' private expertise.

7.2.2 Model-Based Analysis

The goal of model-based analysis is to use established theories in science and engineering to build a predictive model. A classic example is **GOMS analysis** (goals, operators, methods, and selection rules; Card, Moran, & Newell 1983). A GOMS model is organized into goals that name the user's current intention, methods that list the steps needed to achieve the goal (e.g., an idealized action plan; Chapter 5), the operators that implement the methods, and any selection rules needed to choose among multiple possible methods or operators. This rep-resentation of users' goals and knowledge is commonly known as a **user model**.

A portion of a GOMS model is shown in Figure 7.2; it was extracted from an analysis of document editing on the Macintosh (Kieras 1997). This part of the model begins with the goal to move some text. The method for this goal includes four steps; two of the steps instantiate subgoals (`cut text`, and `paste text`). It also includes the perceptual operator `verify`. Each of the subgoals is decom-posed into its own method. Both of these include a selection subgoal and a men-tal operator indicated as `Retain`. The first step of the cut-text method also includes a selection rule, modeled in the right-hand column of the figure. This rule can be interpreted as "if the text to cut is a word, then use the word selection method; otherwise, use the arbitrary text-selection method"). The rest of the analysis (not shown here) models the subtasks of selecting a word, selecting arbi-trary text, selecting the insertion point, and issuing a command.

Once a GOMS model has been fully specified, human performance data can be used to estimate the time required to perform a task. For example, a but-ton press takes about 250 milliseconds, moving a hand from keyboard to mouse takes about 400 milliseconds, pointing the mouse takes about 1,100 millisec-onds, and a mental operation (e.g., choosing between two methods) takes about 1,350 milliseconds. The GOMS model would be converted into an executable program, and parameters such as these could be used to calculate times for dif-ferent versions of document editing tasks.

Goals, Methods, and Operators

```
Method for goal: move text.
   Step 1. Accomplish goal: cut text.
   Step 2. Accomplish goal: paste text.
   Step 3. Verify correct text moved.
   Step 4. Return with goal accomplished.

Method for goal: cut text.
   Step 1. Accomplish goal: select text.
   Step 2. Retain that the command is CUT,
   and accomplish goal: issue a command.
   Step 3. Return with goal accomplished.

Method for goal: paste text.
   Step 1. Accomplish goal: select
   insertion point.
   Step 2. Accomplish goal: Retain that
   the command is PASTE and accomplish
   goal: use a command.
   Step 3. Return with goal accomplished.

Method for goal: select insertion point.
   Step 1. Accomplish goal: cut text.
   Step 2. Accomplish goal: paste text.
   Step 3. Verify correct text moved.
   Step 4. Return with goal accomplished.
```

Selection Rules

```
Selection rule set for goal:
select text.
   If text-is-word, then
   accomplish goal: select word.
   If text-is-arbitrary, then
   accomplish goal: select
   arbitrary text.
   Return with goal accomplished.
```

Figure 7.2 Goals, operators, methods, and selection rules for the subtask of moving text on a Macintosh computer (Kieras 1997, 755–56).

GOMS analysts can also use models such as these to consider issues such as complexity or consistency. For example, in Microsoft Word clicking at the left border of a cell in a table selects the entire cell, but clicking at the left border of a paragraph selects just the closest line. A detailed GOMS analysis might uncover the different uses of this selection technique, perhaps sparking discussion (or empirical tests) of whether the methods create inconsistency problems for users. The models can also be used to interpret empirical data; users may not do exactly what is predicted, but comparing their behavior to the model's prediction can help evaluators understand why.

Model-based analyses must be focused and explicit so that they can produce precise and quantifiable predictions. But because approaches like GOMS focus on the individual operators that constitute user tasks, they tend to ignore significant aspects of human behavior—namely the structure of work and organizations, and the experiences of learning and problem solving (Tradeoff 7.2). At the same time, a GOMS analysis (which was simplified in our example) can seem like a lot of work to obtain advice about fine adjustments to mouse selections or keystrokes.

TRADEOFF 7.2

 Models of performance can yield precise predictions of user behavior, BUT the time spent building such models can take attention away from higher-level human behavior such as learning, problem solving, and social relationships.

Recent enhancements to user modeling have addressed these issues. The original GOMS model assumes sequential task execution, although humans regularly work on multiple tasks at once. Current approaches have been extended to include parallel task execution (Gray, John, & Atwood 1992). Current approaches also address learning, perception, and errors (Kieras 1997). A simplified notation was developed to reduce the tedium of developing detailed symbolic descriptions (Kieras 1988). Finally, the practical use of these models has been demonstrated for niche applications. A well-known example is evaluation of a telephone operator workstation, a computer application in which keystrokes are worth millions of dollars (Gray, John, & Atwood 1992).

Not all model-based analysis is aimed at performance estimates. In a task-action grammar (Payne & Green 1986), the focus is how users' task knowledge is mapped to system objects and actions. The analyst begins by creating a **grammar** (a set of rules) describing the tasks a system supports. For document editing, an example rule might be:

```
Move Paragraph => Select/Cut Text + Cut at Destination
+ Splice/Paste Text
```

The action sequence on the right describes how cut-and-paste can be used to move a paragraph in a paper document. A user interface design for a text editor can then also be described by a grammar, and the mapping between the two sets of rules examined. A simple mapping suggests less difficulty for users learning or using the proposed system.

User interface metaphors can also be used for model-based analysis (Carroll, Mack, & Kellogg 1988). People try to understand new systems by analogy to situations they already know about. Designers take advantage of this by conveying that a metaphor will be helpful in learning about a system (e.g., the concept of a library helps when learning to use a digital archive). A metaphor-based analysis is similar to a task-action grammar, but it highlights the extent to which significant objects, actions, and relationships in the system match or mismatch the structures of the metaphor domain. This leads to predictions about which tasks will be more or less easy to learn or perform, where and what kinds of errors may occur, and so on.

7.3   Empirical Methods

The gold standard for usability evaluation is empirical data. Heuristic evaluation produces a list of possible problems, but they are really no more than suggestions. Claims analysis produces a set of design tradeoffs, but the designers must decide whether the tradeoffs are really dilemmas, and if so, which are most problematic. A model-based approach such as GOMS leads to precise predictions about user performance, but has limited application. What usability evaluators really need to know is what happens when people use the system in real situations.

Unfortunately, empirical evaluation is not simple. If we wait to study users until they have the finished system in their workplace, we will maximize the chance for a real disaster. Finding significant problems at that stage means starting over. The whole point of formative evaluation is to support parallel development and evaluation, so as to avoid such disasters. On the other hand, any compromise we make—such as asking users to work with an incomplete prototype in a laboratory—raises issues concerning the validity of the evaluation (i.e., do laboratory tasks adequately represent realistic use?).

The validity of the testing situation is just one problem. Rarely do empirical results point to a single obvious conclusion. A feature that confuses one user in one circumstance might save another user in a different situation. What should we do? What conclusion can we draw? There are technical tools to help manage these problems. For example, we can calculate the mean number of users who experience a problem with some feature, or contrast the proportion who like the feature to the proportion who dislike it. However, the interpretation of descriptive statistics such as these depends very much on the number and characteristics of the users who are studied.

7.3.1   Field Studies

One way to ensure the validity of empirical evaluation is to use **field study** methods, where normal work activities are studied in a normal work environment. As we emphasized in Chapters 2 and 3, people often adapt new technology in unexpected ways to their existing work practices. The adaptations that they invent and their descriptions of how and why they use the technology in these ways can provide detailed guidance to designers trying to refine a system's basic functions and user interface. Thus, field studies can be valuable in formative evaluation, just as they are in requirements analysis. A field study is often the only way to carry out a **longitudinal study** of a computer system in use, where the emphasis is on effects of the system over an extended period of time.

Suchman's (1987) study of document copier systems is a classic example of a field study. Suchman observed people using a sophisticated photocopier equipped with sensors to track users' actions, and the system offers helpful prompts and feedback. In one example, a person starts to copy a multipage document by placing the first page in the document handler. The copier senses the page and prompts the user to press Start. She does so, and four copies are produced. The user is then prompted to remove the original document from the handler. She does this as well, then waits for further direction. However, the copier next senses the pages in the output tray, and prompts the user to remove them. At this point, the interaction breaks down: The prompt about the output tray does not connect to the user's current goal. She ignores it and instead places a second page into the document handler, triggering a repeat of the earlier prompt to remove the originals. Trying to understand, she misinterprets: "Remove the original—Okay, I've re- . . . , I've moved the original. And put in the second copy."

This simple example vividly shows how a photocopier designer's best efforts to provide helpful and "smart" instructions backfired, actually misleading and confusing the user. As is typical of field studies like this, the details of the episode also suggest design remedies. In this case, providing less help via the prompts led to a better design.

In a comprehensive field study, hundreds of such episodes might be collected. The amount and richness of the data emphasize the key disadvantage of fieldwork—the data obtained has high validity but can be extremely difficult to condense and understand (Tradeoff 7.3). One approach to this is **content analysis**—the evaluator organizes related observations or problems into categories. For instance, one category might be problems with system prompts, another might be button layout, another might be feedback indicators, and so forth. Data reduction of this sort helps to focus later redesign work.

TRADEOFF 7.3

Field studies ensure validity of the usability problems discovered, BUT field study results are extensive, qualitative, and difficult to summarize and interpret.

Field study observations may also be rated for **severity**—each episode is judged with respect to its significance for the user(s). These ratings help to prioritize the data, so that designers can direct most attention to issues of most importance. For example, episodes could be rated on a three-point scale: successful use, inconvenience, and total **breakdown**. While breakdown episodes are clearly most useful in identifying and guiding design changes, it is useful to also include successful episodes in the data sample. Successful episodes may seem uninteresting, but they help to establish a user interaction **baseline** (i.e., what can be expected under normal conditions).

Ethnographic observation attends to actual user experiences in real-world situations. Thus, it addresses many of the concerns about the validity of empirical findings (although the presence of an ethnographer may also influence people's behavior). But this style of work is costly. Collecting field data is very time consuming, and analyzing many pages of notes and observations can be laborious.

A compromise is **retrospective interviews**, where people are asked to recall use episodes that they remember as particularly successful or unsuccessful. This method is based on Flanagan's (1954) original work with **critical incidents**—he asked test pilots to report incidents that stood out in their memory of a recent flight. The critical incidents reported by users should not be considered representative or typical; the point is to identify what seems to be important. However, this makes retrospective interviews an extremely efficient method for producing a collection of problem reports.

Unfortunately, self-reported incidents have their own validity problems. It is well known that people reconstruct their memories of events (Bartlett 1964; Tradeoff 7.4). For example, someone might remember a task goal that makes more sense given the result they obtained. The tendency to reconstruct memories becomes stronger as time elapses, so it is best to gather critical incident reports immediately after an activity. Even then, users are often just mistaken about what happened and what caused what, making their retrospective reports difficult to interpret (Carroll 1990). Self-reported critical incidents should never be taken at face value.

TRADEOFF 7.4

 Users often possess valuable insight into their own usability problems, BUT humans often reconstruct rather than recall experiences.

Just as users can contribute to requirements analysis and design, they can participate in evaluation. In field studies and retrospective interviewing, they participate as actors or reporters. But they can also become analysts themselves through **self-reflection**—a person is asked to interpret his or her own behaviors. In such a situation, the evaluator ends up with two sorts of data—the original episode and the actors' thoughts about what it means. We are currently exploring this approach with a collaborative critical incident tool, in which a community of users and designers post and discuss usage episodes (Neale, et al. 2000).

7.3.2   Usability Testing in a Laboratory

A significant obstacle for field studies is that systems are often not fielded until development is complete. Even if a preliminary field trial is conducted, it may be costly to travel to the site to collect observational data. There are also specific technical reasons for evaluating usability in a laboratory setting: Laboratory studies can be small in scope and scale, and they can be controlled to focus on particular tasks, features, and user consequences. Laboratory studies do not have the overhead of installing or updating a system in a real work site, so they permit rapid cycles of user feedback and prototyping. In fact, laboratory tests can be useful well before any design work has been done—for example, by studying users' performance on comparable systems using standardized **benchmark tasks**.

Because laboratory studies can only simulate real-world usage situations, test validity becomes a major concern (Tradeoff 7.5). For example, it is important that the users be representative—they should be similar to the target users in terms of background, age, ability, and so on (Figure 7.3). A team may inadvertently recruit test participants who know a lot about spreadsheet programs but very little about Web browsers, relative to the intended user population.

TRADEOFF 7.5

Laboratory studies enable focused attention on specific usage concerns, BUT the settings observed may be unrepresentative and thus misleading.

It is also important to recognize and interpret differences among individuals. For example, a novice user may like a system with extensive support for direct manipulation, but an expert user may be frustrated and critical. This is the general problem of **variability** in test results; dealing with variability is a challenge for all empirical work. Evaluators can address these concerns by studying a large enough set of users that general patterns emerge, or by carefully documenting user characteristics and restricting their conclusions to people who have these characteristics.

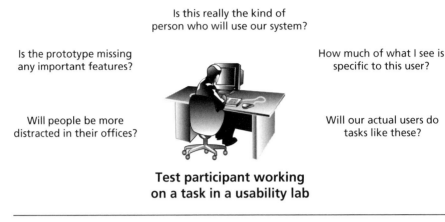

**Test participant working
on a task in a usability lab**

Figure 7.3   Validity concerns that arise in usability testing done in a laboratory.

The prototype or mock-up tested in a laboratory study may also differ from the final system in key respects. The IBM PCjr failed in part because of the rubbery feel of its keyboard. Studies of keyboard prototypes focusing only on the small size of the miniature keyboard would have missed this critical element. The printed graphics pasted onto a cardboard mock-up may have a higher resolution than the resolution real users will experience with cheap displays. What if users working with such displays cannot see the critical cues?

The tasks tested in the laboratory may not be the ones that people will ultimately undertake with the system. Initially, the significance of the World Wide Web was thought to be its improved user interface for transferring files over the network. Spreadsheets were thought to be tools for arithmetic calculation; only later did it become clear that users would also use spreadsheets for planning, reporting, and communication tasks (Nielsen, et al. 1986).

Ironically, another concern for usability testing is the usability laboratory itself! A **usability lab** is a specially constructed observation room that is set up to simulate a work environment (e.g., an office), and instrumented with various data collection devices (e.g., video, one-way observation windows, and screen capture). Users are brought into the lab to perform and comment about carefully constructed test tasks. However, the participants in these studies are insulated from normal work distractions and deprived of many of their daily workplace resources. For example, most work environments involve significant interaction among employees, but this is very difficult to simulate in a laboratory environment.

Sometimes a usability test can approximate a field study. Gould, et al. (1987) describe **storefront testing**, in which a prototype is placed in a semi-public place, such as a hallway near the developers' workroom. Colleagues passing by are invited to try out the prototype and provide feedback. Such user interactions are not examples of real work. The passersby do not have realistic user goals; they are just curious or are trying to be helpful. The usage context may also not be realistic. Gould, et al. were designing a system for a noisy environment, but tested it in the relatively quiet halls of an industrial research laboratory. Nonetheless, a storefront prototype can literally be wheeled out of the developers' laboratory and into a usage setting. The method generates user feedback instantly and supports very rapid prototype refinement and iterative testing.

An important issue for laboratory studies is deciding what data to collect. Most studies gather task performance times, videotapes of user actions, screen displays, and so on. But much of a user's experience is unobservable, taking place inside his or her head as information is interpreted and plans are constructed. Thus, it is also common for usability evaluators to gather **think-aloud protocols**: Users narrate their goals, plans, reactions, and concerns as they work through the test tasks (Ericsson & Simon 1993). The think-aloud protocol can then be analyzed to determine when the person became confused or experienced usage difficulties; the narration before and after a problem often provides insight into the causes and consequences of usability problems.

Usability testing is often conducted in usability labs designed to look like workplace settings (e.g., an office), and evaluators seek to make test participants feel as comfortable as possible. At the same time, it is important to realize that thinking out loud while working is not natural behavior for most computer users! Tracking and narrating mental activity are tasks in and of themselves, and they compete with the application task the user is trying to perform (Tradeoff 7.6). Task performance times and errors are much less meaningful in think-aloud studies. The reporting process also leads users to pay careful attention to their actions and to system responses, which may influence how they plan or execute their tasks.

TRADEOFF 7.6

Externalizing one's goals, plans, and reactions reveals unobservable cognitive sources of usability problems, BUT self-reflection may alter what people do.

Think-aloud studies produce a lot of data, just like field observations. In making sense of the data, evaluators use some of the same techniques they would apply to field data. For example, they may identify critical incidents directly from the data record (e.g., Mack, Lewis, & Carroll 1983). A more systematic analysis might produce behavior graphs, in which each user action is indicated, along with comments revealing associated mental states (Rosson & Carroll 1996). Because the evaluator controls the requirements of the test tasks, this method can be used to carry out very detailed investigations of how users plan, execute, and make sense of their own behavior.

Almost all usability studies measure time and errors for users performing tasks. To ensure that the times collected are meaningful, evaluators must specify the test tasks precisely enough so that all participants will try to accomplish the same goal. For example, an email task might be "searching for a message received in spring 1997 from Kanazan Lebole that may have mentioned ACM SIGCHI." Discovering that such a task is difficult or error prone would cause designers to think about how to better support message retrieval in this email system. (Remember that task times and errors collected during think-aloud studies are influenced by the demands of the reporting task.)

Most usability tests also gather users' **subjective reactions** to a system. Users may be queried in a general fashion (e.g., "What did you [dis]like most?") or they may be asked to rate the usability of specific tasks or features. An interesting and challenging aspect of user testing is that subjective reactions do not always correspond to performance data. A feature may improve efficiency but also annoy users, or it may slow users down but make them feel more comfortable. For example, early formative evaluation of the Xerox Star revealed that users spent a considerable time adjusting window location—they tried to keep their windows arranged so as to not overlap (Miller & Johnson 1996). As a result, designers decided to not allow overlapping windows. Soon after, however, it became clear that overlapping windows are preferred by most users; this is now the default for most windowing systems. The Star was perhaps so far in front of user and designer experience that it was impossible to make reliable formative inferences from time and error measures.

7.3.3   Controlled Experiments

Most usability evaluation examines performance or satisfaction with the current version of the system or prototype. It tries to answer questions about what is working well or poorly, what parts of the system need attention, and how close developers are to meeting overall usability objectives. On occasion, however, a more controlled study may be used to investigate a specific question. For example, suppose a team needs to understand the performance implications of three different joystick designs. A controlled experiment can be designed to compare and contrast the devices.

The first step in planning an experiment is to identify the variables that will be manipulated or measured. An **independent variable** is a characteristic that is manipulated to create different experimental conditions. It is very important to think carefully about how each variable will be manipulated or **operationalized**, to form a set of different test conditions. Participants (subjects) are then exposed to these varying conditions to see if different conditions lead to different behavior. In our example, the independent variable is joystick design. The three different designs represent three different **levels** of this variable. Attributes of study participants—for example, degree of experience with video games—could also be measured and incorporated as independent variables.

A **dependent variable** is an experiment outcome; it is chosen to reveal effects of one or more independent variables. In our example, a likely dependent variable is time to carry out a set of navigation tasks. Experimenters often include multiple independent and dependent variables in an experiment, so that they can learn as much as possible. For instance, task complexity might be manipulated as a second independent variable, so that the effects of joystick design can be examined over a broad range of user behavior. Other dependent variables could be performance accuracy or users' subjective reactions. For complex tasks requiring many steps, an evaluator may implement some form of **software logging**, where user input events are captured automatically for later review (Rosson 1983).

Experimenters must specify how a dependent variable will be measured. Some cases are straightforward. Performance time is measured simply by deciding when to start and stop a timer, and choosing a level of timing precision. Other cases are less obvious. If task errors are to be measured, advance planning will be needed to decide what will count as an error. If subjective reactions are being assessed, questionnaires or rating scales must be developed to measure participants' feelings about a system.

The independent and dependent variables of an experiment are logically connected through **hypotheses** that predict what causal effects the independent variables will have on dependent variables. In our example, the experimenter might predict faster performance times for one joystick but no performance differences for the other two. As the number of variables increases, the experimental hypotheses can become quite complex: For example, one joystick might be predicted to improve performance for simple tasks, while a second is predicted to improve complex tasks. Hypothesis testing requires the use of inferential statistics (see Appendix).

Once the experiment variables have been identified, experimenters must choose how participants will be exposed to the different experimental conditions. In a **within-subjects design** (also called repeated measures), the same participants are exposed to all levels of an independent variable. In contrast, a **between-subjects design** uses independent groups of participants for each test condition. In our example, we might have one group of users who work with all three joysticks (within subjects), or we might bring in different groups for each device.

A within-subjects design has the advantage that the variability in data due to differences among users (e.g., some people respond more quickly in general) can be statistically removed (controlled for). This makes it easier to detect effects of the independent variable(s). However, exposure to one level of an independent variable may influence people's reactions to another (Tradeoff 7.7). For example, it is quite possible that experience with one joystick will cause people to learn physical strategies that would influence their success with a second.

TRADEOFF 7.7

 Using the same participants in multiple testing conditions helps to control for individual differences, BUT may lead to task ordering or other unwanted effects.

Such concerns are often addressed by a **mixed design**, where some independent variables are manipulated within subjects and others are manipulated between subjects. For example, the different joysticks could be used by different groups of people, but task complexity could be left as a within-subjects variable.

Within-subjects designs are popular and convenient—fewer participants are required, and potentially large effects of individual variability are controlled. Exposing the same participants to two different conditions also allows for direct comparison (e.g., in a series of rating scales). However, experimenters must anticipate nuisance effects, such as task order, and counterbalance the testing conditions as necessary. In complex designs having many independent variables with multiple levels of each, preventing nuisance effects can be challenging.

In any usability evaluation, it is important to recruit subjects who are representative of the target population. But for experimental studies, there are also important questions of how participants are assigned to different conditions, and how many participants will be needed to measure the expected differences among conditions.

The simplest method is **random assignment**: Each participant is placed randomly in a group, with the constraint that groups end up being the same size (or as close as possible to equal sizes; unequal group sizes reduce the sensitivity of statistical tests). Under this strategy, nuisance variables such as age, background, or general motivation are randomly distributed across the different experimental conditions. Randomization increases the "noisiness" of the data but does not bias the results.

Random assignment is most effective when the number of participants is large; a rule of thumb is to have at least ten individuals in each condition. As the number of participants (the sample, or n) increases, the statistical estimate of random variation is more accurate, creating a more sensitive test of the independent variables. However, this can lead to a dilemma—an experiment with results of borderline significance can often be repeated with a larger number of participants to create a more powerful test, but results may not be worth the extra cost and effort (Tradeoff 7.8). Usability practitioners must carefully balance the needs of their work setting with the lure of reporting a "statistically significant" result. Ironically, a very large experiment may produce statistically significant differences that account for a very small portion of the overall variance in the data. Experimenters should be careful to report not only the statistical tests of differences, but also the proportion of the overall variability accounted for by these differences (see Appendix).

TRADEOFF 7.8

 The sensitivity of a statistical test is enhanced by increasing sample size, BUT obtaining a statistically significant result may not be worth the cost and effort of running a very large experiment.

Another assignment strategy is to combine random assignment with control of one or more participant variables. For example, experimenters often randomly assign an equal number of men and women to each group because they worry that gender will influence the results. This helps to ensure that any effects of this particular nuisance variable will be equally distributed across the conditions of interest.

7.4 Science Fair Case Study: Usability Evaluation

Evaluation is central and continuous in SBD. From the first step of activity design, the use context provided by the scenarios serves as an implicit test of the emerging design ideas. The "what-if" reasoning used in analyzing claims expands and generalizes the situations that are envisioned and considered. The focus on design feature impacts is an ongoing source of formative evaluation feedback.

Evaluation becomes more systematic when usability specifications are created from design scenarios and their associated claims (Figure 7.4). The scenarios

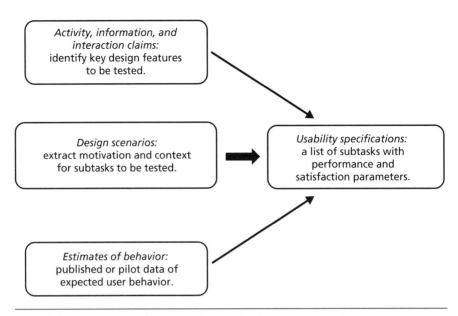

Figure 7.4   Developing usability specifications for formative evaluation.

provide the motivation and activity context for a set of sequential subtasks that will be evaluated repeatedly as benchmarks of the system's usability. The claims analyses are used to identify the subtasks to be tested—recall that claims have been used throughout to track design features with important usability implications. For each subtask, outcome measures of users' performance and satisfaction are defined, creating a testable set of usability specifications (Carroll & Rosson 1985).

The high-level goal of any usability evaluation is to determine to what extent a design is easy or hard to learn and use, and is more or less satisfying. Usability specifications make this high-level goal more precise, transforming it into a set of empirically testable questions. The repeated testing of these tasks ascertains whether the project is meeting its usability goals, and if not, which design features are most in need of attention.

7.4.1   Usability Inspection

As we have seen, analytic evaluation takes place constantly in SBD when writing scenarios and claims. This ongoing analytic work forms a skeleton for empirical studies. Other analytic evaluation methods can be useful as well. For example,

Table 7.3 VSF usability problems identified through heuristic evaluation.

Guideline	Potential VSF Usability Problems
Use simple and natural dialog	Control+F used to synchronize views; Control+I to query activity
Speak the user's language	Young or inexperienced students may not understand "Nested Components"
Minimize user memory load	Chat bubbles stay on the screen only for 20 seconds
Be consistent	People appear as avatars in exhibit space, but as a text list at exhibit; map is replaced by miniaturized windows in exhibit display
Provide feedback	Information on others' activities only available with extra effort; chat bubbles in room overlap for large groups; red color used for alerts will not be detectable by color-blind individuals
Provide clearly marked exits	Relationship between exhibit and nested components not clear; when you change view, what happens to nested component?
Provide shortcuts	Must open each nested component individually, i.e., no "display all"
Provide good error messages	"File type not recognized" doesn't indicate how to fix problem when Excel or other source applications are not installed on client machine
Prevent errors	Multiple independent windows are difficult to distinguish and manage
Include good help and documentation	Help information on how to extend file types assumes familiarity with similar dialogs in Web browsers

we carried out an informal usability inspection using the guidelines suggested by Nielsen (1994); Table 7.3 summarizes usability issues raised during this inspection.

The inspection was carried out as an informal "walk-through" of the design scenarios. We stepped through each scenario and considered whether the actors might have problems in any of the ten areas identified by Nielsen's (1994) guidelines (left column). We did not worry about the severity of the problems at this point, so some of the problems listed in the table may be unlikely or have little impact. For example, few people will have difficulty recognizing that avatars and text names are different views of the same individuals. However, a visitor forced to carry out many selections and double-clicks to open many nested components may become very frustrated.

A usability inspection such as in Table 7.3 provides an early indication of possible problems, similar to that provided by a claims analysis. Even if no empirical studies were carried out, this list of problems could be prioritized and handed back to the design team for their consideration and possible redesign. Of course, as for any inspection technique, the list of problems identified is meaningful only to the extent the problems will arise in actual use, and without empirical data these judgments can only be based on opinion.

7.4.2 Developing Usability Specifications

In parallel with ongoing inspection and claims analysis, usability specifications were developed for each of the science fair design scenarios. Table 7.4 illustrates the first step in developing usability specifications (we have focused on the two interaction design scenarios presented in Chapter 5; see Figures 5.5 and 5.6).

Each scenario was decomposed into **critical subtasks**—the key features of the system that are influencing people's experience. The claims analyzed during design were used as a guide in identifying the subtasks. The list is not exhaustive, but rather highlights the system functionality most likely to affect system usefulness, ease of learning or use, or satisfaction. Thus, the subtasks cover a number of the open issues discussed during design (e.g., nested components and use of the control-key commands). This is the sense in which usability specifications support mediated evaluation—the results of analytic evaluation are used to set up an empirical evaluation plan.

Table 7.4 Subtasks analyzed from the VSF design scenarios.

Interaction Design Scenario	Subtasks Identified from Claims Analysis
Mr. King coaches Sally	Identify and synchronize views; Upload local file; Open and work with source application; Create nested component
Alicia and Delia visit the fair	Find location of specified visitor; Join an exhibit; View specified exhibit element; Open and work with source application; Review and modify FAQ; Access and view nested component

Table 7.5 presents two fully elaborated usability specifications. Each scenario has been broken into subtasks, and target levels for users' performance and subjective reactions have been specified. The performance measures are based on time to perform a subtask and the number of errors made. Satisfaction is measured on a 5-point attitude scale. For example, "confusion" after the first subtask is rated on a scale from 1 = "not at all confusing" to 5 = "extremely confusing."

Table 7.5   Detailed usability specifications for two scenario contexts.

Scenario and Subtasks	Worst Case	Planned	Best Case
Interaction Scenario: Mr. King coaches Sally	2.5 on usefulness, ease of use, and satisfaction	4 on usefulness, ease of use, and satisfaction	5 on usefulness, ease of use, and satisfaction
1. Identify Sally's view and synchronize	1 minute, 1 error 3 on confusion	30 seconds, 0 errors 2 on confusion	10 seconds, 0 errors 1 on confusion
2. Upload file from the PC	3 minutes, 2 errors 3 on familiarity	1 minute, 1 error 4 on familiarity	30 seconds, 0 errors 5 on familiarity
3. Open, modify, attempt to save Excel file	2 minutes, 1 error 3 on confidence	1 minute, 0 errors 4.5 on confidence	30 seconds, 0 errors 5 on confidence
4. Create nested exhibit component	5 minutes, 3 errors 3 on complexity	1 minute, 1 error 2 on complexity	30 seconds, 0 errors 1 on complexity
Interaction Scenario: Alicia and Delia visit the fair	3 on usefulness and ease of use	4 on usefulness and ease of use	5 on usefulness and ease of use
5. Find Marge at the VSF	15 seconds, 1 error 3 on awareness	5 seconds, 0 errors 4 on awareness	1 second, 0 errors 5 on awareness
6. Open Sally's exhibit	60 seconds, 1 error 3 on directness	15 seconds, 1 error 4 on directness	5 seconds, 0 errors 5 on directness
7. View data analysis	30 seconds, 2 errors 3 on predictability	15 seconds, 1 error 4.5 on predictability	3 seconds, 0 errors 5 on predictability
8. Open and manipulate Excel charts	5 minutes, 2 errors 3 on engagement	1 minute, 0 errors 4 on engagement	30 seconds, 0 errors 5 on engagement
9. Review and contribute to FAQs	2 minutes, 2 errors 3 on tedium	1 minute, 0 errors 2 on tedium	30 seconds, 0 errors 1 on tedium
10. Access and view Martin's experiment	1.5 minutes, 2 errors 3 on obscurity	45 seconds, 0 errors 2 on obscurity	20 seconds, 0 errors 1 on obscurity

Some scales are written so that a higher number means a more positive rating, while some are reversed. In all cases, the target levels are interpreted as an average across all test participants.

It is important that the usability outcomes in the specification are concrete and testable. Each subtask names a test task that will be observed; the target performance and satisfaction levels specify exactly what measures should be collected. These subtasks are evaluated over and over during development as a benchmark of progress toward agreed usability objectives.

The three levels of outcomes bound the iterative development process: "Best case" is determined by having an expert carry out the task; anything below "worst case" indicates failure. "Planned level" is the actual target, and should be a feasible and realistic statement of usability objectives. Initially, these usability outcomes reflect an educated guess and are based on the design team's experience with the prototype or with other systems having similar functionality. It is possible that these levels will change slightly as users' actual performance and reactions are studied, but it is crucial that a team (and its management) take the numbers seriously as targets to be achieved.

Notice that along with time, errors, and satisfaction measures for each subtask, Table 7.5 specifies satisfaction judgments for the interaction design scenario itself. A full scenario includes so many features that it would be difficult to predict precise performance measures. However, the team can certainly ask test users to try out the functionality described in a scenario, and measure subjective reactions to this experience. Measures like these can be used to specify usability outcomes even for a rather open-ended scenario exploration.

7.4.3   Testing Usability Specifications

Usability testing should not be restricted to the design scenarios. Early in development, if a scenario machine is the only available prototype, empirical evaluation may necessarily be limited to these tasks. But when a more general-purpose prototype is ready, new activities and subtasks should be introduced into the evaluation. This is important in SBD, because exclusive attention to a small set of design scenarios can lead to a system that has been optimized for these situations at the expense of others.

Figure 7.5 shows one technique for generating new activity scenarios. The left column summarizes the five design scenarios developed in Chapters 3 through 5. The scenarios on the right were created by bringing in actors with differing backgrounds and motivations, but with overlapping system functionality and user interface features. This strategy works well early in a system's lifecycle, when only some of a system's features are available (i.e., that specified in the

Original Scenario	Extension or Generalization
Sally plans her exhibit on black holes: An experienced science fair participant organizes her many diverse elements using the template. She pays special attention to components that will make her exhibit more interactive because she knows this will give her points with the judges.	*Ben and Marissa collaborate on a project:* Two students participate in the science fair for the first time. They work independently, and then come together to organize and integrate their sections. Neither is familiar with how to organize or present a science project, so they rely a lot on the templates and help information, and they revise their project a lot as they work.
Mr. King coaches Sally: An experienced science fair advisor coaches Sally from home in the evening. He goes over each piece of the exhibit, then helps her make it less complex by finding a way to nest materials.	*Cheryl makes some suggestions:* Cheryl is a retired biochemist who is part of the online seniors group. She sees the VSF advertised in MOOsburg and visits several weeks before the exhibits are done. She browses several biology exhibits under construction and leaves comments on the message boards.
Alicia and Delia go to the fair: A busy mother and her daughter log into the fair after school. They see other people there and join an old friend at Sally's exhibit. They see Sally's exhibit, and Delia gets interested and asks questions.	*Delia brings her friend Stacy back to Sally's exhibit:* In school the next day, Delia takes her lab partner Stacy to Sally's exhibit. Sally isn't there, so Delia shows the stored discussion to Stacy, and demonstrates how to use the spreadsheet and the black hole simulation.
Ralph judges the high school physics projects: Ralph is an experienced judge with well-developed strategies. He has enough experience with judging and with technology to propose and provide the rationale for a modification to the judges' ratings form.	*Mark judges for the first time:* Because this is his first year, Mark is unsure how to proceed. He spends most of one day on the task, sending out a number of emails for guidance. At certain points he chats online with his peers. Because of his uncertainty, he edits his ratings and comments many times, and prints them out for final review before he submits them.
Rachel prepares a summary for Carlisle: The superintendent wants an impressive summary	*School board member Jenkins thinks about resources:* Jim Jenkins thinks the VSF has

(continued)

Figure 7.5 User interaction scenarios form the basis of usability evaluations.

Figure 7.5   *(continued)*

to use in asking for more science fair resources. Rachel first takes him on a virtual tour, then goes back herself to select and copy out visuals from winning projects.

plenty of resources based on Superintendent Carlisle's presentation. But he goes back to study the site more carefully. He is not very familiar with MOOsburg, so it takes him a while to find and browse just a few exhibits, but he confirms to himself that the fair needs no further support for next year.

design scenarios), but the team wants to evaluate multiple use contexts. Later on, test scenarios representing more radical extensions of the core design (e.g., a teacher who takes her students on a "virtual tour" of the fair) can be developed and evaluated.

The scenarios in Figure 7.5 were used in two sorts of usability testing. Early on, we simply asked test participants to adopt the perspective of an actor (e.g., Sally or Mr. King), and to simulate the scenario activity. For example, a simple introduction such as the following was given:

> Imagine that you are Alicia Sampson, owner of a hardware store in Blacksburg. You are already familiar with MOOsburg, but have not visited the Virtual Science Fair. You are busy and somewhat ambivalent about attending science fairs in general, but this year your neighbor Jeff is a participant and your daughter Delia has shown some interest. One afternoon Delia shows you a URL and the two of you decide to log on and visit together. Go to the fair, locate your friend Marge who is already there, join her, and explore the exhibit she is browsing.

The test participants then explored the system with these instructions in mind. We asked the participants to think out loud as they used the system, and we observed their actions with the system. After each scenario we asked them to rate their experience with respect to usefulness, ease of use, and satisfaction (see Table 7.5). The goals of these early tests were very informal—we tried to understand whether the system supported the scenarios as intended, and if not, the major problem areas. In the rest of this section, we describe the more careful testing we conducted on individual subtasks.

Recruiting Test Participants

The participants in usability studies represent the population the system is designed to support. This often means that evaluators will need to recruit individuals from multiple stakeholder groups. For example, our science fair scenarios include students, parents, teachers, community members, and school administrators as actors. The scenarios also assume certain experience and knowledge (recall the stakeholder profiles in Chapter 2). Sometimes it is difficult to recruit participants from each of these groups (e.g., there are not very many school administrators to draw from). A compromise is to ask individuals from one group to role play the perspective and concerns of another group.

Even when a team can identify representative users, persuading them to participate in a usability session can be challenging. Sometimes a system is novel enough that users will agree to work with it just for the experience. More typically, spending time evaluating a system means taking time away from something else (e.g., work or leisure time). Offering a small stipend will attract some individuals, but ironically, the most appropriate users are often those who are least available—they are busy doing just the tasks your system is designed to enhance! Participatory design addresses some of these problems, because stakeholders are involved in a variety of analysis and design activities. Unfortunately, end users who contribute to design are no longer good representatives of their peers; they are members of the design team.

Regardless of how participants are recruited, it is important to remember that they are just a sample of the entire population of users. Personality, experience, socioeconomic background, or other factors will naturally influence users' behavior and reactions. Gathering relevant background information can demonstrate that a test group is (or is not) a representative sample of the target population. It also aids in interpretation of observed differences among individuals.

Developing Test Materials

Prior to beginning a usability test, the team must develop the instructions, surveys, and data collection forms that will be used to coordinate the test sessions. In this section, we illustrate the test materials developed for the science fair usability tests.

An important concern in any test with human participants is that they be treated fairly. The guidelines for ethical treatment of human subjects developed by the American Psychiatric Association emphasize **informed consent**: The study's goals and procedures are summarized for each participant, questions if any are answered, and the person is asked to sign a form affirming that he or she is participating voluntarily and can withdraw at any time without penalty (Figure 7.6). In practice, this agreement often reads like a legal document—for example, it may promise that videotapes will not be used for commercial purposes, or that the participant will not disclose details of the prototype systems to other people.

User Study of a Virtual Science Fair: Consent Form
Virginia Tech Computer Science Department and Center for Human-Computer Interaction

Study Goals: This research is being conducted to explore the usefulness, ease of learning and use, and satisfaction experienced by students, teachers, and community members interacting with a Virtual Science Fair (VSF). The VSF is an extension of physical science fairs, in that exhibits can be created and browsed online, communication can take place among visitors and exhibitors, judging takes place online, and so on. We will use the results of the study to refine the VSF. **Note**: We are interested in how well the system performs, not how well any individual is able to use it.

Procedures: You will begin by filling out a brief background survey. Then, after reading some brief instructions you will work through several tasks designed to introduce you to features of the VSF. These instructions will be deliberately brief, in order to see how well the system can support use on its own. After the tasks, you will fill out a user reaction survey, and then will be given an opportunity to ask any questions you have about this study's goals, procedures, or outcomes.

Throughout your interactions with the VSF, we will be collecting several sorts of information: We will be videotaping your actions with the system, as well as recording what happens on each screen of the VSF. One or more evaluators will be taking notes, measuring task start and stop time, and noting any problems that you encounter. To help us gather as much information about the VSF as possible, we also will be asking you to *think aloud* about your goals, expectations, and reactions to the system as you work. At times we may prompt you to tell us what you are thinking. We realize that providing a think-aloud commentary may be distracting, but it is important for us to know what you are thinking as you carry out the tasks.

Participant Consent: Your participation in this experiment is entirely voluntary; there will be no remuneration for the time you spend evaluating it. All data gathered from the usability study will be treated in a confidential fashion: It will be archived in a secure location and will be interpreted only for purposes of this evaluation. When your data are reported or described, all identifying information will be removed. There are no known risks to participation in this experiment, and you may withdraw at any point. Please feel free to ask the evaluators if you have any other questions; otherwise, if you are willing to participate, please sign and date this form.

_____   _____

Name   Date

If there are any questions, please contact Dr. Mary Beth Rosson, 231-6470, rosson@vt.edu.

Figure 7.6 Sample informed consent form used in VSF formative evaluation.

In these situations, the wording must be developed even more carefully to ensure that participants understand their role and responsibilities.

A **user background survey** collects information about participants' background and expectations prior to using a system. Typically, this survey will be completed at the beginning of a usability test session, but on occasion a usability team may recruit participants in an ongoing fashion, so that they always have a panel of users from which they select individuals for specific evaluation sessions. The background survey need not be extensive; indeed, if the users are asked to spend a lot of time in advance filling out a questionnaire, their interest in working on the system may decline or disappear. Consider carefully what participant characteristics are most likely to influence users' interactions with the system.

Figure 7.7 shows the background survey developed for the science fair studies. We ask about participants' occupations and their experience with science fairs so that we can categorize them into one of our major stakeholder groups. Their general computing experience, and more specifically their experience with MOOs, help us to understand their technology background and is useful in understanding any personal variations we might observe (e.g., a very successful experience of a high school student who has been using MOOs for several years). The final open-ended question gives participants a chance to disclose any other personal data that they believe might be relevant.

The background survey also measures pre-test attitudes about online science fairs. We developed three **Likert scales**—an assertion followed by a response scale ranging from Strongly Agree to Strongly Disagree—to measure pre-test expectations about online science fairs and science education. We will repeat these rating scales in a user reaction survey administered after the test tasks (i.e., a post-test), so that we can look for changes relative to the pre-test judgments.

Figures 7.8 and 7.9 present instructions developed for the VSF testing. We show both general instructions (provided once at the beginning of the testing) and task-specific instructions (provided at the beginning of each subtask). The general instructions provide an overview of the procedure and communicate requirements shared by all tasks (e.g., thinking aloud and indicating task start and stop).

The task instructions should motivate and guide participants through the two groups of subtasks detailed in the earlier usability specifications (Table 7.5). In this example, the subtasks are the four elements selected from the coaching scenario. A brief context description sets the scene, specifying details of the actors and situation that are relevant to the individual tasks that will follow.

Each subtask is presented as briefly as possible—again, remember that the goal of the testing is to see how well the system supports the tasks, not how well

User Background Survey

Virginia Tech Computer Science Department and Center for Human-Computer Interaction

Thank you for agreeing to participate in the study. Before we begin, it will be useful for us to know more about your background—your experience with science fairs, with technology, and so on. This will help us to better understand your interactions and reactions to the system. Remember that all personal data will be treated confidentially and reported with no identifying information.

Name: _____   Occupation: _____

Age: ____   Years of Education: _____   Years a resident in Blacksburg: _____

For how many years have you been using computers? ____
Please describe your typical computer use (e.g., over a period of a week). As part of the description, please indicate the type(s) of computer(s) that you use on a regular basis:

Have you had any experience with science fairs? If yes, please describe:

Have you had any experience with virtual worlds (MOOs, MUDs, other online communities)? If yes, please describe:

Please respond to the following 3 items by *circling the opinion* that best corresponds to your own. Note that in some cases, this may require you to make a prediction about online activities.

1. Browsing an online science exhibit is like visiting a science fair in the real world.

| Strongly Disagree | Disagree | Neutral | Agree | Strongly Agree |

2. Online science exhibits are diverse and of interest to a wide range of visitors.

| Strongly Disagree | Disagree | Neutral | Agree | Strongly Agree |

3. There are many opportunities for me to become involved in students' science projects.

| Strongly Disagree | Disagree | Neutral | Agree | Strongly Agree |

Is there anything else we should know about your interests or background? If yes, briefly describe:

Figure 7.7   Sample user background survey for a VSF usability test.

General Instructions for Science Fair Study

In the next 30 minutes or so, you will be carrying out ten tasks within the Virtual Science Fair. These tasks are organized into two groups of four and six. Each group will be introduced with a story line that describes the role and situation we would like you to adopt for that set of tasks, and then each task is specified individually. Note that we intentionally leave out some of the detailed task steps so that we can determine how well the system can guide your interactions with it. If you are confused at any point, please just make your best guess about how to proceed, using the information that you have been given. We will intervene if necessary to help you make progress.

At the start of each task, please say out loud: "Beginning Task" followed by the number of the task. When you are done, please say: "Task Complete." Also, please remember to *think out loud* as you work. It is very important for us to understand your goals, expectations, and reactions as you work through the tasks. Any further questions?

Figure 7.8   General instructions for the VSF usability testing.

Specific Task Instructions for Science Fair Study

Background to Tasks 1 through 4
Imagine that you are Mr. King, an experienced science teacher who has coached many student projects in the past. This year you are advising Sally Harris on her black holes project. You are both very busy, but have arranged to meet in the VSF at 8 PM tonight. When you arrive, Sally is already there working.

Task 1:
Find out what exhibit component Sally is working on and synchronize your view with hers.

Task 2:
While Sally works on her Title Page, upload the Word file "Bibliography.doc" (on your desktop) into the exhibit element named "Bibliography."

Task 3:
Open the exhibit element that is an Excel document and modify the title of the chart to be "Interaction of Mass and Movement." Save your change.

Task 4:
Open the simulation element and add a nested folder named "Visitor Experiments."

Figure 7.9   Task-specific instructions for the coaching scenario subtasks.

the evaluator can describe what steps to take. However, it is important to supply the details needed to carry out a step, such as the name of a file to be uploaded. Each task assumes that the system is in an appropriate starting state. For example, when the user begins Task 1, he or she should see Sally's exhibit as it would appear when Mr. King first arrives; a co-evaluator should be online playing the role of Sally.

The task instructions guide users' interactions with the prototype, and evaluators collect various pieces of data as these interactions take place. In some cases, the data collected by hand will be minimal. Software systems can be instrumented to collect user input events and system responses, and a video camera can easily capture visible user behavior and comments. However, the review and analysis of these comprehensive data records are very time consuming (e.g., two to four hours for each hour of videotape recorded), so most evaluations will also employ one or more human observers (perhaps hidden behind a one-way mirror). In the science fair study, we used the simple **data collection form** in Figure 7.10 to record times, errors, and other interesting behavior.

Figure 7.11 shows part of the **user reaction survey** we developed to assess participants' subjective impressions of the science fair system. A reaction survey is usually more extensive than a background survey; by the time users complete this form, they have worked through a number of test tasks, and are primed to

Data Collection Form for VSF Study

Date: _____   Participant ID: _____   Evaluator: _____

Task Number: _____   Start time: _____   Stop time: _____

Comments made by participant:

Errors or problems observed (including assistance offered):

Other relevant observations:

Figure 7.10   A data collection form developed for VSF usability testing.

User Reactions Survey

Virginia Tech Computer Science Department and Center for Human-Computer Interaction

Now that you have completed the VSF tasks, we would like to know some of your reactions, both in general and to specific features of the system.

Name: _____

What three things did you like most about the VSF? Why?

What three things did you like least about the VSF? Why?

If the VSF was made available to you, would you use it or not? Why?

Please respond to the following 10 items by circling the opinion that best corresponds to your own.

1. Browsing an online science exhibit is like visiting a science fair in the real world.

Strongly Disagree   Disagree   Neutral   Agree   Strongly Agree

2. Online science exhibits are diverse and of interest to a wide range of visitors.

Strongly Disagree   Disagree   Neutral   Agree   Strongly Agree

3. There are many opportunities for me to become involved in students' science projects.

Strongly Disagree   Disagree   Neutral   Agree   Strongly Agreee

4. I was confused by the commands used to synchronize and unsynchronize my view with others.

Strongly Disagree   Disagree   Neutral   Agree   Strongly Agree

5. The procedure for uploading files into exhibit components is familiar to me.

Strongly Disagree   Disagree   Neutral   Agree   Strongly Agree

6. Learning that I could not make permanent changes to project data increased my confidence.

Strongly Disagree   Disagree   Neutral   Agree   Strongly Agree

7. Creating a new exhibit element that is nested behind another element is complex.

Strongly Disagree   Disagree   Neutral   Agree   Strongly Agree

8. It was easy to stay aware of what other co-present users were doing.

Strongly Disagree   Disagree   Neutral   Agree   Strongly Agree

< more Likert scales, testing the satisfaction specifications for the other subtasks . . . >

What would you suggest as changes to the design of the VSF (including the projects you browsed)?

Do you have any other final comments or reactions?

Thanks again for your participation!!

Figure 7.11 Part of the user reaction survey used in the science fair testing.

report their reactions. This particular survey combines several open-ended questions with a set of Likert rating scales. The former are probes similar to those used in critical incident interviews, where the goal is to discover what stands out in users' memories.

The Likert scales used in the pre-test survey are repeated, along with scales designed to measure the satisfaction outcomes specified earlier (Table 7.5). For example, Item 4 queries users' confusion stemming from the Control +F mechanism for sychronizing views; Item 5 measures the extent to which the file-uploading procedure is familiar to users; and so on. The final open-ended questions again enable participants to voice any additional reactions or suggestions.

Conducting the Usability Test

For a usability test to be meaningful, participants must feel comfortable and able to concentrate on their assigned tasks. The evaluators must be certain that participants know what is expected, but once this is established, they should make themselves as invisible as possible. Usability labs equipped with remote video or one-way mirrors for observation help to distance evaluators from participants. If one or more evaluators stay in the room to observe and take notes, they should step back out of the participants' peripheral vision and refrain from distracting movements or noises.

It is understandably difficult to keep an appropriate distance when participants have difficulty with a task—the natural human reaction is to offer assistance or advice. For this reason, it is essential to consider in advance which steps in a task are most likely to cause difficulties, and to develop an **assistance policy** that specifies when and how much help to provide.

The assistance policy should take into account the quality of the prototype and the goals of the test. If the prototype has a help system, experimenters may not intervene at all; participants are told to rely on the help documentation just as they would in the real world. However, prototypes are often incomplete. Sometimes an intervention is necessary simply to enable a participant to continue.

A good general strategy is to intervene in a graduated fashion: The first time a participant experiences a problem, direct him or her back to the task instructions and the screen display. If the problem persists or worsens, point to the specific instruction(s) or screen display that is most likely to help. Finally, if nothing else helps, specify exactly what to do (sometimes an evaluator must physically intervene to help the participant recover from an error).

A related issue arises when participants are asked to think aloud as they work. At the start of the session, individuals often need to be prompted, "What

are you thinking?" to remind them to share their thoughts. As the test progresses, it is up to the evaluators to recognize when significant events take place
(either successful or problematic), and to probe the users' thoughts at that point
if commentary is not provided. After testing, a semi-structured interview, or **debriefing**, helps to resolve any questions that come up during the evaluation.

Knowing when and how to intervene (whether for assistance or for prompting think-aloud commentary) requires extensive familiarity with task steps and
with the current state of the prototype. For this reason, and to ensure that the
instructions and survey questions are working as planned, evaluators should carry
out one or more **pilot tests**—practice sessions in which one or two participants
try out the materials, while the evaluators look for ways to refine the instructions,
data-gathering procedures, and so on. Pilot tests can usually be carried out quite
informally; for example, colleagues can be asked to test-drive the materials.

Reporting Test Results

The goal of an empirical evaluation is to discover as much as possible about
whether and how a system is meeting its usability specifications, and to develop
suggestions for improving the design. To fulfill this goal, the evaluators must
understand not just *what* test participants did during the test tasks, but *why* they
behaved and reacted as they did. This is accomplished by first characterizing the
test participants, and then examining in detail their behavior (e.g., time, errors,
and interaction episodes), and subjective reactions (e.g., comments while using
the system and ratings or opinions provided after the tests).

Participant Background   Several types of user characteristics were measured in our
user background survey. Occupation is a **categorical variable**; the response of
each participant is grouped into categories such as student or community member. Categorical variables are normally summarized as a frequency or count for
each category (e.g., 5 students, 2 professionals, 3 housewives) and are often displayed in a bar chart (Figure 7.12). Categorical variables may also be expressed as
percents or proportions, if the goal is to contrast different categories. Sometimes
the data from more than one variable is graphed in the same chart, to illustrate
relationships between variables.

Participants' occupation responses on the background survey were used to
assign them to one of four stakeholder groups; the chart on the left of Figure
7.12 shows that we tested 12 students, 8 community members, 4 teachers, and 2
school administrators. The histogram on the right summarizes computer use
across the different user groups. It shows that, as expected, the students and

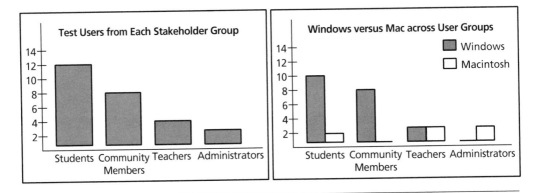

Figure 7.12   Categorical data from the VSF usability test. Each histogram shows the frequency of responses in that category.

community members are most likely to be using PCs, but that the education professionals are just as likely to use Macintosh computers.

An **ordinal variable** has values that have an inherent order, such as a scale that measures reactions from "positive" to "neutral" to "negative." These variables are also summarized with frequencies and histograms. In contrast, the values of an **interval variable** represent an ordered scale where the difference between any two neighboring values is known to be equal. Examples of these variables are age, years of education, and years of residency. These data are normally summarized with descriptive statistics such as means, modes, medians, and measures of variability.

Table 7.6 reports descriptive statistics for several questions about user background; each cell reports the mean and standard deviation for users in that group (the number or *n* in each group is shown in the header). A summary such as Table 7.6, combined with charts such as those those in Figure 7.12, provides a comprehensive description of the people serving as test participants. Notice that both the students and community members tend to be longtime residents, despite their wide variation in age and level of education.

Task Performance and Satisfaction   The results from the usability test fall into two general groups: objective data concerning users' performance (generally time and errors, sometimes an inventory of behaviors), and subjective data concerning their attitudes and reactions (the ratings and comments they make during or after their interactions with the system).

Table 7.6 Means (and standard deviations) for three background measures, broken down by user group.

Participant characteristics (in years)	Students (n = 12)	Community (n = 8)	Teachers (n = 4)	Administrators (n = 2)
Age	14.5 (1.18)	54.7 (7.69)	38.3 (5.41)	45.8 (2.44)
Education	10.0 (1.55)	17.8 (4.43)	16.5 (1.94)	17.3 (3.44)
Residency	10.8 (2.65)	12.3 (3.01)	8.3 (2.87)	5.9 (5.22)

Table 7.7 Summary of time (and standard deviations) and errors on four VSF test tasks (across all 26 participants).

VSF Task	Mean Time (seconds)	Mean Errors
1. Synchronizing views	40.20 (3.12)	1.6
2. Uploading a file	115.30 (15.33)	2.2
3. Interacting with Excel	62.55 (2.30)	0.9
4. Adding a nested element	143.13 (20.41)	2.8
Combined total	361.18 (10.29)	5.2

Summarizing performance data is straightforward. Task times are easy to report with means and measures of variability. Errors are counted and reported as total frequencies, or as an average frequency across users. If there are many errors, it may be useful to first categorize them into groups (e.g., navigation or editing).

Table 7.7 summarizes performance on the four subtasks from the coaching scenario. Generally, results are summarized task by task (e.g., the average time to complete Task 1 was 40.20 seconds, with an average of 1.6 errors made across the 26 participants). This allows easy comparison to the usability specifications developed earlier (Table 7.5), and makes clear which tasks are particularly problematic or successful. For example, we can see that creating a nested component took much longer than specified, and that most of the tasks produced some degree of error.

When there are many tasks, or when the tasks fall into natural groupings (e.g., by source scenario), it may be helpful to combine task times and errors,

Table 7.8 Summary of satisfaction ratings for VSF test tasks (across 26 participants).
Strongly Disagree = 1; Disagree = 2; Neutral = 3; Agree = 4; and Strongly Agree = 5.

Likert Item	Mean Rating	Change
1. VSF is like real world	3.2 (1.55)	+1.01 (0.15)
2. Exhibits diverse, interesting	4.1 (1.67)	+0.55 (0.25)
3. Opportunities for science project involvement	2.9 (2.11)	+0.10 (0.09)
4. Confusion about synchronization	3.5 (0.91)	
5. Familiarity of file-uploading dialog	4.2 (1.02)	
6. Confidence when interacting with project data	3.7 (2.24)	
7. Complexity of creating a nested element	4.0 (1.94)	

developing composite performance measures that represent more complex inter-action sequences. If the evaluators suspect or observe differences related to user background, the data may also be decomposed and summarized as a function of the various user characteristics.

In summarizing satisfaction outcomes, usability evaluators often treat rating scales as if they are interval variables—in other words, they treat each scale position as if it were a number, and assume that the difference between any two positions is always the same. Even though experts agree that rating scales are not as precise a measure as implied here, treating ratings as interval data makes it much easier to summarize test results and to compare outcomes for different user groups or versions of a system. Thus, in Table 7.8 we use means and standard deviations of the data from seven Likert scales.

Table 7.8 also presents **change scores** for the rating scales that were in-cluded in both surveys. These attitude items were of a general nature, probing views of an online science fair and involvement in science fair activities. The assumption is that a positive experience overall should increase the positive re-sponses on these scales; such an effect would appear as an overall positive differ-ence. The data in the table suggest that while participants' interactions with the system may have enhanced their concept of a virtual science fair, they were not persuaded that it will change their opportunities for becoming more involved in science fairs.

Sometimes it is also useful to explore the relationship between user char-acteristics and the performance or attitude measures collected. For example, an evaluation team might be interested in task time for experienced versus inexperienced computer users. Indeed, even if there was no deliberate sampling of users with varying backgrounds, the performance or attitude data collected may be highly variable across individuals. Such diversity is often a signal that personal characteristics are influencing users' experiences, and a careful examination of user background variables may be essential to fully understand the results obtained.

Verbal Protocols and User Behavior A more challenging data summary task is the organization and interpretation of the comments made by participants. Some of these comments emerge during the test tasks, as participants think aloud about their activities. Others are offered in response to open-ended questions included on the user reaction survey. It is the great diversity and subjective nature of these data that make them difficult to summarize.

The simplest approach is to develop categories that capture major themes in the comments. For example, comments might be categorized as positive or negative, or they might be divided into function areas, such as navigation, error recovery, and so on. For survey questions asking for "the three worst things," a summary of this sort can be very helpful in guiding redesign, particularly if users are also asked why they highlighted a particular feature. Categorical data such as these could be summarized with frequency, percentage, or proportion scores (e.g., in a table or histogram).

A more detailed analysis may be developed to understand individual users' interactions with a system. The raw data in this case are behaviors documented through observers' notes, videotape or screen capture, and corresponding think-aloud protocols. Figure 7.13 shows such an episode from the science fair testing. Such episodes can be examined for events that reveal misunderstandings (or correct inferences) about the system. For example, this particular episode suggests that the user did not at first realize that she could double-click on the miniature windows to open the underlying application. If this same problem were observed for a number of users, the design team might consider a redesign that makes the "application-launch" functionality more apparent (e.g., recall the icon design discussion in Chapter 4).

This sort of qualitative analysis demonstrates a form of critical incident analysis that is very common and very useful in formative usability evaluation. The data obtained through observation and think-aloud studies, although qualitative and somewhat anecdotal in character, can have a tremendous influence on software developers, simply because the usage experience it conveys is so rich.

00:00 <begins spreadsheet task>

"That looks like an Excel chart, I guess that's what I'm supposed to work on."

00:15 <clicks on Excel miniature window>

"So I see the chart up there, but how am I supposed to change it?

Maybe I can type directly on that screen?"

<gesturing at main viewing area>

00:50 <tries to type into the main screen, nothing happens>

"Uh-oh, I hope I didn't break this, I can't type anything here. Is it frozen?"

<tries selecting another element, it works, then back to Excel>

"But I still can't do anything!"

<stops and looks around, not clear what thoughts are>

01:35 <starts looking at menu bar>

"So maybe this is just to look at and I need to use a menu or something."

. . . Or maybe—ah, that's it!"

<double-clicks on icon, it opens . . . continues the task>

Figure 7.13   A partial episode transcript from Task 3, merging records of what the user was doing with her think-aloud commentary.

7.4.4   Assessing and Refining Usability Specifications

It is easy to become lost in the details of data collected in an empirical study. The team must always keep in mind the relative costs and benefits of the techniques they are using—for instance, early in system development, control and precision may be less critical than seeing if a particular scenario or subtask is even possible for users. In such cases, it is perfectly reasonable to rely on informal testing situations, as long as the team understands the limitations of these more informal methods (e.g., lower test validity).

However, in the longer term, it is the development and constant reference to a set of usability specifications that guides a usability engineering process. Participants' performance and subjective reactions are compared to the expected levels. When test data are considerably worse than the projected levels, a warning flag is raised; the evaluators must then carefully analyze the detailed usage data to determine how to resolve the problem. If the test data are considerably better than expected, a different warning flag is raised—in this case, the team may have been too conservative in their usability objectives, or may have inadvertently developed instructions or test procedures that oversimplified or trivialized a task.

Summary and Review

This chapter has presented the rationales and examples of usability evaluation in the design of interactive systems. The discussion was organized by Scriven's (1967) contrasts of formative and summative evaluation, and of analytic and empirical evaluation. The science fair project was used to demonstrate how design scenarios and claims can be directed toward the goals of usability evaluation. Central points to remember include:

- Formative evaluation emphasizes guidance for redesign, whereas summative evaluation emphasizes assessment of a system's overall quality.

- Scenarios can be reformulated as usability specifications, because they describe the usability consequences of specific system features. For testing purposes, scenarios are broken into subtasks that serve as usability benchmarks in development.

- Analytic methods such as inspection or model building can take place at any time in development, but may not reflect the issues that emerge during actual use.

- Important concerns in empirical evaluations include representative users, realistic tasks and work environment, and the quality of the prototype tested.

- Asking users to think aloud as they work through test tasks provides important insights into how they are forming and pursuing goals, and how they are making sense of what happens when they attempt actions.

- Summarizing user behavior and think-aloud reports in terms of critical incidents (both positive and negative) can be a highly evocative (albeit anecdotal) mechanism for educating and influencing software developers.

- Independent variables are the factors expected to have an effect on users' experience; dependent variables are the behaviors or reactions measured to assess these effects.

- Claims analysis and other analytic methods (e.g., usability inspection) can be used to identify and prioritize subtasks for detailed analysis in usability testing.

- Writing new scenarios just for the purposes of usability testing is important to ensure generality and coverage of the design work.

- During usability testing, it is important to gather relevant background information about each user, so as to best interpret the behavior and satisfaction data obtained.

- Careful planning must be directed at all aspects of the usability test (e.g., instructions, assistance policy, background and reaction surveys) to ensure that useful and interpretable data are collected.

Exercises
_____

1. Carry out a usability inspection of the Web site for Amazon.com. Using the example in Table 7.3 as a model, play the role of a usability expert working from Nielsen's guidelines. Scope the analysis by first choosing two concrete tasks (e.g., finding a particular product), and then identify usability problems associated with each task. Be sure to describe the tasks you focused on along with the problems that you identify.

2. Discuss the problem of recruiting representative users for a usability test of a Java development environment. Suggest some strategies you might use to address these problems. What would you do if you could not recruit expert Java programmers?

3. Think back over your last few weeks of surfing the Web. Can you remember any episodes that you would report as "critical incidents"? If so, what makes them critical? If you can't remember any, interview friends and see what they remember.

4. Complete the set of Likert scales in Figure 7.11. Using items 4 through 8 as models, write one additional rating scale for subtasks 6 through 10 in Table 7.5. Remember that the scale should be specific to the aspect of satisfaction singled out in the specification (i.e., directness, predictability, engagement, tedium, and obscurity).

5. Add another column of new scenarios to Figure 7.5. Use the same technique demonstrated there, working with similar functionality in each case, but bringing in the goals and concerns of sets of actors.

6. Collect a brief think-aloud protocol of a friend searching the Web for information about the International Space Station. Provide a version of the general instructions in Figure 7.8, and then record (preferably using a

tape recorder) all remarks made. Create a transcript like the one in Figure 7.13, and then look for evidence of how your friend thinks about this task. What does it tell you about his or her mental model of the Web and understanding of search machines? What organizations and people are concerned with space stations?

Project Ideas

Plan, conduct, and report on a usability evaluation of your online shopping system:

- Use your scenarios and claims to define subtasks and create usability specifications. Discuss and select realistic performance and satisfaction levels, using performance on similar systems as a guide.

- Design and construct testing materials (consent form, instructions, background and reaction surveys, and data collection forms).

- Recruit five or six participants (subjects) and carry out the study. Be sure to plan all procedures in advance, including how errors will be recognized, what other data will be collected, when and how much assistance will be provided, and so on.

- Develop summary presentations and discussions of your test results. Focus on the findings that are most out of line with the specifications, and consider what you might do in redesign to address these issues.

Recommended Reading

Dix, A., J. Finlay, G. Abowd, & R. Beale. 1998. *Human-Computer Interaction*. 2d ed. (chapter 11). London: Prentice-Hall.

Lewis, C., & J. Rieman. 1993. *Task-Centered User Interface Design*. Shareware book available by FTP at *ftp.cs.colorado.edu*.

Monk. A., P. Wright, J. Haber, & L. Davenport. 1992. *Improving Your Human-Computer Interface: A Practical Approach*. London: Prentice-Hall.

Nielsen, J. 1992. *Usability Engineering*. New York: Academic Press.

Preece, J., Y. Rogers, H. Sharp, D. Benyon, S. Holland, & T. Carey. 1994. *Human-Computer Interaction* (chapters from section entitled Interaction design: Evaluation). Reading, MA: Addison-Wesley.

Robson, C. 1999. *Experiment, Design and Statistics in Psychology*. 3rd ed. Penguin.

User
Documentation

In the early 1980s, our group at the IBM Watson Research Center investigated the difficulties people experienced getting started with personal computers. In these studies, we provided all required software, hardware, and documentation, and then watched quietly. Our observations illustrated how people did not, and perhaps could not, make effective use of what appeared to be carefully designed documentation and self-instruction material. As part of this project, we carried out a study of the Apple Lisa, one of the first systems to incorporate a graphical user interface, an interactive tutorial, and an extensive library of manuals specifically designed for end users.

One of our volunteer users turned out to be a linguist working as a documentation developer. He was fairly knowledgeable about the state of the art in documentation, and was quite impressed with the Lisa manuals and interactive tutorial. He declared to us at the outset of the session, "You're going to be watching a lot of reading. I am the kind of person who reads everything before doing anything." However, within a few minutes, he had discarded the manuals and was improvising with the tutorial exercises, actively exploring the system, and making lots of errors (Carroll & Mazur 1986).

———⟨∞∞⟩———

User documentation is stored information about how to use a system. There are many forms of documentation and many purposes served by documentation. The most typical example is the traditional bound reference manual. But documentation also includes online help utilities, intelligent tutoring systems, and user forums. It can be a standalone subsystem, like an interactive tutorial or a frequently asked questions (FAQ) forum, or it can be tightly integrated with core system functionality, such as input prompts and error messages. It can support new users just getting started with a system, experienced users recovering from errors, or expert users refining their knowledge and use of advanced options.

The main problem that defines or frames documentation design is that people interacting with software systems have a wide variety of information needs. They need to know what a piece of software is for and what tasks it supports. For example, a spreadsheet program is for table-based calculation, not for document preparation or real-time conferencing. People need to know how the software supports those tasks and what procedures are possible. For instance, the spreadsheet probably supports graphing and macro definition. People need to know how to carry out various procedures, such as how to specify cells for a graph and how to reference cell indices in a macro.

People also need to know something about how the software works (i.e., they need a mental model). One reason for this is that a mental model will help them make sense of their interactions with the software. Take a simple word processing example: It is obvious that paragraph formatting is represented by a character, once you know it. But if you do not already know it, text manipulation can be confusing and frustrating. Some text insertions will reformat and some will not, some text deletions will remove paragraph formatting and some will not, and so forth. Another reason for providing how-it-works documentation is that people will spontaneously generate mental models for how things work. Without guidance, they often produce incorrect models.

Each of these information needs is itself a complex documentation problem. None of the problems can be satisfied once and for all with a single description or explanation, presented in a single manner. For example, the graphing capabilities of a spreadsheet program should be presented in a way that reinforces an appropriate mental model of what the system can do and how it works. At the same time, graphing procedures (action plans) must be guided by prompts and error messages in the user interface. Graphing capabilities must be described in instructional materials—the manuals, the interactive tutorial, and the online help. The information needed for a given usage situation must be easily accessible, and it must be presented in a way that aids interpretation and sense making (Chapter 4).

From these initial considerations it might seem that documentation design should be a lively and attractive topic in computing—and, to some extent, it is. However, documentation is also dogged by paradox. One of the well-known clichés of computing is that nobody reads documentation. Indeed, it is worse than that: The cliché should be that nobody reads documentation and nobody writes documentation, but everybody needs documentation.

8.1   The Production Paradox

Attitudes toward and use of documentation are described by a principle of human cognition called the **production paradox**: People want to produce things, and they want to achieve meaningful results. This is not an issue of job performance, that is, of pleasing managers and bosses; it is a more fundamental issue of self-perception. People want to see themselves as competent, engaged, and productive. However, in order to be productive in the long term, people often must carry out activities that undermine their short-term productivity, such as reading or writing documentation (Carroll & Rosson 1987).

Users want to achieve task goals that are meaningful to them, goals they already understand and expect to achieve, such as finding a particular piece of information or document, or communicating something to someone. Sometimes the software they use facilitates these goals, and sometimes it obstructs them, but the act of reading documentation about the software is *always* a distraction (Tradeoff 8.1). An analogous account can be given as to why software developers devalue the task of writing documentation.

TRADEOFF 8.1

Documentation helps people to use systems more productively, BUT people do not experience reading documentation as meaningful work activity.

The production paradox helps in understanding many of the problems people have using documentation. People often skip around. Instead of carefully reading explanations and following procedures, they browse and scan sections, perhaps alternating among several manuals. Documentation designers know that people skip around in documentation, and they attempt to discourage this, such as with the somewhat pathetic plea to "Read everything before doing anything." A more drastic technique in online training is to require specific actions before moving to the next step. Users do not like this technique.

An alternative approach to the skipping-around problem starts with asking why it happens. Skipping around can be seen as a way to transform the passive tasks of reading and following instructions into the more meaningful tasks of exploration, diagnosis, and hypothesis testing. Skipping around is an attempt to **learn by doing**, rather than by reading. People want to learn about a system while they are trying things out; this follows directly from the production paradox. Skipping around is not a problem, but a symptom: Users do this to create more meaningful tasks for themselves. The problem is that skipping around can lead to tangled errors that are difficult to analyze or correct.

Error management is another example of the production paradox. Most people do not try to make errors, but errors often help them to explore the boundaries of what they know. In our studies of people using systems and documentation, we have observed people who almost roll up their sleeves in anticipation when they recognize a nontrivial error state. As in the case of skipping around, error diagnosis and recovery are active and meaningful tasks.

Traditional documentation design treated error as rare and problematic, addressed via troubleshooting appendices. In reality, error and error recovery are frequent and common. Even experts spend about a quarter of their time in error states (Card, Moran, & Newell 1983); novices often spend more than half their time recovering from errors (Carroll & Carrithers 1984). The variety and sophistication of contemporary documentation technologies, especially context-sensitive and intelligent help, permit ambitious approaches to learning from error—using errors to help people understand what the system is for, what they might want to do with it, and how to pursue both of these goals.

A theme in modern documentation design is the integration of documentation with meaningful activities. Instead of simply defining operations and options, documentation should explain how to accomplish a real task with the software, a task that incorporates the use of particular operations, while illustrating respective options and their interactions. Key guidelines for writing effective documentation are the tight coupling between people's goals and strategies and the presentation of information that enables these goals and strategies.

8.2   Paper and Online Manuals

A person's first encounter with documentation for a system is often a self-paced tutorial. Instruction-oriented documentation became common in the 1980s with personal computing. Classroom approaches to training were not economically viable for inexpensive personal computers, whose users varied greatly in technical background and application needs. The computing industry adopted the concept of **self-instruction**, so that users could teach themselves how to use new software. Computers and software were bundled with comprehensive training materials (see "Systematic Documentation" sidebar).

The first examples of self-instruction were paper manuals. People worked through lessons following procedures, reading explanations, and carrying out self-test exercises. The design of such manuals has evolved to address the production paradox in a variety of ways. For example, it is common for instruction manuals to emphasize hands-on activity, to be organized in terms of people's tasks instead of system functions and operations, to coordinate the textual material with other information such as associated screen images, and to provide error-recovery procedures (see Figure 8.1).

People's diverse learning needs have also promoted a lively third-party industry providing a variety of specialized paper documentation. For example, a user might obtain:

- A getting-started manual that introduces a few core tasks.

- A comprehensive self-study tutorial covering all application tasks.

Systematic Documentation

Documentation design is not just writing. Every piece of documentation—every label, prompt, and error message; every help frame; and every paragraph of every manual—is constrained by every other piece. Terminology and assumptions about people's prior knowledge must be consistent throughout. In this sense, the documentation is itself a system. Like the software it describes, the documentation has an overall design that can be systematically analyzed and decomposed into an implementation. Recent documentation technologies, such as hypertext and multimedia, make this point emphatically: They provide a much richer design space for documentation, and thus many more ways to achieve poor documentation design!

Systematic documentation emerged in the 1960s as an example of hierarchical decomposition; task analysis and structured programming are other examples (Gagne & Briggs 1979). It models human knowledge and task-oriented goals as hierarchies: For example, the concept of a spreadsheet involves subconcepts such as cell, column, and equation. The goal of graphing a set of spreadsheet cells involves the subgoals of selecting the cells and formatting the graph; the latter decomposes into selecting a graph template and specifying labels for axes, and so on. The de-

composition can be carried to arbitrary levels of detail.

After the documentation designer constructs a comprehensive task hierarchy, explanatory material is created to address each terminal node as a separate information objective. Subsequent references in the documentation to a given concept or task can then repeat or point to the relevant piece of the hierarchy. An important strength of this approach is that it ensures that prerequisite information is incorporated into documentation.

But systematic documentation has important weaknesses as well (Tradeoff 8.3). People do not always experience systematic documentation as meaningful when they read it. An overall decomposition of task knowledge and goals may not correspond to the way anyone thinks about a particular task. Indeed, general-purpose decompositions often emphasize subgoals too much, at the expense of conveying the bigger picture. A focus on low-level goals (e.g., formatting the text in a spreadsheet cell), with only secondary attention to the larger task context (e.g., creating a budget report) can frustrate and de-motivate people. Decomposing a task into subtasks allows a complex activity to be built up from its parts, but the knowledge gained may not be useful in real task settings.

- Job aids presented as cards that briefly define a specific function or operation.

- A comprehensive reference manual that defines all features, functions, and operations.

Paper has a number of advantages and disadvantages (Table 8.1). Turning pages is not a meaningful activity for people who want to use software. Bulky manuals (indeed libraries of manuals) are intimidating and de-motivating (Tradeoff 8.2). Their sheer mass emphasizes how much the person does not yet know,

Select a GOO brush and apply the effect directly to your image with your cursor.

Reset   Reset removes all GOO effects from your image.

Grow/Shrink   Painting with Grow/Shrink in a clockwise motion enlarges the painted area of the image. Painting in a counter-clockwise motion shrinks the painted area.

Move   One of four "push" brushes. Move has the largest area of effect but the least pressure. Use it to create subtle distortion effects.

Smear   Smear is smaller than Move and exerts a high level of distortion pressure for creating quick, dramatic distortions.

Smudge   Smudge affects a slightly smaller area than Smear, but with decreased pressure. Use it to create small, subtle distortion effects.

Nudge   The extremely small size and high pressure of Nudge makes it useful for creating a finger-painting effect.

Mirror/Toggle   When Mirror/Toggle is active, brushstrokes are mirrored along the vertical axis.

Smooth   Smooth gradually and selectively undos the distortion effects of the GOO brushes.

UnGOO   UnGOO quickly undos the distortion effects of the GOO brushes. It is the ultimate "selective undo" brush.

Grow/Shrink   Move

Smear   Smudge   Nudge

Mirror/Toggle   Smooth   UnGOO

Figure 8.1   This page from the manual for *Kai's Power GOO* (Torzewski & Sullivan 1997) illustrates explicit coordination (the gallery of image transformation effects are coordinated with the names for the effects) and error management (the first command defined is Reset and the last is UnGOO). The manual addresses the user requirement for a meaningful task in an interesting way: The image to which the transformations is applied is highly recognizable, and the examples immediately suggest the open-ended and engaging task of creating one's own reinterpretation of Mona Lisa.

and how many pages remain to be turned. It is difficult to coordinate the information in manuals with system activity, because people become absorbed in system interactions and forget to check the manual in their laps. This increases the possibility that errors will not be recognized and addressed when they first occur and that multiple errors may accumulate, creating a tangle of errors that is difficult to diagnose and recover from.

TRADEOFF 8.2

   Online manuals facilitate information access, navigation, and search, BUT are harder to read and browse than paper, and less convenient to annotate.

Table 8.1 Commonly cited advantages and disadvantages of paper-based documentation.

Advantages	Disadvantages
Highly portable, can be used anywhere	Finding and turning to a page is an extra task
Easy to scan at varying levels of detail	Paper is bulky, takes up office or desk space
Can be annotated with normal writing tools	Large manuals may seem intimidating to novices
Familiarity, based on well-practiced reading habits	Lack of coordination between paper and software
Reading is faster from paper than screens	Fixed organization of content
People like owning books and other manuals	Paper and print deteriorate over time with use

Nevertheless, paper manuals remain an important delivery medium for user documentation. Paper is highly portable, easy to scan, and convenient to annotate. Despite the reluctance people often have toward reading manuals, they seem to like having manuals. Some of the downsides of paper can be addressed merely by making paper documentation available online. People always have the manual content ready to hand, and they do not need to dedicate desk space to a physical manual. They can navigate the manual with links, instead of turning pages; for example, an online index can be a list of links. Even better, they can use string searches, or sophisticated information retrieval tools (Egan, et al. 1989a, 1989b) to access relevant content, instead of laboriously scanning physical pages.

However, there are also downsides to placing information online. Displays produce poorer images than printed materials; they can be as much as 25% less readable. Displays often present less information than a printed page, particularly, of course, when the online information is allocated only a portion of the display. This means that online manuals usually have more frames than the number of pages in a paper version. This makes navigation more difficult. Finally, online information structures are more difficult to grasp; browsing online information is typically less effective than browsing a paper manual. Because of issues such as these, optimal online and paper designs for the same information content tend to be different.

TRADEOFF 8.3

 Documenting tasks as components that combine systematically into larger tasks organizes complex information, BUT may not match real-world tasks.

8.3   Demonstrations and Tutorials

All manuals have inescapable usability problems. For example, they tell rather than show. For graphical user interfaces, it is often easier and more effective to show people what to do or what will happen than to describe it in words. **Demonstrations** are scripted user-system interactions. A demonstration captures a user's attention with animation, and shows brief but intriguing interaction episodes. The idea is motivated by video games, such as PacMan, that present documentation as an animation which plays over and over, attracting and training new users at the same time. Demonstrations are very good at expressing simple and dynamic information (Waterson & O'Malley 1992). They orient users to important elements of a user interface display and illustrate typical behaviors with this information. Demonstrations motivate people to try out software, while removing the possibility of error (Palmiter & Elkerton 1991; Payne, Chesworth, & Hill 1992).

The key disadvantage of demonstrations derives from one of their strengths: Learners do nothing but watch (Tradeoff 8.4). Often even simple requests—stop, replay, back up, or skip—are not possible. Demonstrations may offer a realistic view of the software in use, but they provide little opportunity for goals, planning, action, or sense making. This weakness can be addressed by enabling at least a small degree of interaction. For example, a demonstration might display a brief description of a screen object when it is selected, or prompt viewers to provide the next command in a sequence. Such techniques make learners more active and enhance learning.

TRADEOFF 8.4

 Demonstrations provide attractive and safe previews of functions, BUT people cannot learn how to find, execute, and control a function by viewing its effects.

A problem for both manuals and demonstrations is that they do not respond to people's behavior. Manuals can coordinate illustrative screen shots with error-recovery information, but this may not help if the reader is viewing a different screen or page. A demonstration executes with little or no regard for what the viewer is doing. This lack of responsiveness is a key motivation for interactive documentation. An **interactive tutorial** is similar to an online manual. It presents a sequence of presentations and exercises designed to promote learning, but using digital media. Because these tutorials are online, they can incorporate built-in demonstrations; they can illustrate typical user–system interactions, often by running actual system code. An interactive tutorial can also provide **scaffolding** (learning supports that enable new users to do more interesting tasks than they can do on their own) in the form of prompts, special feedback, reflective questions, and so on.

In an interactive tutorial, the display of information is triggered by system states and input events. Instead of showing a screen image and asking the learner to verify that the system is in this state, the tutorial determines the state itself. This is enormously useful in error management: An interactive tutorial can monitor for specific errors and provide immediate feedback and recovery guidance, cutting down the possibility of tangled errors that are difficult to diagnose and address.

Online tutorials can also be specialized to address differences among learners. For example, scientists and accountants use spreadsheets in different ways—accountants do not need inferential statistics, while scientists make limited use of percentages. Mathematicians and Web designers make different uses of word processors—mathematicians make extensive use of symbols, while Web designers need to worry about what can be translated into HTML.

Substantial differences in domain knowledge and usage interests such as these are relatively easy for people to self-diagnose, so different tutorials can be designed around different basic tasks. The learner can indicate a domain preference at the start of an instructional program, and thus obtain the version appropriate to this interest. This version specificity leverages a learner's prior knowledge in acquiring new information and makes the learning process more personally interesting and meaningful.

Tutorials can also provide alternate learning tracks for different types of learners. For example, a fast track can be created for people who learn quickly, who want only a quick overview, or who are relearning to use a program. Remedial tracks can be provided for people who experience difficulty with portions of the tutorial. And, of course, error-recovery support should be available from any point in the tutorial experience. Figure 8.2 suggests some of the control-flow possibilities for an interactive tutorial.

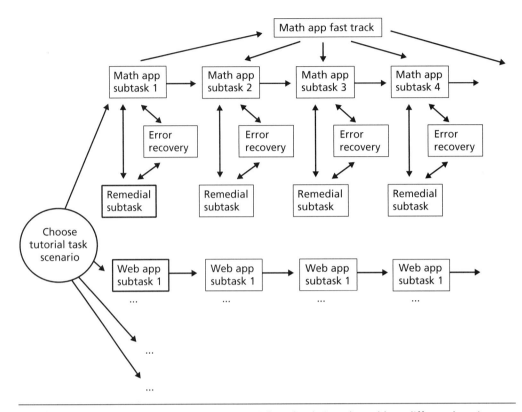

Figure 8.2 Multiple tracks in an interactive tutorial can be designed to address different learning needs.

Tutorials can be designed to simulate the real system, or they can be directly integrated into the system. An advantage of integration is that it helps to ensure a smooth transition from learning about the system to using it. In a tutorial we created for the Smalltalk language, learners developed Smalltalk classes in their tutorial exercises. At the end of the tutorial, these classes were part of their Smalltalk class library; the tutorial was not just similar to real programming, it was real programming (Rosson, Carroll, & Bellamy 1990). Of course, a disadvantage of this approach is that the range and complexity of potential errors is greater when working with the full system.

The greatest challenge in designing interactive tutorials is staying focused on the most important concepts and operations. The possibilities for interactive learning are many and are increasing. It is easy to overwhelm users with graphical animations, video images, and sound, while teaching very little (Tradeoff 8.5). It is also tempting to provide a tutorial that is too thorough: For even a modest application program, there are far too many possible tasks and variations to provide a tutorial for each. Instead, an analysis and iterative design process should identify the tasks most people want to do most of the time, and then prepare materials that guide them through these tasks (see "Minimalism" sidebar).

Minimalism

The minimalist model for documentation is an attempt to move beyond systematic design. It emphasizes the iterative design of documentation that learners can use to learn by doing (Carroll 1990, 1998; Meij & Carroll 1995). The following key principles guide the design of minimalist instruction.

1. Documentation should be *action oriented*: People should be continuously encouraged and supported to act as they work with information. In a practical sense, this means that most of the learner's time should be spent interacting with the system rather than reading about how to achieve these interactions. Verbiage should be kept to a minimum, and prompts for action and analysis should be common.

2. Documentation should leverage learners' prior knowledge of work domains. The material should be presented in familiar task contexts, such as, for example, construction of a budget report or analysis of a budget discrepancy. The content and structure of the documentation and the tools that present it should correspond to the content and structure of real tasks. When possible, connect the learning tasks to the learner's real-world activities, such as analyzing and modifying information that supports actual work.

3. Documentation should *anticipate and manage errors*: Nuisance mistakes (e.g., mistyping a file name) should be prevented when possible. However, common conceptual errors (e.g., confusing a data file with an application file) should be discovered and analyzed through empirical testing, and adequate and timely error detection and recovery information should be provided. When possible, these likely error episodes should be treated as opportunities for reflection and greater understanding of how the system works.

The design of minimalist instruction shares some similarities with systematic documentation design, but it is more demanding. For example, in minimalist design it is crucial to investigate the domain knowledge people bring to their use of systems and software, and the sorts of inferences people are likely to make in given circumstances. Information that users are likely to already know or can infer need not be made explicit; such information clutters the documentation and discourages user activity.

Of course, minimalist documentation has its own set of disadvantages (Tradeoff 8.6). People who expect documentation to be sequential and explanatory may be intimidated if they are asked to make sense of open-ended and incomplete instructions. Many people do not see error recovery as a learning opportunity, but rather as an irritating distraction. Documentation designers also can be intimidated by the need to analyze, and take into account what they discover, about learners' prior knowledge, as opposed to merely describing how the software works.

TRADEOFF 8.5

Interactive tutorials allow documentation to be dynamically linked to users' needs and activities, BUT can overwhelm users by trying to do too much.

In recent years, many applications have begun to build wizards into their online help systems. A wizard is somewhat like an interactive tutorial, in that it guides users through the steps of a new task. However, each wizard is very task specific, making it more like a help system than a general training system. Wizards are particularly common during installation or customization procedures, where a task is done only rarely, and then in a very scripted (and thus easily supported) fashion.

TRADEOFF 8.6

Meaningful activities motivate and orient people to apply information, BUT may lead to anxiety about continually making sense and taking appropriate action.

8.4   Information in the Interface

One thing that manuals, demonstrations, and tutorials have in common is that they are *not* what users want to do. People install a spreadsheet to carry out spreadsheet tasks, not to read manuals, watch demonstrations, or work through the sequential tasks of an interactive tutorial. Fortunately, contemporary user interfaces provide many options for embedding information so that it can be incidentally encountered by people as they work on their own tasks. User interfaces that do a good job at this are often characterized as **walk-up-and-use systems**, emphasizing that users are not expected to first read about or learn the system but rather can get right down to work.

One large category of information in the interface is system messages. User interfaces include labels for many task objects such as programs and files, they prompt for user input, and they notify users of progress and errors. When these messages are specific and action oriented, they can be important documentation resources. When a new Macintosh user clicks on "Register With Apple," a Web browser opens on the "Apple Product Registration" Web site, making it very clear what actions to take next (including canceling the task). At other times, a message is too general to guide action. An error message such as #VALUE! in a spreadsheet indicates that something could not be calculated. A more action-oriented message would indicate why the calculation is not possible (X is an unbound variable) or what would make it possible (assign a value).

Of course, there are design tradeoffs lurking. A message such as "Application cannot open" provides useful information, but less so than "Insufficient memory to open application." The latter is longer and more specific, but requires more screen space to display and more reading time to comprehend (Tradeoff 8.7). The message "There is not enough memory available to open 'Microsoft Excel'. Do you want to quit the application 'Microsoft PowerPoint' and open 'Microsoft Excel' instead?" is even more action oriented, but even longer (Figure 8.3). Where should message content stop? Is it helpful to say how memory is allocated among applications? Should a message explain memory allocation, and perhaps provide information on how to install additional RAM? At some point, calling such documentation a system message becomes a stretch.

TRADEOFF 8.7

 System messages integrate documentation with ordinary interaction, BUT messages that are specific and task oriented may be lengthy and consume screen space.

Information layering allows system information to be rich but still consume only modest screen space. Information is organized into different levels, with each level providing more detailed help or explanation. For example, a special key combination invoked on an icon might open a small information window stating what the program does and what it assumes about the operating environment. This would allow people to find out enough about an unfamiliar program to start it up. But the information box might also provide access to more

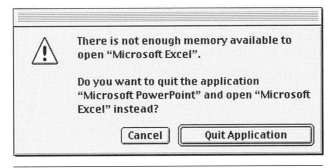

Figure 8.3 System message that provides specific and action-oriented documentation.

detailed information, such as a button for additional feature summaries, a demonstration, even a tutorial. Similarly, a more lengthy explanation of the error message "X is an unbound variable," for example, could be accessed by clicking on the error message.

Layering is a very general technique. Farkas (1998) describes procedure prompts that have links to (1) conceptual background information, (2) an example, (3) detailed steps, (4) little-used options and infrequently encountered circumstances, (5) tips for efficient use, and (6) links to related topics. Of course, such an approach has disadvantages. The layering structure can become complex enough that it becomes a learning and control obstacle itself. Second, it could be quite expensive to develop documentation in which every error message, prompt, or display object has its own small hypertext information model.

Another technique for documenting a system via its user interface is to define special interaction modes. In a **training-wheels** environment, a filter causes many system states to be inaccessible. The learner can do less—just as one can do less with a bicycle that has training wheels—but is protected from the consequences of serious mistakes. In one system using this technique, just a few core system functions were enabled. Selecting other functions produced the message "<name of function> is not available in the Training Displaywriter." This message recognizes that the learner has taken a specific action, but redirects planning and acting back to the core functions. Training-wheels interfaces have been shown to help learners get started more rapidly, spend less time in error recovery, and more quickly learn advanced functions later on (Carroll 1990).

Icon **tooltips** is a pervasive technique for embedding documentation in the interface. A function name or brief description appears in a pop-up label box when the user pauses the mouse pointer over the icon. This is an example of dynamic presentation of information discussed in Chapter 4; the additional documentation becomes visible only when implicitly requested (though sometimes a user is only pausing to think!). If designed with care, a set of tooltips can provide just enough additional information that a relatively experienced user can make use of unfamiliar icons or buttons. Unfortunately, these bits of information are often included as afterthoughts and sometimes provide little or no new information (Johnson 2000, 235–36).

The tooltip mechanism is a descendant of Macintosh **balloon help**. In contrast to tooltips, balloon help is turned on and off explicitly through a menu choice. When it is on, information about user interface objects is presented in a balloon when the mouse pointer passes over it (Figure 8.4). Although the level of assistance provided is up to the documentation designer, balloon help tends to provide assistance at one level of detail beyond a tooltip. In the figure, the text explains what will happen if the user chooses the option in question. Some

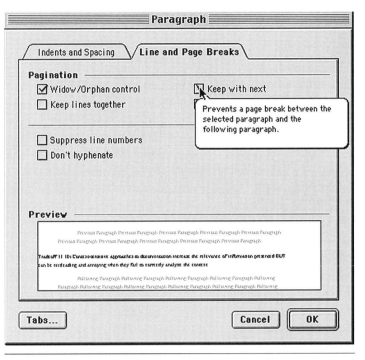

Figure 8.4 Macintosh balloon help explaining the effect of selecting a particular pagination option in Microsoft Word.

implementations of balloon help incorporate layering through hypertext links, raising the richer possibilities and tradeoffs discussed above.

8.5 Socially Mediated Documentation

Manuals, help systems, tutorials, and system messages are designed by professionals. But much of the information we acquire about software comes from other people. People like to help others, and they like personalized attention to their own information needs. Indeed, one-on-one human coaching is the gold standard for instruction—it is dramatically more effective than methods such as classroom instruction (Bloom 1984). User groups often organize themselves so that individuals who master a subset of advanced functions provide guidance when other group members need to use these functions (Nardi & Miller 1991; Nardi 1993). User groups create a form of information exchange that is also a social interaction, which in turn can form a basis for friendship, confidence, trust, empathy, and fun. Documentation, however effective, cannot evoke these qualities.

A key requirement in socially mediated information is access to knowledgeable colleagues. But some users work alone, and others work in small organizations. What happens when a colleague with special knowledge is not around? One approach is to search for a **newsgroup**, a structured email discussion that is distributed worldwide by a network of news servers. Replies to posted messages are displayed along with the messages they reply to, forming a threaded discussion. This approach creates a sort of ad hoc Internet help desk; answers to and discussion of a question become part of an information archive accessible to everyone. Figure 8.5 shows part of a technical newsgroup moderated by Microsoft. The interactions from newsgroups like these are sometimes summarized as a list of **FAQs** (frequently asked questions). These information repositories can often be browsed or accessed by keyword search.

Many examples of socially mediated documentation reflect a culture of knowledge sharing. USENET newsgroups are moderated by the users themselves (if moderated at all). This allows, and even encourages, people to pursue their interests in technical documentation in concert with pursuing their social lives. For example, Rheingold (1993) refers to USENET newsgroups as "virtual communities." Many newsgroup discussions reflect rather diverse content. For example, people may contribute stories of personal experiences, as well as focused technical descriptions and queries. Irrelevant postings are not uncommon, and occasionally there are extensive meta-discussions about what is and is not an appropriate posting for a given newsgroup.

Newsgroup communities raise new documentation challenges (Tradeoff 8.8). A group of expert programmers might enjoy interacting personally and professionally in a newsgroup; the quality of their discussion is likely to attract less expert programmers. However, novice questions might then dilute the discussion and drive off the experts who originally attracted the novices. Thus, one might have to trace the experts as they move from site to site on the Internet! Other problems with informal newsgroups include the difficulty of finding a relevant newsgroup and newsgroup thread for a query, the possibility that no one will respond to a specific problem or help request, and the chance that incorrect or suboptimal (even if well-intentioned) help will be provided.

TRADEOFF 8.8

 Socially mediated documentation can be fun and empowering, BUT the offered advice may be wrong or suboptimal, and it may be difficult to find relevant resources.

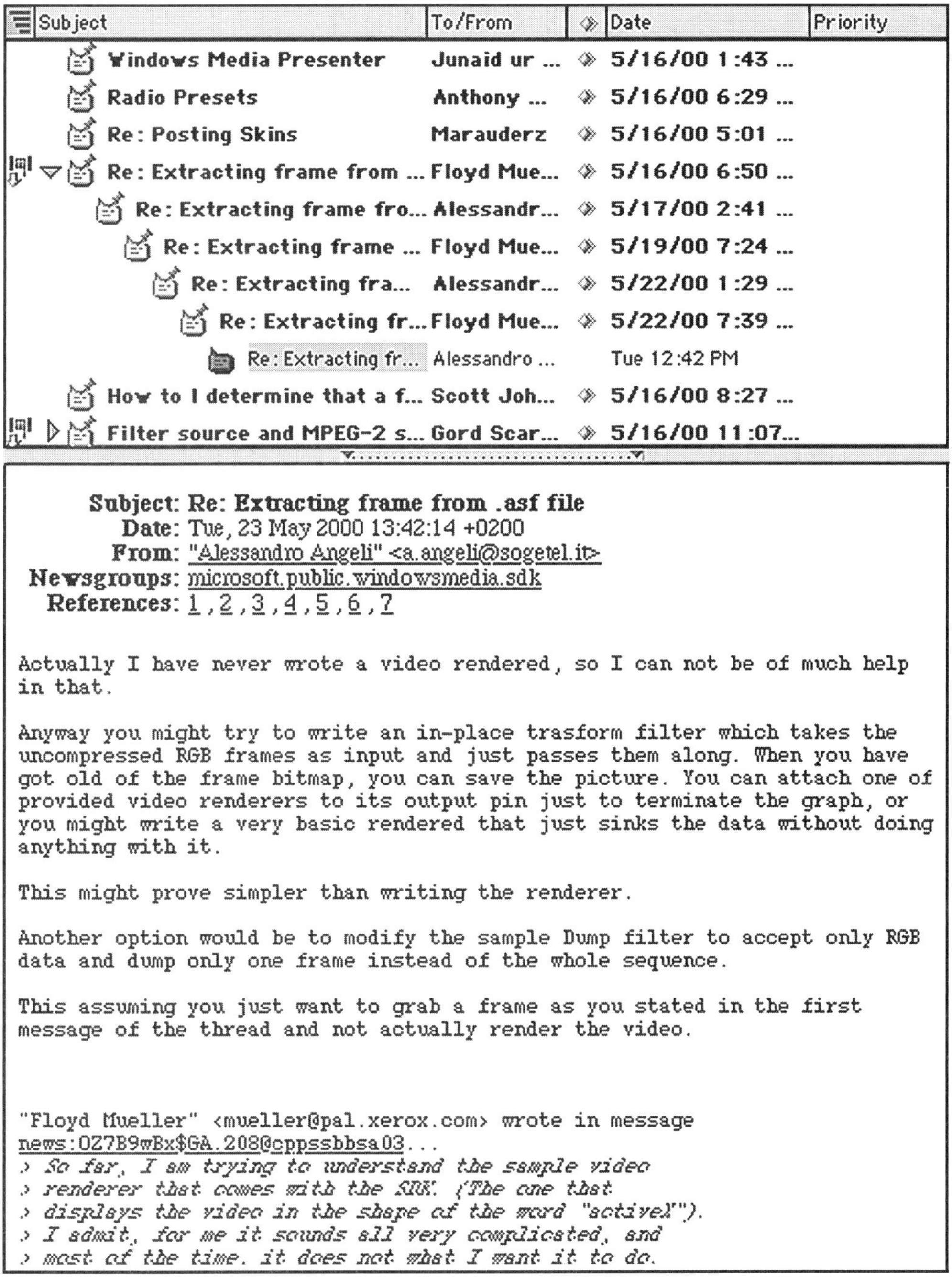

Subject	To/From	◈	Date	Priority
☒ Windows Media Presenter	Junaid ur ...	◈	5/16/00 1:43 ...	
☒ Radio Presets	Anthony ...	◈	5/16/00 6:29 ...	
☒ Re: Posting Skins	Marauderz	◈	5/16/00 5:01 ...	
▽ ☒ Re: Extracting frame from ...	Floyd Mue...	◈	5/16/00 6:50 ...	
☒ Re: Extracting fro...	Alessandr...	◈	5/17/00 2:41 ...	
☒ Re: Extracting frame ...	Floyd Mue...	◈	5/19/00 7:24 ...	
☒ Re: Extracting fra...	Alessandr...	◈	5/22/00 1:29 ...	
☒ Re: Extracting fr...	Floyd Mue...	◈	5/22/00 7:39 ...	
☒ Re: Extracting fr...	Alessandro ...		Tue 12:42 PM	
☒ How to I determine that a f...	Scott Joh...	◈	5/16/00 8:27 ...	
▷ ☒ Filter source and MPEG-2 s...	Gord Scar...	◈	5/16/00 11:07...	

Subject: Re: Extracting frame from .asf file
Date: Tue, 23 May 2000 13:42:14 +0200
From: "Alessandro Angeli" <a.angeli@sogetel.it>
Newsgroups: microsoft.public.windowsmedia.sdk
References: 1 , 2 , 3 , 4 , 5 , 6 , 7

Actually I have never wrote a video rendered, so I can not be of much help
in that.

Anyway you might try to write an in-place trasform filter which takes the
uncompressed RGB frames as input and just passes them along. When you have
got old of the frame bitmap, you can save the picture. You can attach one of
provided video renderers to its output pin just to terminate the graph, or
you might write a very basic rendered that just sinks the data without doing
anything with it.

This might prove simpler than writing the renderer.

Another option would be to modify the sample Dump filter to accept only RGB
data and dump only one frame instead of the whole sequence.

This assuming you just want to grab a frame as you stated in the first
message of the thread and not actually render the video.

"Floyd Mueller" <mueller@pal.xerox.com> wrote in message
news:OZ7B9wBx$GA.208@cppssbbsa03...
> So far, I am trying to understand the sample video
> renderer that comes with the SDK. (The one that
> displays the video in the shape of the word "activeX").
> I admit, for me it sounds all very complicated, and
> most of the time, it does not what I want it to do.

Figure 8.5 Portion of Microsoft public newsgroup for Windows Media Presenter.

8.6   Using Context and Intelligence

A prime motivation for interactive documentation is responsiveness to the user's current situation. However, the information available (i.e., system state) corresponds only roughly to the task context understood by the learner. A person understands things in a task-oriented vocabulary that may not map directly to system states; for example, a learner may think "I am creating a letter," but the system state is that a text file is being edited. A person thinks he or she is "recovering from an error," but the system state is that a file has just been deleted. The basic problem in using task context to enhance documentation is that what a person is thinking is always underdetermined by what the person is doing.

In the past three decades there have been many attempts to better diagnose and support users' activities. The greatest progress has been made by focusing on very specific tasks and system states. An example is **intelligent tutoring systems** (Anderson, et al. 1992). Intelligent tutors guide a user through tasks that are carefully designed to provide information about what a user has and has not done, and what they have seen in response to their actions. This information enables the system to simulate a user's mental model and to predict what this user will and will not understand at any point. On the basis of the simulated model, the tutor selects tasks that lead the user to practice missing skills and concepts, clarify misconceptions, and explore new areas of knowledge.

One problem in building intelligent tutor software is that it requires extensive task analysis. Users also are not able to pursue their own work with an intelligent tutoring system (Tradeoff 8.9). If an unanalyzed task is undertaken, learning support collapses. A complementary approach is to provide more broad and flexible responses to context, with less effort directed at being specific and thorough in the help offered. For example, **software agents** can recognize key features in people's circumstances and activity, and provide guidance related to these features (Chapter 9). An example of an agent is the Microsoft Office Assistant, which appears as a paperclip, a display monitor, a butler, a dog, and so forth, offering specific help triggered by specific user behavior. For example, if a user is working with Microsoft Word, typing "Dear Frodo, <return key>" triggers the help offering in Figure 8.6.

TRADEOFF 8.9

 Intelligent tutors can provide guidance specific to a learner's current situation, BUT the person must work within the system's limited task repertoire.

Figure 8.6

A help agent in
Microsoft Word.

A strength of agents is that they operate within the user's task context. The agent does not dictate a task, and does not collapse if a person behaves creatively. A corresponding weakness is that agents are often wrong (Tradeoff 8.10). For example, we typed "Dear Frodo, <return>" right here in this textbook file, and an agent popped up. This was inappropriate, even funny. But it is annoying to be offered help on writing a letter when that isn't what is happening.

TRADEOFF 8.10

Help agents provide specific support triggered by task actions and events, BUT can be misleading and annoying when they are wrong or not helpful.

A second disadvantage is that agents can fail to be helpful. The letter-writing agent provides a form for the recipient's address and so forth, but the assumptions about address format and so forth can conflict with what is actually needed. An agent that seems to work better is the spelling agent. It flags possible misspellings with a red underscore as a person types. It still makes a wrong analysis on occasion, but it seems more forgivable to diagnose "Frodo" as a misspelling than to wrongly guess that a letter-writing task is underway.

There is always a significant risk when software implies that it is intelligent (Chapter 9). People view intelligence as a characteristic of human beings, and perhaps some animals. Intelligence in software, at least at present, is a good deal more brittle and narrow, and less reliable and insightful. From the standpoint of effective HCI, this seems to be largely a matter of expectations: There is a risk in conveying intelligence, such as jumping in with a guess that letter writing is underway, and then being exposed as wrong. It is probably better to be more modest in offering assistance, such as using a simple underscore to indicate possible misspellings, and then pleasing users by often being correct.

8.7   Science Fair Case Study: Documentation Design

Some of the issues regarding documentation for the online fair have already been discussed in Chapter 4 during information design. For example, labels selected for buttons, menu choices, and instructions on a screen are all part of the overall system documentation. Walk-up-and-use systems rely solely on such information to guide use, so that they can be self-explanatory and require no learning effort. Examples are kiosk information systems commonly found in shopping malls, airports, or other large public spaces.

The science fair is somewhat like a kiosk information system, because it assumes that use will be discretionary. Thus, it must be immediately useful and usable. If students or community members try to do something with the system and fail, they may never return. The basic functionality must be as self-evident as possible. At the same time, the science fair is not a simplistic system. As illustrated by the scenarios in Chapters 3 through 5, the system is designed to support a wide range of services for exhibit construction, browsing and interacting with exhibits, and general support for community interaction and discussion. Help and information systems must be designed for introducing and guiding use of the full range of services.

As we indicated earlier, documentation design can be viewed as a specialized design problem embedded within the design of the system as a whole (Figure 8.7). One product of requirements analysis is an understanding of stakeholders' technology background and domain experience that will influence their learning about the system. The design scenarios create an activity background for analyzing the learning needs of users. Usability evaluation should test the effectiveness of the user documentation along with other aspects of the user interface. Indeed, treating documentation as a separate topic is artificial; training and help scenarios should be raised and developed in parallel with other design scenarios.

8.7.1   Exploring the Documentation Design Space

The metaphors useful to documentation design for the science fair overlap to some extent with those we explored during information design. The general information model and its components should be comprehensible and self-

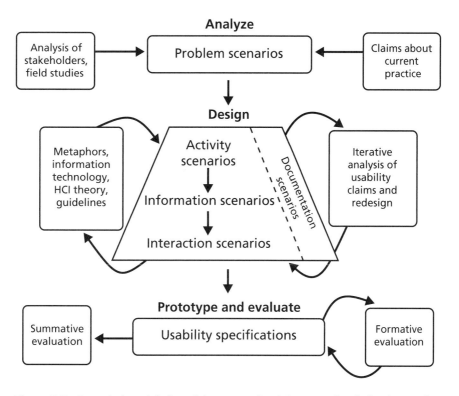

Figure 8.7 Scenario-based design of documentation is integrated with the design of other services and activities.

explanatory, and certainly this is also true for user documentation. However, the design emphasis when planning user documentation is slightly different—the goal is to envision and respond to situations where an unexpected need arises, where people do not have the necessary background, or where they need specific guidance of some sort.

Table 8.2 lists some of the real-world metaphors we explored when thinking about documentation for the virtual science fair. The ideas suggested by the metaphors are often specific to one or two aspects of user documentation. For example, a warning sign is a common metaphor applied in designing error messages or other task-specific feedback and prompts. A police-officer metaphor is similar, but directs design attention to the "rules" of user interactions within the system. For example, this metaphor caused us to brainstorm about unplanned situations that would be experienced as inappropriate in some way, perhaps rudeness or disruption at an exhibit.

Table 8.2 Metaphors used to explore the design of documentation for the virtual science fair.

Metaphor	Implications for Documentation Design
Warning sign	Specific attention-grabbing signal that something has gone wrong or is about to happen
Police officer	Posting and applying generally accepted rules of conduct
Neighbor	Watching for interesting or problematic information, and then telling friends about it
Coach	Specific attention to an individual with suggestions for improvement or refinement
Teacher	Lectures, demonstrations, and discussions of novel, important, or complicated ideas

In contrast, the neighbor, coach, and teacher metaphors are more comprehensive. Thinking about how neighbors treat one another emphasizes a socially mediated view of documentation. It caused us to think of ways in which participants might look out for one another's interests and help others who run into difficulties. The coach metaphor is similar, but with a slight shift in focus toward an individual's behavior and development. The teacher metaphor led us to think about information that might have been pre-analyzed and shared via a structured presentation or group discussion.

MOOsburg does not yet have a user documentation design; currently, new users discover how to use the system by exploring what is there, modeling on other people's use, and so on. Thus, we explored more general technology options in thinking about documentation for the science fair activity in MOOsburg (Table 8.3). For example, hypermedia is pervasive in user documentation. This general linking technique is very useful in providing context-specific information or help—the idea is to analyze documentation needs into bundles of information that are attached to the locations where help is most likely to be needed. The information itself can be of different forms, although textual descriptions are easiest and most common. Indeed, one form of such information might be an animated procedure or demonstration of a more abstract concept.

The online book and forum are more comprehensive technologies. Rather than trying to guess where information will be needed, the focus shifts to organizing the information in a way that will be useful to people accessing it from a

Table 8.3 Technology explored during documentation design for the virtual science fair.

Technology	Implications for Documentation Design
Hypermedia	Links to context-specific information distributed throughout a system's services
Animation	Scripted and stored demonstrations of small procedures or interaction episodes
Online book	Comprehensive set of descriptive information with index, chapters, etc.
Online forum	Dynamic and evolving multiparty discussion of problems, issues, and approaches
Chat, video	Real-time communication about a problem or opportunity

variety of task contexts. In an online book, a professional analyzes and implements the organization, whereas in an online forum the organization grows out of people's experiences with a system (e.g., FAQs). Chat or video technology could be used to support a more personal style of help access and retrieval, such as a version of the coach metaphor described above.

8.7.2 Documentation Scenarios and Claims

Rather than create documentation versions for each design, we focus here on just the scenarios that raised specific needs for help information, and we consider how best to provide that information given the rest of the design and our analysis of stakeholders and their activities (Chapter 2). Another way to develop ideas about documentation design is to envision new scenarios that take the perspective of other actors, such as actors who have less experience with computing or with science fairs in general. But for the sake of simplicity, we continue to develop our small set of scenarios. Also for simplicity, we abbreviate much of the surrounding scenario activity, describing only the information-seeking episode.

When we examined the five design scenarios for points at which help or training needs were apparent, we found the following episodes:

- Sally worries about how she will add her star lifecycle simulation to the standard template. Thus far, we have finessed this issue, simply indicating that she finds out how to do this (from "Sally plans her exhibit on black holes").

- Mr. King is concerned about the complexity of Sally's display. He looks for ideas to address this and discovers the option to create nested elements. He and Sally then work through an example of nesting a folder (from "Mr. King coaches Sally on her project").

- Ralph wants to make a change in the judging form and isn't sure whether and how to do this. He experiments and finds out that he can do this (from "Ralph judges the high school physics projects at the science fair").

Figure 8.8 contains the relevant parts of these three scenarios, extended to address these documentation needs. The first scenario illustrates the use of an action-oriented error message; this can be seen as a mix of the warning sign and the coach metaphor, in that an alert is provided but it contains a sugggestion for what to do next. The scenario also takes advantage of our requirements analysis studies that indicated most science fair students are quite familiar with Web browsers and Web applications; the interaction technique used to extend the capabilities of the science fair template is analogous to what is used for extending the file types recognized and handled by Web browsers. At the same time, the design uses information layering to provide a backup for less sophisticated users, presenting a `More Information . . .` button in the same group as the other options.

The second scenario illustrates a more conventional help system, an "online book" organized by topics and searchable, the same type of help system provided for most modern applications. Of course, this scenario represents a wealth of similar scenarios, because the help system Mr. King accesses is designed to be comprehensive. The third scenario illustrates the use of socially mediated information, in this case an annotation that was created by the science fair organizers. It also reflects the police officer metaphor, in that the organizers are conveying the rules for what is and is not allowed when judging.

Like other design activities, these scenario elaborations were developed in parallel with claims that documented important issues (Table 8.4). The claims encouraged us to consider users with different skill sets. For example, the information layering used in the first scenario has a number of consequences. For people like Sally, who is relatively sophisticated, the brief message requires minimal reading and thought, and the option to move immediately on to the specification dialog is just what is desired. Because she was envisioned as a typical example of a student building a science exhibit (i.e., with good technology skills), the design opted for this relatively brief and action-oriented message that assumes background knowledge of helper applications. At the same time, it is important to realize that not all students will have this background, and to provide the two backups of either getting more information or canceling the request altogether.

1) Sally plans her exhibit on black holes.

<Background context introducing Sally and her motivations and expectations about her online exhibit, her reaction to the template, and her plans and concerns for how to organize her exhibit using this template.>

Sally hopes that she will be able to attach her star lifecycle simulation, but isn't sure yet how this will work. After initializing her project and adding some Word documents, an Excel spreadsheet, and a PowerPoint slide show, she is ready to add her Authorware simulation. She selects the "Results" element in the template, and then tries to upload the simulation using the same dialog box she used for the others. But when she presses the OK button, an error message pops up: "Unrecognized exhibit content. Please select a helper application to use for this content type." The message box includes three buttons at the bottom: Browse Applications, More Information, and Cancel. Sally remembers doing something like this when she adds helper applications for her Web browser, so she presses Browse Applications. This action opens a file browser on the science fair server machine. She browses the folder structure until she finds an Authorware player, and then she selects it. A message box confirms that her simulation has been imported as an element, and that the Authorware application will be used to present this exhibit element. She wonders if her action will enable other students to upload Authorware simulations.

<Continuing discussion about Sally's actual construction of her exhibit, and her subsequent decisions and planning for how to make the simulation portion more interactive.>

2) Mr. King coaches Sally on her science fair exhibit.

<Background context introducing Mr. King and his expectations, and his and initial work with Sally.>

Mr. King sees that Sally has already added quite a few elements to her exhibit, including some he doesn't recognize. He is concerned that the exhibit is becoming too complex, and he reminds her that even though this is an unlimited space, visitors and judges have limited time and will be very influenced by first impressions. Sally agrees and they start browsing her elements and choosing the ones that are most revealing at first glance. When he asks about an unfamiliar element, she shows him the star simulation, explaining that it was created with Authorware and that she had to extend the science fair template to include it.

Mr. King is impressed, but again worries that Sally's idea for visitors to add their own experiments will make her display look messy, with more and more contributions. He decides to look around for possibilities, so he opens the Help system. It opens off to the side, and seems to have the familiar structure of an initial index and a text field where he

(continued)

Figure 8.8 Documentation design elaborations for three virtual science fair scenarios.

Figure 8.8 *(continued)*

---

can type a search string. He tries several strings before he finds one that retrieves something that looks useful: "Nested Elements" is returned in response to his query, "Nesting." He opens the topic and reads a brief description of how nesting works, and the menu item that is used to set it up. He waits for Sally to finish her current task, and then works through the process with her, keeping the help instruction up on the side.

<Continuation of the planning and refinement Mr. King and Sally do together.>

4) Ralph judges the high school physics projects at the science fair.

<Background context on Ralph, his motivations, expectations about what it will be like to judge online exhibits, his initial efforts at scanning and adding comments to the forms.>

Ralph spends an hour on Thursday morning scanning each of the five exhibits, making informal notes on the forms that were provided for each. He recognizes the categories and structure of the form from previous years, and figures that as usual he will need to make annotations explaining the numerical judgments he is required to provide at the end. And in fact, when he returns later in the day to complete the work, this is just the problem he faces: Jeff Smith's exhibit on window coatings is very solid on research methods, but Sally Harris's exhibit on black holes is just as high on innovation.

As he is trying to decide how to contrast the two exhibits, he wonders if he can edit the form in place. He would like to change the weighting so that Sally's form gives the same weighting to innovation that Jeff's gives to methods. He can see that the sum at the bottom is controlled by a formula, just as in a spreadsheet, so he tries editing the values of the formula. He is able to do this, but then when he tries to save the file, he is shown a message stating that formula editing is allowed but only under some circumstances. When he presses the `More Information...` link, a science fair FAQ browser opens, positioned at an entry written by Rachel, the fair organizer. She explains that judges are allowed to revise the weighting for individual exhibits, as long as they include an explanation in the comment section. Relieved, Ralph makes the change and adds his explanatory comment.

<Continuing discussion of Ralph's completing and submitting the forms>

Some of the other claims reflect an influence of the more general tradeoffs discussed earlier in this chapter. For example, the help system that Mr. King consults opens in a separate browser. But it is not organized as an online manual; rather it is a hypertext system, with a table of contents provided as an overview, and keyword searching offered for more direct access (Tradeoff 8.2). The disadvantages indicated are not serious in the cases we have considered, but could

Table 8.4 Claims analyzed during VSF documentation design.

Scenario Feature	Possible Pros (+) or Cons (–) of the Feature
Action-oriented error messages	+ encourage people to continue their activity rather than to stop and read
	– but people may decide to take action when they lack prerequisite knowledge
Using Web browsers as a model for file type extension	+ makes users familiar with this process feel competent and in control
	– but users not familiar with the process may be uncertain about what to do
	– but users may be uncertain about the scope of their modifications
Offering a "More Information . . ." option on an error message	+ conveys that users may be able to use background knowledge to solve the problem
	+ minimizes screen space and text comprehension demands
	– but novice users may be leery of following an open-ended prompt like this
Table of contents as a default view of help information	+ offers a familiar overview of what people will find in the help system
	– but may be disappointing or frustrating in its lack of specific details
Keyword search in help information	+ encourages the asking of detailed specific or technical questions
	+ provides direct access to relevant content in a large information repository
	– but may be frustrating when users do not know in advance the right words to use
Forums for contributing comments and helpful advice	+ remind users that assistance is a shared community activity
	+ suggest that use and learning of the system is open ended and evolutionary
	– but if everyone contributes, the information may become complex and awkward to navigate and understand

be problematic for people who have no experience with online help or hypertext structures in general.

The science fair FAQ feature is a particularly important extension to the overall design. Because the fair is part of MOOsburg—an environment designed to support community interaction—it makes sense that we should provide corresponding mechanisms that enable participants to help and inform one another. By providing a virtual science fair FAQ, we both encourage and support explicit and deliberate sharing of concerns and ideas. The disadvantage is one discussed earlier, namely, that if many people contribute to such a forum, the quality of the content may suffer, making the forum less useful (Tradeoff 8.8).

8.7.3   Refining the Documentation

Like any other design activity, the development of user documentation is an iterative process. The error messages or other prompts are an extension of the information model developed in Chapter 4 and should be carefully examined to ensure that they reflect consistent style, use of language and graphics, and so on. Usability specifications can be written specifically to capture the goals of documentation—for example, using the file type extension dialog could be analyzed as a subtask in the usability specifications (Chapter 7, Table 7.5). Users' performance on this subtask would then be tested along with other tasks to determine the usability of this part of the design.

Summary and Review

This chapter discussed issues and approaches to the design of user documentation for a system. A broad view of documentation was presented, including information incorporated into the system (prompts and error messages), printed materials, and online help and references. Three of the virtual science fair scenarios were elaborated to illustrate the design of documentation for this system. Central points to remember include:

- People's attitudes about learning and the use of documentation are paradoxical. They want to produce results of a high quality, but often are unwilling or unable to use the documentation that could help them to achieve their goals.

- Putting documentation online gives readers more flexibility in access, but most people are more comfortable with paper and find it easier to read.

- Learning by doing increases people's motivation and their subsequent ability to apply what they have learned, but it makes the learning process more demanding.

- Making messages specific and action oriented supports learning by doing, but the amount of detail required in such messages may make them so lengthy that people will ignore them or find them irritating.

- Other users of a system are a valuable source of ongoing information and help.

- Intelligent tutors are developed by modeling and tracking a set of well-defined tasks, whereas help agents are triggered by specific user or system events.

- Documentation design should be approached as a design problem on its own, with training or help scenarios developed and refined and prototypes built and iterated, in parallel with the design of the system as a whole.

Exercises

1. Compare the training needs of a hypothetical Star Wars video arcade game with those of a control system for a nuclear power plant. Make a list of similarities and differences with respect to user population, tasks, and use situations. What does this analysis suggest in terms of documentation for new users? Why?

2. Open one of your own documents in your favorite word processor. Explore the buttons and menu systems until you find an unfamiliar feature. Try out the new function without referring to the help system. Keep doing this until you make a mistake, and then try to correct the mistake. Afterward, write down an analysis of what happened:
   - What feature did you try?
   - How did you think it would work and what happened instead?
   - How could tell you had made a mistake?
   - What did you have to do to correct the mistake?
   - What did you learn overall about the system as a result?

3. Surf the Web looking for links that no longer work (i.e., a target page does not exist). Find at least two different examples of an error screen produced in response to following the nonworking link. Use claims analysis to compare the two screens: What are their key features, and what positive and negative consequences do these features have for the people who follow the nonworking link?

4. Study the user guide for an electronic appliance (video recorder, digital camera, microwave, etc.). Critique and discuss it as an example (or not) of minimalist documentation. Be sure to cover the three main principles summarized in the module on minimalism—suggesting and supporting

action, encouraging users to apply prior knowledge, and anticipating and managing errors.

Project Ideas

Analyze and design user documentation for your online shopping project. Consider both first-time or casual users, and people who use it regularly but need help for more advanced functions. Add documentation support where relevant to your online shopping scenarios, sketching screens or individual message boxes to provide supporting details. As you go, develop claims that document key features of your information design.

Recommended Reading

Carroll, J. M. 1990. *The Nurnberg Funnel: Designing Minimalist Instruction for Practical Computer Skill.* Cambridge, MA: MIT Press.

Carroll, J. M., ed. 1995. *Scenario-Based Design: Envisioning Work and Technology in System Development.* New York: John Wiley & Sons.

Carroll, J. M., ed. 1998. *Minimalism Beyond "The Nurnberg Funnel."* Cambridge, MA: MIT Press.

Corbett, A. T., K. R. Koedinger, & J. R. Anderson. 1997. Intelligent tutoring systems. In *Handbook of Human-Computer Interaction*, 2d ed., eds. M. G. Helander, T. K. Landauer, & P. V. Pradhu, 849–74. Amsterdam: North-Holland.

Horton, W. K. 1994. *Designing and Writing Online Documentation.* New York: John Wiley & Sons.

Selber, S. A., J. Johnson-Eilola, & B. Mehlenbacher. 1997. On-line support systems: Tutorials, documentation, and help. In *Handbook of Computer Science and Engineering,* ed. A. B. Tucker, 1619–43. Boca Raton, FL: CRC Press.

9

Emerging Paradigms
for User Interaction

It can be surprisingly easy to simulate intelligence in a computer. In the 1960s Joseph Weizenbaum developed the famous ELIZA program, a conversational system that uses simple language rules to simulate a Rogerian psychotherapist (Weizenbaum 1976). It responds in particular ways to mentions of keywords or phrases (e.g., "mother," "I think"), rephrases stated concerns in a questioning fashion designed to draw people out, makes mild remarks about assertions, and so on. Weizenbaum made no claims of intelligence in ELIZA, but interactions with its simple teletype interface were sometimes quite convincing. Appearing below is an excerpt from a continuing dialog between ELIZA and a patient (available at *www.word.com/newstaff/tclark/three/index.html*):

E: HELLO. MY NAME IS ELIZA. WHAT'S YOURS?

T: Tomas.

E: ALRIGHT, TOMAS, WHAT WOULD YOU LIKE TO TALK ABOUT TODAY?

T: I am sorry I got angry at you earlier, Eliza.

E: DO YOU ENJOY BEING SORRY YOU GOT ANGRY AT I EARLIER?

T: Enjoy it? No, I am feeling guilty.

E: I WOULD CONCUR, YOU ARE FEELING GUILTY.

T: Thank you for that confirmation.

E: PLEASE DON'T MENTION IT.

T: All right. I am feeling less angry now.

E: OH, YOU ARE?

T: I think so. Maybe it has just bubbled beneath the surface again.

E: YOU SEEM TO BE A RATHER PENSIVE INDIVIDUAL.

T: When I am talking to you, I try to examine myself.

E: LET'S MOVE ON NOW, IF YOU PLEASE.

Once you know how ELIZA works, it's easy to trick it into saying silly things, or using language that is awkward or unlikely. Indeed, part of the fun of talking to ELIZA or its modern "chat-bot" descendants is seeing how your words are misconstrued. Weizenbaum's personal goal was to highlight his growing concern about overattribution of intelligence to machines. His message was one of alarm at how engaged people were by this poor imitation of a human:

I was startled to see how very deeply people conversing with [the program] became emotionally involved with the computer and how unequivocally they anthropomorphised it. . . . Once my secretary, who had watched me work on the program for many months and therefore surely knew it to be merely a computer program, started conversing with it. After only a few interchanges, she asked me to leave the room. (Weizenbaum 1976, 76)

The last decade has been one of tremendous growth in information technology. Computer chips have become microscopically small while at the same time providing phenomenal increases in processing speed. Output displays exist for devices as small as a watch or as large as a wall. A robust network backbone interconnects diverse resources and enormous information stores. Complex models of people's behavior can be built to aid task performance or to predict preferences and decisions. These developments enable a wide variety of interaction paradigms beyond the familiar WIMP user interface style. As user interface designers, it is easy to be swept up in the excitement of new interaction technology; as usability engineers, it is crucial to examine the implications of new technology for usefulness, ease of learning and use, and satisfaction (see "Updating the WIMP User Interface" sidebar).

Figure 9.1 revisits Norman's (1986) framework in light of emerging paradigms for human-computer interaction. For example, the figure suggests some of the ways that new technologies will influence the process of planning and making sense of computer-based activities. A system with artificial intelligence may actively suggest likely goals. At the same time, the pervasive connectivity provided by networks adds group and organizational elements to goal selection and sense making. For instance, the figure shows an accountant planning for a budget meeting. But if he is collaborating with others over a network, the accountant may be expected to coordinate his actions with those of other people in his team or company, or to compare his results with work produced by others.

New interaction paradigms are also beginning to change the lower-level processes of action planning, execution, perception, and interpretation. Intelligent systems often support more natural human-computer interaction, such as speech or gesture recognition and, in general, the more complex multimodal behavior that we take for granted in the world (i.e., simultaneous processing and

Updating the WIMP User Interface

Several years ago, Don Gentner and Jakob Nielsen wrote a brief paper designed to provoke debate about the status quo in user interface design (Gentner & Nielsen 1996). The article critiques the pervasive WIMP user interface style. The authors use the direct-manipulation interface popularized by the Apple Macintosh in the mid-1980s as an operational definition of this style, analyzing the relevance of the Macintosh user interface guidelines (Apple Computer 1992) for modern computing applications.

The general argument that Gentner and Nielsen make is simple: End user populations, their tasks, and computing technology have matured and gained sufficient sophistication that WIMP interfaces are no longer necessary. They argue that WIMP interfaces have been optimized for ease of learning and use, that is, for people just learning to use personal computers. Today's users want more from their computing platforms and are willing to do extra work to enjoy extra functionality.

The following table lists the original Mac principles alongside the authors' proposed revisions. Many of the Mac guidelines name usability issues discussed in earlier chapters. The alternatives they suggest have occasionally been raised as tradeoffs or discussion, but will be illustrated more

elaborately in this chapter on emerging paradigms. Indeed, many of revised principles can be summarized as "build smarter systems." Such systems are more likely to know what people really want, which means that people might be more willing to share control, let the system handle more of the details, and so on. At the same time, the principles imply much greater power and diversity in the computing platform, as illustrated in the sections on multimodal interfaces and virtual reality.

A new look for user interfaces (adapted from Gentner & Nielsen 1996, table 1, 72).

Macintosh GUI	The New Look
Metaphors	Reality
Direct manipulation	Delegation
See and point	Describe and command
Consistency	Diversity
WYSIWYG	Represent meaning
User control	Shared control
Feedback and dialog	System handles details
Forgiveness	Model user actions
Aesthetic integrity	Graphic variety
Modelessness	Richer cues

generating information through our senses). As the computer-based world becomes more nearly a simulation of the real world, the need to learn new ways of communicating with the system is significantly decreased. Of course, as we discussed in Chapter 3, this can be a double-edged sword—if we seek to simulate reality too closely, we will impose unwanted boundaries or restrictions on users' expectations and behavior.

The increasingly broad concept of what counts as a "computer"—from mainframes and desktop workstations to tiny portable computers to the processing

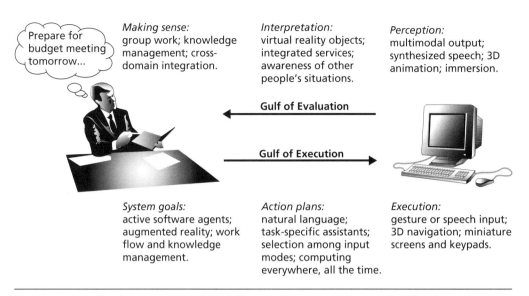

Figure 9.1 Emerging interaction paradigms influence all aspects of Norman's (1986) action cycle.

capacity that has been embedded in everyday objects—also has important implications for human-computer action. A typical handheld computer has a very small display with poor resolution, which severely restricts the range of interaction and display options possible. But its size and portability increase the flexibility of when and where computing will happen.

The opportunities raised by the emerging interaction paradigms are exciting and have created a flurry of technology-centered research projects and scientific communities. In a brief chapter such as this, it is impossible to summarize this work. In fact, attempting such a summary would be pointless, because the technology and context are evolving so quickly that the discussion would soon be obsolete. Thus, we restrict our discussion to four themes that are already having significant impact on the design of new activities and user interaction techniques—collaborative systems, ubiquitous computing, intelligent systems, and virtual reality.

9.1   Collaborative Systems

Group interaction takes place in many different settings, each with its own needs for collaboration support. Two general distinctions are the location of the group (whether the members are co-located or remote) and the timing of the work. Collaboration that takes place in real time is **synchronous**, while collaboration that takes place through interactions at different times is **asynchronous** (Ellis, Gibbs, & Rein 1991). To some extent these distinctions are artificial—a co-located group is not always in the same room, or conversations that start out in real time may be pursued through email or some other asynchronous channel. However, the distinctions help to organize the wide range of technologies that support collaborative work (see Figure 9.2).

A typical example of co-located synchronous collaboration is **electronic brainstorming**. A group gathers in a room and each member is given a networked workstation; ideas are collected in parallel and issues are prioritized, as members vote or provide feedback by other means (Nunamaker, et al. 1991). An important issue for these synchronous sessions is **floor control**—the collaboration software must provide some mechanism for turn-taking if people are making changes to shared data. Of course, the same group may collaborate asynchronously as well, reviewing and contributing ideas at different points in time, but such an interaction will be experienced more as a considered discussion than as a rapid and free-flowing brainstorming session.

For asynchronous interactions, the distinction between co-located and remote groups becomes somewhat blurred. It refers to people who are able to engage in informal face-to-face communication versus those who can "get together"

	Synchronous	Asynchronous
Co-located	Decision-support software Electronic brainstorming Digital whiteboards Voting, real-time comments	Shared file system Group intranet Version control Knowledge management Work-flow systems
Remote	Video/audio conferencing Text chat, messaging Shared editors MUDs and MOOs Virtual meeting rooms	Email, listservs Newsgroups Web forums MUDs and MOOs Document annotations

Figure 9.2 Collaborative activities can be classified according to whether they take place in the same or different locations, and at the same or different points in time.

only by virtue of technology. At the other extreme from a co-located meeting is collaborative activity associated with Web-based virtual communities (Preece 2000). **MUD**s (multiuser domains) and MOOs are popular among online communities (Rheingold 1993; Turkle 1995). A MUD is a text-based virtual world that people visit for real-time chat and other activities. But because MUDs and MOOs also contain persistent objects and characters, they enable the long-term interaction needed to form and maintain a community.

Regardless of geographic or temporal characteristics, all groups must coordinate their activities. This is often referred to as **articulation work**, which includes writing down and sharing plans, accommodating schedules or other personal constraints, following up on missing information, and so on. The key point is that articulation work is not concerned with the task goal (e.g., preparing a budget report), but rather with tracking and integrating the individual efforts comprising the shared task. For co-located groups, articulation work often takes place informally—for example, through visits to a co-worker's office or catching people as they walk down the hall (Fish, et al. 1993; Whittaker 1996). But for groups collaborating over a network, it can be quite difficult to maintain an ongoing awareness of what group members are doing, have done, or plan to do.

In face-to-face interaction, people rely on a variety of **nonverbal communication** cues—hand or arm gestures, eye gaze, body posture, facial expression, and so on—to maintain awareness of what communication partners are doing, and whether they understand what has been said or done. This information is often absent in remote collaboration. The ClearBoard system (Figure 9.3) is an experimental system in which collaborators can see each other's faces and hand gestures, via a video stream layered behind the work surface. The experience is like working with someone who is on the other side of a window. ClearBoard users are able to follow their partners' gaze and hand movements and use this information in managing a shared task (Ishii, Kobayashi, & Arita 1994).

ClearBoard is an interesting approach, but it depends on special hardware and is restricted to pairs of collaborators. Other efforts to enhance collaboration awareness have focused on simpler information, such as the objects or work area currently in view by a collaborator. A **radar view** is an overview of a large shared workspace that includes rectangles outlining the part of the workspace in view by all collaborators (Figure 9.4). By glancing at an overview of this sort, group members can keep track of what others are working on, particularly if this visual information is supplemented by a communication channel such as text or audio chat (Gutwin & Greenberg 1998).

From a usability point of view, adding awareness information to a display raises a familiar tradeoff. The added information helps in coordinating work, but

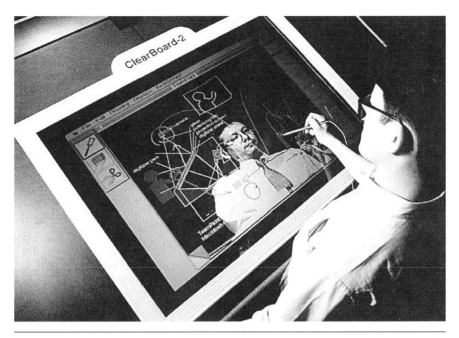

Figure 9.3 ClearBoard, another system that addresses awareness issues, by merging video of a collaborator's face with a shared drawing surface (Ishii, Kobayashi, & Arita 1994).

it becomes one more thing in the user interface that people must perceive, interpret, and make sense of (Tradeoff 9.1). When a collaborative activity becomes complex—for example, when the group is large or its members come and go often—it can be very difficult to present enough information to convey what is happening without cluttering a display. Suppose that the radar view in the upper left of Figure 9.4 contained five or six overlapping rectangles. Would it still be useful?

TRADEOFF 9.1

 Awareness of collaborators' plans and actions facilitates task coordination, BUT extensive or perceptually salient awareness information may be distracting.

A related issue concerns awareness of collaborators' contributions over time. In Microsoft Word, coauthors use different colors to identify individual input to a shared document. These visual cues may work well for a small group,

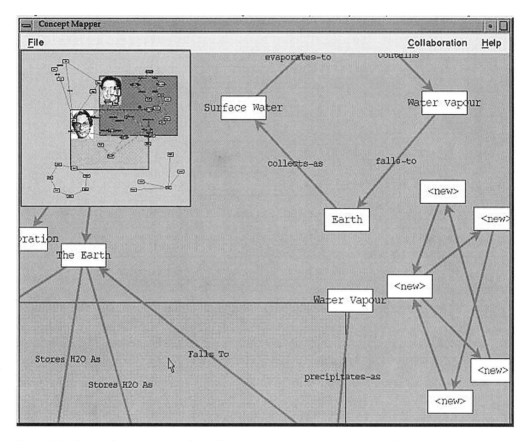

Figure 9.4 Supporting awareness of collaborators during remote synchronous interactions. The upper-left corner shows a radar view—an overview of the shared workspace that also shows partners' locations (GroupLab team, University of Calgary, available at *http://www.cpsc.ucalgary.ca/Research/ grouplab/project_snapshot/radar_groupware/radar_groupware.html*).

but as the number of colors increases, their effectiveness as an organizing scheme decreases.

In the Virtual School project summarized in Chapter 1, students collaborate remotely on science projects over an extended period of time, sometimes in real time, but more often through asynchronous work in a shared notebook (the Virtual School was pictured in Figure 1.3). The environment promotes awareness of synchronous activity through buddy lists, video links, and by showing who has a "lock" on a page. It supports asynchronous awareness through a notice board that logs Virtual School interactions over time, text input that is colored to indicate authorship, and information about when and by whom an annotation was made. A good case can be made for any one of these mechanisms, but they combine to create a considerable amount of coordination information. It is still an open question which pieces of awareness information are worth the cost of screen space and complexity (Isenhour, et al. 2000).

Networks and computer-mediated communication allow distributed groups to work together. These systems increase the flexibility of work: Resources can be shared more effectively, and individual group members can enjoy a customized work setting (e.g., a teleworker who participates from home). But whenever technology is introduced as an intermediary in human communication, one side effect is that some degree of virtuality or anonymity in the communication is also introduced. Even in a telephone conversation, participants must recognize one another's voices to confirm identity. Communicating through email or text chat increases the interpersonal distance even more.

An increase in interpersonal distance can lead individuals to exhibit personality characteristics or attitudes that they would not display in person (Sproull & Kiesler 1991). A worker who might never confront a manager about a raise or a personnel issue might feel much more comfortable doing so through email, where nonverbal feedback cues are avoided (Markus 1994). Members of Internet newsgroups or forums may be quite willing to disclose details of personal problems or challenges (Rosson 1999a). Unfortunately, the same loss of inhibition that makes it easier to discuss difficult topics also makes it easier to behave in rude or inappropriate ways (Tradeoff 9.2). Sometimes this simply means it will be more difficult to reach a consensus in a heated debate. But studies of virtual communities also report cases in which members act out fantasies or hostilities that are disconcerting or even psychologically damaging to the rest of the community (Cherny 1995; Rheingold 1993; Turkle 1995).

TRADEOFF 9.2

Reduced interpersonal communication cues aid discussion of awkward or risky concerns, BUT may encourage inappropriate or abusive ideas and activities.

Deciding whether and how much anonymity to allow in a collaborative setting is a critical design issue. If a system is designed to promote creativity or expression of diverse or controversial opinions, anonymous participation may be desirable, even if this increases the chance of socially inappropriate behavior. More generally, however, groups expect that each member is accountable for his or her own behavior, and individuals expect credit or blame for the contributions they make. These expectations demand some level of identification, commonly through a personal log-in and authentication procedure, or through the association of individuals to one or more roles within a group. Once a participant is recognized as a system-defined presence, other coordination mechanisms can be activated, such as managing access to shared resources, organizing the tasks expected of him or her, and so on.

One side effect of supporting online collaboration is that recording shared information becomes trivial. Email exchanges can be stored, frequently asked questions (FAQs) tabulated, project versions archived, and procedures of all sorts documented. The process of identifying, recording, and managing the business procedures and products of an organization is often called **knowledge management**. Although it is hard to put a finger on what exactly constitutes the "knowledge" held by an organization, there is a growing sense that a great deal of valuable information is embedded in people's everyday work tasks and artifacts.

Having a record of a shared task can be helpful in tracing an activity's history—determining when, how, and why decisions were made—or when reusing the information or procedures created by the group. Historical information is particularly useful when new members join a group. But simply recording information is usually not enough; a large and unorganized folder of email or series of project versions is so tedious to investigate that it may well not be worth the effort. Group archives are much more useful if participants filter and organize them as they go. The problem is that such archives are often most useful to people other than those who create and organize them—for example, new project members or people working on similar tasks in the future (Tradeoff 9.3).

TRADEOFF 9.3

 Archiving shared work helps to manage group decisions and rationales, BUT archiving costs must often be borne by people who will not receive direct benefits.

What can be done to ensure that the people creating the archives enjoy some benefit? To some extent, this is a cultural issue. If everyone in an organization contributes equally to a historical database, then chances are higher that everyone will benefit at some point. On a smaller scale, the problem might be addressed by rotating members through a history-recording role, or by giving special recognition to individuals who step forward to take on the role of developing and maintaining the shared records.

9.2 Ubiquitous Computing

A decade ago Mark Weiser (1991) coined the term **ubiquitous computing** to describe a vision of the future in which computers are integrated into the world around us, supporting our everyday tasks. In Weiser's vision, people do not interact with "boxes" on a desk. Instead, we carry small digital devices (e.g., a smart card or a personal digital assistant) just as we now carry drivers' licenses or credit cards. When we enter a new setting, these devices interact with other devices placed within the environment to register our interests, access useful information, and initiate processes in support of task goals.

Current technology has moved us surprisingly close to Weiser's vision. A range of small devices—such as pocket PCs, portable digital assitants (PDAs), and mobile phones (see Figure 9.5)—are already in common use. Such devices enable **mobile computing**, computer-based activities that take place while a person is away from his or her computer workstation. Laptop and pocket PCs offer services similar to those of a desktop system, but with hardware emphasizing portability and wireless network connections. PDAs such as the Palm series use simple character recognition or software buttons and a low-resolution display. They provide much less functionality than a desktop PC, but are convenient and easy to learn. PDAs are often used as mobile input devices, such as when keeping records of notes or appointments that are subsequently transferred to a full-featured desktop computer.

Some of the most important advances in ubiquitous computing are occurring in the telecommunications industry. People are comfortable with telephones; most already use phones to access information services (e.g., reservations

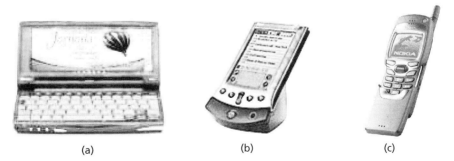

(a) (b) (c)

Figure 9.5 Several portable computing devices: (a) The Jornada 680 pocket PC made by Hewlett Packard; (b) the Palm V from 3Com; and (c) a Nokia mobile phone.

and account status), so adding email or Web browsing is not a large conceptual leap. Mobile phones have become extremely popular, particularly in northern Europe—in Finland, 90% of the population owns a mobile phone! People's general comfort level with telephones, combined with emerging protocols for wireless communication, makes them very attractive as a pervasive mobile computing device.

But these small mobile devices raise major challenges for usability engineers. People are used to interacting with computers in a workstation environment—a dedicated client machine with an Ethernet connection, a large color bitmap display, a mouse or other fine-grained input device, and a full-size keyboard. They take for granted that they will enjoy rich information displays and flexible options for user input. Many common tasks, such as checking email, finding stored documents, or accessing Web pages, have been practiced and even automated in such environments. A small display and simple input mechanisms are a constant frustration to these well-learned expectations and interaction strategies (Tradeoff 9.4).

TRADEOFF 9.4

Small mobile interaction devices increase portability and flexibility, BUT these devices do not support the rich interaction bandwidth needed for complex tasks.

One solution to limitations in display and communication bandwidth is to cut back on the services provided—for example, PDAs are often used for personal databases of calendars, contact information, or brief notes, and these tasks have relatively modest bandwidth requirements. The problem is that as people use PDAs more and more, they want to do more and more things with them. Thus, user interface researchers are exploring techniques for scaling complex information models (such as Web sites) to a form appropriate for smaller devices.

One approach is to employ a **proxy server** (an intermediate processor) to fetch and summarize multiple Web pages, presenting them on the PDA in a reduced form specially designed for easy browsing. For example, in the WEST system (WEb browser for Small Terminals; Björk, et al. 1999), Web pages are chunked into components, keywords are extracted, and a focus+context visualization is used to provide an overview suitable for a small display. Specialized interaction techniques are provided for navigating among and expanding the chunks of information.

When mobile phones are used to access and manipulate information, designers are faced with the special task of designing an auditory user interface that uses spoken menus and voice or telephone keypad input. Of course, such systems have been in use for many years in the telecommunications industry, but the increasing use of mobile phones to access a variety of information services has made the usability problems with spoken interfaces much more salient.

As discussed in Chapter 5, people have a limited working memory, which means that we can keep in mind only a small number of menu options at any one time. When the overall set of options is large, the menu system will be a hierarchy with many levels of options and selections. Because an auditory menu is presented in a strictly linear fashion (i.e., it is read aloud), users may navigate quite deeply into a set of embedded menus before realizing that they are in the wrong portion of the tree. Usually, there is no way to undo a menu selection, so the user is forced to start all over, but now with the additional task of remembering what not to select. Because of the lack of control in these interfaces, the design of the menu hierarchy should be very carefully designed to satisfy users' most frequent needs and expectations.

Access to small or portable computers is an important element of the ubiquitous computing vision. But another piece of the vision is that the support is distributed throughout the environment, or incorporated into objects and tools not normally considered to be computing devices. This is often termed **augmented reality**; the concept here is to take a physical object in the real world—a classroom whiteboard, a kitchen appliance, an office desk, or a car—and extend it with computational characteristics.

Much current work on augmented reality is directed toward novel input or output mechanisms. Researchers at MIT's Media Lab have demonstrated ambient displays that convey status information (e.g., traffic flow and weather) as background "pictures" composed of visual or auditory information (Ishii & Ullmer 1997; see "Tangible Bits" sidebar). A new category of interactive services known as **roomware** provides enhancements to chairs, walls, tables, and so on; the intention is that the people in a room can access useful information and services at just the right moment, and in just the right place (Streitz, et al. 1999). Many researchers are investigating the possibilities for devices and services that are **context aware**, such that features of a person's current setting, personal preferences, or usage history can be obtained and processed to provide situation-specific functions and interaction techniques (Abowd & Mynatt 2000).

An important practical problem for augmented reality is the highly distributed infrastructure of sensors or information displays that are needed to capture and process people's actions in the world. For example, in the NaviCam system, a handheld device recognizes real-world objects from special tags placed on them, and then uses this information to create a context-specific visual overlay (Rekimoto & Nagao 1995). But this application assumes that the relevant objects have somehow been tagged. Bar codes might be used as one source of such

---

Tangible Bits

Hiroshi Ishii and colleagues at the MIT Media Lab are researching ways to bridge the gap between cyberspace and the physical environment (Underkoffler & Ishii 1999; Ishii & Ullmer 1997; Yarin & Ishii 1999). They are working with three key concepts: *interactive surfaces,* where the ordinary surfaces of architectural space (walls, doors, and windows) serve as an active interface between the physical and virtual worlds; *coupling of bits and atoms,* emphasizing the integration of everyday objects that can be grasped (cards and containers) with relevant digital information; and *ambient models,* the use of background media such as sound, light, or water movement to present information in the periphery of human perception. The following table summarizes several projects that illustrate these concepts.

Examples of projects that are exploring the concept of tangible bits.

Project Name	Brief Description
metaDesk	A nearly horizontal back-projected graphical surface with embedded sensors that enables interaction with digital objects displayed on the surface, in concert with physical objects (including "phicons" or physical icons) that are grasped and placed on the desk
transBoard	A networked, digitally enhanced whiteboard that supports distributed access to physical whiteboard activity, including attachment of special-purpose phicons
ambientRoom	A 6′ × 8′ room augmented with digital controls; auditory and visual background displays render ongoing activity such as Web-page hits or changes in the weather
URP	Urban planning environment that creates light and wind flow to simulate time-specific shadow, reflection, and pedestrian traffic for a physical model on a table
TouchCounters	Physical sensors and local displays integrated into physical storage containers and shelves, for recording and presenting usage history, including network-based access

information, but are normally available only for consumer retail items. Researchers are now exploring the more general concept of **glyphs**, coded graphical elements that can be integrated into a wide variety of displayed or printed documents (Moran, et al. 1999).

The integration of computational devices with everyday objects raises many exciting opportunities for situation- and task-specific information and activities. But even if the infrastructure problem can be resolved, the vision also raises important usability issues (Tradeoff 9.5). Few people will expect to find computational functionality in the objects that surround them. In the case of passive displays such as the experiments summarized in the "Tangible Bits" sidebar, this may not be too problematic. People may not understand what the display is communicating, but at worst they will be annoyed by the extraneous input. But for interactive elements such as a chair, wall, or kitchen appliance, the problems are likely to be more complex. Indeed, when a problem arises, people may be unable to determine which device is responsible, much less debug the problem!

TRADEOFF 9.5

 Distributing interaction technology throughout the environment ties computing power to task-specific resources, BUT people may not expect or appreciate such services.

Another concern hiding beneath the excitement over ubiquitous computing is the extent to which people really want to bring computers into their personal lives. Many companies are exploring flexible working arrangements that allow employees to work partially or entirely from home offices. This necessarily blurs the dividing line between work and home, and the advances in mobile computing and ubiquitous devices do so even more. As homes and other locations are wired for data and communication exchange, individuals and families will have less and less privacy and fewer options for escaping the pressures and interruptions of their working lives. The general public may not recognize such concerns until it is too late, so it is important for usability professionals to investigate these future scenarios now, *before* the supporting technology has been developed and broadly deployed.

9.3   Intelligent User Interfaces

What is an intelligent system? In the classic Turing test, a computer system is deemed intelligent if its user is fooled into thinking he or she is talking to another human. However, most designers of intelligent human-computer interfaces strive for much less. The goal is to collect and organize enough information about a user, task, or situation, to enable an accurate prediction about what the users want to see or do. As with any user interaction technology, the hope is that providing such intelligence in the computer will make users' tasks easier and more satisfying.

9.3.1   Natural Language and Multimodal Interaction

Science fiction offers a persuasive vision of computers in the future: For instance, in *Star Trek*, Captain Kirk poses a question, and the computer immediately responds in a cooperative and respectful fashion. At the same time, there has always been a dark side to the vision, as illustrated by HAL's efforts to overthrow the humans in *2001: A Space Odyssey*. People want computers to be helpful and easy to talk to, but with a clearly defined boundary between the machine and its human controller.

From an HCI perspective, an interactive system that successfully understands and produces natural language short-circuits the Gulfs of Execution and Evaluation. People only have to say what is on their minds—there is no need to map task goals to system goals, or to retrieve or construct action plans. When the computer responds, there is no need to perceive and interpret novel graphical shapes or terminology. The problem, of course, is that there are not yet systems with enough intelligence to reliably interpret or produce natural language. Thus, a crucial design question becomes just how much intelligence to incorporate into (and imply as part of) an interactive system.

The challenges of understanding natural language are many. For example, when people talk to one another, they quickly establish and rely on **common ground**. Common ground refers to the expectations that communication partners have about each other, the history of their conversation so far, and anything else that helps to predict and understand what the other person says (Clark & Brennan 1991; Monk in press). For example, a brief introductory statement such as "Right, we met at last year's CHI conference," brings with it a wealth of shared experiences and memories that enrich the common ground. One partner in such an exchange can now expect the other to understand a comment such as "That design panel was great, wasn't it?" The speaker assumes that the listener knows that CHI conferences have panel discussions, and that this particular meeting had a memorable panel on the topic of design.

Related problems stem from the inherent ambiguity of natural language. Suppose that the comment about a design panel was uttered in a conversation between two graphic artists or electrical engineers; rather different interpretations of the words "design" and "panel" would be intended in the two cases. Listeners use the current situational context and their knowledge of the real world to disambiguate words and phrases in a fluent and unconscious fashion.

Even if an intelligent system could accurately interpret natural language requests, interaction with natural language can be more tedious than with artificial languages (Tradeoff 9.6). As discussed in Chapter 5, the naturalness of human-computer communication very often trades off with power. Imagine describing to a computer your request that a particular document should be printed on a particular printer in your building—and then compare this to dragging a document icon onto a desktop printer icon.

TRADEOFF 9.6

Natural language interaction simplifies planning and interpretation, BUT it may be less precise and take more time than artificial language interaction.

One approach to the problems of understanding natural language is to enable multiple communication modes. In a **multimodal user interface**, a user might make a spoken natural language request, but supplement it with one or more gestures. For example, the user might say "Put that there," while also pointing with the hand or pressing a button (Bolt 1980). Pointing or scoping gestures can be very useful for inherently spatial requests such as group specification (e.g., removing the need for requests such as "Select the six blue boxes next to each other in the top left corner of the screen but skip the first one"). Interpreting and merging simultaneous input channels is a complex process, but multimodal user interface architectures and technology have become robust enough to enable a variety of demanding real-world applications (Oviatt, et al., 2002; see "Multimodal User Interfaces" sidebar).

Usability engineers often worry about the degree to which a computer system appears human or friendly to its users. A system that has even a little bit of information about a user can adjust its style to create a more personal interaction. For example, many Web applications collect and use personal information in this way. An online shopping system may keep customer databases that can be very helpful in pre-filling the tedious forms required for shipping address, billing address, and so on. However, the same information is also often used to construct a personalized dialog ("Welcome back, Mary Beth!"), with a sales pitch customized for the kinds of products previously purchased.

Current guidelines for user interface design stress that overly personal dialogs should be avoided (Shneiderman 1998). Novice users may not mind an overfriendly dialog, but they may conclude that the system is more intelligent than it really is and trust it too much. The ELIZA system (see starting vignette) is a classic example of how little intelligence is required to pass Turing's test. This

Multimodal User Interfaces

Multimodal user interaction is motivated by tasks that are complex or variable, and by the desire to provide people with the freedom to choose an input modality (modality refers to types of sensations, such as vision, sound, smell, and pressure) that is most suitable for the current task or environment. For example, speech input is quick, convenient, and keeps the hands free for other actions. Pens can be used for drawing, as well as pointing, signing one's name, and so on. The combination of pens with speech can lead to extremely effective performance in tasks with significant spatial components such as geographical information systems (Oviatt 1997). Pens and speech are particularly useful in mobile computing, where size and flexibility are at a premium.

In addition to increasing interaction flexibility, multimodal interaction can re-

duce errors by increasing redundancy. Someone who names an object but also points to it is more likely to enjoy accurate responses; a warning that flashes on the screen but also sounds a beep is more likely to be received by a person engaged in complex activities. The option to switch among modalities also alleviates individual differences such as handicaps, and can minimize fatigue in lengthy interactions.

Recent advances in spoken language technology, natural language processing, and in pen-based handwriting and gesture recognition have enabled the emergence of realistic multimodal applications that combine speech and pen input (Oviatt, et al., 2002). The table below lists several such projects underway at the Oregon Graduate Institute (OGI); IBM; Boeing; NCR; and Bolt, Beranek, & Newman (BBN).

Examples of systems using multimodal input and output interaction techniques.

System Name	Use of Multimodal Input and Output
QuickSet (OGI)	Speech recognition, pen-based gestures, and direct manipulation are combined to initialize the objects and parameters of a spatial (map-based) simulation.
Human-Centric Word Processor (IBM)	Continuous, real-time speech recognition and natural language understanding, combined with pen-based pointing and selection, for medical dictation and editing.
Virtual Reality Aircraft Maintenance Training (Boeing)	Speech understanding and generation are combined with a data glove for detecting hand gestures. Controls a 3D simulated aircraft in which maintenance procedures can be demonstrated and practiced.
Field Medic Information System (NCR)	Mobile computer worn around the waist of medical personnel, using speech recognition and audio feedback to access and manipulate patient records. Used in alternation with a handheld tablet supporting pen and speech input.
Portable Voice Assistant (BBN)	Handheld device supporting speech and pen recognition, using a wireless network to browse and interact with Web forms and repositories.

simple simulation of a psychiatrist asks questions and appears to follow up on people's responses. But it uses a very simple language model (e.g., a set of key vocabulary words and the repetition of phrases) to create this perception.

Users today are more sophisticated than the people Weizenbaum (1976) observed using ELIZA. Most computer users are unlikely to believe that computers have human-like intelligence, and they often find simulated "friendliness" annoying or misleading (Tradeoff 9.7). A well-known failure of this sort was Microsoft Bob, a highly graphical operating system that included the pervasive use of human-like language (Microsoft 1992). Although young or inexperienced home users seemed to like the interface, the general public reacted poorly and Microsoft Bob was quietly withdrawn.

TRADEOFF 9.7

 Personal and "friendly" language can make an interaction more engaging or fun, BUT human-like qualities may mislead novices and irritate sophisticated users.

At the same time, it is wrong to reject this style of user interface entirely. Particularly as entertainment, commerce, and education applications of computing become more pervasive, issues of **affective** or **social computing** are a serious topic of research and development (see "Social Computing" sidebar). The concept of "fun" is also gaining focus in HCI, as the scope of computing increases (Hassenzahl, et al. 2000). If a primary requirement for a user interface is to persuade a highly discretionary user to pause long enough to investigate a new service, or to take a break from a busy workday, the pleasure or humor evoked by the user interface clearly becomes much more important.

9.3.2   Software Agents

One very salient consequence of the expansion of the World Wide Web is that computing services have become much more complex. People now can browse or search huge databases of information distributed in locations all over the world. Some of this information will be relevant to a person's current goals, but most of it will not. Some of the information obtained will be trustworthy, and some will not. Some of the useful information will be usable as is, and some will need further processing to obtain summaries or other intermediate representations. Finding the right information and services and organizing the found materials to be as useful as possible are significant chores, and many researchers and businesses are exploring the use of software agents that can do all or part of the work.

Social Computing

As the ELIZA system showed, humans are quite willing to think of a computer in social terms, or as an intelligent and helpful conversation partner. Many user interface designers have been alarmed by this, and try to minimize the social character of systems as much as possible (Shneiderman 1998). But recent work by Clifford Nass and colleagues on social responses to communication technologies has documented a number of ways in which people respond to computers in the same way that they respond to other people. For example, users react to politeness, flattery, and simulated personality traits (Nass & Gong 2000). These researchers argue that people will respond this way regardless of designers' intentions, so we should focus our efforts on understanding when and how such reactions are formed, so as to improve rather than interfere with their usage experience.

In one recent set of experiments, these researchers studied people's responses to humor in a computer user interface, as compared with the same humor injected into interactions with another person (Morkes, Kernal, & Nass 1999). In the experiment, people were told that they were connected to another person remotely and would be able to see this person's comments and contributions to a task (ranking items for relevance to desert survival). In fact, all of the information they saw was generated by a computer; half of the participants were shown jokes interspersed with the other comments and ratings. Other people were told that they were connected to a computer, and that the computer would make suggestions. Again, half of the participants received input that included jokes.

The reactions to the "funny" versus "not funny" computer were similar in many respects to those of people who thought they were communicating with another person. For example, people working with the joking computer claimed to like it more, made more jokes themselves, and made more comments of a purely sociable nature. These reactions took place without any measurable cost in terms of task time or accuracy. Although these findings were obtained under rather artificial conditions, the researchers suggest that they have implications for HCI, namely, that designers should consider building more fun and humor into user interactions, even for systems designed for "serious" work.

Software agents come in many varieties and forms (Maes [1997] provides a good overview). For example, agents vary in the target of their assistance—an email filter is user specific, but a Web crawler provides a general service to benefit everyone. Agents also vary in the source of their intelligence; they may be developed by end users, built by professional knowledge engineers, or collect data and learn on their own. Agents vary in location; some reside entirely in a user's environment, others are hosted by servers, and others are mobile, moving around as needed. Finally, there is great variation in the roles played by agents. Example roles include a personal assistant, a guide to complex information, a memory aid for past experiences, a filter or critic, a notification or referral service, and even a buyer or seller of resources (Table 9.1).

A usability issue for all intelligent systems is how the assistance will impact users' own task expectations and performance. As intelligent systems technology has matured, engineers are able to build systems that monitor and integrate data to assist in complex tasks—for example, air traffic control or engineering and construction tasks. Such systems are clearly desirable, but usability professionals worry that people may come to rely on them so much that they cede control or become less vigilant in their own areas of responsibility (Tradeoff 9.8). This can be especially problematic in safety-critical situations such as power plants or aircraft control (Casey 1993). Dialogs that are abrupt and "machine-like," or that include regular alerts or reminders, may help to combat such problems.

Table 9.1 Software agents developed at the MIT Media Lab, illustrating a number of variations in target of assistance, source of intelligence, location, and task role.

Software Agent	Brief Description
Cartalk	Cars equipped with PCs, GPS, and radio communicate with each other and stationary network nodes to form a constantly reconfigured network
Trafficopter	Uses Cartalk to collect traffic-related information for route recommendations; no external (e.g., road) infrastructure required
Shopping on the run	Uses Cartalk network to broadcast the interests from car occupants, and then receive specific driving directions to spots predicted to be of interest
Yenta	Finds and introduces people with shared interests, based on careful collection/analysis of personal data (email, interest lists)
Kasbah	User-created agents given directions for what to look for in an agent marketplace, seeks out sellers or buyers, negotiates to try to make the "best deal" based on user-specified constraints
BUZZwatch	Distills and tracks trends and topics in text collections over time, e.g., in Internet discussions or print media archives
Footprints	Observes and stores navigation paths of people to help other people find their way around

---

TRADEOFF 9.8

Building user models that can automate or assist tasks can simplify use, BUT may reduce feelings of control, or raise concerns about storage of personal data.

An overeager digital assistant that offers help too often, or in unwanted ways, is more irritating than dangerous. For example, the popular press has made fun of "Clippy," the Microsoft Windows help agent that seems to interrupt users more than help them (Noteboom 1998). Auto-correction in document or presentation creation can be particularly frustrating if it sometimes works, but at other times introduces unwelcome changes that take time and attention to correct. Reasoning through scenarios that seem most likely or important can be extremely valuable in finding the right level of intelligent support to provide by default in a software system.

A more specific issue arises when agents learn by observing people's behavior. For example, it is now common to record online shopping behavior and use it as the basis for future recommendations. This, of course, is nothing new—marketing firms also collect behavior about buying patterns and target their campaigns accordingly. The usability concerns are simply that there is so much online data that is now easily collected, and that much of the data collection happens invisibly. These concerns might be addressed by making personal data collection more visible and enabling access to the models that are created.

Finally, software agents are often a focus for the continuing debates about anthropomorphic user interfaces, because it is common to render digital assistants as **conversational agents**. Thus, many researchers are exploring language characteristics, facial expressions, or other nonverbal behavior that can be applied to cartoon-like characters to make them seem friendly and helpful (Lieberman 1997). A particularly well-developed example is Rea, an agent that helps real estate clients learn about available real estate properties. Rea uses information about the buyer to make recommendations. However, the recommendations are presented in a simulated natural language dialog that includes a variety of nonverbal communication cues to her output (e.g., glancing away, hand gestures, and pausing slightly; see Figure 9.6), to make the interaction seem more realistic (Cassell 2000).

The earlier point about the emergence of entertainment-oriented computing is relevant to the discussion here as well. For example, one Web-based "chatbot" provided for visitors' enjoyment is the John Lennon AI project, a modern

Rea's domain of expertise is real estate; she has access to a database of available condominiums and houses for sale in Boston. She can display pictures of these properties and their various rooms and point out and discuss their salient features. The following is an excerpt from an actual interaction.

Mike approaches the projection screen while Rea is gazing about idly. As Mike moves within range of the two cameras mounted above the screen, Rea turns to face him and says:
Hello. How can I help you?
Mike. I'm looking to buy a place near MIT.
Rea nods, indicating that she is following.
Rea. I have a house to show you.
A picture of a house appears on the screen behind Rea, who blinks and looks at the house and then at Mike.
Rea. It's in Somerville.
Mike. Tell me about it.
Rea looks up and away while she plans what to say.
Rea. It's big.
Rea makes an expansive gesture with her hands.
Mike brings his hands up as if he is about to speak, so Rea does not continue, waiting for him to speak.
Mike. Tell me more about it.
Rea. Sure thing. It has a nice garden.
Rea sketches a curved gesture with her hands, indicating the garden extends along two sides of the house.
Mike. How far is it?
Rea. It is five minutes to the Porter Square T station.
Rea makes it clear it is five minutes on foot from the T station by making a walking gesture with her fingers.
Mike. How big is the house?
Rea. It has four bedrooms, three bathrooms...
Mike interrupts Rea, who stops speaking immediately.
Mike. Wait. Tell me, where is the master bedrooom?
Rea. I'm sorry, I didn't catch that. What did you ask me?
Mike. Where is the master bedroom?
Rea. It's upstairs.
Rea points up.
Mike. Where is the master bathroom?
Rea. It's next to the bedroom.
Rea brings her hands together to indicate the relationship between the bedroom and the bathroom.
And the house tour continues.

Figure 9.6 A brief conversation with an embodied conversational agent that is programmed to assist in real estate tasks (Cassell 2000, 73).

variant of the ELIZA program (available at *http://www.triumphpc.com/john-lennon*). People can talk to this agent to see if it reacts as they would expect Lennon to react; they can critique or discuss its capabilities, but there is little personal consequence in its failures or successes. In this sense, the entertainment domain may be an excellent test bed for new agent technologies and interaction styles—the cost of an inaccurate model or an offensive interaction style is simply that people will not buy (or use for free) the proffered service.

9.4   Simulation and Virtual Reality

Like the natural language computer on Captain Kirk's bridge, *Star Trek* offers an engaging vision of simulated reality—crew members can simply select an alternate reality, and then enter the "holodeck" for a fully immersive interaction within the simulated world. Once they enter the holodeck, the participants experience all the physical stimulation and sensory reactions that they would encounter in a real-world version of the computer-generated world. A darker vision is conveyed by *The Matrix* film, where *all* human perception and experience is specified and simulated by all-powerful computers.

Virtual reality (VR) environments are still very much a research topic, but the simulation techniques have become refined enough to support real-world applications. Examples of successful application domains are skill training (e.g., airplane or automobile operation and surgical techniques), behavioral therapy (e.g., phobia desensitization), and design (e.g., architectural or engineering walkthroughs). None of these attempt to provide a truly realistic experience (i.e., including all the details of sensory perception), but they simulate important features well enough to carry out training, analysis, or exploration activities.

Figure 9.7 shows two examples of VR applications: the Web-based desktop simulation on the left uses VRML (Virtual Reality Markup Language) to simulate a space capsule in the middle of an ocean. Viewers can "fly around," go in and out of the capsule, and so on (available at *http://www.cosmo.com*). On the right is an example from the Virginia Tech CAVE (Collaborative Automatic Virtual Environment). This is a room equipped with special projection facilities to provide a visual model that viewers can walk around in and explore, in this case a DNA molecule (available at *http://www.cave.vt.edu*).

A constant tension in virtual environments is designing and implementing an appropriate degree of **veridicality**, or correspondence to the real world. Because our interactions with the world are so rich in sensory information, it is

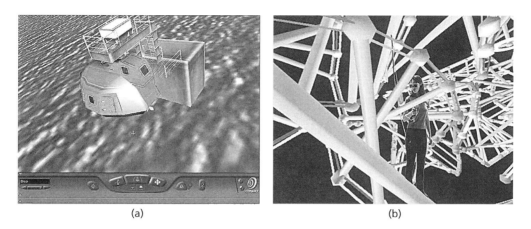

(a)   (b)

Figure 9.7 Sample virtual reality applications: (a) VRML model of a space capsule floating on water, and (b) a molecular structure inside a CAVE.

impossible to simulate everything. And because the simulated world is artificial, the experiences can be as removed from reality as desired (e.g., acceleration or gravity simulations that could never be achieved in real life). Indeed, a popular VR application is games where players interact with exciting but impossible worlds.

From a usability perspective, maintaining a close correspondence between the simulated and real worlds has obvious advantages. *Star Trek's* holodeck illustrates how a comprehensive real-world simulation is the ultimate in direct manipulation: Every object and service provided by the computer looks and behaves exactly as it would if encountered in the real world. No learning is required beyond that needed for interacting with any new artifact encountered in the world; there are no user interface objects or symbols intruding between people and the resources they need to pursue their goals.

But as many VR designers point out, a key advantage in simulating reality is the ability to deliberately introduce mismatches with the real world (Tradeoff 9.9). Examples of useful mismatches (also called "magic"; Smith 1987) include allowing people to grow or shrink, have long arms or fingers to point or grab at things, an ability to fly, and so on (Bowman in press). The objects or physical characteristics of a simulated world can also be deliberately manipulated to produce impossible or boundary conditions of real-world phenomena (e.g., turning gravity "off" as part of a physics learning environment).

TRADEOFF 9.9

Interaction techniques that simulate the real world may aid learning and naturalness, BUT "magic" realities may be more engaging and effective for some tasks.

Reasoning from scenarios that emphasize people's task goals helps to determine the level of realism to include in a VR model. In a skill-training simulation, learning transfer to real-world situations is the most important goal. This suggests that the simulation should be as realistic as possible given processing and device constraints. In contrast, if the task is to explore a DNA molecule, realism and response time are much less critical; instead, the goal is to visualize and improve access to interesting patterns in the environment. In an entertainment setting, a mixed approach in which some features are very realistic but others are mismatched may lead to feelings of curiosity or humor. In all cases, careful analysis of the knowledge and expectations that people will bring to the task is required to understand when and how to add "magic" into the world.

Many people equate VR with **immersive environments**, where the simulated reality is experienced as "all around" the user. Immersive VR requires multimodal input and output. For example, a head-mounted display provides surround vision, including peripheral details; data gloves or body suits process physical movements as well as providing **haptic** (pressure) **feedback**; speech recognition and generation allows convenient and direct requests for services; and an eye-gaze or facial gesture analysis tool can respond automatically to nonverbal communication. All of these devices work in parallel to produce the sensation of looking, moving, and interacting within the simulated physical setting. The degree to which participants feel they are actually "in" the artificial setting is often referred to as **presence**.

The overhead in developing and maintaining immersive VR systems is enormous, and usage can be intimidating, awkward, or fatiguing (Tradeoff 9.10). Stumbling over equipment, losing one's balance, and walking into walls are common in these environments. If a simulation introduces visual motion or movement cues that are inconsistent, or that differ significantly from reality, participants can become disoriented or even get physically sick.

TRADEOFF 9.10

Immersive multimodal input and displays may enhance presence and situation awareness, BUT can lead to crowded work areas, fatigue, or motion sickness.

Fortunately, many VR applications work quite well in desktop environments. The space capsule on the left of Figure 9.7 was built in VRML, a markup language developed for VR applications on the World Wide Web. Large displays and input devices that move in three dimensions (e.g., a joystick rather than a mouse; see Chapter 5) can increase the sense of presence in desktop simulations. Again, scenarios of use are important in choosing among options. When input or output to hands or other body parts are crucial elements of a task, desktop simulations will not suffice. Desktop VR will never elicit the degree of presence produced by immersive systems, so it is less effective in tasks demanding a high level of physical engagement. But even in these situations, desktop simulations can be very useful in prototyping and iterating the underlying simulation models.

9.5   Science Fair Case Study: Emerging Interaction Paradigms

The four interaction paradigms discussed in the first half of the chapter can be seen as a combination of interaction metaphors and technology. Table 9.2 summarizes this view and serves as a launching point for exploring how these ideas might extend the activities of the science fair. For example, the intelligent system paradigm can be viewed as combining a "personal-assistant" metaphor with technology that recognizes natural language and builds models of users' behavior. For simplicity, we have restricted our design exploration to just one design scenario for each interaction paradigm.

Table 9.2   Viewing the emerging paradigms as a combination of metaphor and technology.

Interaction Paradigm	Associated Metaphors	Associated Technology
Coordinating work	Management, interpersonal nonverbal communication	Network services, multimedia displays, database management
Ubiquitous computing	Just-in-time information and services	Wireless networks, handheld devices, microchip controllers
Intelligent systems	Personal assistant	Speech, gesture, handwriting recognition, artificial intelligence models and inference engines, data mining of historical records
Simulation and virtual reality	Real-world objects and interactions	High-resolution or immersive displays, haptic devices

9.5.1   Collaboration in the Science Fair

Coordinating work in the science fair raises questions of multiparty interaction—what do people involved in the fair want to do together, in groupings of two or more, that could benefit from greater awareness and coordination of one another's activities? Of course, to a great extent we have been considering these questions all along, because the science fair has been a group- and community-oriented concept from the start.

For instance, we have many example of coordination features in the design—a mechanism that "welcomes" new arrivals, information about where other people are, an archive of people's comments, and so on. However, in reviewing the design proposed thus far, we recognized that the judging scenario could benefit from further analysis of coordination mechanisms:

- Ralph decides to make changes on the judging form. The judging scenario describes Ralph's desire to make this change and indicates that he is allowed to do it, as long as he includes a rationale. We did not yet consider the larger picture implied by this scenario, specifically, that a group of other judges or administrators might be involved in reviewing Ralph's request for a change.

This coordination concern also provides a good activity context from which to explore the tradeoffs discussed earlier—awareness of shared plans and activities (Tradeoff 9.1), consequences of computer-mediated communication (Tradeoff 9.2), and managing group history (Tradeoff 9.3).

Figure 9.8 presents the judging scenario with most of the surrounding context abbreviated, and just the form editing activity elaborated. Table 9.3 presents the corresponding collaboration claims that were analyzed in the course of revising the scenario. Note that the elaboration of this subtask could be extracted and considered as a scenario on its own, but with a connection to the originating scenario that provided Ralph's goals and concerns as motivation.

This elaboration is relatively modest and builds on the services already designed. For example, Ralph is able to check for other judges because the room metaphor of the science fair has been customized for the judging activity. He had easily noticed other judges on arrival and is quickly able to check to see if they are still there. When he decides to make the change on his own, the automatic notification simplifies the process for him—he does not need to remember to tell the other judges about it. At the same time, he may feel a bit concerned that now others will be checking on his work. His colleagues in turn may feel compelled to review the change and respond. This possible disadvantage echoes a general tradeoff discussed earlier, namely, that being "made aware" of a collaborator's

---

4) Ralph judges the high school physics projects at the science fair.

<Background context on Ralph, his motivations and expectations about serving as judge at the VSF.>

<Narrative of Ralph's initial exploration of the VSF, seeing what exhibits he has been assigned, his first visit to the exhibits, and the subsequent visit where he does the more detailed comparisons and ratings, including a rather complex episode where he works with multiple forms and exhibits.>

As Ralph considers the exhibits in more detail, he begins to worry that the forms are not quite right for the points he needs to make about Sally Harris and Jeff Smith. Sally has gone all out for creativity while Jeff is very strong on methods. Ralph would like to weight the two subsections differently in the two forms, and when he checks the total, he sees that it is calculated as a formula.

He starts to edit the formula, then remembers that several other judges were also in the judging room when he arrived. He looks back in the main view of the judging room but they are no longer there. Since he needs to get the work done, he decides to go ahead and make the change and check with everyone else later. He edits the formula in both forms and writes a comment explaining his rationale. Then he saves the new forms. He notices when he does this that email notices have been sent to all of the other judges. A copy has been sent to him as well, and when he views it, he sees that it indicates a change to the evaluation form has been made, and asks the other judges to review the changes. A link back to the two forms is also included.

When he goes back to finish his work, he sees that several judges have left their own comments. No one has disagreed with his change, although one person questioned whether the science fair instructions might need revising in the future. He feels much better about his decision knowing that others have reviewed and confirmed his argument.

<Narrative describing his completion of the ratings, the submission and authorization process, and his subsequent ability to browse the temporary results.>

Figure 9.8 Collaboration support for the science fair judging activity.

plans or activities may be felt as an unwanted demand for time and attention (Tradeoff 9.1).

The review process itself is supported by annotations on the judging form, which are essentially comments on Ralph's explanation. This is nice because the result is a group-created piece of rationale. But because the annotations appear directly on the form, there is the risk that they compromise the form's main job, which is to document one judge's evaluation of a project.

Table 9.3   Collaboration-oriented claims analyzed during scenario generation.

Design Feature	Possible Pros (+) or Cons (−) of the Feature
Automatic requests for change review	+ emphasizes that changes are a shared concern
	+ simplifies notification of and access to changes
	− but the change maker may feel that his or her work is being audited
	− but recipients may feel that immediate review is expected
Group annotation of an editing form	+ promotes consensus and confidence about individual proposals
	− but annotation sets that are long or complex may make the form more difficult to read and process

9.5.2   Ubiquitous Computing in the Science Fair

According to the vision of ubiquitous computing, humans will be able to access and enjoy computer-based functionality whenever, wherever, and however it is relevant. For the science fair, this caused us to think about how we might push on the "containment" boundaries of the fair event, distributing parts of the fair into the world, or bringing parts of the world into the fair.

Again, we considered these options in light of the scenarios and claims already developed. Do constraints exist that are imposed by the virtual fair concept in general, or are there problems with specific features? One interesting issue that we have ignored is the implicit constraint that fair participants will have access to a computer for their activities. All of the scenarios assume this, even though they take place in school labs, home environments, office environments, and so on. But remember that a central goal for the project was to make access and participation more convenient and flexible. Does requiring access to a conventional computer really accomplish this goal?

This line of thought caused us to think about situations in which people might want to "visit" the fair without actually sitting down at a computer. Are there occasions when a participant might want to check in briefly, look at a specific piece of information, and then move on? If so, the simple act of moving to a computer and turning it on might not be worth the effort. We explored this general notion in the scenario where Mr. King coaches Sally, envisioning how he might use a mobile phone to check to see if Sally was at the fair before logging on to work with her. The resulting scenario segment appears in Figure 9.9, and the associated claims in Table 9.4.

1) Mr. King coaches Sally on her exhibit on black holes.

<Background context introducing Mr. King and his prior experience and interest in science fairs.>

After school Mr. King did a bit of grading, and then headed for the gym to work out. Halfway there, he remembered that he had told Sally he would work with her on her virtual science fair project. He didn't want to disappoint her, but he also didn't want to miss his workout if she was already done and didn't need his help. He decided to quickly check and see if she was there working, so he dialed up the science fair information number on his cell phone. The system answered in its distinct synthetic speech voice: "Welcome to Virtual Science Fair 2000! To hear new announcements, press 1; to leave a message for fair organizers, press 2; to search the fair for a person or object, press 3."

Mr. King pressed 3, then listened again: "Use the keypad to type the name of a science fair object or person; press the pound sign when done." This time he didn't wait for the prompt to finish, because he is so used to these phone systems he already knows about the pound sign. So he interrupts and types in Sally's userid, sharris, followed by the pound sign. Immediately, the synthetic voice responded: "Sally Harris is at black hole exhibit. Sally Harris has been active for about five minutes." With this information, Mr. King headed home, where he got online right away to talk to Sally.

<Continuing description of how Mr. King works with Sally to evaluate her materials and think about how best to select among them and lay them out.>

Figure 9.9 Adding a ubiquitous computing element to Mr. King's coaching experience.

Table 9.4 Claims analyzed while generating the ubiquitous computing scenario.

Design Feature	Possible Pros (+) or Cons (−) of the Feature
Supporting a search with a telephone keypad	+ builds on people's experience with other phone-based applications + provides an important preview function when away from the full system − but it will be tedious when entering long or arbitrary search strings
Text-to-speech output	+ makes it clear that a computer rather than a human is providing the service + reinforces that any arbitrary object or person can be checked and reported − but listening to long utterances may be difficult or unpleasant

This scenario highlights the "just-in-time" concept associated with ubiquitous computing. The information Mr. King needs is available when and where he realizes he needs it—in the car on his way to do something else. It also suggests that the phone has become familiar as an alternate input device; Mr. King already knows the convention of "closing off" an open-ended entry with a pound sign. However, the claims in Table 9.4 document the negative aspects of the proposed phone interface. The telephone buttons do not map well to typing out long names. Although the use of a speech synthesizer enables the system to speak the names of arbitrary objects and people, the pronunciation and intonation of synthetic speech can be difficult or tedious to understand.

9.5.3   Intelligence in the Science Fair

The most general metaphor of an intelligent system paradigm is assistance. So, in thinking about what this interaction paradigm might contribute to the science fair, the obvious candidates are tasks or subtasks that have special knowledge or complexities associated with them, particularly if these tasks have been affected by the introduction of online activities or information. Scanning the earlier scenarios and claims, we found the following issue:

- The selection of material for the highlights summary. It was easy for Rachel to identify the winning exhibits, because they had colored ribbons attached to them. But she then had to open each exhibit and explore it to find interesting examples of material.

We considered what sorts of models or guidance might be provided to reduce the tedium of browsing all the material in the winning exhibits. It seemed unlikely that the science fair could have an intelligent model of what is "interesting." However, it seemed quite possible that the fair could record viewers' interactions with the exhibits and use this information to make recommendations about what material was more or less popular. This could be a useful heuristic for Rachel (we are assuming that the people who visited the exhibits have good taste!).

The resulting scenario and claims appear in Figure 9.10 and Table 9.5. The concerns they raise are related to one of the general tradeoffs for intelligent systems—when an automated system collects and presents information about people's activities, it is possible to base one's own behavior on "data" rather than personal judgment, with the possible cost of ignoring the values normally used to make such judgments, or feeling less in control and less involved (Tradeoff

9.8). There is also the more general downside that some people (e.g., the exhibitors in this case) may not want these "objective" data collected and shared.

The related problem of evoking too much trust in a software agent is addressed to some extent by designing an interaction that offers different sorting options. Each button reveals a piece of the model that calculates "interest" rankings. Playing with them helps to demystify the process—Rachel is able to make some analysis of how the advice is generated. The agent is also not introduced as an "assistant"; there is no effort to anthropomorphize the service, but rather it is treated simply as a normal science fair service.

---

5) Superintendent Mark Carlisle reports on the 1999 science fair to the school board.

<Background context on Carlisle, his motivations and expectations about summarizing the VSF to the school board.>

Rachel would have normally built a customized presentation for Carlisle, but because he needs it tomorrow, she decided to use the "What's interesting?" service. This service keeps a record of all visits and interaction within the fair; visitors can check with it at any time to get recommendations about exhibits or activities that people find most interesting. Rachel hasn't tried it out yet, so she's not sure how it decides what is "interesting," but she figures it must be based on something meaningful, because why else would it be offered as part of the system?

She goes to the main view screen and opens the "What's interesting?" object. A separate window opens to the side with histograms of about 20 objects ordered by Viewing frequency. At the top of the window are three buttons labeled "Viewing frequency," "Viewing length," and "Length & Frequency"; the first seems to be in effect by default. She infers that these buttons must map somehow to the system's judgments of what counts as interesting. She sees that she gets a very different ordering when she uses the length-based ordering; more of the "winning" exhibits (with ribbons) are at the top. This makes sense to her, because these activities probably had richer information and activity associated with them. She figures that the frequency order may also include exhibits from students who are well known or popular. She decides to work from the length-based listing.

<Narrative describing creation of the nontemplate board and the dragging of content onto it.>

<Concluding narrative describing Carlisle's use of the highlights board and his unsuccessful efforts to persuade the school board to contribute more resources to next year's fair.>

Figure 9.10 Construction of a highlights board, as aided by a "What's interesting?" agent.

Table 9.5   Claims analyzed while generating the intelligent system scenario.

Scenario Feature	Possible Upsides (+) or Downsides (−) of the Feature
Using browsing and interaction history as an "interest" indicator	+ emphasizes that perceived value of activities is a community issue + simplifies access to, and influence of, the behavior of a community − but may interfere with more traditional exhibit evaluation criteria − but may reduce people's feeling of judgment and control − but students with exhibits judged less interesting may be demoralized
Multiple options for ranking activities by interest level	+ reveals something about how interest rankings may be calculated + stimulates comparison and reasoning about the implied criteria − but may be confusing if widely disparate orderings are produced

9.5.4   Simulating Reality in the Science Fair

The virtual reality paradigm has an obvious relationship to the current VSF design: It can be seen as an end point of the physical science fair metaphor. Our design uses a two-dimensional information model; maps and exhibit spaces evoke the physical world, but do not simulate it. We could have envisioned a three-dimensional information model in which visitors and judges walk around to get to the individual exhibits, with the exhibit components themselves arrayed in three dimensions.

We chose not to pursue the 3D model because it wasn't clear what the simulated reality would add to the experience. We decided instead to expand one piece of Sally's black hole exhibit. In lieu of the Authorware simulation, we considered what it would be like if she had created a demonstration in VRML. In this case, there seemed to be a legitimate application of the extra realism: By providing visitors with a vivid three-dimensional experience of being "sucked into" a black hole, the overall exhibit would have much more impact.

We explored this elaboration in the visit scenario of Alicia and Delia, focusing on just their encounter with this new black hole simulation. The resulting scenario and associated claims appear in Figure 9.11 and Table 9.6.

For this particular application, we did not want to consider highly immersive virtual reality, because most visitors will be coming from home and will not have any special input or output devices. Thus, we proposed a simple mapping of the three dimensions to the arrows found on all computer keyboards. This ensures that anyone with a normal keyboard can navigate in Sally's virtual model.

3) Alicia and Delia go to the science fair.

> <Background context introducing Alicia and Delia, their motivations, expectations, decision to go to the fair, initial experiences finding Marge and joining her at Sally's exhibit, decision to look around while Marge and Sally chat. . . .>
>
> Delia noticed a miniature window on the bottom with the intriguing title, "The Visit." When she clicked on it, a very dark sky with a few stars strewn around appeared in the main view. A key at the bottom indicated that the keyboard up/down arrow keys would move her up and down in the sky, but that the left/right keys would move her out away from, and closer into, the scene. She was not much into video games and wasn't quite sure what to do, but Alicia encouraged her to give it a try.
>
> It didn't take long to get the hang of it. Moving up and down was easy, but she had to keep remembering how the in/out keys worked. She could see as she moved around that what had seemed to be stars were actually planets and other space objects with different characteristics. She was heading for one that had some blue and green on it, when all of a sudden she was sucked into an invisible black hole! She tried and tried but couldn't get out. Alicia was laughing as Delia gave up, congratulating Sally on a very successful demonstration.
>
> <Continuation of narrative describing their discussions with Sally, Alicia's positive response.>

Figure 9.11   A portion of the visit scenario transformed to emphasize virtual reality.

Table 9.6   Claims analyzed for the virtual reality interaction.

Scenario Feature	Possible Upsides (+) or Downsides (−) of the Feature
Using keyboard arrow for 3D controls	+ makes it possible for all viewers to explore the visual model + leverages familiarity with arrow keys in other spatial tasks − but provides a poor mapping to the third (depth) dimension
Three-dimensional movement through a simulated space	+ reinforces the connection of the scientific phenomenon to the real world − but some viewers may not know how to move in space − but it may be tedious to identify and navigate to the "interesting" spots

But we made this decision with the understanding that it was not a terrific match to the task, and that some individuals might have considerable trouble figuring out how to carry out these navigation movements.

In the miniscenario described here, Delia actually enjoys her exploration of the three-dimensional space, and at some point simply finds herself "sucked into" the black hole. But during claims analysis we also imagined someone who spent considerable time in the space but never encountered the black hole. Would this person have been as satisfied as Delia? Probably not. In fact, this is a common issue in virtual reality systems. People get around these spaces by walking or flying. If a task consists of searching a large open space for a few key elements, the simple task of navigating the space can become quite tedious.

9.5.5   Refining the Interaction Design

The emphasis in the chapter has been on emerging interaction paradigms. By definition, these interaction techniques are not yet standard practice; much of the underlying technology is still being developed. As a result, many of the design ideas they inspire may be not feasible for immediate refinement and implementation. They are more likely to be useful in discussions that take a longer view, or in thinking about how a system may evolve in future releases.

The science fair elaborations described in this chapter are not extreme, and they vary considerably in how much extra work is implied. For example, the mobile access via cell phone implies an entirely new user interface customized for that device. We have glossed over the extensive design process that would be necessary to define the features such an extension to the normal science fair should have. In contrast, the "What's interesting" service would be relatively straightforward to design or implement, because people and their activities are already being stored as part of the overall MOOsburg infrastructure. Similarly, the proposed VRML extension to the black hole exhibit requires only that the science fair be prepared to support documents of this type, and there are already browsers available that do this.

Summary and Review

This chapter has explored interaction paradigms that go beyond the conventional WIMP style of user interface. The case study was elaborated to demonstrate how the metaphors and technology of computer-supported cooperative work, ubiquitous computing, intelligent systems, and virtual reality might be used to extend the science fair design. Central points to remember include:

- Emerging interaction paradigms influence all aspects of action planning and evaluation.

- Facilitating awareness of collaborators' activities, both current and past, is a key challenge in the design of collaborative systems.

- As computers become smaller and more distributed, user interfaces are becoming more specialized, and the services provided less predictable to their users.

- People often treat computer systems as if they had human characteristics or intelligence, particularly when the system uses natural language or personalized user interfaces.

- The automatic storage and analysis of personal data are becoming a social issue as software agents are being developed to assist in many different service areas.

- An important challenge for virtual reality environments is determining when to go beyond a simple simulation of reality.

Exercises

1. Analyze the collaborative project work you have been doing in this course. List the tasks that you carry out on a regular basis, and the roles and responsibilities of the group members in each task. Then describe the techniques that you use to coordinate your work, to stay in touch, share progress or status, distribute updates or documents, and so on. What are the biggest problems in coordinating your team's work?

2. Develop a proposal for a "smart kitchen." Draw (by hand or using a graphics editor) your hypothetical kitchen, using arrows and labels to identify devices. Provide a key to the drawing that names each device and briefly describes its function.

3. Try out the ELIZA program (or a more modern chat-bot). Experiment with it enough to make and test some hypotheses about how it is processing your input. Write up your hypotheses and how you tested them.

4. Surf the Web to find two examples of VRML in use, including one that you judge to be a useful application, and a second where the VR is gratuitous or even contrary to task goals. Describe the two cases and provide a rationale for your comparative judgment. (Be careful not to fall into the trap of thinking that if it "looks good," then it must be useful.)

Project Ideas

Elaborate your online shopping scenarios to explore the four interaction paradigms discussed in this chapter. Try to create at least one example of coordinating work, ubiquitous computing, intelligent systems, and virtual reality in the context of your current design. Be careful not to force the new interaction techniques—use claims analysis to reason about the situations where the alternative interaction styles can be of most benefit. Illustrate your proposals with sketches or storyboards if relevant.

Recommended Reading

Beaudouin-Lafon, M., ed. 1999. *Computer Supported Co-operative Work.* Chichester, England: John Wiley & Sons.

Gellerson, H.-W., & P. J. Thomas, eds. 2000. *Proceedings of Handheld and Ubiquitous Computing: HUC 2000.* Amsterdam: Springer-Verlag.

Heim, M. 1997. *Virtual Realism.* Oxford: Oxford University Press.

Huhns, M. N., & M. P. Singh, eds. 1998. *Readings in Agents.* San Francisco: Morgan Kaufmann.

Maybury, M. T., & W. Wahlster, eds. 1998. *Readings in Intelligent User Interfaces.* San Francisco: Morgan Kaufmann.

Rheingold, H. 1992. *Virtual Reality.* New York: Touchstone Books.

10

Usability Engineering in Practice

Digital Equipment Corporation's TeamLinks software supports heterogeneous intranets within an organization. The product was originally developed for Windows PC platforms and then ported to the Macintosh platform. Instead of simply porting the Windows interface, the development team engaged in an informal process of customer interviews and iterative prototyping. Through this process, many of the initial assumptions about the product were quickly discarded. For example, users of the Windows version access the TeamLinks application through a special-purpose control window, but the Macintosh version leverages native Macintosh-style document views and navigation. Macintosh users access the application's shared data through the Chooser, using the same techniques they apply to other shared data. Afterward, the developers reported that if they had not taken the time to consider what their Macintosh users would want, they would have wasted the first half of their redevelopment effort (see Wixon, et al.1996).

∞∞∞

Usability is not just a nice concept. It determines, whether products and companies succeed or fail. It determines whether some products can be sold at all in international markets. It determines whether people can find the information they need, communicate effectively, and enjoy their work life. It can be a factor in workplace injuries and other safety-related hazards. It determines whether children, the elderly, and others with special needs are able to participate in the larger culture.

In the real world of software development, it is not enough to have creative ideas and all the right skills. The development plan for TeamLinks (see opening vignette) was quite sophisticated from a usability perspective. It emphasized user interface metaphors, consistent displays, and tight integration. Fortunately, it also included a strong process of customer participation, which enabled the developers to discover that they were wrong. Not every product development effort is like this. The DEC group had established credibility within their organization over more than a decade of effective cooperation. They state that their group's effectiveness, and the effectiveness of usability engineering methods in general, depend on the organizational context.

Through most of this book we have examined particular aspects of usability engineering in isolation, so that we could focus on specific issues and relationships. This final chapter returns to the broader role and implications of usability engineering. We will look at usability in organizations, internationalization, and the ethics of usability.

10.1   Usability in Organizations

Usability engineering has a broad basis in science and in evaluation methods. It relies on the psychology of learning, perception, problem solving, and skill; the sociology and anthropology of groups and organizations; human physiology; biomechanics and the ergonomics of seating, lighting, and equipment; computer science tools and methods; and graphical and industrial design. Practicing usability engineers must also interact with representatives of other disciplines who contribute to the definition, refinement, and implementation of the products they work on.

Software development teams are composed of people with a range of talents and skills, and many of these colleagues may not share the usability engineer's focus on user needs and preferences. Usability engineers must be able to make the case for usability to these individuals. To do that, they need to understand the bigger picture of system development. They must be able to cooperate with—so as to support and lead—other development team members.

10.1.1   Usability Specialists in a Development Team

The organizational role of usability engineering in system development is a longstanding issue. In the 1970s, it was common to schedule controlled user tests of nearly final system products. This was not effective. When usability is assessed only toward the end of a development process, the impact of the test results is limited to cosmetic improvements, calls for additional training materials, or requirements for future versions of the product. Through the 1980s, as the computing industry became more competitive and product cycles became shorter, usability issues were raised and addressed at earlier points in development. One response to this was to form and maintain separate usability groups, which acted as a general resource to a number of development teams. Another approach was to integrate usability specialists into the development team.

Figure 10.1 contrasts these two approaches to usability in organizations and summarizes some of the advantages and disadvantages associated with each

 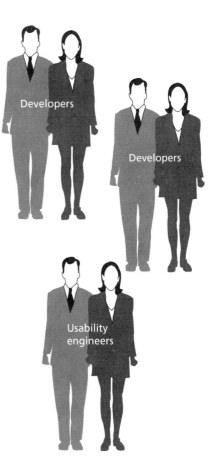

Advantages: tightly integrated, focused work, appreciation of project-specific constraints
Disadvantages: less objectivity, hard to take a general perspective

Advantages: resource sharing, cross-product insights, and organizational learning
Disadvantages: communication overhead, time-sharing, and prioritization

Figure 10.1 Alternative organizational structures for integrating usability concerns into product development teams.

(Tradeoff 10.1). From a pure design perspective, integration of a usability professional into a project team increases the likelihood that the right use-related questions will be raised and addressed throughout the product development lifecycle. The usability specialist becomes immersed in the problem domain, which helps him or her to produce a design solution that is optimized for the users and tasks of this domain.

TRADEOFF 10.1

Integrating usability engineers into individual project teams increases immersion and attention to project-specific usability issues, BUT usability engineers may become so immersed that they miss opportunities for cross-project relationships.

However, many organizations cannot (or will not) employ enough usability specialists for every project to have at least one, so assigning a specialist to one project may mean less usability engineering for other projects. There is also a possibility that a usability engineer will become so engaged in project development that he or she begins to think and act more as a designer than as a user advocate. Gathering usability professionals into a separate group that consults with a variety of projects can address these issues, but is likely to lead to a less comprehensive usability engineering process for any one project. The most effective structure for a company depends on many factors: the resources it is willing to spend on usability engineering, the similarities and differences among projects, the experience of its usability professionals, and its own organizational culture.

In the 1990s, usability engineers came to play major roles in both requirements development—a role traditionally assigned to marketing—and design. One trend in this history is that usability has moved steadily "upstream" in the development process, from the evaluation of functional systems, to defining objectives and designing prototypes. A second trend is that usability is beginning to be seen as a critical skill for development teams, rather than as a consulting resource.

A key job requirement for usability specialists is communication. A development team must be able to express a range of technical issues in a common language to understand tradeoffs and resolve conflicts. Because scenarios rely on natural language to describe and elaborate many different kinds of design issues, usability engineers may find them to be very useful for supporting communication among different team members throughout the development process.

One likely trajectory for usability engineering as a profession is further integration into system development. In the past, usability specialists emerged from many different disciplines, including anthropology, computer science, industrial engineering, management science, psychology, and sociology. In contrast, most other members of development teams were trained in computer science. But in the 1990s, human-computer interaction was identified as a core area within computer science and was recommended as a required element in computer science programs (Tucker, et al. 1991). It is likely that in the future usability engineering will become a specialty area of computer science.

10.1.2   Cost-Justifying Usability

If every software developer were trained in the concepts and techniques of usability engineering, we still would not have perfect usability. The reason is that in product development there are inescapable tradeoffs. Some of the tradeoffs are associated with the design issues discussed throughout this book; other tradeoffs arise from finite resources or other management concerns. Producing software that costs more to develop than it can ever return through sales and services does not make sense. The reality of the marketplace not only affects resources for usability engineering, but applies to all costs in system development. Product managers must make tradeoff decisions every day, investing more resources in some aspects and less in others.

Usability engineers must be prepared to argue that any resources invested in usability will provide a profitable return. How can they do this? Cost-justifying usability is a business planning process in which costs and benefits are explicitly planned and quantified (Conklin 1991; Karat 1997). Any planning projection involves assumptions, some of which may later prove to be incorrect. But the point of cost justifying is to be explicit about the assumptions, and to defend them with data, models, and science.

When estimating costs and benefits of usability work, the usability practitioner is faced with a dilemma. To justify resources for analysis, evaluation, and redesign, a clear case for the resulting benefits must be presented. But because these benefits are only predictions, and may often involve intangible consequences such as customer satisfaction, the benefit estimation process must be highly conservative (Tradeoff 10.2). Because benefit predictions are more likely to be wrong, cost predictions are easier to make. Also, contention is more likely on the benefits side, because they are clearly predictions. Unfortunately, the result may be that fewer resources are allotted than necessary to achieve a successful result.

TRADEOFF 10.2

 Cost-benefit analysis of usability activities contributes to more systematic usability engineering, BUT benefits are difficult to quantify, so estimates will often be overly conservative.

Costs are mainly personnel time and equipment. An estimate can be developed by enumerating specific usability engineering activities that will be carried out. For example, the following list is typical of the usability engineering activities advocated in this book:

- development of requirements scenarios
- validation/refinement of scenarios with users and customers
- development of basic-level task scenarios
- refinement of design scenarios with development team members and customers
- development of information model
- review with team members
- development of paper prototypes
- walk-throughs with users of paper prototypes
- analysis of transcripts/report preparation
- development of interaction model
- review with team members
- development of running prototypes
- formative evaluation
- analysis of transcripts/report preparation
- detailed design and prototype-driven iteration of previous three steps

The costs for each usability engineering activity depend on the scope of the product, the range of functionality, the number of scenarios, the number of users studied, and, of course, the skill and experience of the usability specialists. Each activity can be further detailed and quantified in terms of time and material required. For example, formative evaluation can be decomposed into specific tests, which in turn can be decomposed into the time required to design and set up for each test, the equipment and space required for each, and the time per test session. In addition to the salaries of the usability engineers, reimbursement of the test participants' time may be an expense.

Usability costs also vary with the facilities available; investment in a permanent usability lab is a large initial expenditure, but significantly decreases the cost of subsequent tests. Organizational factors may aid or impede cooperation with the developers, such as physical co-location with the product development group. Such factors can be quite important, because there is a perception that one major cost of usability engineering is to delay the development process, resulting in lost revenue due to reduced market share. Of course, this concern applies to *all* product development activities. One remedy is to carry out usability engineering activities in parallel with other development activities, so as not to lengthen total development time.

Benefits are harder to estimate, but there are many positive outcomes that can be attributed to usability engineering:

- fewer downstream design changes
- increased sales (and consequently reduced time to profitability)
- reduced need for user training
- enhanced customer productivity
- reduced resources spent on customer support
- increased loyalty in customer base (repeat and referral sales)

The key to preparing a benefits analysis is to make a set of conservative assumptions about outcomes. For example, one source of benefit is addressing design changes early. Changes made early in the development process cost far less than those made later; for instance, changes made in early prototyping cost about 25% of those made after installation (Mantei & Teorey 1988). Thus, in a benefits projection, it might be assumed that five design changes, each requiring four to eight hours to address, will be identified through formative evaluation and addressed in early stages of development. This could save the development team a week of effort. Although planning for five early design changes of this magnitude is very conservative, it might turn out that three or ten design changes are actually identified, or that they each require two days of redesign work. One way to manage the estimation process is to develop a prediction based on several possible outcomes.

Other benefits of usability work include reduced need for user training and customer support, as well as increased user productivity. Impacts on user productivity can be estimated by projecting average user performance for a set of typical design scenarios, and then calculating the benefits of reducing these performance times by small amounts. For a core scenario—one that users in the workplace would perform at least 20 to 30 times per day—reducing performance time by even half a minute could provide an enormous cost savings for customers. Every user would save 10 to 15 minutes a day, every day for the life of the product. A similar line of argument can be used for designing error-recovery mechanisms, by estimating the time it takes to correct errors. The benefit in these cases is the total time saved multiplied by the salaries of the users.

One major question concerns how to estimate benefit parameters. How can the degree of performance streamlining or error elimination be projected before the project is carried out? This is a reasonable question, but one that applies to all other benefit projections in product development. For example, new product functions must also be justified in terms of their development costs and market value, but it is difficult to do this before the function even exists.

Many of these concerns can be addressed by prior experience. For example, an organization may have a history of developing self-study tutorials or training courses. Cost reductions in these areas are part of the expected benefit of usability engineering and can be explicitly planned. Indeed, the organization's own track record with respect to sales, new customers, customer support, design changes, and user training is a useful baseline for planning benefits. Another way to add substance to benefit estimations is to review published case studies. Unfortunately, product development case studies are usually not published in enough detail to make the necessary estimates.

Table 10.1 summarizes a retrospective cost-benefit analysis cited in Karat (1997, 774). The project is described as an "internal product built to replace a manual process," so the value of a successful product should be quite high. However, the cost-benefit analysis of the usability engineering process is limited to the improvement that can be attributed to iterative testing and refinement of the software, not the general move from manual to computer-based support. The projected savings is a function of the task-time reduction, the number of times a task will be repeated in a year, and the costs of personnel who carry out the task.

Table 10.1   Example usability cost-benefit analysis (Karat 1997, 774).

Estimated Benefits	Estimated Costs	Cost-Benefit Ratio
Reduction in task time from initial to final version of the software: **9.67 minutes**	Usability resource: **$23,000**	For the first year of application deployment:
Task repetitions per year: **1,308,000**	Study participant travel: **$9,750**	$68,000 / $6,800,000, for a ratio of **1:100**
Projected savings: **$6,800,000**	Test-related development work: **$34,950**	
	Total cost: **$68,000**	

The corresponding costs of the project are based on the actual usability engineering activities carried out in support of the project. These costs included a field test, development of a high-fidelity prototype, and three iterations of usability evaluation and iterative design. The activities took place over a period of 21 months. The final ratio is very high, and though it may not be typical, it could be used as part of a general argument to set aside resources for usability engineering activities.

Some benefits of usability engineering are indirect and cannot be quantified, but are nonetheless useful to consider when cost justifying the usability process. One of these benefits is a better understanding of customer attitudes and workplace practices; this knowledge may be very useful in future development projects. Moreover, because the general public now regards attention to usability as a positive thing, simply being careful to practice usability engineering may have value in terms of customer relations.

10.2   Internationalization and Localization

Software development is not just people writing programs for one another. It is a huge and complex business, and a global one, in the inspiring sense that it brings people from all over the world together. But this globalization aspect raises many issues. Should there be a standard approach to user interface design or usability engineering? Companies, nations, and international bodies are establishing software standards, including standards for user interface design. At the same time, a global approach to user interfaces might conflict with well-established cultural differences (Prabhu & del Galdo 1999). How can such conflict or cultural strain be prevented while still allowing some degree of standardization and economy of scale?

10.2.1   User Interface Standards

Standardization sometimes has a bad connotation to designers; it may imply constraints on creativity, raising concerns that good ideas may be blocked by standards that lead to mediocre results. This is certainly a possible negative effect of standardization, but there are strong advantages as well (Tradeoff 10.3). Standards for memory chips, operating systems, network protocols, programming languages, image formats, and, of course, for applications and user interfaces make modern computing possible. Standards have transformed the world, connecting people and information resources inexpensively, reliably, and transparently.

TRADEOFF 10.3

Standardized user interfaces simplify the design process and facilitate transfer of learning for users, BUT at the cost of restricting the design space and making design results less innovative.

There are many standardization efforts. The most visible is the International Organization for Standardization (ISO; *http://www.iso.ch/*). This standardization effort started in the 1970s and has produced an important document: *Ergonomic Requirements for Office Work with Visual Display Terminals* (ISO 9241). Many individual countries also have their own standards organizations. Corporate standards document specific user-interface design techniques—Apple Computer's *Macintosh Human Interface Guidelines* (1992) was an early example, along with the OSF/Motif Style Guide and the Windows interface design guide (Microsoft 1992).

From a development perspective, the rationale for standards is to avoid reinventing the wheel, to more easily and reliably incorporate best practices into future design work. When standards become established, they can be used to certify products. For example, a customer might require compliance to one or more standards in software contracting. The U.S. government regularly does this. Products that fail to meet government standards can be refused access to the government market, a potentially devastating penalty.

From a user experience perspective, standards are intended to facilitate transfer of learning from one system to another. The pervasive WIMP user interface has become so familiar to many users that they do not even bother to read help or user documentation, preferring instead to explore the user interface controls of a new application until they find what they want. And, of course, if a standard captures best practices as intended, it should increase the usability of user interfaces that conform to it.

Most user interface standards describe specific features such as color assignments, keyboard shortcuts, and so forth. Some are grounded in properties of human psychology and physiology. However, it is difficult to keep the standards current. For example, much of the rationale behind the ISO standard for menu design is based on the systems used in the mid-1980s, but the standard was not ready for publication until 1997.

Recently, the process of usability engineering itself has become a topic of standardization. Standards organizations have recognized that many user interface design issues depend on the context of use. Checklists of features will not ensure usability and may distract attention away from more important issues.

ISO 9241-11 requires that the context of use be analyzed during product development. Dzida and Freitag (1998) suggest that one method for implementing such analysis is to develop scenarios in cooperation with domain experts.

10.2.2   Localization

Standardization is a tool for addressing internationalization concerns, but also a challenge for the same concerns. The Internet has created a global computing community. However, the world is not a homogeneous community with a single culture. Indeed, people throughout the world are concerned that regional variation is being threatened by a global computing paradigm. It is easy to see how this could happen. In the limiting case, software costs will be minimized by providing one spreadsheet package for every user in the world: one set of commands and icons, one color palette and color assignment, one keyboard mapping, and, of course, one language—English.

This has already happened to some extent, but there are reasons to rethink this trend. First, the world will become less interesting if regional variations disappear. Second, designing user interfaces that respect cultural knowledge and practices is analogous to designing systems that are appropriate for specific workplace contexts, a widely accepted principle in user interface design.

Some user interfaces employ terms, images, and other elements that would be unacceptable in some cultures. A classic example is the `kill` command—and various iconic representations of such concepts. In the American computing culture, this concept is fun and vivid, and has become quite standard. However, it may be perceived as violent and disturbing by people from other cultures. A less extreme case would be a dog image in an icon or logo. Some Islamic cultures view dogs as unclean, which would make such imagery unappealing. These examples are relatively easy to address; the offensive command names or images can be changed to a more universally acceptable variant with little or no cost to overall user interaction.

Other examples are more difficult to resolve, because there is no single user interface design that will be effective for all users. A typical example is mailboxes, which are differently shaped and colored in various countries. Even simple attributes such as color may have cultural implications: Black signifies death in Western countries, but rebirth in Egypt; and white signifies purity and life in the West, but death and mourning in China. Date formats vary, as do assumptions about currency, weights, and measures. And, of course, there are many natural languages, including those that are read left to right instead of right to left; and different alphabets, grammatical conventions, and keyboard layouts.

Choong and Salvendy (1999) describe more complex variations among cultures. They have demonstrated that Americans tend to classify things by functions, focus on components, and look for common features. In contrast, Chinese tend to classify things by relationships within wholes, and they rely on subjective experiences. These researchers suggest that such differences are caused in part by family culture: Chinese see themselves as integral parts of their families, whereas Americans are more independent.

Localization refers to a design strategy in which the global computing community is supported with systematic variation among regions and cultures. For example, interfaces for China might emphasize concrete metaphors that rely on the user's subjective experience; they might also avoid using the color white for meaningful distinctions. Interfaces for North America might do the reverse. Of course, the effectiveness of these particular contrasts is a question for scientific analysis. Localization simply says that the differences should be identified and addressed in design (Fernandes 1995).

A challenge for localization arises from the cost and ambiguity in identifying and characterizing cultural boundaries (Tradeoff 10.4). China is a different culture than North America, but is it a single culture? For that matter, is North America a single culture? There may also be transient differences among cultures; it may be important to track cultural trends. For example, the culture of Coke versus Pepsi has become very salient in contemporary India, but only since 1998. Nevertheless, the slogans and iconography of this marketing battle are pervasive and might provide great leverage to user interface designers pursuing the Indian market.

TRADEOFF 10.4

Localizing user interfaces strengthens cultural diversity, BUT is more expensive than designing global user interfaces that are culturally monolithic.

10.3   Ethics of Usability

Technical professionals appreciate technical rationales. Thus, usability engineering is usually motivated by technical arguments: faster learning, increased productivity, fewer errors, and greater satisfaction. However, there is also a strong moral basis for usability engineering. It is wrong to provide people with tools that are more difficult to learn and use than they have to be. In 1981, we were studying office personnel as they learned to use word processing equipment. In one of these sessions, a study participant who was experiencing significant difficulties suddenly got up, put on her coat, and walked out. She was visibly shaking and nearly incoherent as she tried to explain to us that she just could not continue. This episode is more than a data point, and more than an error-recovery failure; it was a personal calamity.

One can respond that word processing, and office automation more generally, has come a long way since then. And this is true. But moral and ethical issues in usability are becoming more rather than less widespread, and they are becoming more complex.

10.3.1 Changing Scope of Computing

Computing is no longer about computers; it pervades our lives. Computing is embedded in our cars and homes, and in classrooms and libraries; we are using computers in some way almost all of the time. Data and programs are not matrices, storage media, and instructions. They are now our personal safety, the security of our savings, and our very identities. This joining of computing with the world is exciting, but not always comfortable. There are many implications for public safety, education, and access—and for the concept of usability.

Safety is a good example. Concerns about software safety have increased recently, motivated by several horrendous accidents (see "The Therac-25" sidebar). People seem to expect software systems to be safer than mechanical systems. In part, this may be because mechanical failures such as the Tacoma Narrows Bridge incident are easier to see and understand. It may also be due to the cultural myth that software is built from infallible logic, and because it is held in digital storage, it cannot degrade. But, in fact, software systems are *more* dangerous than mechanical systems because their behavior is more complex, less observable, and more difficult to diagnose. The potential for unanticipated interactions in software is enormous.

Safety has remained a side issue in usability engineering, perhaps because the origins of usability engineering were largely in studies of programming, data processing, and office automation. However, designing for safety and for ease of use are similar in many respects. The challenge in both cases is anticipating combinations of circumstances that may lead to problems. Indeed, safety-oriented requirements have long been a driving force in studies of the human factors of human-machine interfaces. Examples include simple and appropriate underlying conceptual models; clear warnings and prompts; prevention of errors whenever possible; rapid feedback, especially when error is likely; availability of diagnostic information; and support for error recovery.

Unfortunately, designing for safety is much more complex than detecting and correcting user interface problems (Tradeoff 10.5). Like ease of use or

The Therac-25

The Therac-25 was a medical linear accelerator used in radiation therapy in the mid-1980s. It was an expensive machine that had evolved from earlier models. One of its innovations was software-based control and monitoring. Safety mechanisms and interlocks used by predecessor designs were removed. It was assumed that software errors could be comprehensively identified in testing and that software-based safety would avoid risks of system degradation due to wear. From 1985 to 1987 there were six accidents in which massive radiation overdoses were administered. Most of the affected patients died as a direct result.

The Therac-25 is a paradigm case of bad software engineering. Its design was carried over from a much simpler predecessor system. This resulted in critical design flaws. For example, the software permitted concurrent access to shared memory, and provided synchronization only through the values of shared variables. Furthermore, the specifications and testing of the new software were not documented. Almost no component testing was performed, because the developers considered system use to be testing.

A Therac-25 operator controlled the machine through a DEC VT100 terminal. After positioning the patient on the treatment table, the operator entered patient and treatment parameters, including one of two energy modes. Under certain circumstances, energy mode entries were displayed on the screen but were not sensed by the data entry subroutine. This happened when the operator changed a value too rapidly, presumably when fixing a typing error. When the mismatch was detected, the system displayed the message "Malfunction 54" and paused. The documentation for this message indicated that the energy level was either too high or too low. Because of the strange wording of the Malfunction 54 message, operators sometimes concluded that too small a dose had been delivered, and initiated a second treatment.

This example offers a new perspective on bad user interface design. The developers did not understand the user's task, in this case, the likelihood of typos and rapid correction for treatment specifications. They provided poor coordination of screen information with underlying program states and events, and inscrutable error messages with inadequate reference documentation, and failed to fully test either the basic functionality or use of the system. In this case, these practices killed people. (See Leveson [1995] for additional discussion.)

satisfaction, safety must be achieved through a comprehensive process in which risks are documented and actively and persistently monitored throughout design, development, and deployment (Leveson 1995). The Therac-25 incident resulted from a combination of failures in software engineering, usability engineering, and project management. Again, as with usability, an effective approach to safety concerns is the collection and analysis of "critical incidents" (in this case, safety-related episodes) during software development. Such reports make the factors that affect safety more concrete. This approach in turn helps team members to recognize other situations that may raise safety concerns, as well as helping to reinforce an organizational culture of safety.

TRADEOFF 10.5

 Designing for safety requires identification of specific user interface features that cause errors, BUT the observed problems may in fact be caused by the complex interactions of parallel development activities.

Incident reports can be represented as scenarios, and as such can incorporate many of the usability engineering techniques discussed throughout this book. Scenarios help to project and analyze future possibilities. For example, what sorts of failures are possible, how can they be recognized and diagnosed, and how can a failure be contained? These questions can be addressed in "what-if" variants of incident reports, where the engineers consider the safety consequences of a particular component failure. Indeed, such consequences might be represented as claims, perhaps enabling safety risks to be integrated with other usability risks.

10.3.2   The Digital Divide

A generation ago, computing belonged to computer professionals and a small population of hobbyists. Computing is no longer remote from the culture at large. The use of computing is now required for full participation in society. In industrialized societies, computing skills such as word processing, spreadsheets, and Web browsing are increasingly seen as basic literacy. People must use computing to have access to banking, shopping, communication systems, and even government services.

This has made computing very important socially and economically, but has also made computing mandatory. People who want to have good job opportunities and economic security are not able to *choose* to use computers any more than they can choose to read and write. People who do not use computers can only be marginal members of society. And yet meaningful access to computing is not available to all (Tradeoff 10.6).

TRADEOFF 10.6

 Internet-based access to education, commerce, communications, and government services distributes political and economic control, BUT penalizes and excludes those who do not or cannot participate in the Internet.

A new phrase has been coined to refer to the disparity in access to computers and networking: the **digital divide**. For example, 80% of Internet users live in the 15 countries with highest per capita incomes. Asian Americans have the highest level of home Internet access in the United States at 57%; African Americans are at the other end of the spectrum with 23%. People with disabilities are half as likely to have access to the Internet as those without disabilities (National Telecommunications and Information Administration 2000).

In education, computing and networks are the newest panacea. There is a massive initiative in the United States to wire all classrooms, accompanied with exciting visions of lifelong learning supported by the Internet. But it is far from clear just how technology will transform education. Most of the research involves small-scale twiddling with curriculum and delivery, whereas the problems of education are large-scale and systemic. A U.S. Department of Education survey indicates that 45 million Americans—a quarter of the population—are functionally illiterate (National Center for Education Statistics 1999). Most of the early and encouraging results of educational technology may be due to simply providing students and teachers with new and exciting experiences. Whether this novelty will mature into new educational practices and opportunities is a serious question.

Whatever benefits technology may bring to education, it is clear they are now concentrated in wealthy, suburban school districts. Rural and inner-city schools have much less access to computing and network technologies. The U.S. Commerce Department has estimated that a child's chance of being excluded from information technology is 20 times greater if the child is poor and lives in a rural area (National Telecommunications and Information Administration 2000).

There are many initiatives underway to address the digital divide. Some of these provide public access to the Internet, for example, in public libraries. Many local initiatives can be grouped under the concept of community networks. Indeed, the virtual science fair example used in this book is a community network application.

10.3.3   Meeting the Needs of Special Populations

People are not all the same. Individuals vary in many ways, and these differences can have implications for their technology needs. Large or small people may need special keyboards; one size does not always fit all. It is important to keep special needs in mind when designing and evaluating user interfaces and applications, seeking to provide new opportunities and minimizing the challenges faced by these populations. Addressing the needs of special populations may also help in developing generally useful innovations.

An important category of special needs is users with disabilities. Of course, computers already provide significant new opportunities for some types of disabilities (Edwards 1995). For example, people with hearing impairments suffer greatly from social isolation. But they can now participate much more fully in the social world through email and other computer-based communication tools. User interfaces can be modified to convert tones into visual display elements, providing access to most of the information typically conveyed in user interfaces.

In many cases, accommodations for disabled users are applicable to other user interface situations. For example, head-mounted pointing devices are often designed for people with limited mobility, and speech recognition and speech synthesis are provided for visually impaired people. The development of these input and output technologies was driven to a considerable extent by special needs. But the resulting techniques are also useful to anyone with a hands-free requirement (e.g., industrial and military applications). Dynamic enlargement of display elements is effective for users with vision impairments, but also serves a general need of elderly users, many of whom experience gradual but progressive visual impairment. A user interface for a hearing-impaired person may also be useful in noisy environments such as factories or airport runways.

Elderly users are often discussed as a special population, but they are a major demographic segment. Age-related changes in vision begin to appear in the early forties. Thus, for vision-related issues, the elderly constitute 40% of the population in Western countries. In general, aging entails progressive decline in physical strength, speed, flexibility, perceptual acuity and recognition, and some kinds of memory and learning. Despite such impairments, many elderly people are eager and able to carry out complex activities. However, if the needs and preferences of elderly users are not factored into the usability engineering process, the resulting user interfaces may be unsuitable or unattractive to them (Tradeoff 10.7). The same is true for any user population with special needs.

TRADEOFF 10.7

 Computing offers new opportunities to persons with special needs, BUT these opportunities may never be realized if user interfaces are developed and tested only with normal user populations.

Some accommodations are straightforward: larger fonts and greater contrast in display elements, low-pitched voices for speech output (hearing acuity declines more for high-pitched sounds), slower blink rates on cursors and warnings, adjustable parameters for double-clicks and menu manipulation, and larger mouse targets (Hawthorn 2000). Older users are more disrupted by errors and may benefit from a finer level of confirmation dialog. Older users have difficulties with new behaviors that conflict with existing habits; they cannot replace over-learned behaviors as easily as younger people. Thus, the cognitive "cost" of adopting new user interfaces may be higher for an older user.

In many cases, accommodations for the elderly result in general and robust user interface characteristics. Because older users have a reduced capacity for managing complex window layouts, designing simple window management schemes and avoiding purely decorative graphical embellishments are useful strategies. But as discussed in Chapter 4, this is a desirable approach for user interface design in general (Mullet & Sano 1995). Speech recognition for older users must cope with slow and less fluent speech, hesitations, interruptions, and filled pauses. But again, these phenomena are not limited to older users, and addressing such problems will create more robust speech technology.

Elderly users often perform far better than one might expect based on the progressive declines associated with aging. Thus, we need to better understand the compensatory strategies developed by successful elderly users, since these strategies could help other users, including younger users who experience difficulties with various aspects of user interfaces (Czaja 1990).

Computing also offers new possibilities for seniors. It allows many activities to be undertaken at home, without walking or driving to a new location. Computing enables connections with peers through Internet services such as SeniorNet, opportunities to participate in a wide range of online activities, and easy access to the wealth of information available over the Internet. From December 1998 to August 2000, individuals 50 years of age and older—while less likely than younger Americans to use the Internet—experienced a 53% growth rate in Internet usage, compared to a 35% growth rate for individual Internet usage nationwide.

10.3.4   Technology Evolution and Unintended Consequences

There will always be unexpected costs that come along with exciting technology visions and innovations (Tradeoff 10.8). Over the past 40 years computing has dramatically improved reliability and access in record keeping, but at the same time it has raised new challenges of privacy and security for legal, medical, and financial records. The Internet in particular has provoked many tradeoffs. It enables easy access to an unprecedented volume of information. But much of this information is unreliable, some is unwelcome, and people feel the stress of information overload. The Internet has provided many new ways for people to interact and form groups, but people who use the Internet more may have fewer face-to-face meetings with family, friends, and colleagues.

TRADEOFF 10.8

New technologies and systems make possible new tasks and activities, BUT they invariably require people to develop and learn new skills, and change how people think about their tasks and themselves.

The very term "technology evolution" suggests a somewhat hit-or-miss process of innovation and selection. It uses an analogy to biological evolution, suggesting random mutation and subsequent survival of the fittest. It is indeed possible to look at the history of technology through this analogy. But it is not desirable. Random mutation is a wasteful way of managing innovation. As with biological evolution, it could take millions of trials to achieve good design. And survival of the fittest entails that people will have to try out and finally reject many inappropriate technological innovations in order to find a few that are appropriate. As we look to the future, we should consider how technology development can become more rational, deliberate, and efficient.

One key is to cultivate a system development process that integrates consideration of requirements for new technology with analysis of how people will use and experience the technology. Ultimately, designers enable scenarios. They create tools and environments that enable new ways of carrying out tasks and entirely new possibilities for tasks. If technology is seriously thought about as enabling support for human activities, then technology development can be far more efficient than mere evolution. Designers can find out what people expect, what they value most in what they currently do and know, what their needs and desires are, and so forth.

This is what scenario-based usability engineering is for. No design method can guarantee good solutions, but a design method should at least guarantee good questions. Scenario-based design tries to identify the critical and typical things that people do or want to do and the tradeoffs associated with design features that enable these activities. Many of these tradeoffs are inherent. Increasing the efficiency of user interactions improves ease of use, but conveys to people that their activities are less complex and less valuable. Designers can address such tradeoffs, finding good balance points for particular issues, but design tradeoffs are never just problems that are solved once and for all.

Usability is a broad concept. It will become broader as computer systems continue to pervade and transform human experience and activity. Computers should ease and enrich people's lives, not through a stumbling evolution that creates and then fixes unintended consequences, but through a thoughtful and systematic engineering process. Designers and users should expect nothing less.

Summary and Review
_____

This chapter has discussed some of the more complex issues surrounding the practice of usability engineering in software development organizations. Earlier chapters have presented a somewhat idealized view of problem analysis, scenario generation and revision, and evaluation, but in practice these activities are carried out in the context of many other impinging concerns. Central points to remember include:

- Usability specialists are becoming increasingly integrated within software development teams, which means that the emphasis on communication skills is greater than ever.

- Usability engineers are often expected to cost justify the usability process they plan to conduct, including the development of quantitative estimates of usability benefits.

- The trend toward greater standardization is opening up possibilities for computing on a global level, but development efforts must at the same time take care to respect the local needs and culture of their target users.

- Beyond the concrete goals of creating fluent and pleasant user interface techniques, usability engineers must consider broader issues such as the safety of computing and access by diverse populations with special needs.

- Attending to the needs of disabled users or other special populations is often an indirect strategy for discovering more robust and generally useful interaction techniques.

- Technology will evolve whether we want it to or not. Scenario-based design techniques force attention to intended and unintended consequences of technology features, which in turn help to guide this evolution in appropriate directions.

Exercises
_____

1. Critique your favorite Web site for use by people with visual impairments. Assess it with respect to:

   - font style and size—small and highly decorative fonts are difficult to perceive,

   - number and intensity of color distinctions—many subtle distinctions are hard to detect,

- use of white space—crowded displays are hard to decompose and organize, and

- visual contrast—low-intensity contrasts are more difficult to perceive.

Respond to your critique with suggestions for redesign. Discuss the extent to which your suggested changes would improve the quality of the information design for users in general (with respect to both performance and satisfaction).

2. Design of the controls on an automobile dashboard clearly has safety implications that must be addressed during development. What additional activities or structures would you include in scenario-based development of such a display? Use as a contrast the process used to develop the virtual science fair.

3. Choose a central screen from your class project (if you did not do a class project, choose some other simple application, such as a Web information system). Invite an international student or other foreign visitor to help you analyze the screen and interaction techniques from the perspective of his or her culture. Is it possible to translate the terms directly? Why or why not? Do the images on the screen have the intended meaning? Are there higher-level characteristics (e.g., ordering or layout of different components) that lead to different interpretations for this person than are intended by the design?

Project Ideas

Develop a cost-benefit analysis for your online shopping project. If you have been able to do at least one design iteration and test, use the costs of the iteration, and the resulting task performance and user satisfaction improvements, as a basis for the analysis. Otherwise, establish a set of assumptions about costs and benefits. Remember to make your benefit predictions conservative, but be as detailed and accurate as possible in your cost estimates. Once the analysis is complete, discuss how you would present it to a project manager. Would he or she be persuaded to give you more resources for this project (or future ones)? Why or why not?

Recommended Readings

Bias, R., & D. Mayhew, eds. 1994. *Cost-Justifying Usability*. New York: Academic Press.

Buie, E. 1999. HCI standards: A mixed blessing. *interactions* 6(2): 36–42.

Casey, S. 1993. *Set Phasers on Stun*. Santa Barbara, CA: Aegean Publishing Company.

Czaja, S. J., ed. 1990. *Human Factors Research Needs for an Aging Population*. Washington, DC: National Academy Press.

Edwards, A. 1995. *Extra-Ordinary Human-Computer Interaction: Interfaces for Users with Disabilities*. Cambridge: Cambridge University Press.

Johnson, J. 1993. Scenarios of people using the NII. *Newsletter of Computer Professionals for Social Responsibility*. Available at *http://www.cpsr.org/program/nii/niiscen.html*.

Kallman, E. A., & J. P. Grillo. 1996. *Ethical Decision Making and Information Technology: An Introduction with Cases*. New York: McGraw-Hill.

Nielsen, J., & E. M. del Galdo, eds. 1996. *International User Interfaces*. New York: John Wiley & Sons.

Olson, J. S., & T. P. Moran. 1995. Mapping the method muddle: Guidance in using methods for user interface design. In *Human-Computer Interface Design: Success Stories, Emerging Methods, Real-World Context*, eds. M. Rudisill, C. Lewis, P. B. Polson, & T. D. McKay, 269–300. San Francisco: Morgan Kaufmann.

Inferential Statistics

Chapter 7 described a range of evaluation goals and methods that are commonly used in usability engineering. However, while we discussed the major concepts of experimental design—for example, the concepts of variables, hypotheses, and validity—we did not present the methods or techniques of inferential statistics. These methods are required when evaluators wish to claim that the results they have obtained are due to the conditions of the experiment rather than chance variation.

There are many statistical tests that can be used to assess the significance of the patterns observed in usability outcomes. Some common tests are listed in Table A.1, along with sample questions they might be used to answer. For example, a t-test compares two independent data sets to see if their means are different, whereas analysis of variance (ANOVA) compares mean differences for the case of multiple independent variables (each of which may have two or more levels). In linear regression, a mathematical equation is constructed to show whether and to what extent each independent variable contributes to the prediction of a dependent variable.

The result of a statistical test is usually reported with respect to its "significance"—the probability that an observed difference or relationship is the result of chance variation. The lower the probability figure, the more confident an evaluator can be that the observed effect is genuine. By convention, researchers use a probability level of 0.05 as a cut-off for reporting that an effect is statistically significant (this cut-off point is called the alpha level). A simple way to think about a probability level is in terms of faulty conclusions: If a finding is reported as significant at the 0.05 level, then the experimenters are stating that the chance they are wrong is no more than 5 out of 100.

Statistical tests vary in how well they can detect differences. The most powerful are parametric statistics, which are used to analyze continuous variables with a normal distribution (the familiar bell-shaped curve). A normal distribution has a single measure of central tendency (i.e., the mean, mode, and median are the same); most observations are clustered symmetrically around the mean (Figure A.1).

Table A.1   Statistical tests commonly used in summative evaluation activities.

Statistical Test	Illustrative Usability Evaluation Question
Single sample t-test	Is users' average time to perform a task different than a published or accepted baseline value for similar systems?
Two-sample t-test	Are times to issue commands for a user interface with on-screen buttons faster than another with pull-down menus?
Analysis of variance (ANOVA)	Are there differences in performance time for multiple versions of a user interface (e.g., on-screen buttons, pull-down menus, and gesture recognition)?
	Do the performance benefits of a direct-manipulation user interface depend on the task complexity?
Correlation or linear regression	How much do individual differences in visual acuity influence performance time?
	After age is removed as a covariate, are there differences in performance time for two versions of a user interface?
Mann-Whitney	Is user satisfaction (measured on a 7-point rating scale) different for the user groups who worked with two different prototypes?
Wilcoxon *U*	Are users more satisfied (as measured by a 7-point rating scale) with one user interface prototype than a second one (i.e., after using both)?
Sign test	When users are asked to choose between two prototypes, do they choose one more frequently than chance alone would predict?
Chi square (χ^2)	Is body posture (rated rigid, normal, or relaxed by expert judges) affected by the use of natural language prompts in a user interface?

Unfortunately, data collected in usability tests are not always normally distributed (Figure A.1). Measures with a natural lower bound (e.g., user response times) are often skewed around the low end; measures with a natural upper bound (e.g., percentage correct on a memory test) may be skewed in the opposite direction. It is also possible to observe bimodal distributions in a data set—for example, when a user characteristic such as gender influences system interactions.

Data sets that do not follow a normal distribution should be analyzed with nonparametric statistical procedures, which make few assumptions about the

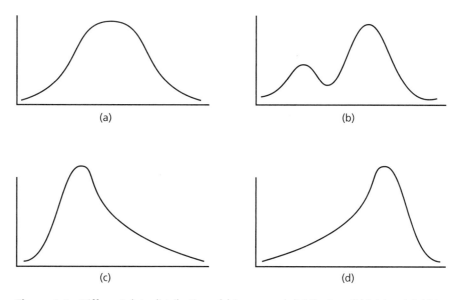

Figure A.1 Different data distributions: (a) is a normal distribution; (b) is bimodal; (c) is skewed positively, and (d) is skewed negatively.

underlying data distribution. These tests are usually based on the ranks of the data (i.e., each number is converted to its ordinal position). As a result, nonparametric statistics are also very useful for measures that are inherently ordinal (e.g., a rating scale) or for qualitative data that have been coded using an ordinal scheme (e.g., energy level). The Mann-Whitney test and the Wilcoxon U in Table A.1 are nonparametric statistics often used to test for differences in rating-scale judgments.

Categorical data (i.e., the values have no relative ordering) can be analyzed via binomial probabilities or contingency tables. For example, a sign test can determine whether the number of users who select one of two shortcut options is greater than that expected by chance. A chi-square test can be used to test similar questions for categories that have more than two possible values.

There are many textbooks and software packages covering the concepts, methods, and calculations of behavioral statistics. Richard Lowry, Professor of Psychology at Vassar College, has developed useful online resources, including an introductory online text, available at *http://faculty.vassar.edu/~lowry/webtext.html*; and a set of corresponding statistical software procedures, available at *http://faculty.vassar.edu/~lowry/VassarStats.html*. In the following, we use the science fair example to illustrate common statistical techniques applied to usability studies.

A.1   Science Fair Case Study: How to Represent Visitors?

An ongoing concern in the design of the online science fair has been the complexity of the initial view, where projects, avatars of visitors, and other objects such as message boards are arrayed on a panoramic view of the high school gymnasium. One issue concerns whether the user interface will scale up to situations in which there are more than one or two visitors and a full complement of student projects. In this brief example, we report an experiment carried out to examine this issue, where we studied the impacts of a redundant source of user information (a visitors list) as a function of the number of people present at the exhibit.

A.1.1   Experimental Design

The experiment was designed to test two independent variables: two user interface styles (avatars-only versus avatars+list) and the number of visitors in the welcome area. Group size was set at 4, 8, or 16 to cover a reasonable spectrum of sizes. The number of exhibits in the welcome area was fixed at 10.

A number of complementary dependent variables were defined (Table A.2). One concern was conversation fluency: How quickly would participants be able to respond to questions directed at them by other visitors? This variable was

Table A.2   Dependent variables and hypotheses for the avatar experiment.

Variable	How Measured	Hypotheses
Conversation fluency	Time from when a question appears to the initiation of a typed response	Response times will be faster for the avatars+list condition
Partner recognition	Percent correct on post-test identifying the users who had been in conversation with the participant (out of 20 names)	Percent correct will be higher for users in the avatars+list condition
Satisfaction	Judgments on three 7-point scales measuring feelings of awareness, directness, confusion	Satisfaction ratings will be lower for the avatars+list condition
Conversation initiative	Choice of yes or no response to question about conversation initiation	Participants in the avatars+list condition will be more likely to say yes

defined as the time between the appearance of a question directed to a participant and his or her initiation of a typed reply.

A second concern was group memory: Would participants be able to keep track of who had been part of the ongoing conversation? We measured this variable through a memory test administered at the end of the study, in which participants indicated for a list of 20 user names whether each individual had participated in the ongoing conversation (half of the people had, half had not, but all were present at one time or another).

Two other dependent variables were defined to measure subjective outcomes. Three Likert scales were developed (Figure A.2). The first questioned participants' feelings of awareness of others, the second asked whether they felt their interactions with others to be direct, and the third measured confusion about conversation partners. The final dependent variable was a simple yes-no judgment, indicating whether the user would feel comfortable initiating a conversation in the welcome area.

Hypotheses were developed for each combination of independent and dependent variables. Based on our formative evaluations, we expected that:

- Conversation fluency and memory will be improved for avatars+list. The list provides redundant information about who is there, and we expected this to aid users in keeping track of what was happening and in remembering what happened afterward.

- Subjective reactions will be more positive for the avatars alone. Although the list provides useful information, it does so by pulling attention away from the overall scene, thereby reducing levels of awareness and engagement and increasing confusion.

- Both of the above effects will vary with the size of the group. Specifically, the facilitating effects of the visitor list will be stronger for the larger group

1. During my conversations I was aware of the visitors present with me at the fair.

Strongly Agree   Agree   Neither Agree nor Disagree   Disagree   Strongly Disagree

2. I felt that I was in direct conversation with the other visitors at the fair.

Strongly Agree   Agree   Neither Agree nor Disagree   Disagree   Strongly Disagree

3. I found it confusing to keep track of who was talking to whom at the fair.

Strongly Agree   Agree   Neither Agree nor Disagree   Disagree   Strongly Disagree

Figure A.2   Likert scales assessing three aspects of satisfaction with two user interfaces.

sizes, and the preference for the avatars will be stronger for the smaller group sizes.

- For the yes-no question, there will be a preference for the avatars+list, because the combination offers more options for conversation management.

Participants were randomly assigned to sample groups in a mixed design: The (visitor) group-size variable was manipulated as a repeated measure (i.e., all users were exposed to groups of all three sizes), while user interface style was between-groups (i.e., two independent groups of test users worked with the two versions of the software). A total of 24 participants were recruited, with 6 men and 6 women assigned to each group.

A.1.2   Procedures

Participants first read and signed an informed consent form (similar to the one shown in Figure 7.6). They completed a user background survey that assessed their general computer background, their experience with virtual environments in particular, and their experience with science fairs (similar to that in Figure 7.7). Each participant then read printed instructions that described the tasks they were about to carry out: The instructions included a screen shot of the welcome area with 10 exhibits and 4 visitors. The different elements of the screen were described with reference to this screen.

The participants were told that they would be playing the role of Alicia, a community member visiting the fair for the first time. Other visitors would be arriving and leaving during her visit. Alicia's main goal is to explore the 10 exhibits. However, the participants were also told that on occasion another visitor will direct a question to Alicia, and they should respond to these questions as quickly and accurately as possible.

The experimental trials then proceeded. Over a period of about 10 minutes, a total of 30 other visitors arrived at the fair; some moved on while others stayed and chatted. During this time, Alicia was asked to respond to three questions. The order and precise timing of the questions was determined quasi-randomly for each participant. One question appeared when 3 other people were present, one when 7 others were present, and one when 15 other visitors were in the welcome area.

The "other visitors" who arrived, chatted, and directed questions to Alicia were simulated by the computer; the questions asked were balanced for length and complexity. This control of the simulated visitors and their questions was an important feature of the experiment design. It eliminated any possible **confound** due to personality or conversation skill of real visitors. Response times were collected automatically; the clock was started when a question was displayed and stopped as soon as the test participant typed a character in the input area of the chat tool. Participants' responses to the questions were recorded for later review.

Following the science fair activity, the participants first completed a user reaction questionnaire that included the three Likert scales, along with more general comments and suggestions for improvement. They then completed a memory test of conversation partners that indicated whether each of 20 names had participated in the conversation at the fair; no advance warning was given of this test.

A.1.3   Results and Analysis

The effects of group size and user interface style on conversation fluency were assessed with a two-factor, repeated-measures ANOVA. The raw data appear in Table A.3, and the means for each test condition are graphed in Figure A.3. The ANOVA revealed a main effect of user interface style ($F(1,66) = 10.68$, $p < 0.01$), with the avatar+list interface producing faster times overall. There was also a main effect of group size, with response times increasing as the number of visitors increased ($F(2,66) = 42.02$, $p < 0.001$). However, as the graph conveys, the analysis also revealed the predicted interaction of user interface style with group size ($F(2,66) = 11.12$, $p < 0.001$). The advantage for the avatar+list interface was significant only for the largest group size.

Table A.3   Raw data for response times to answer question directed to test participants. Note that group size is a repeated measure, and user interface style is between-subjects.

	Group Size: 4	Group Size: 8	Group Size: 16	
Avatars	2100, 1898, 2256, 2314, 1764, 2109, 2512, 2045, 2451, 1998, 1999, 2254	2409, 2455, 2455, 2755, 1966, 2338, 2466, 2489, 2669, 2377, 2201, 2487	3212, 2976, 2788, 2997, 2698, 2661, 3088, 2975, 3311, 3087, 2666, 2913	*Mean = 2504.0*
Avatars+List	2211, 2020, 2315, 2400, 1818, 2399, 2411, 2112, 2597, 2121, 1959, 2265	2300, 2199, 2401, 2403, 1988, 2514, 2506, 2288, 2619, 2287, 2177, 2368	2400, 2351, 2471, 2599, 2100, 2589, 2587, 2389, 2888, 2578, 2388, 2455	*Mean = 2346.7*
	Mean = 2180.5	*Mean = 2380.0*	*Mean = 2715.5*	

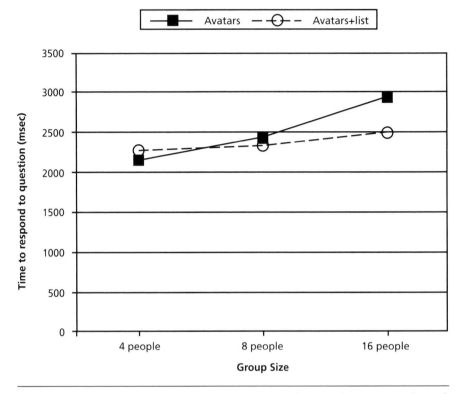

Figure A.3 Average time to respond to questions in conditions with varying numbers of other visitors and different user interface styles.

The raw data for percentage correct on the memory test appear in Table A.4. As the difference in means suggests, the participants using the avatars+list user interface were more accurate in identifying the names of visitors who had participated in the ongoing conversation. A one-tailed t-test for independent samples confirms this conclusion: $t(22) = 1.78$, $p < 0.05$.

Participants' responses to the rating scales appear in Table A.5, broken down by user interface style and the reaction assessed by the rating scale (see Figure A.2). Judgments have been converted to an ordinal scale (from 1 = Strongly Disagree to 5 = Strongly Agree). Note that for the third scale, the assertion was worded negatively—a lower rating reflects a more positive response. The mean differences in the answers to questions 1 and 2 are consistent with the predicted preference for avatars alone. However, the effect was reversed for the confusion scale, with participants using the avatars alone reporting a greater sense of confusion.

Table A.4 Percentage correct on conversation partner identification for participants using the two user interfaces. Scores are percentage correct for 20 names.

Avatars	85, 70, 80, 80, 75, 90, 70, 65, 75, 90, 90, 60	*Mean = 77.5, SD = 10.44*
Avatars+List	90, 75, 95, 80, 90, 95, 80, 70, 80, 95, 100, 70, 85	*Mean = 85.0, SD = 10.11*

Because the rating scale data are ordinal in nature, the data were analyzed with the nonparametric Wilcoxon *U* statistic. The rank of each rating across the two user interface conditions was calculated for each of the three scales. The statistic calculates an estimate of what the average rank for each group would be by chance alone, and tests to see if the average rank obtained is different from the estimate. The Wilcoxon *U* for the avatar-only condition was 20 for the awareness scale, 33 for the directness scale, and 18 for the confusion scale. All of these differences are significant at $p < 0.05$.

The final analysis examined participants' response to whether they would choose to initiate a conversation in the welcome area. Answers to this question are tabulated in Table A.6. These categorical data were analyzed with a chi-square test, which compares the observed frequency in each cell with the frequency expected by chance. The expected frequency is estimated from the margin values (e.g., the expected frequency of the upper left cell is equal to 12/24*14, or 7). This analysis revealed that there was no significant relationship between user interface style and likelihood of initiating a conversation ($\chi^2(1) = 0.38$, ns).

Table A.5 Judgments made on satisfaction rating scales; judgments have been converted to an ordinal scale (1 = Strongly Disagree to 5 = Strongly Agree).

	Awareness	Directness	Confusion
Avatar	4, 5, 5, 4, 4, 5, 5, 4, 5, 5, 4, 5 *Mean = 4.58*	5, 5, 5, 5, 4, 5, 5, 5, 5, 4, 4, 5 *Mean = 4.75*	2, 2, 2, 2, 2, 2, 3, 2, 2, 3, 2, 2, 3 *Mean = 2.25*
Avatars+List	3, 4, 4, 3, 4, 4, 4, 3, 4, 4, 3, 4 *Mean = 3.67*	4, 4, 4, 4, 5, 5, 5, 4, 4, 3, 3, 4 *Mean = 4.08*	1, 1, 2, 1, 1, 2, 1, 1, 2, 1, 1, 2 *Mean = 1.33*

Table A.6 Frequency of responses regarding likelihood of initiating a conversation in the welcome area of the virtual science fair.

	Would initiate a conversation	Would *not* initiate a conversation
Avatar	7	5
Avatars+List	6	6

A.1.4   Drawing Conclusions

The findings of the comparative study confirmed most of the experimental hypotheses. Participants using the avatars-only version of the user interface felt greater awareness and directness in their conversations. However, they also seemed to experience greater confusion, perhaps because the speech bubbles are distributed around the "room," and it is difficult to keep track of the entire population of visitors and of what is being said. In the avatars+list condition, the list is a stable indicator of who is present and more attention can be focused on the content of the speech bubbles.

The performance data are also generally consistent with the hypotheses: Response times and vistor group memory were better in general for the users working with the avatars+list interface. Importantly, however, the response time advantage was present only for the largest visitor group size. In combination with the satisfaction results, this suggests that the issue is more complex than deciding whether or not to provide the secondary list view. In most cases, users will prefer avatars alone and perform just as well without the extra list support. Only when the visitor group size is large is a redundant information display needed. Display of a visitor list might thus be made contingent on the current visitor group size, or perhaps as an option under user control.

The findings regarding conversation initiation contribute little information. It seems likely that other factors are more important in determining users' conversation behavior (e.g., who is visiting and users' general personality). Despite the lack of a difference between test conditions, this result should be seen as good news, in that the choice of user interface will not bias people one way or the other in taking conversational initiative.

Glossary

action plan a sequence of actions selected to achieve a goal

activities the collective ventures that provide context and meaning for people's interactions with computers and other tools

activity design the first phase of reasoning about a new software system, in which the problems and opportunities of current practice are transformed into new ways of behaving

affective computing the study and design of user interfaces that explicitly engage and respond to people's emotions or affective experiences

affordance perceptual characteristics of an object that make it obvious what the object can do and how it can be manipulated

analytic method usability evaluation based on a careful analysis or theoretical modeling of user interface features, usually carried out by usability experts

anthropomorphism considering machines (especially computers) as if they have human capabilities or responsibilities

area a gestalt perceptual principle stating that visual elements are likely to be grouped so as to create larger structures with the smallest possible areas

articulation work the collaborative effort required to document, exchange, schedule, refine, and otherwise coordinate shared activities

articulatory directness the extent to which the physical behaviors carried out with a user interface map to the goals and intentions of the user's current task

artifact a designed object or tool used in support of an activity

assistance policy a predetemined set of rules that usability evaluators develop and apply to decide when and how to intervene during a usability test

asynchronous collaboration computer-mediated shared activity that does not take place in real time (see **synchronous collaboration**)

augmented reality distributing computational power among objects in the real world; the new capability may be achieved by embedding input sensors or other processors, or by attaching information that is processed by external computational devices

avatar an icon or other visual depiction used to represent the user in an information display

balloon help a technique for embedding documentation in the user interface; when balloon help is turned on, a small "balloon" containing descriptive information appears when the mouse pointer moves over a display object

baseline task performance or other usability outcomes that are measured under normal conditions and then used as a basis for comparison to other conditions

benchmark task a standard task that is used to comparatively evaluate designs, measuring users' performance on the task with different versions or systems

between-subjects design a usability test structure in which a separate group of participants is exposed to each level of an independent variable

breadth   (of a hierarchy) the average number of choices at any level in a hierarchical information structure

breakdown   an episode of interaction in which a system does not work in the real world as planned or expected

categorical variable   user choices or other measures that can be classified and tabulated but not converted to a numeric value

change score   a difference between two numerical measures gathered from the same participant, one measured before a usage experience takes place, and one afterward

chauffered prototype   a user interface prototype that is not used directly by a test user, but instead is used by a designer under the user's direction

chord keyboard   an input device in which alphanumeric information is entered by conjointly pressing groups of keys

chunk   a structured collection of information that acts as a single unit with respect to storage and information processing capacity

claims analysis   an analytic evaluation method involving the identification of scenario features that have significant positive and negative usability consequences

claims feature   an element of a situation or an interactive system that has positive or negative consequences for people in this or similar situations

closure   a gestalt perceptual principle stating that perceivers are likely to fill in small gaps in a figure in order to see it as complete (and thus simpler)

cognitive walk-through   an expert critique of a user interface that involves simulating the use of a system and analyzing possible problems in goal selection, planning, or action execution

command language   a structured set of expressions that a computer interprets as requests for information and services

common ground   mutual expectations of communication partners that help them predict and interpret what is said

confound   a problem in experimental design in which two variables are correlated, making the interpretation of observed effects ambiguous

content analysis   a summarization and interpretation method in which qualitative data such as behavioral observations or user comments are grouped by similarity and labeled

context-aware computing   computer functionality and user interaction options that are selected and presented as a function of what is known about the use setting

contextual inquiry   a method used in requirements analysis and formative evaluation, in which people are observed as they carry out their normal tasks and are questioned about interesting or confusing episodes

continuity   a gestalt perceptual principle stating that objects positioned along a smooth curve are more likely to be seen as a group

conversational agents   software agents that interact with the user using natural language, and which are often given a human-like appearance

cooperative design   a variant of user-centered design that emphasizes the direct involvement of users in analysis and design activities (also called participatory design)

critical incident   an event reported by a user as having a significant effect, either positive or negative, on task performance or satisfaction

critical subtasks   the key features of a scenario that are expected to influence usability, and thus are carefully specified and evaluated continuously during iterative design

data collection form   a planning and observation form designed to guide an evaluator's note taking, time measurement, and so on, during a usability test

debriefing a planned interaction after a user test, in which the test participant is allowed to ask and receive answers to questions about the system, tasks, or goals of the study

default (in a user interface) a pre-set input string or other user input that is offered as a likely input value; users can simply accept this input rather than generating their own

demonstration a documentation technique in which a sequence of user inputs and system responses are animated, so that the user can see what actions to perform and what system response to expect in return

dependent variable a usability outcome that is measured to determine if there are effects of system variations or other test characteristics (see **independent variable**)

depth (of a hierarchy) the average number of intermediate nodes between the root of a hierarchical information structure and a terminating node

design rationale arguments for why (or why not) a feature or set of features should be incorporated into a design

designer's model the mental representation of a design held by a designer, sometimes shared via design documentation such as scenarios or feature lists

dialog design the specification of each step of user input and system response during a user interaction sequence

digital divide the gap in opportunities for education, jobs, and wealth, between those who have and use computers and those who do not

direct manipulation a user interface style in which system objects are represented visually and can be manipulated in ways analogous to how objects are manipulated in the real world (e.g., pointing, grabbing, dragging)

distributed cognition a framework analyzing how information and processing activitiy are distributed throughout a situation—across the mental states of collaborating individuals,

their communications with each other, and the states of task-relevant artifacts and tools

electronic brainstorming a computer-mediated discussion in which participants are able to contribute ideas freely and in parallel, often anonymously so as to minimize social inhibitions

empirical method usability evaluation based on collection of data from users working with an interactive system or prototype

ethnography in-depth study of individuals and groups, their practices, and their artifacts, in the context of their normal work environment

evolutionary development an approach to system development in which a version of the system is created as early as possible and then expanded or refined in an incremental fashion as more system requirements and constraints are discovered

external consistency the use of similar (or identical) interface actions and objects in a system for similar task actions and objects encountered in other systems or in the real world

FAQs (frequently asked questions) questions about a system that are asked and answered multiple times that are collected and made easily accessible to all users

feedback information generated and communicated by a computer system in response to input from the user; typically it is provided to guide or confirm task-relevant behavior

field study a usability evaluation of an installed system carried out in a workplace context, often involving surveys or observational methods

fish-eye view a visualization in which one part of an information structure is presented in detail relative to the surrounding context

Fitts's Law time to point to a target is proportional to the distance from the target divided by the width of the target

floor control   the mechanism by which users take and relinquish input control in a shared work system

focus+context   a visualization in which one part of an information structure is presented in detail relative to the surrounding context

formative evaluation   usability analyses carried out during system development with the goal of identifying usability problems and guiding redesign

Gestalt principles   principles of human perception that emphasize the holistic relationships among visual features that identify objects and configurations

glyph   a visual symbol or code that is attached to a physical object, to be recognized by a computer as task-relevant input

GOMS analyis   an analytic evaluation method that involves describing users' goals, operators, methods, and selection rules for computer tasks

grammar   composition rules that describe how commands or other language elements can be combined to form syntactically correct expressions

grid-based design   an information-design strategy in which a grid is defined to specify the physical scale of visual elements, their relative position, and axes of symmetry

Gulf of Evaluation   the psychological distance between what is displayed by a computer and the user's understanding of how it relates to current task goals

Gulf of Execution   the psychological distance between the task goals of a user and the physical actions required to achieve these goals with a computer system

haptic feedback   kinesthetic or force feedback provided by a user interface, often to convey physical characteristics of computational objects and media

heuristic evaluation   a user interface critiquing process carried out by experts applying common usability guidelines

hierarchical task analysis   decomposition of a complex task into a structure of constituent subtasks, annotated with the logic needed to perform the subtasks at each level

hierarchy   an information structure in which a root concept is successively decomposed, such that every child concept is the descendant of one and only one parent concept

horizontal prototype   a user interface prototype that illustrates all or most of a software system at a high level but provides little if any details about the functionality or user interaction

human-computer interaction   situations in which people understand and make requests of a software system, and the system interprets and responds to these requests

human factors   the study of variables that influence human performance in work contexts

hypothesis   a prediction of a causal relation between one or more independent variables and one or more dependent variables

hypothetical stakeholders   imaginary persons with characteristics that are typical of a stakeholder group, developed to serve as actors in analysis and design scenarios

immersive environment   a virtual reality simulation in which the user wears special headgear, eyeglasses, or other input devices so that the simulated world is experienced as a three-dimensional space

independent variable   an attribute of a usability test situation that is manipulated to determine if it influences outcome measures (see **dependent variable**)

information design   presentation and organization of task objects and actions in a way that facilitates the user's perception, interpretation, and understanding

information layering   a documentation technique wherein help information is organized into successively more detailed levels accessed on an as-needed basis

information model   a set of concepts, relationships, and representations that are developed to help users make sense of large data sets and complex functionality

information visualization   a representational technique in which properties of data are mapped to visual features and rendered as a spatial display

informed consent   participants in usability studies must be informed in advance of the procedures and risks, and must feel free to withdraw from the study at any time

inheritance   a technique used in object-oriented programming to share attributes and behavior among related classes; superclasses specify common behaviors, and subclasses extend the superclasses with specialized attributes or behaviors

inquiry method   an analysis method in which the goal is to raise questions and prompt discussion that will lead to a richer understanding of a problem

intelligent tutoring system   an online training system that models user knowledge and progress through pre-analyzed learning tasks, and uses this model to make suggestions, correct errors, answer questions, or provide other learning support

interaction design   mechanisms for accessing and manipulating the elements of an information design to facilitate the user's goal selection, action planning, and action execution

interactive tutorial   an online series of presentations and exercises designed to introduce and practice system concepts and skills

interference (in memory)   when information learned earlier causes difficulty in learning or errors in remembering new information

internal consistency   the use of similar (or identical) interface actions and objects within

a system to represent similar task actions and objects

interpretation   (of an information display) the process of recognizing how perceived information is related to the objects and actions provided by a user interface

interval variable   data measured on a scale for which any two contiguous values are equidistant

iterative design   a cyclical approach in which design ideas are prototyped and tested, with the results used to guide the next cycle of redesign

iterative development   an approach to software development in which the design specification is continually modified through prototyping and testing activities

keyboard shortcut   a brief sequence of key presses that is assigned to, and can be substituted for, a graphical user interaction sequence

knowledge management   the activity of identifying, documenting, archiving, maintaining, and reusing the concepts and skills developed by the members of an organization

knowledge work   work involving significant expertise and intellectual decision making

layout appropriateness   a design heuristic in which interface controls (e.g., a button in a dialog box) are laid out to optimize travel time for the most common usage cases

learn by doing   a strategy exhibited by many learners (especially those with task-domain or computer experience) in which they try to accomplish tasks as they learn

level   (of a variable) one of multiple possible values of an experimental variable used in a usability test; the levels of independent variables form the experimental conditions

Likert scale   a rating scale used to gather subjective judgments, in which an assertion about the task or system is made and users rate the level of their agreement

localization   a design strategy in which global interaction and exchange is supported by adapting information and user interface designs to particular regions and cultures

longitudinal study   analysis of one or more user behaviors or attitudes over an extended period of time, often in a real-world usage setting

macro   a user-defined sequence of events that is stored, labeled, and subsequently executed as a single command

mediated evaluation   an empirical usability evaluation in which the content and structure of the usability test materials are guided by a prior analytic evaluation

mental model   a cognitive structure of concepts and procedures that users refer to when selecting relevant goals, choosing and executing appropriate actions, and understanding what happens when they interact with a computer system (or other tool)

metaphor   a known concept that is used to understand a new concept by analogy

minimalism   an approach to instruction and documentation that emphasizes realistic tasks, minimal verbiage, thinking and improvization by the user, and the recognition of and recovery from errors

mistake   when an inappropriate system goal is selected and pursued

mixed design   a usability test structure in which the independent variables are manipulated in a combination of within-subjects and between-subjects conditions

mobile computing   use of computing systems outside normal office or work environments, particularly while moving around in the physical world

mode   (of a user interface) a user interface state that provides a special context for interpretation of user input, including ignoring some input

MOO (multiuser domain object-oriented)   a MUD in which the characters, their behavior, and all other services are built and extended using an object-oriented programming language

MUD (multiuser domain)   a persistent collaborative environment that is modeled on a geographic space

multimodal user interface   user interaction that integrates multiple input and output channels, either in parallel or in sequence

multiple coordinated views   a visualization technique in which complementary views of an underlying information structure are presented, manipulated, and updated simultaneously (see also **tiled display**)

multiple overlapping windows   a user interface technique in which parallel tasks are presented and pursued in different windows open simultaneously; the layering of windows mirrors the activity history of each task

newsgroup   an online threaded discussion where people post positions, questions, comments, or answers

nonfunctional requirements   qualities of a system under development that are not directly related to its function (e.g., maintainability or reliability)

nonverbal communication   the body language, facial expressions, gestures, and other nonlanguage cues that extend and aid interpretation of normal conversations

operationalize   to specify how a variable of interest will be manipulated or measured

opportunistic behavior   the tendency for users to generate and pursue goals suggested by manifest elements of the user interface

ordinal variable   data measured on a scale that has an inherent linear sequence or order

participatory analysis   a phase of cooperative or participatory design where users are presented with records of their own or other users' behavior and asked to reflect on features of interest

participatory design a variant of user-centered design that emphasizes the direct involvement of users in analysis and design activities (also called cooperative design)

PICTIVE plastic interface for technology initiatives through video exploration, a participatory design technique addressing user interface layout

pilot test a small study carried out prior to a large-scale study in order to practice and refine usability test materials, procedures, or data collection techniques

pluralistic walk-through a variant of a usability inspection where usability engineers, designers, and end users collaboratively step through and critique a user interface

point of view a technique used during the design of interactive systems in which the designer adopts a computational perspective on the task objects in a scenario

pragmatics (of a user interaction device) the physical behaviors that are required to manipulate the input or output devices in a user interface

presence (in a simulated world) the extent to which users of a virtual reality system feel as if they are moving within and experiencing the simulated environment

problem scenario a story of current practice developed to reveal aspects of the stakeholders and their activities that have implications for design

production paradox many users are highly motivated to continually accomplish real results, and as a result are often unwilling to take time to learn how to best achieve any given result

property sheet a secondary window activated to present and manipulate the attributes of task objects or user interface controls

prototype an operational model of a design or software development proposal, usually created for testing and feedback purposes

proximity a gestalt perceptual principle stating that objects positioned near one another are more likely to be seen as comprising a group

proxy server an intermediate server that intercepts and assists in processing the requests sent by a client to a server on a network; the technique is often used to improve the quality or latency of a server's response

radar view an overview of a shared workspace that includes an outline or other indication of the portion of the workspace that is being viewed by each collaborator

random assignment test participants are allocated to test conditions on a random basis

redundant coding multiple perceptual cues signal the same information

requirements analysis the detailed study of stakeholders and their current situation that is used to identify problems and opportunities to be addressed by a new system

requirements specification a document listing and describing the features that a system under development is expected to provide

retrospective interview a user interview conducted soon after a task has been completed to determine what usability issues stand out in a user's memory of the interaction; sometimes the user's memory may be prompted with a videotape or other records of activity

roomware furniture or other objects in a room that have been augmented with computational powers designed to be useful for the activities conducted in the room

root concept a multifaceted description of the starting premises of a design project that includes a high-level vision, basic rationale, stakeholders, and starting assumptions

scaffolding an instructional technique in which people are given support of some kind (often tool based) that allows them to carry out, and thereby learn about, tasks that they otherwise would be unable to do

scenario a narrative or story that describes the activities of one or more persons, including information about goals, expectations, actions, and reactions

scenario machine a special-purpose user interface prototype that can be used to enact a user interaction scenario, that is, a single thread of execution given a starting state

scenario mock-up one or more screen designs or other physical artifacts, created to illustrate key system states described by a scenario

self-instruction an approach in which people learn on their own using standalone documentation, tutorials, and tools

self-reflection a usability evaluation method in which users are asked to remember and reflect about their own goals, plans, behaviors, and reactions

semantic directness the extent to which a user interface allows users to pursue their goals in a direct fashion

semantic filtering a dynamic information visualization technique in which the semantic attributes of each data point are used to determine whether the element is visible, and where and how it is rendered if visible

severity (of a usability problem) a judgment about how much impact an observed or analyzed usability problem will have on actual use

similarity a gestalt perceptual principle stating that objects that look alike are more likely to be perceived as comprising a group

site map an overview of a large information space (typically a Web site) that may be of a textual form (e.g., a table of contents), a diagram, or an image

slip an error that occurs during action planning or execution even though an appropriate system goal was selected

social computing the study and design of user interfaces that explicitly engage and respond to people's social expectations

social context the personal and organizational relationships among people in a situation, including their roles and their knowledge of one another's history, goals, and preferences

sociotechnical systems theory an approach to software development in which the information technology system and the surrounding organization are analyzed, designed, and iterated as a single co-evolving system.

software agent a computational entity that observes users' behavior, makes inferences about their goals and needs, and offers suggestions or other helpful advice

software crisis the failure of the software industry to keep up with the demand for systems and applications of greater complexity, reflected in cost overruns, late delivery, and ineffective and unreliable systems

software logging instrumentation of a system such that it automatically records and time-stamps user actions and system reactions

squint test an assessment of a display's "gestalt" made by squinting the eyes to blur the visual details of a display and allow the layout of major structures to stand out

stakeholder any individual or organization with an interest in the process or product of an analysis or design project

stakeholder diagram a sketch of major stakeholders with interconnections indicating the relations and dependencies among the different groups

stakeholder profile a summary of the general characteristics of a stakeholder group, including background, expectations, and technology preferences

storefront testing a usability evaluation method in which a prototype of an interactive system is placed in a hallway or other public area so that people passing by can try out the system and provide feedback

storyboard   a graphical event-by-event enactment of all or part of a scenario, developed to communicate or analyze a user interface design; the enactment may be at a high level (e.g., major screen changes) or at a detailed level (e.g., mouse selections), depending on the usability issue being explored

subjective reactions   a user's personal responses, judgments, or opinions before, during, or after interaction with a computer system

summative evaluation   usability analyses carried out at milestones during system development with the goal of assessing whether and how well a system has met its usability objectives

symmetry   a gestalt perceptual principle stating that similar or identical objects seen on either side of a possible axis of rotation are more likely to be seen as a group

synchronous collaboration   computer-mediated communication or shared work that takes place in real time (see **asynchronous collaboration**)

system functionality   the information a system holds or accesses, the kinds of operations permitted on this information, and the results returned by these operations

system goal   a task-related goal expressed in terms of the objects and actions offered by a software system

systematic documentation   an approach to user documentation that analyzes knowledge about a system into hierarchies, and then systematically introduces and builds up component skills and concepts one by one

tacit knowledge   knowledge that people have in an inarticulate form, which they may not be able to produce or explain on demand, but which they can enact, such as know-how about exceptions that arise in a work setting

technological determinism   the view that technology is the single most important factor in determining the success of an organization

think-aloud protocol   a usability evaluation method in which the user speaks out loud his or her goals, plans, behaviors, and reactions while using an interactive system

tiled display   a user interface style in which parallel tasks or subtasks are presented in separate windows that are sized and arranged to prevent overlapping (see also **multiple coordinated views**)

tooltips   a method for embedding small snippets of documentation in a user interface; usually a brief statement of a display object's name or function appears when the mouse pointer rests over it

tradeoff   an issue (often in design) that is understood to have competing arguments, usually contrasting positive and negative impacts of an option

training wheels   an approach to user training that involves temporary deactivation (but not hiding) of functionality deemed unnecessary or inappropriate for use by novices

transfer of learning   a learning and memory phenomenon in which what is learned in one situation facilitates understanding and behavior in a similar situation

ubiquitous computing   a term used to refer to the increasingly pervasive availability of computational processing in the world around us

usability   the quality of an interactive computer system with respect to ease of learning, ease of use, and user satisfaction

usability engineering   an approach to software development in which target levels of system usability are specified in advance, and the system is engineered toward these measures

usability evaluation   any activity, either analytic or empirical, directed at assessing or understanding the usability of an interactive system or prototype

usability inspection   an analytic method in which usability experts examine the user interaction required to perform central or critical tasks with an interactive system or prototype, looking for problematic aspects of user input or system response

usability lab   one or more rooms designed to simulate office or other computer use settings, usually instrumented with software and hardware for capturing the user's behavior as he or she works through a set of tasks

usability specifications   critical or typical user tasks that are decomposed into subtasks associated with target usability outcomes and iteratively evaluated to guide redesign work

use case   an enumeration of the complete course of events that can take place in response to some user input; the case specifies all possible interactions between the user and the system

user background survey   a questionnaire (usually brief) completed by a usability test participant prior to interaction with a system or prototype (sometimes called a pre-test)

user documentation   stored training and help information provided to assist users in carrying out activities with a computer system

user model   a representation (typically computer based) of the knowledge and mental activities involved in use of a computer system, often used to make predictions about system usability

user interface   the physical representations and procedures that are provided for viewing and interacting with the system functionality

user interface prototype   an operational version or mock-up of a system that supports interaction between the user and the system that is used for user testing and iterative design

user reaction survey   a questionnaire completed by a usability test participant during or after interaction with a system or prototype (sometimes called a post-test)

user-system conversation   a scenario-based analysis technique in which user input is specified as one side of a conversation and the system's interpretation, processing, and response to this input is specified on the other

validity   (of a usability evaluation) the extent to which the conditions of an evaluation (users, setting, tasks) are representative of real-world use

variability   (of usability test data) the amount of diversity in a sample of data; high variability makes detecting and interpreting differences among test conditions more difficult

veridicality   (of virtual reality) the extent to which a simulated world matches the structures, information, and actions possible in the real world

vertical prototype   a user interface prototype that illustrates all of a system's functionality and user interface but for just one task or a small set of tasks

visual design program   a set of visual design features and relationships that are deliberately repeated to create consistency and coherence among screens, dialog boxes, and other user interface elements

visual language   the features of an information design (e.g., menu style, font type and size, button shape and size) that are repeated across visual displays to create a sense of consistency and coherence

walk-up-and-use system   a computer system that requires no explicit user training; the functionality and user interaction procedures are designed to be self-evident and intuitive

waterfall   an approach to software development that organizes activities into a series of modular phases, beginning with the analysis of functional requirements, and continuing through software design, implementation, testing, and maintenance

white space   the parts of a graphical display that contain no graphical elements

widget   a user interface control (e.g., a menu or scroll bar), often predefined by the windowing system used to build a user interface

WIMP   (windows, icons, menus, pointer) the graphical user interface style popularized by the Xerox Star and the Apple Macintosh in the 1980s

within-subjects design   a usability test structure in which the same subjects are exposed to different levels of an independent variable (also called repeated measures)

wizard   (help documentation) online assistance wherein a computer system recognizes that the user is attempting a specific task and offers step-by-step guidance through the procedure

Wizard of Oz   (prototype) a software system simulation, in which someone hides behind the scenes to interpret and generate meaningful responses to a user's input

workflow system   a business support system that operates on an explicit model of task procedures; this model is used to plan, coordinate, and track interrelated tasks

workplace themes   labeled categories used to group related observations, stakeholder comments, or other data collected in a field study

References

Abowd, G. D., & E. D. Mynatt. 2000. Charting past, present, and future research in ubiquitous computing. *Transactions on Computer-Human Interaction* 7(1): 29–58.

Anderson, J. R. 1983. *The Architecture of Cognition*. Cambridge, MA: Harvard University Press.

Anderson, J. R., A. T. Corbett, J. Fincham, D. Hoffman, & R. Pelletier. 1992. General principles for an intelligent tutoring architecture. In *Cognitive Approaches to Automated Instruction*, eds. V. Shute & W. Regian, 81–106. Hillsdale, NJ: Lawrence Erlbaum.

Andrews, K. 1995. Visualizing cyberspace: Information visualization in the Harmony internet browser. In *Proceedings of the IEEE Symposium on Information Visualization '95*, 97–104. New York: IEEE Computer Press.

Apple Computer. 1992. *Macintosh Human Interface Guidelines*. Reading, MA: Addison-Wesley.

Bannon, L., & Schmidt, K. 1991. CSCW: Four characters in search of a context. In *Proceedings of European Conference on Computer-Supported Cooperative Work: ECSCW '91*, eds. J. M. Bowers & D. D. Benford, 3–16. Amsterdam: North-Holland.

Bartlett, F. C. 1964. *Remembering*. Cambridge: Cambridge University Press.

Beaudouin-Lafon, M., ed. 1999. *Computer Supported Co-operative Work*. Chichester and New York: John Wiley & Sons.

Beck, K. 1999. *Extreme Programming Explained: Embrace Change*. Reading, MA: Addison-Wesley.

Bederson, B., & J. Hollan. 1994. Pad++: A zooming graphical interface for exploring alternate interface physics. In *Proceedings of User Interface Software: UIST '94*, 17–26. New York: ACM.

Bennett, J. 1984. Managing to meet usability requirements. In *Visual Display Terminals: Usability Issues and Health Concerns*, eds. J. Bennett, D. Case, J. Sandelin, & M. Smith, 161–84. Englewood Cliffs, NJ: Prentice-Hall.

Beyer, H., & K. Holtzblatt. 1998. *Contextual Design: Defining Customer-Centered Systems*. San Francisco: Morgan Kaufmann.

Bias, R. G. 1991. Walkthroughs: Efficient collaborative testing. *IEEE Software* (September): 4–5.

Bias, R. G., & D. Mayhew, eds. 1994. *Cost-Justifying Usability*. New York: Academic Press.

Bjerknes, G., P. Ehn, & M. Kyng, eds. 1983. *Computers and Democracy*. Aldershot Hants, England, and Brookfield, VT: Avebury.

Björk, S., L. E. Holmquist, J. Redström, I. Bretan, R. Danielsson, J. Karlgren, & K. Franzén. 1999. WEST: A Web browser for small terminals. In *Proceedings of User Interface Software and Technology: UIST '99*, 187–96. New York: ACM.

Blomberg, J. L. 1995. Ethnography: Aligning field studies of work and system design. In *Perspectives on HCI: Diverse Approaches,* eds. A. F. Monk & N. Gilbert, 175–98. London: Academic Press.

Blomberg, J. L., L. Suchman, & R. Trigg. 1996. Reflections on a work-oriented design project. *Human-Computer Interactions,* 11(3): 237–65.

Bloom, B. S. 1984. The 2 sigma problem: The search for methods of group instruction as effective as one-to-one tutoring. *Educational Researcher* 13: 3–16.

Bødker, S. 1991. *Through the Interface: A Human Activity Approach to User Interface Design.* Hillsdale, NJ: Lawrence Erlbaum Associates.

Boehm, B. 1988. The spiral model of software development and enhancement. *IEEE Computer* 21(5): 61–72.

Bolt, R. A. 1980. Put-that-there: Voice and gesture at the graphics interface. *Computer Graphics,* 14(3): 262–70.

Boutkin, P., D. Poremsky, K. Slovak, & J. Bock. 2000. *Beginning Visual Basic 6 Application Development.* Birmingham, UK: Wrox Press.

Bowman, D. In press. Principles for the design of performance-oriented interaction techniques. In *Handbook of Virtual Environment Technology,* ed. K. Stanney. Hillsdale, NJ: Lawrence Erlbaum Associates.

Brooks, F. 1987. No silver bullet: Essence and accidents of software engineering. *IEEE Computer* 20(4): 10–19.

Brooks, F. 1995. *The Mythical Man-Month: Essays on Software Engineering.* Anniversary ed. Reading, MA: Addison-Wesley.

Buie, E. 1999. HCI standards: A mixed blessing. *interactions* 6(2): 36–42.

Buxton, W. 1983. Lexical and pragmatic considerations of input structure. *Computer Graphics* 17(1): 31–37.

Buxton, W. 1986. There's more to interaction than meets the eye: Some issues in manual input. In *User-Centered System Design: New Perspectives in Human-Computer Interaction,* eds. D. A. Norman & S. D. Draper, 319–38. Hillsdale, NJ: Lawrence Erlbaum Associates.

Card, S. K., J. D. Mackinlay, & B. Shneiderman, eds. 1999. *Readings in Information Visualization.* San Francisco: Morgan Kaufmann.

Card, S. K., T. P. Moran, & A. Newell. 1980. The keystroke-level model for user performance with interactive systems. *Communications of the ACM* 23: 396–410.

Card, S. K., T. P. Moran, & A. Newell. 1983. *The Psychology of Human-Computer Interaction.* Hillsdale, NJ: Lawrence Erlbaum Associates.

Card, S. K., G. G. Robertson, & J. D. Mackinlay. 1991. The Information Visualizer, an information workspace. In *Proceedings of Human Factors in Computing Systems: CHI '91,* eds. S. P. Robertson, G. M. Olson, & J. S. Olson, 181–86. New York: ACM.

Carroll, J. M. 1985. *What's in a Name: An Essay in the Psychology of Reference.* New York: W. H. Freeman.

Carroll, J. M. 1990. *The Nurnberg Funnel: Designing Minimalist Instruction for Practical Computer Skill.* Cambridge, MA: MIT Press.

Carroll, J. M., ed. 1991. *Designing Interaction: Psychology at the Human-Computer Interface.* New York: Cambridge University Press.

Carroll, J. M., ed. 1995. *Scenario-Based Design: Envisioning Work and Technology in System Development.* New York: John Wiley & Sons.

Carroll, J. M., ed. 1998. *Minimalism Beyond "The Nurnberg Funnel."* Cambridge, MA: MIT Press.

Carroll, J. M. 2000. *Making Use: Scenario-Based Design of Human-Computer Interactions.* Cambridge, MA: MIT Press.

Carroll, J. M., & A. P. Aaronson. 1988. Learning by doing with simulated intelligent help. *Communications of the Association for Computing Machinery* 31: 1064–79.

Carroll, J. M., & R. L. Campbell. 1989. Artifacts as psychological theories: The case of human-computer interaction. *Behaviour and Information Technology* 8: 247–56.

Carroll, J. M., & C. Carrithers. 1984. Blocking learner errors in a training wheels system. *Human Factors* 26(4): 377–89.

Carroll, J. M., G. Chin, M. B. Rosson, & D. C. Neale. 2000. The development of cooperation: Five years of participatory design in the Virtual School. *DIS 2000: Designing Interactive Systems,* 239–51. New York: ACM.

Carroll, J. M., & D. S. Kay. 1985. Prompting, feedback, and error correction in the design of a scenario machine. In *Proceedings of Human Factors in Computing Systems: CHI '85,* eds. B. Curtis & L. Borman, 149–54. New York: ACM.

Carroll, J. M., & R. L. Mack. 1985. Metaphors, computing systems, and active learning. *International Journal of Man-Machine Studies* 22: 39–57.

Carroll, J. M., R. L. Mack, & W. A. Kellogg. 1988. Interface metaphors and user interface design. In *Handbook of Human-Computer Interaction,* ed. M. Helander, 67–85. Amsterdam: North-Holland.

Carroll, J. M., & S. A. Mazur. 1986. LisaLearning. *IEEE Computer* 19(11): 35–49.

Carroll, J. M., & J. R. Olson. 1988. Mental models in human-computer interaction: Research issues about what the user of software knows. In *Handbook of Human-Computer Interaction,* ed. M. Helander, 45–65. Amsterdam: North-Holland.

Carroll, J. M., & M. B. Rosson. 1985. Usability specifications as a tool in iterative development. In *Advances in Human-Computer Interaction,* Vol. 1, ed. R. Hartson, 1–28. New York: Ablex.

Carroll, J. M., & M. B. Rosson. 1987. The paradox of the active user. In *Interfacing Thought: Cognitive Aspects of Human-Computer Interaction,* ed. J. M. Carroll, 80–111). Cambridge, MA: MIT Press.

Carroll, J. M., & M. B. Rosson. 1990. Human-computer interaction scenarios as a design representation. In *Proceedings, Volume II of HICSS-23: 23rd Hawaii International Conference on System Sciences, Software Track,* ed. B. D. Shriver, 555–61. Los Alamitos, CA: IEEE Computer Society Press.

Carroll, J. M., & M. B. Rosson. 1991. Deliberated evolution: Stalking the View Matcher in design space. *Human-Computer Interaction* 6: 281–318.

Carroll, J. M., & M. B. Rosson. 1992. Getting around the task-artifact cycle: How to make claims and design by scenario. *ACM Transactions on Information Systems* 10(2): 181–212.

Carroll, J. M., M. B. Rosson, G. Chin, & J. Koenemann. 1998. Requirements development in scenario-based design. *IEEE Transactions on Software Engineering* 24(12): 1156–70.

Carroll, J. M., M. B. Rosson, P. L. Isenhour, C. H. Ganoe, D. Dunlap, J. Fogarty, W. Schafer, C. Van Metre. 2001a. Designing our town: MOOsburg. *International Journal of Human-Computer Studies* 54: 725–51.

Carroll, J. M., M. B. Rosson, P. L. Isenhour, C. VanMetre, W. A. Schafer, & C. H. Ganoe. 2001b. MOOsburg: Multi-user domain support for a community network. *Internet Research* 11(1): 65–73.

Carroll, J. M., M. B. Rosson, D. C. Neale, P. L. Isenhour, D. Dunlap, C. H. Ganoe, C. VanMetre, et al. 2000. The LiNC Project: Learning in Networked Communities. *Learning Technology* 2(1). Available at *http://lttf.ieee.org/learn_tech/issues/january2000/*.

Carroll, J. M., J. A. Singer, R. K. E. Bellamy, & S. R. Alpert. 1990. A View Matcher for Learning Smalltalk. In *Proceedings of Human Factors in Computing Systems: CHI '90*, eds. J. C. Chew & J. Whiteside, 431–37. New York: ACM.

Carroll, J. M., & J. C. Thomas. 1982. Metaphors and the cognitive representation of computing systems. *IEEE Transactions on Systems, Man, and Cybernetics* 12(2): 107–16.

Casey, S. 1993. *Set Phasers on Stun*. Santa Barbara, CA: Aegean Publishing Company.

Cassell, J. 2000. Embodied conversational interface agents. *Comunications of the ACM* 43(4): 70–78.

Checkland, P. B. 1981. *Systems Thinking, Systems Practice*. Chichester and New York: John Wiley.

Checkland, P. B. & J. Scholes. 1990. *Soft Systems Methodology in Action*. Chichester, England: John Wiley.

Cherny, L. 1995. Mud community. In *The Mud Register: Conversational Modes of Action in a Text-Based Virtual Reality*, 42–126. Ph.D. diss., Stanford University.

Chin, G., M. B. Rosson, & J. M. Carroll. 1997. Participatory analysis: Shared development of requirements from scenarios. In *Proceedings of Human Factors in Computing Systems, CHI '97 Conference*, 162–69. New York: ACM.

Chin, G., & M. B. Rosson. 1998. Progressive design: Staged evolution of scenarios in the design of a collaborative science learning environment. In *Proceedings of Human Factors in Computing Systems, CHI '98 Conference*, 611–18. New York: ACM.

Choong, Y-Y., & G. Salvendy. 1999. Implications for design of computer interfaces for Chinese users in mainland China. *International Journal of Human-Computer Interaction* 11(1): 29–46.

Clark, H. H., & S. E. Brennan. 1991. Grounding in communication. In *Socially Shared Cognition*, eds. L. B. Resnick, J. Levine, & S. D. Behreno, 127–49. Washington, DC: American Psychological Association.

Collins, D. 1995. *Designing Object-Oriented User Interfaces*. Redwood City, CA: Benjamin Cummings.

Conklin, P. F. 1991. Bringing usability effectively into product development. In *Human-Computer Interface Design: Success Stories, Emerging Methods, Real-World Context*, eds. M. Rudisill, C. Lewis, P. Polson, & T. McKay, 367–85. San Francisco: Morgan Kaufmann.

Constantine, L. L., & L. A. D. Lockwood. 1999. *Software for Use: A Practical Guide to the Models and Methods of Usage-Centered Design*. Reading, MA: Addison-Wesley.

Cooper, A. 1999. *The Inmates Are Running the Asylum: Why High-Tech Products Drive Us Crazy and How to Restore the Sanity*. Indianapolis: Sams Press.

Corbett, A. T., K. R. Koedinger, & J. R. Anderson. 1997. Intelligent tutoring systems. In *Handbook of Human-Computer Interaction,* 2d ed., eds. M. G. Helander, T. K. Landauer, & P. V. Pradhu, 849–74. Amsterdam: North-Holland.

Curtis, P., T. Heiserman, D. Jobusch, M. Notess, & J. Webb. 1999. Customer-focused design data in a large, multi-site organization. In *Proceedings of Human Factors in Computing Systems: CHI '99,* eds. M. G. Williams, M. W. Altom, K. Ehrlich, & W. Newman, 608–15. New York: ACM.

Cypher, A., ed. 1993. *Watch What I Do: Programming by Demonstration.* Cambridge, MA: MIT Press.

Czaja, S. J., ed. 1990. *Human Factors Research Needs for an Aging Population.* Washington, DC: National Academy Press.

DeGrace, P., & L. H. Stahl. 1990. *Wicked Problems, Righteous Solutions.* Englewood Cliffs, NJ: Prentice-Hall.

Diaper, D. 1989. Task analysis for knowledge-based descriptions (TAKD): The method and an example. In *Task Analysis for Human-Computer Interaction,* ed. D. Diaper, 108–59. Chichester, England: Ellis-Horwood.

Dix, A., J. Finlay, G. Abowd, & R. Beale. 1998. *Human-Computer Interaction.* 2d ed. London: Prentice-Hall.

Djajadiningrat, J. P., W. W. Gaver, & J. W. Frens. 2000. Interaction relabelling and extreme characters: Methods for exploring aesthetic interactions. In *Proceedings of Designing Interactive Systems: DIS 2000,* eds. D. Boyarski & W. A. Kellogg, 66–71. New York: ACM Press.

Douglas, S. A., & T. P. Moran. 1983. Learning text editor semantics by analogy. In *Proceedings of Human Factors in Computing Systems: CHI '83,* ed. A. Janda, 207–11. New York: ACM.

Dubberly, H., & D. Mitch. 1987. *The Knowledge Navigator.* Cupertino, CA: Apple Computer, Inc. Videocassette.

Dzida, W., & R. Freitag. 1998. Making use of scenarios for validating analysis and design. *IEEE Transactions on Software Engineering* 24(12): 1182–96.

Eason, K. D. 1988. *Information Technology and Organizational Change.* London: Taylor & Francis.

Eason, K. D. & S. Harker. 1989. *An Open Systems Approach to Task Analysis.* Internal Report, HUSAT Research Centre. Loughborough University of Technology. Loughborough, England.

Edwards, A. 1995. *Extra-Ordinary Human-Computer Interaction: Interfaces for Users with Disabilities.* Cambridge: Cambridge University Press.

Egan, D. E., J. R. Remde, T. K. Landauer, L. M. Gomez, J. Eberhart, & C. C. Lochbaum. 1989a. Formative design evaluation of "SuperBook." *ACM Transactions on Office Information Systems* 7(1): 30–57.

Egan, D. E., J. R. Remde, T. K. Landauer, C. C. Lochbaum, & L. M. Gomez. 1989b. Behavioral evaluation and analysis of a hypertext browser. In *Proceedings of Human Factors in Computing Systems: CHI '89,* eds. K. Bice & C. Lewis, 205–10. New York: ACM.

Ehrlich, S. F. 1987a. Social and psychological factors influencing the design of office communication systems. In *Proceedings of Human Factors in Computing Systems: CHI+GI '87,* eds. J. M. Carroll & P. P. Tanner, 323–29. New York: ACM.

Ehrlich, S. F. 1987b. Strategies for encouraging successful adoption of office communication systems. *ACM Transactions on Office Systems* 5: 340–57.

Ellis, C. A., S. J. Gibbs, & G. L. Rein. 1991. Groupware: Some issues and experiences. *Communications of the ACM* 34(1): 38–58.

Erickson, T. 1990. Working with interface metaphors. In *The Art of Human-Computer Interface Design,* ed. B. Laurel, 65–73. Reading, MA: Addison-Wesley.

Erickson, T. 1995. Notes on design practice: Stories and prototypes as catalysts for communication. In *Scenario-Based Design: Envisioning Work and Technology in System Development,* ed. J. M. Carroll, 37–58. New York: John Wiley & Sons.

Erickson, T. 2000. Position paper for panel: Stories and storytelling in the design of interactive systems. In *Proceedings of Designing Interactive Systems: DIS 2000,* eds. D. Boyarski & W. A. Kellogg, 446–48. New York: ACM.

Ericsson, K. A., & H. A. Simon. 1981. Sources of evidence on cognition: A historical overview. In *Cognitive Assessment,* eds. T. V. Merluzzi, C. R. Glass, & M. Genest, 16–51. New York: Guilford Press.

Ericsson, K. A., & H. A. Simon. 1993. *Protocol Analysis: Verbal Reports as Data.* 2d ed. Cambridge, MA: MIT Press.

Farkas, D. 1998. Layering as a "safety net" for minimalist documentation. In *Minimalism Beyond "The Nurnberg Funnel,"* ed. J. M. Carroll, 247–74. Cambridge, MA: MIT Press.

Fernandes, T. 1995. *Global Interface Design.* San Francisco: Morgan Kaufmann.

Fish, R. S., R. E. Kraut, R. W. Root, & R. E. Rice. 1993. Video as a technology for informal communication. *Communications of the ACM* 36(1): 48–61.

Fitts, P. M. 1954. The information capacity of the human motor system in controlling the amplitude of movements. *Journal of Experimental Psychology* 47: 381–91.

Fitts, P. M., & J. R. Peterson. 1964. Information capacity of discrete motor responses. *Journal of Experimental Psychology* 67: 103–12.

Fitts, P., & M. I. Posner. 1967. *Human Performance.* Wokingham, England: Wadsworth.

Flanagan, J. C. 1954. The critical incident technique. *Psychological Bulletin* 51: 28–35.

Furnas, G. W. 1986. Generalized fisheye views. In *Proceedings of Human Factors in Computing Systems: CHI '86,* eds. M. Mantei & P. Oberton, 16–23. New York: ACM.

Gagne, R. M., & L. J. Briggs. 1979. *Principles of Instructional Design.* 2d ed. New York: Holt, Rinehart, & Winston.

Gaver, W. 1986. Auditory icons: Using sound in computer interfaces. *Human-Computer Interaction* 2(2): 167–77.

Gaver, W. 1989. The SonicFinder: An interface that uses auditory icons. *Human-Computer Interaction* 4(1): 67–94.

Gaver, W., R. B. Smith, & T. O'Shea. 1991. Effective sounds in complex situations: The ARKola simulation. In *Proceedings of Human Factors in Computing Systems: CHI '91,* eds. S. P. Robertson, G. M. Olson, & J. S. Olson, 85–90. New York: ACM.

Gellerson, H.-W., & P. J. Thomas, eds. 2000. *Proceedings of Handheld and Ubiquitous Computing: HUC 2000.* Amsterdam: Springer-Verlag.

Gentner, D., & J. Nielsen. 1996. The Anti-Mac interface. *Communications of the ACM* 39(8): 70–82.

Gick, M. L., & K. J. Holyoak. 1980. Analogical problem solving. *Cognitive Psychology* 12: 306–55.

Gilb, T. 1984. The "Impact Analysis Table" applied to human factors design. In *Proceedings of the 1st IFIP Conference on Human-Computer Interaction—INTERACT '84,* ed. B. Shackel, 655–59. Amsterdam: North-Holland.

Good, M., T. M. Spine, J. Whiteside, & P. George. 1986. User-derived impact analysis as a tool for usability engineering. In *Proceedings of Human Factors in Computing Systems: CHI '86,* eds. M. Mantei & P. Oberton, 241–46. New York: ACM.

Gould, J. D., & C. Lewis. 1985. Designing for usability: Key principles and what designers think. *Communications of the ACM* 28: 300–311.

Gould, J. D., S. J. Boies, S. Levy, J. T. Richards, & J. Schoonard. 1987. The 1984 Olympic Message System: A test of behavioral principles of system design. *Communications of the ACM* 30(9): 758–69.

Gray, W. D., B. E. John, & M. E. Atwood. 1992. The precis of Project Ernestine, or an overview of a validation of GOMS. In *Proceedings of Human Factors in Computing Systems: CHI '92,* eds. P. Bauersfeld, J. Bennett, & G. Lynch, 307–12. New York: ACM.

Greenbaum, J., & M. Kyng. 1991. *Design at Work: Cooperative Design of Computer Systems.* Hillsdale, NJ: Lawrence Erlbaum Associates.

Greenstein, J. S. 1997. Pointing devices. In *Handbook of Human-Computer Interaction* 2d ed., eds. M. G. Helander, T. K. Landauer, & P. V. Pradhu, 1317–48. Amsterdam: North-Holland.

Grudin, J. 1988. Why CSCW applications fail: Problems in the design and evaluation of organizational interfaces. In *Proceedings of Computer Supported Cooperative Work: CSCW '88,* 85–94. New York: ACM.

Grudin, J. 1989. The case against user interface consistency. *Communications of the ACM* 4(3): 245–64.

Grudin, J. 1990. Groupware and cooperative work: Problems and prospects. In *The Art of Human Computer Interface Design,* ed. B. Laurel, 171–185. Reading MA: Addison-Wesley.

Grudin, J. 1994. Groupware and social dynamics: Eight challenges for developers. *Communications of the ACM* 37(1): 92–105.

Guindon, R. 1990. Designing the design process: Exploiting opportunistic thoughts. *Human-Computer Interaction* 5: 305–44.

Gutwin, C., & S. Greenberg. 1998. Design for individuals, design for groups: Tradeoffs between power and workspace awareness. In *Proceedings of Computer Supported Cooperative Work: CSCW '98,* 207–16. New York: ACM.

Guzdial, M. 2001. *Squeak: Object-Oriented Design with Multimedia Applications.* Upper Saddle River, NJ: Prentice-Hall.

Hackos, J. T., & J. C. Redish. 1998. *User and Task Analysis for Interface Design.* New York: John Wiley & Sons.

Halasz, F., & T. P. Moran. 1982. Analogy considered harmful. In *Proceedings of Human Factors in Computing Systems: CHI '92,* ed. A. Janda, 383–86. New York: ACM.

Hassenzahl, M., A. Platz, M. Burmester, & K. Lehner. 2000. Hedonic and ergonomic quality aspects determine a software's appeal. In *Proceedings of Human Factors in Computing*

Systems: CHI 2000, eds. T. Turner, G. Swillus, M. Czerwinski, & R. Paternò, 201–208. New York: ACM.

Hawthorn, D. 2000. Possible implications of aging for interface designers. *Interacting with Computers* 12: 507–28.

Heim, M. 1997. *Virtual Realism.* Oxford: Oxford University Press.

Hendley, R. J., A. J. Drew, A. M. Wood, & R. Beale. 1995. Narcissus: Visualizing information. In *Proceedings of Information Visualization '95,* 90–96. New York: IEEE Computer Society Press.

Holtzblatt, K., & H. Beyer. 1993. Making customer-centered design work for teams. *Communications of the ACM* 10: 93–103.

Holyoak, K. J., & P. Thagard. 1995. *Mental Leaps: Analogy in Creative Thought.* Cambridge, MA: MIT Press.

Horton, W. K. 1994. *Designing and Writing Online Documentation.* New York: John Wiley & Sons.

Howlett, V. 1996. *Visual Interface Design for Windows.* New York: John Wiley & Sons.

Hudson, S. E., B. E. John, K. Knudsen, & M. D. Byrne. 1999. A tool for creating predictive performance models from user interface demonstrations. In *Proceedings of User Interface Software and Technology: UIST '99,* 93–102. New York: ACM.

Hughes, J. A., D. Randall, & D. Shapiro. 1992. Faltering from ethnography to design. In *Proceedings of Computer Supported Cooperative Work: CSCW '92,* eds. J. Turner & R. Kraut, 115–22. New York: ACM Press.

Hughes, J., V. King, T. Rodden, & H. Andersen. 1996. Moving out from the control room: Ethnography in system design. In *CSCW '94: Proceedings of the Conference on Computer Supported Cooperative Work,* eds. R. Furata & C. Neuwirth, 429–39. New York: ACM.

Huhns, M. N., & M. P. Singh, eds. 1998. *Readings in Agents.* San Francisco: Morgan Kaufmann.

Hutchins, E. 1995. *Distributed Cognition.* Cambridge, MA: MIT Press.

Hutchins, E. L., J. D. Hollan, & D. A. Norman. 1986. Direct manipulation interfaces. In *User Centered System Design,* eds. D. A. Norman & S. W. Draper, 87–124. Hillsdale, NJ: Lawrence Erlbaum Associates.

Hutchins, E., & T. Klausen. 1996. Distributed cognition in an airline cockpit. In *Cognition and Communication at Work,* eds. Y. Engeström & D. Middleton, 15–34. New York: Cambridge University Press.

IBM. 1991. *Common User Access Guide to User Interface Design.* Carey, NC: IBM Corporation.

Isenhour, P., J. M. Carroll, D. Neale, M. B. Rosson, & D. Dunlap. 2000. The Virtual School: An integrated collaborative environment for the classroom. *Educational Technology & Society* 3(3): 74–86.

Isenhour, P., M. B. Rosson, & J. M. Carroll. In press. Supporting interactive collaboration on the Web with CORK. *Interacting with Computers.*

Ishii, H., M. Kobayashi, & K. Arita. 1994. Iterative design of seamless collaboration media. *Communications of the ACM* 37(8): 83–97.

Ishii, H., & B. Ullmer. 1997. Tangible bits: Towards seamless interfaces between people, bits and atoms. In *Proceedings of Human Factors in Computing Systems: CHI '97,* ed. S. Pemberton, 234–41. New York: ACM.

Jacobson, I. 1990. *Object-Oriented Development in an Industrial Environment.* Research Report. Kista, Sweden: Objective Systems SF AB (Box 1128, S-164 22 KISTA, Sweden).

Jacobson, I. 1995. Use cases and scenarios. In *Scenario-Based Design: Envisioning Work and Technology,* ed. J. M.Carroll. New York: John Wiley & Sons.

Jacobson, I., M. Christersson, P. Jonsson, & G. Övergaard., 1992. *Object-Oriented Software Engineering: A Use Case Driven Approach.* Reading, MA: Addison-Wesley.

Jeffs, T., & M. K. Smith. 1996. *Informal Education: Conversation, Democracy and Learning.* Ticknall, UK: Education Now Books.

Johnson, J. 1993. Scenarios of people using the NII. *Newsletter of Computer Professionals for Social Responsibility.* Available at *http://www.cpsr.org/program/nii/niiscen.html.*

Johnson, J. 2000. *GUI Bloopers: Don'ts and Do's for Software Developers and Web Designers.* San Francisco: Morgan Kaufmann.

Kallman, E. A., & J. P. Grillo. 1996. *Ethical Decision Making and Information Technology: An Introduction with Cases.* New York: McGraw-Hill.

Karat, C. 1997. Cost-justifying usability. In *Handbook of Human-Computer Interaction*, 2d ed., eds. M. G. Helander, T. K. Landauer, & P. V. Pradhu, 767–81. Amsterdam: North-Holland.

Karat, C. 1993. Usability engineering in dollars and cents. *IEEE Software* 10(3): 88–89.

Kieras, D. 1988. Towards a practical GOMS model methodology for user interface design. In *Handbook of Human-Computer Interaction,* ed. M. Helander, 135–58. Amsterdam: North-Holland Elsevier.

Kieras, D. 1997. A guide to GOMS model usability evaluation using NGOMSL. In *Handbook of Human-Computer Interaction,* 2d ed, eds. M. G. Helander, T. K. Landauer, & P. V. Pradhu, 733–66. Amsterdam: North-Holland.

Kreitzberg, C. 1996. Managing for usability. In *Multimedia: A Management Perspective,* ed. A. F. Alber, 65–88. Belmont, CA: Wadsworth.

Kuutti, K., & T. Arvonen. 1992. Identifying potential CSCW applications by means of activity theory concepts: A case example. In *Proceedings of Computer-Supported Cooperative Work: CSCW '92,* eds. J. Turner & R. Kraut, 233–40. New York: ACM.

Kyng, M. 1995. Creating contexts for design. In *Scenario-Based Design: Envisioning Work and Technology in System Development,* ed. J. Carroll, 85–108. New York: John Wiley & Sons.

Lamping, J., R. Rao, & P. Pirolli. 1995. A focus+context technique based on hyperbolic geometry for visualizing large hierarchies. In *Proceedings of Human Factors in Computing Systems: CHI '95,* eds. I. R. Katz, R. Mack, L. Mark, M. B. Rosson, & J. Nielsen, 401–408. New York: ACM.

Leveson, N. 1995. *Safeware: System Safety and Computers.* Reading, MA: Addison-Wesley.

Lewis, C., & D. A. Norman. 1986. Designing for error. In *User-Centered System Design,* eds. D. A. Norman & S. Draper, 411–32. Hillsdale, NJ: Lawrence Erlbaum Associates.

Lewis, C., & J. Rieman. 1993. *Task-Centered User Interface Design*. Shareware book available via FTP at *ftp.cs.colorado.edu*.

Lieberman, H. 1997. Autonomous interface agents. In *Proceedings of Human Factors in Computing Systems: CHI '97,* ed. S. Pemberton, 67–74. New York: ACM.

Lieberman, H., ed. 2001. *Programming by Example.* San Francisco: Morgan Kaufmann.

Lowery, J. 2000. *Dreamweaver 3: Gold Edition.* Indianapolis: Hungry Minds.

Mack, R. L., C. H. Lewis, & J. M. Carroll. 1983. Learning to use office systems: Problems and prospects. *ACM Transactions on Office Information Systems* 1: 254–71.

Madsen, K. H. 1994. A guide to metaphorical design. *Communications of the ACM* 37(12): 57–62.

Maes, P. 1997. Tutorial: Introduction to software agents. In *CHI 97 Companion.* Available at *http://pattie.www.media.mit.edu/people/pattie/CHI97*.

Mantei, M. M., & T. J. Teorey. 1988. Cost/benefit analysis for incorporating human factors in the software lifecycle. *Communications of the ACM* 31(4): 428–39.

Markus, M. L. 1994. Finding a happy medium: Explaining the negative effects of electronic communication on social life at work. *ACM Transactions on Information Systems* 12(2): 119–49.

Maulsby, D., S. Greenberg, & R. Mander. 1993. Prototyping an intelligent agent through Wizard of Oz. *Proceedings of the ACM CHI '93 Conference on Human Factors in Computing Systems.* Amsterdam: ACM Press.

Maybury, M. T. & W. Wahlster, eds. 1998. *Readings in Intelligent User Interfaces.* San Francisco: Morgan Kaufmann.

Mayhew, D. J. 1999. *The Usability Engineering Lifecycle: A Practitioner's Handbook for User Interface Design.* San Francisco: Morgan Kaufmann.

Meij, H. van der, & J. M. Carroll. 1995. Principles and heuristics for designing minimalist instruction. *Technical Communication* 42: 243–61.

Meyer, B. 1988. *Object-Oriented Software Construction.* Englewood Cliffs, NJ: Prentice-Hall.

Microsoft. 1992. *The Windows Interface: An Application Design Guide.* Microsoft Press.

Miller, G. A. 1956. The magical number seven, plus or minus two: Some limits on our capacity to process information. *Psychological Review* 63(2): 81–97.

Miller, L., & J. Johnson. 1996. The Xerox Star: An influential user interface design. In *Human-Computer Interface Design: Success Stories, Emerging Methods, Real-World Context,* eds. M. Rudisill, C. Lewis, P. Polson, & T. McKay, 70–100. San Francisco: Morgan Kaufmann.

Mills, H. 1971. Top-down programming in large systems. In *Debugging Techniques in Large Systems,* ed. R. Rustin. Englewood Cliffs, NJ: Prentice-Hall.

Monk, A. In press. Common ground in electronically mediated communication: Clark's theory of language use. *Toward a Multidisciplinary Science of Human-Computer Interaction.* San Francisco: Morgan Kaufmann.

Monk, A., P. Wright, J. Haber, & L. Davenport. 1992. *Improving Your Human-Computer Interface: A Practical Approach.* London: Prentice-Hall.

Moran, T. P. 1983. Getting into the system: External task–internal task mapping analysis. In *Proceedings of Human Factors in Computing Systems: CHI '83,* ed. A. Janda, 45–49. New York: ACM.

Moran, T., & J. M. Carroll, eds. 1995. *Design Rationale: Concepts, Techniques, and Use.* Hillsdale, NJ: Lawrence Erlbaum Associates.

Moran, T. P., E. Saund, W. Van Melle, A. U. Gujar, K. P. Fishkin, & B. Harrison. 1999. Design and technology for collaborage: Collaborative collages of information on physical walls. In *Proceedings of User Interface Software and Technology: UIST '99,* 197–206. New York: ACM.

Morkes, J., H. K. Kernal, & C. Nass. 1999. Effects of humor in task-oriented human-computer interaction and computer-mediated communication: A direct test of SRCT theory. *Human-Computer Interaction* 14(4): 395–436.

Muller, M. K. 1991. PICTIVE—An exploration in participatory design. In *Proceedings of Human Factors in Computing Systems: CHI '91,* eds. S. P. Robertson, G. M. Olson, & J. S. Olson, 225–31. New York: ACM.

Muller, M. K. 1992. Retrospective on a year of participatory design using the PICTIVE technique. In *Proceedings of Human Factors of Computing Systems: CHI '92,* ed. A. Janda, 455–62. New York: ACM.

Muller, M. J., R. Carr, C. Ashworth, B. Diekmann, C. Wharton, C. Eickstaedt, & J. Clonts. 1995. Telephone operators as knowledge workers: Consultants who meet customer needs. In *Proceedings of Human Factors in Computing Systems: CHI '95,* eds. I. R. Katz, R. Mack, L. Marks, M. B. Rosson, & J. Nielsen, 130–37. New York: ACM.

Muller, M. J., D. M. Wildman, & E. A. White. 1993. "Equal Opportunity" PD Using PICTIVE. *Communications of the ACM* 36(4): 54–66.

Mullet, K., & D. Sano. 1995. *Designing Visual Interfaces: Communication Oriented Techniques.* Englewood Cliffs, NJ: Sunsoft Press.

Mumford, E. 1987. Socio-technical systems design: Evolving theory and practice. In *Computers and Democracy,* eds. G. Bjerknes, P. Ehn, & M. Kyng, 59–77. Aldershot Hants, England: Avebury.

Myers, B. A., & M. B. Rosson. 1992. Survey on user interface programming. In *Proceedings of Human Factors in Computing Systems, CHI '92 Conference,* eds. P. Bauersfeld, J. Bennett, & G. Lynch, 195–202. New York: ACM.

Nardi, B. A. 1993. *A Small Matter of Programming.* Cambridge, MA: MIT Press.

Nardi, B. A., ed. 1996. *Context and Consciousness: Activity Theory and Human-Computer Interaction.* Cambridge, MA: MIT Press.

Nardi, B. A. 1997. The use of ethnographic methods in design and evaluation. In *Handbook of Human-Computer Interaction,* 2d ed., eds. M. G. Helander, T. K. Landauer, & P. V. Pradhu, 361–67. Amsterdam: North-Holland.

Nardi, B. A., & J. R. Miller. 1991. Twinkling lights and nested loops: Distributed problem solving and spreadsheet development. *International Journal of Man-Machine Studies* 34: 161–84.

Nardi, B. A., & V. L. O'Day. 1999. *Information Ecologies: Using Technology with Heart.* Cambridge, MA: MIT Press.

Nass, C. A., & L. Gong. 2000. Speech interfaces from an evolutionary perspective. *Communications of the ACM* 43(9): 36–43.

National Center for Education Statistics. 1999. *Literacy in the Labor Force: Results from the National Adult Literacy Survey.* Office of Educational Research and Improvement, U.S. Department of Education (available at *http://nces.ed.gov/pubs99/1999470.pdf*).

National Telecommunications and Information Administration. 2000. *Falling Through the Net: Toward Digital Inclusion*. Washington, DC: U.S. Department of Commerce (available at *http://www.ntia.doc.gov/pdf/fttnoo.pdf*).

Neale, D. C., D. R. Dunlap, P. Isenhour, & J. M. Carroll. 2000. Collaborative critical incident development. In *Proceedings of the 40th Annual Meeting of the Human Factors and Ergonomics Society*, 598–601. Santa Monica, CA: Human Factors and Ergonomics Society.

Neuschotz, N. 2000. *Introduction to Director and Lingo: Multimedia and Internet Applications*. Upper Saddle River, NJ: Prentice-Hall.

Newell, A., & S. K. Card. 1985. The prospects for psychological science in human-computer interaction. *Human-Computer Interaction* 1: 209–42.

Nielsen, J. 1992. *Usability Engineering*. New York: Academic Press.

Nielsen, J. 1994. Heuristic evaluation. In *Usability Inspection Methods*, eds. J. Nielsen & R. L. Mack. New York: John Wiley.

Nielsen, J. 1995. Scenarios in discount usability engineering. In *Scenario-Based Design: Envisioning Work and Technology in System Development*, ed. J. M. Carroll, 59–84. New York: John Wiley & Sons.

Nielsen, J. 1999. *Designing Web Usability: The Practice of Simplicity*. Indianapolis: New Riders.

Nielsen, J., & E. M. del Galdo, eds. 1996. *International User Interfaces*. New York: John Wiley & Sons.

Nielsen, J., & R. L. Mack. 1994. *Usability Inspection Methods*. New York: John Wiley & Sons.

Nielsen, J., R. L. Mack, K. H. Bergendorff, & N. L. Grischkowsky. 1986. Integrated software usage in the professional work environment. In *Proceedings of Human Factors in Computing Systems: CHI '86*, eds. M. Mantei & P. Oberton, 162–67. New York: ACM.

Norman, D. A. 1981a. Categorization of action slips. *Psychological Review* 88: 1–15.

Norman, D. A. 1981b. The trouble with UNIX: The user interface is horrid. *Datamation* (November): 139–50.

Norman, D. A. 1986. Cognitive engineering. In *User Centered System Design*, eds. D. A. Norman & S. D. Draper, 31–61. Hillsdale, NJ: Lawrence Erlbaum Associates.

Norman, D. A. 1987. Cognitive artifacts. In *Designing Interaction: Psychology at the Human-Computer Interface*, ed. J. M. Carroll, 17–38. Cambridge, MA: MIT Press.

Norman, D. A. 1988. *The Psychology of Everyday Things*. New York: Basic Books.

Norman, D. A., & S. D. Draper, eds. 1986. *User Centered System Design: New Perspectives on Human-Computer Interaction*. Hillsdale, NJ: Lawrence Erlbaum Associates.

Noteboom, N. 1998. Die Clippy, Die. *ZDNet AnchorDesk*, 29 September 1998. Available at *http://www.zdnet.com/anchordesk/story/story_2589.html*.

Nunamaker, J. F., A. R. Dennis, J. S. Valacich, D. R. Vogel, & J. F. George. 1991. Electronic meeting systems to support group work. *Communications of the ACM* 34(7): 40–61.

Olson, J. S., & T. P. Moran. 1995. Mapping the method muddle: Guidance in using methods for user interface design. In *Human-Computer Interface Design: Success Stories, Emerging Methods, Real-World Context*, eds. M. Rudisill, C. Lewis, P. B. Polson, & T. D. McKay, 269–300. San Francisco: Morgan Kaufmann.

Oviatt, S. L. 1997. Multimodal interactive maps: Designing for human performance. *Human-Computer Interaction* 12: 93–129.

Oviatt, S., P. Cohen, L. Wu, J. Vergo, L. Duncan, B. Suhm, J. Bers, et al. 2002. Designing the user interface for multimodal speech and pen-based gesture applications: State-of-the-art systems and future research directions. In *Human-Computer Interaction in the New Millennium,* ed. J. M. Carroll, 419-56. Reading, MA: Addison-Wesley.

Palmiter, S., & J. Elkerton. 1991. An evaluation of animated demonstrations for learning computer-based tasks. In *Human Factors in Computing Systems: CHI '91 Conference Proceedings,* eds. S. P. Robertson, G. M. Olson, & J. S. Olson, 257–63. New York: ACM.

Payne, S. J. 1991. Display-based action at the user interface. *International Journal of Man-Machine Studies* 35: 279–89.

Payne, S. J., L. Chesworth, & E. Hill. 1992. Animated demonstrations for exploratory learners. *Interacting with Computers* 4: 3–22.

Payne, S. J., & T. R. G. Green. 1986. Task-action grammars: A model of mental representation of task languages. *Human-Computer Interaction* 2(2): 93–133.

Plaisant, C., B. Milash, A. Rose, S. Widoff, & B. Shneiderman. 1996. Lifelines: Visualizing personal histories. In *Proceedings of Human Factors in Computing Systems: CHI '96,* ed. M. J. Tauber, 221–27. New York: ACM.

Polson, P. G., C. Lewis, J. Rieman, & C. Wharton. 1992. Cognitive walkthroughs: A method for theory-based evaluation of user interfaces. *International Journal of Man-Machine Studies* 36: 741–73.

Prabhu, G. V., & E. M. del Galdo. 1999. *Designing for Global Markets.* Rochester, NY: Backhouse Press.

Preece, J. 2000. *Online Communities: Designing Usability and Supporting Sociability.* New York: John Wiley & Sons.

Preece, J., Y. Rogers, H. Sharp, D. Benyon, S. Holland, & T. Carey. 1994. *Human-Computer Interaction.* Reading, MA: Addison-Wesley.

Rekimoto, J., & K. Nagao. 1995. The world through the computer: Computer augmented interaction with real world environments. In *Proceedings of Human Factors in Computing Systems: CHI '95,* eds. M. B. Rosson & J. Nielsen, 29–36. New York: ACM.

Rheingold, H. 1992. *Virtual Reality.* New York: Touchstone Books.

Rheingold, H. 1993. *The Virtual Community: Homesteading on the Electronic Frontier.* Reading, MA: Addison-Wesley.

Rissland, E. L. 1984. Examples and learning systems. In *Adaptive Control of Ill-Defined Systems,* eds. O. G. Selfridge, E. L. Rissland, & M. A. Arbib, 149–63. New York: Plenum Press.

Robertson, G., S. K. Card, & J. D. Mackinlay. 1991. Cone trees: Animated 3D visualization of hierarchical information. In *Proceedings of Human Factors in Computing Systems: CHI '91,* eds. S. P. Robertson, G. M. Olson, & J. S. Olson, 184–94. New York: ACM.

Robertson, S. R., J. M. Carroll, R. L. Mack, M. B. Rosson, S. R. Alpert, & J. Koenemann-Belliveau. 1994. ODE: A self-guided, scenario-based learning environment for object-oriented design principles. In *Proceedings of Object-Oriented Programming Systems, Languages, and Applications: OOPSLA '94,* 51–64. New York: ACM.

Robson, C. 1985. *Experiment, Design and Statistics in Psychology.* 3d ed.: Penguin, 1999.

Rosson, M. B. 1983. *Patterns of Experience in Editing.* In *Proceedings of Human Factors in Computing Systems: CH1 '83,* ed. A. Janda, 171–75. New York: ACM.

Rosson, M. B. 1999a. I get by with a little help from my cyber-friends: Sharing stories of good and bad times on the Web. *Journal of Computer-Mediated Communication* 4(4). Available at *http://www.ascusc.org/jcmc/vol4/issue4/rosson.html.*

Rosson, M. B. 1999b. Integrating development of task and object models. *Communications of the ACM* 42(1): 49–56.

Rosson, M. B., & J. M. Carroll. 1995. Integrating task and software development in object-oriented applications. In *Proceedings of Human Factors in Computing Systems: CHI '95,* eds. M. B. Rosson & J. Nielsen, 377–84. New York: ACM Press.

Rosson, M. B., & J. M. Carroll. 1996. The reuse of uses in Smalltalk programming. In *ACM Transactions on Computer-Human Interaction* 3(3): 219–53.

Rosson, M. B., & J. M. Carroll. 2001. Scenarios, objects, and points-of-view in user interface design. In *Object Modeling and User Interface Design,* ed. M. van Harmelen, 39–69. London: Addison-Wesley Longman.

Rosson, M. B., J. M. Carroll, & R. K. E. Bellamy. 1990. Smalltalk scaffolding: A case study in minimalist instruction. In *Proceedings of Human Factors in Computing Systems: CHI '90,* eds. J. C. Chew & J. Whiteside, 423–30. New York: ACM.

Rosson, M. B., & E. Gold. 1989. Problem-solution mapping in object-oriented design. In *Proceedings of OOPSLA '89: Conference on Object-Oriented Programming Systems, Languages, and Applications,* ed. N. Meyrowitz, 7–10. New York: ACM.

Rosson, M. B., S. Maass, & W. A. Kellogg. 1989. The designer as user: Building requirements for design tools from design practice. *Communications of the ACM* 31(11): 1288–97.

Rosson, M. B., & C. D. Seals. 2001. Teachers as programmers: Minimalist learning and reuse. In *Proceedings of Human Factors in Computing Systems: CHI 2001,* eds. J. Jacko & A. Sears, 237–44. New York: ACM.

Rousseau, D. M. 1997. Organizational behavior in the new organizational era. *Annual Review of Psychology* 48: 515–46.

Sachs, P. 1993. Shadows in the soup: Conceptions of work and the nature of evidence. In *Newsletter of the Laboratory for Computer-Human Cognition,* NYNEX Science and Technology, White Plains, NY.

Sachs, P. 1995. Transforming work: Collaboration, learning, and design. *Communications of the ACM* 38(10): 36–44.

Scriven, M. 1967. The methodology of evaluation. In *Perspectives of Curriculum Evaluation,* eds. R. Tyler, R. Gagne, & M. Scriven, 39–83. Chicago: Rand McNally.

Sears, A. 1993. Layout appropriateness: Guiding user interface design with simple task descriptions. *IEEE Transactions on Software Engineering* 19(7): 707–19.

Selber, S. A., J. Johnson-Eilola, & B. Mehlenbacher. 1997. On-line support systems: Tutorials, documentation, and help. In *Handbook of Computer Science and Engineering,* ed. A. B. Tucker, 1619–43. Boca Raton, FL: CRC Press.

Shaw, R., & J. Bransford, eds. 1977. *Perceiving, Acting, and Knowing.* Hillsdale, NJ: Lawrence Erlbaum Associates.

Shepard, R. N. 1967. Recognition memory for words, sentences, and pictures. *Journal of Verbal Learning and Verbal Behavior* 6: 156–63.

Shneiderman, B. 1983. Direct manipulation: A step beyond programming languages. *IEEE Computer* 16(8): 57–69.

Shneiderman, B. 1998. *Designing the User Interface: Strategies for Effective Human-Computer Interaction,* 3d ed. Reading, MA: Addison-Wesley.

Siegel, D. 1997. *Creating Killer Web Sites.* Indianapolis: Hayden Books.

Smith, D., C. Irby, R. Kimball, B. Verplank, & E. Harslem. 1982. Designing the Star interface. *Byte* 7(4): 242–82.

Smith, R. B. 1987. Experiences with the Alternate Reality Kit: An example of the tension between literalism and magic. In *Proceedings of Human Factors in Computing Systems and Graphics Interface: CHI + GI '87,* eds. J. M. Carroll & P. P. Tanner, 61–67. New York: ACM.

Smith, S. L., & J. N. Mosier. 1986. *Guidelines for Designing User Interface Software.* Bedford, MA: MITRE Corporation.

Sommerville, I. 1992. *Software Engineering.* 4th ed. Reading, MA: Addison-Wesley.

Sproull, L., & S. Kiesler. 1991. *Connections: New Ways of Working in the Networked Organization.* Cambridge, MA: MIT Press.

Streitz, N., J. Geissler, T. Holmer, S. Konomi, C. Miller-Tomfelde, W. Reischi, P. Rexroth, et al. 1999. i-LAND: An interactive landscape for creativity and innovation. In *Proceedings of Human Factors in Computing Systems: CHI '99,* eds. M. G. Williams, M. W. Altom, K. Ehrlich, & W. Newman, 120–27. New York: ACM.

Suchman, L. 1987. *Plans and Situated Actions: The Problem of Human-Machine Communication.* Cambridge: Cambridge University Press.

Sun Microsystems. 1990. *Open Look Graphical User Interface Application Style Guidelines.* New York: Addison-Wesley.

Tognazzini, B. 1994. The "Starfire" video prototype project: A case history. In *Proceedings of Human Factors in Computing Systems: CHI '94,* eds. B. Adelson, S. Dumais, & J. Olson, 99–105. New York: ACM.

Torzewski, S., & T. Sullivan. 1997. *Kai's Power GOO.* Carpinteria, CA: MetaTools.

Tucker, A., B. Barnes, R. Aiken, K. Barker, K. Bruce, S. Cain, S. Conry, et al. 1991. *Report of the ACM/IEEE CS Joint Curriculum Task Force: Computing Curricula 1991.* New York: ACM Press/IEEE Press.

Tufte, E. 1983. *The Visual Display of Quantitative Information.* Cheshire, CT: Graphics Press.

Tufte, E. 1990. *Envisioning Information.* Cheshire, CT: Graphics Press.

Tufte, E. 1997. *Visual Explanations: Images and Quantities, Evidence and Narrative.* Cheshire, CT: Graphics Press.

Turkle, S. 1995. *Life on the Screen: Identity in the Age of the Internet.* New York: Simon & Schuster.

Underkoffler, J., & H. Ishii. 1999. Urp: A luminous-tangible workbench for urban planning and design. In *Proceedings of Human Factors in Computing Systems: CHI '99*, eds. M. G. Williams, M. W. Altom, K. Ehrlich, & W. Newman, 386–93. New York: ACM.

Van Harmelen, M., ed. 2001. *Object Modeling and User Interface Design*. London: Addison-Wesley Longman.

VanLehn, K. 1984. Arithmetic procedures are induced from examples. In *Conceptual Procedural Knowledge: The Case of Mathematics*, ed. J. Hiebert. Hillsdale, NJ: Lawrence Erlbaum Associates.

Verplank, W. L. 1988. Graphic challenges in designing object-oriented user interfaces. In *Handbook of Human-Computer Interaction*, ed. M. Helander, 365–76. Amsterdam: North-Holland.

Virzi, R. A., J. L. Sokolov, & D. Karis. 1996. Usability problem identification using both low- and high-fidelity prototypes. In *Proceedings of Human Factors in Computing Systems: CHI '96*, eds. M. J. Taubet, V. Bellotti, R. Jeffries, J. D. Mackinlay, & J. Nielsen, 236–43. New York: ACM.

Ware, C. 1999. *Information Visualization: Perception for Design*. San Francisco: Morgan Kaufmann.

Wasserman, A. I., & D. T. Shewmake. 1982. Rapid prototyping of interactive information systems. *ACM Software Engineering Notes* 7(5): 171–80.

Waterson, P., & C. O'Malley. 1992. Using animated demonstrations to teach graphics skills. In *People and Computers VII: Proceedings of HCI '92*, eds. A. Monk, D. Diaper, & M. D. Harrison, 463–74. Cambridge: Cambridge University Press.

Weidenhaupt, K., K. Pohl, M. Jarke, & P. Haumer. 1998. Scenarios in system development: Current practice. *IEEE Software* 15/2: 34–45.

Weiser, M. 1991. The computer for the 21st century. *Scientific American* (September): 66–75.

Weizenbaum, J. 1976. *Computer Power and Human Reason*. San Francisco: W. H. Freeman.

Whiteside, J., J. Bennett, & K. Holtzblatt. 1988. Usability engineering: Our experience and evolution. In *Handbook of Human-Computer Interaction*, ed. M. Helander, 791–817. Amsterdam: North-Holland.

Whittaker, S. 1996. Talking to strangers: An evaluation of the factors affecting electronic collaboration. In *Proceedings of the Conference on Computer Supported Cooperative Work: CSCW '96*, ed. M. Ackerman, 409–18. New York: ACM.

Williamson, C., & B. Shneiderman. 1992. The Dynamic Homefinder: Evaluating dynamic queries in a real estate information exploration system. In *Proceedings of SIGIR '92*, 339–46. New York: ACM.

Wirfs-Brock, R. 1995. Designing objects and their interactions: A brief look at responsibility-driven design. In *Scenario-Based Design: Envisioning Work and Technology in System Development*, ed. J. M. Carroll, 337–60. New York: John Wiley & Sons.

Wirfs-Brock, R., & B. Wilkerson. 1989. Object-oriented design: A responsibility-driven approach. In *Proceedings of Object-Oriented Programming: Systems, Languages and Applications: OOPSLA '89*, ed. N. Meyrowitz, 71–76. New York: ACM.

Wirfs-Brock, R., B. Wilkerson, & L. Weiner. 1990. *Designing Object-Oriented Software*. Englewood Cliffs, NJ: Prentice-Hall.

Wixon, D., K. Holtzblatt, & S. Knox. 1990. Contextual design: An emergent view of system design. In *Proceedings of Human Factors in Computing Systems: CHI '91*, eds. J. C. Chew & J. Whiteside, 329–36. New York: ACM.

Wixon, D. R., C. M. Pietras, P. K. Huntwork, & D. W. Muzzey. 1996. Changing the rules: A pragmatic approach to product development. In *Field Methods Casebook for Software Design,* eds. D. Wixon & J. Ramey, 57–89. New York: John Wiley & Sons.

Wixon, D., & J. Ramey, eds. 1996. *Field Methods Casebook for Software Design.* New York: John Wiley & Sons.

Woodward, J. 1965. *Industrial Organization: Theory and Practice.* London: Oxford University Press.

Yarin, P., & H. Ishii. 1999. TouchCounters: Designing interactive electronic labels for physical containers. In *Proceedings of Human Factors in Computing Systems: CHI '99,* eds. M. G. Williams, M. W. Altom, K. Ehrlich, & W. Newman, 362–68. New York: ACM.

Figure Credits

Figure 2.3   © ACM, 1992.

Figure 2.5   Photo used by permission of Charles Rencsok.

Figure 4.2   Reprinted with permission from Ho, Powell, and Liley. *Journal of Physical and Chemical Reference Data* 3, Supplement, 1, 1974, American Institute of Physics and National Institute of Science and Technology.

Figure 4.7   © Graphics Press.

Figure 4.8   Courtesy of Human-Computer Interaction Laboratory, University of Maryland, College Park, MD.

Figure 9.3   © ACM, 1994.

Figure 9.4   Greenberg, S. and Gutwin, C. (1998) From Technically Possible to Socially Natural Groupware. In *Proceedings of the 9th NEC Research Symposium: The Human-centric Multimedia Community.* August 31–September 1, Nara, Japan.

Figure 9.6   Courtesy of the ACM from the project of Justine Cassell, MIT Media Lab.

Index

abstract images, 123
action plans, 164–171
    actions, making obvious, 165–166
    as active process, 164
    analogies for, 165
    analysis, 164
    chunks, 166–167
    complexity concerns, 166
    composition, 164
    concept, 164
    corresponding to real-world tasks, 165
    decomposing, 167
    defined, 164
    direct-manipulation interface and, 165
    effects of, 165
    emerging interaction paradigms and, 339
    executing, 171–178
    flexibility, 168–171
    gestural phrases, 172
    internal/external consistency and, 167
    interruption/resumption, 170
    simplifying, 166–168
action sequences
    executing, 171–178
    planning, 164–171
    user interface controls and, 167
actions
    making obvious, 165–166
    reversibility of, 175–176
    stages of, 160
activities
    analyzing, 39, 41
    automation, 89
    collaboration, 46, 307
    communication, 46
    context, emphasis, 84
    costs, 346

    of health care center, 42
    interviewing, 43, 54
    multithreaded, 168
    observation, 43, 54
    simulating, 54
    stakeholder, 48
    workplace, 39
activity design, 79–108
    case study, 91–106
    claims, 91, 92–101
    claims analyzing features of, 100–101
    components, 91
    comprehensible, 84–88
    defined, 79, 81
    effectiveness, 81, 84
    exercises, 107
    general-purpose solutions, 84
    goal, 79
    ideas suggested by MOOsburg tools, 94
    ideas traced to metaphors, 95
    process, 81–84
    project ideas, 107–108
    refining, 101–104
    satisfying, 88–90, 106
    in scenario-based design, 91
    scenarios, 91, 94–101
    scope of, 106
    space, 92–94
    summary, 106–107
    tradeoffs, 84
    See also design
activity scenarios, 26–27
    claims analysis of, 142
    claims generated in parallel with, 99
    elaborating with information design
        details, 143–144
    envisionment of, 107

About the Authors

Mary Beth Rosson has been an associate professor of computer science at Virginia Tech since 1994. Prior to that, she worked at the IBM T. J. Watson Research Center as a research staff member and as manager of tools and architectures. She is the author of many contributed chapters, journal articles, and conference presentations and papers. Her research interests center on the use and design of software systems. She earned her B.A. in psychology *summa cum laude* from Trinity University in Texas and her Ph.D. in human experimental psychology from the University of Texas, Austin.

John M. Carroll is a professor of computer science, education, and psychology, and director of the Center for Human-Computer Interaction at Virginia Tech. He has written more than 250 technical papers, more than 20 conference plenary addresses, and 12 books. He serves on nine editorial boards for journals and handbooks, and in 2000, he served on five conference program committees. In 1994, he won the Rigo Career Achievement Award from ACM (SIGDOC) for contributions to research in documentation, and in 1998, he received the Silver Core Award from IFIP. He manages a research project on networking tools for collaborative learning activities supported by the U.S. National Science Foundation, the U.S. Office of Naval Research, and the Hitachi Foundation. During 2000, he was a visiting scientist at the Xerox Research Centre Europe in Cambridge, England.